The Counter-Reformation in Central Europe

Styria 1580–1630

REGINA PÖRTNER

CLARENDON PRESS · OXFORD

OXFORD
UNIVERSITY PRESS

Great Clarendon Street, Oxford OX2 6DP

Oxford University Press is a department of the University of Oxford.
It furthers the University's objective of excellence in research, scholarship,
and education by publishing worldwide in

Oxford New York

Athens Auckland Bangkok Bogotá Buenos Aires
Cape Town Chennai Dar es Salaam Delhi Florence Hong Kong Istanbul
Karachi Kolkata Kuala Lumpur Madrid Melbourne Mexico City Mumbai
Nairobi Paris São Paulo Singapore Taipei Tokyo Toronto Warsaw
with associated companies in Berlin Ibadan

Oxford is a registered trade mark of Oxford University Press
in the UK and in certain other countries

Published in the United States
by Oxford University Press Inc., New York

© Regina Pörtner 2001

British Library Cataloguing in Publication Data

Data available

Library of Congress Cataloging in Publication Data

Pörtner, Regina.
The counter-Reformation in Central Europe: Styria 1580–1630/Regina Pörtner.
p. cm.—(Oxford historical monographs)
Includes bibliographical references and index.
1. Reformation—Austria—Styria. 2. Counter-Reformation—Austria—Styria. 3. Styria
(Austria)—Church history. I. Title. II. Series.
BR360.5.S7 P67 2001   274.36'506—dc21   2001021695
ISBN 0-19-924615-7

1 3 5 7 9 10 8 6 4 2

Typeset in Ehrhardt by
Cambrian Typesetters, Frimley, Surrey
Printed in Great Britain
on acid-free paper by
Biddles Ltd,
Guildford and King's Lynn

PREFACE

This book is based on a doctoral thesis that was submitted to the Faculty of Modern History at the University of Oxford in December 1997, and accepted in spring 1998. In writing the thesis and preparing the revised text for publication, I have benefited from the help and support of a number of people and institutions in England, Austria, Italy, and Germany, who have turned this project into a truly European undertaking.

First and foremost, I would like to thank my supervisors, Prof. R. J. W. Evans and Prof. P. G. M. Dickson, whose advice and criticism have been of immeasurable value. The magisterial studies of both scholars have been an important source of inspiration, and have helped me develop a better grasp of the general issues involved in the present case study. The revised text has further benefited from constructive criticism by the examiners of the doctoral thesis, Prof. Winfried Schulze (Munich) and Dr Clifford Davies (Oxford), while Prof. Sir John Elliott and Robin Briggs (Oxford) gave important advice during the preliminary stages of my work. While carrying out archival research in Austria, I was most fortunate in receiving expert guidance from the outstanding legal and economic historian of Inner Austria, Prof. Helfried Valentinitsch (Graz), who has encouraged and most generously supported my work in various ways. I was equally lucky in profiting from Prof. Grete Klingenstein's (Graz) wide-ranging knowledge and profound insights into the history of eighteenth-century Austria and Enlightenment Europe. Conversations with Prof. Karl Amon and Prof. Maximilian Liebmann of the Faculty of Theology (Graz) have likewise been instructive in illuminating the ecclesiastical and theological context of my topic. My work in the Austrian archives and libraries in Vienna and Graz in general, and in the Styrian state and ecclesiastical archives in particular, was made both pleasurable and productive by the professional expertise and unfailingly kind response of the staff. In particular, I would like to thank Dr Karl Spreitzhofer, Dr Gernot Obersteiner, Dr Peter Wiesflecker and Ms. Cornelia Ohlsacher of the Steiermärkisches Landesarchiv Graz, and Dr Alois Ruhri of the Diözesanarchiv Graz-Seckau. I further owe special thanks to the directors of both institutions, Hofrat Dr Gerhard Pferschy and Dr Norbert Müller, for supporting my applications for grants. My requests at the General Archive of the Society of Jesus in Rome were handled with characteristic efficiency and patience by the head archivist, Pater Viktor Gramatowski, SJ, to whom I am also indebted for the loan of a powerful magnifying glass. A chance encounter at this archive with the editor of the nuncios' reports from Graz, Prof. Johann Rainer, likewise contributed to the productivity of my enquiries there. While staying in Rome, I enjoyed the hospitality of the British School, and held travel grants from the Rhodes Trust and from my college, Trinity (Oxford). I appreciated and enjoyed being part of the body of graduate students at the latter institution. As a Rhodes Scholar, I was privileged in receiving additional intellectual, moral, and financial support from the Rhodes Trust and its British and German boards. Like many students before me, I benefited from a generous grant from the Austrian government as part of an exchange programme between the Österreichischer and Deutscher Akademischer Austauschdienst, which enabled me to conduct the necessary archival research. During the writing-up stage of my thesis, I held a scholarship at the Institut für Europäische Geschichte in Mainz, where the community of students and scholars under the directorship of Prof. Heinz Duchhardt provided a challenging and stimulating intellectual environment. The revision of this text was completed at the beginning of my term as a Research Fellow at the German Historical Institute in London, and I would like to thank its previous director, Prof. Peter Wende, and the *Beirat* of the Institute in Germany for kindly allowing me to finish this work.

Josephine Moorman and Christoph Schönberger have helped with the layout of the text. I am greatly indebted to the staff of OUP for the production of this book, and would like to thank in particular Ms Jacqueline Pritchard, Ms Anne Gelling, and Mr Michael Watson.

Last but not least, I would like to thank my family and my friends, who have supported my work in many ways. It is to them that I dedicate this book with gratitude.

R. P.

CONTENTS

ABBREVIATIONS

AGDBH	*Archiv zur Geschichte des deutschen Buchhandels*
AGR	Archivio Generale della Compagnia di Gesù, Rome
AÖG	*Archiv für österreichische Geschichte (Archiv für Kunde österreichischer Geschichtsquellen)*
BKSTGQ	*Beiträge zur Kunde steiermärkischer Geschichtsquellen*
DA	Diözesanarchiv Graz-Seckau, Graz
FRA/50, FRA/58, FRA/60	J. Loserth (ed.), *Akten und Korrespondenzen (Fontes rerum Austriacarum)*, 3 vols. (Vienna, 1898, 1906–7)
FVVGST	*Forschungen zur Verfassungs- und Verwaltungsgeschichte der Steiermark*
HbBG	*Handbuch der bayerische Geschichte* ed. H. Lutz and M. Spindler, vol. ii (Munich, 1966)
HJ	*Historical Journal*
HJb	*Historisches Jahrbuch*
HJbG	*Historisches Jahrbuch der Stadt Graz*
HWBH	Eugen Haberkern and Joseph Friedrich Wallach, *Hilfswörterbuch für Historiker*, 2 vols. (4th edn. Munich, 1974)
HZ	*Historische Zeitschrift*
JGGPÖ	*Jahrbuch der Gesellschaft für die Geschichte des Protestantismus in Österreich*
JMH	*Journal of Modern History*
MHVST	*Mitteilungen des historischen Vereins für Steiermark*
MIÖG	*Mitteilungen des Instituts für österreichische Geschichtsforschung*
MÖVBW	*Mitteilungen des österreichischen Vereins für Bibliothekswesen*
MVGDB	*Mitteilungen des Vereins für Geschichte der Deutschen in Böhmen*
Nb i, Nb ii	J. Rainer (ed.), *Nuntiaturberichte*, Sonderreihe: *Grazer Nuntiatur 1582–87*, 2 vols. (Vienna, 1981)
ÖNB	Österreichische Nationalbibliothek, Vienna
P&P	*Past and Present*
QF	*Quellen und Forschungen aus italienischen Archiven und Bibliotheken*
RES	*Revue des études slaves*

STMLA	Steiermärkisches Landesarchiv, Graz
THQS	*Theologische Quartalsschrift*
ZHF	*Zeitschrift für historische Forschung*
ZHVST	*Zeitschrift des historischen Vereins für Steiermark*
ZVGMS	*Zeitschrift des Vereins für die Geschichte Mährens und Schlesiens*

SILESIA

o Prague

BOHEMIA

MORAVIA

o
Brno

PASSAU

BAVARIA

Linz
o

LOWER   Vienna
o

Pozsony
(Preßburg)
o

UPPER
AUSTRIA

AUSTRIA

Salzburg o

1

HABSBURG
HUNGARY

SALZBURG

STYRIA

Graz
o

CARINTHIA
Klagenfurt o

2

3

OTTOMAN
HUNGARY

VENICE

GORIZIA

Liubljana
(Laibach)
o

CARNIOLA

Zagreb
(Agram)
o

4
Trieste o

5

6   7
o   Fiume

CROATIA

OTTOMAN

EMPIRE

1 *Propstei* Berchtesgaden, ecclesiastical
   territory
2 Subject to the bishop of Brixen
3 Subject to the bishop of Freising

4 Trieste
5 Venetian Istria
6 Habsburg Istria
7 Fiume

MAP 1. Inner Austria and adjoining territories, sixteenth to seventeenth centuries

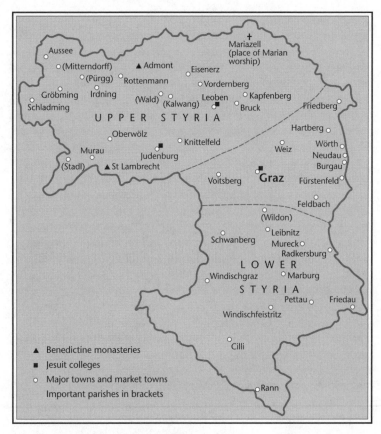

Aussee
○ (Mitterndorff)
▲ Admont
Eisenerz ○
Mariazell + (place of Marian worship)
○ (Pürgg) ○ Rottenmann
○ Vordernberg
Gröbming
Irdning
○ ○
(Wald) (Kalwang)
Leoben ○
○ Kapfenberg
Friedberg ○
Schladming
○

U P P E R   S T Y R I A
Bruck
○ ■

Oberwölz ○
Hartberg ○

Murau
Knittelfeld ○
Weiz ○
Wörth ○

(Stadl) ○
■ Judenburg
Neudau ○

▲ St Lambrecht
Burgau ○

Voitsberg ○
Graz ■
Fürstenfeld ○

Feldbach ○

(Wildon) ○

Leibnitz ○
Schwanberg ○
Mureck ○
Radkersburg ○

L O W E R

Windischgraz ○
Marburg ○

S T Y R I A
Pettau ○
Friedau ○

Windischfeistritz ○

Cilli ○

▲ Benedictine monasteries
■ Jesuit colleges
○ Major towns and market towns
Important parishes in brackets

Rann ○

MAP 2. Major towns and market towns in the duchy of Styria

I

Introduction

The following text is intended as a case study of the Counter-Reformation in one of the provinces of the Habsburg Monarchy from the beginnings of forcible recatholicization in the late sixteenth century to the definite termination of religious persecution by the end of the eighteenth century. The geographical focus of this study reflects Styria's importance as the administrative and political centre from which the complex of Inner Austrian territories in the south-east of the Monarchy was governed directly (until 1619) or indirectly (after that date). Together with the adjoining 'Inner Austrian' duchies of Carinthia and Carniola and the archduchy of Upper and Lower Austria, early modern Styria belonged to the so-called hereditary lands (*Erblande*) which formed the territorial core of the Austrian Habsburgs' Monarchy and the bedrock of the dynasty's political power. The terms of the thirteenth- and four-teenth-century constitutional settlements by which the Inner Austrian estates had pledged themselves permanently to the service of the Habsburgs as hereditary territorial princes invested the latter with a considerable measure of discretionary authority.[1] The ruler of the Inner Austrian duchies thus exerted extensive legislative power and was theor-etically free to declare war or conclude peace without prior consultation

---

[1] In spite of the Inner Austrian nobility's legal and fiscal liberties, which each duke had to confirm at his accession, the duke's scope for action still compared favourably with the Habsburgs' more narrowly circumscribed powers in the subsequently acquired kingdoms of Bohemia and Hungary. This situation changed with the reaction in the lands of the Bohemian crown which set in after the rebels' defeat at the Battle of the White Mountain in 1620. Earlier assumptions about the extent of the indisputably profound social and political changes resulting from punitive action and the absolutist claims of the Ferdinandean 'Verneuerte Landesordnung' of 1627 have recently been slightly modified to take account of continuities; e.g. where the survival of the old elites is concerned, see R. Evans, *The Making of the Habsburg Monarchy 1550–1700* (Oxford, 1979), 198–204 and J. Pánek, 'The Religious Question and the Political System of Bohemia before and after the Battle of the White Mountain', in R. J. W. Evans and T. Thomas (eds.), *Crown, Church and Estates* (Basingstoke, 1991; repr. 1994), 129–48. For the situation in Hungary see the article cited below. References to Karl II and Ferdinand (II) as dukes or archdukes in the following refer to their capacity as Inner Austrian rulers and as members of the dynasty respectively. The title of 'archduke' was assumed by the Habsburg ruler of Inner Austria in 1453 and from the time of Maximilian I applied to all princes of the dynasty, see *HWBH* i. 181.

with his estates, though, like most of his peers among the contemporary European princes, he would normally be expected to seek their counsel on political decisions of major consequence. Of far greater political importance, however, was the limitation of the prince's scope of action by the one powerful right which the nobility had reserved to themselves, that is the right to vote taxes and extraordinary grants. The voluntary nature of these contributions was stressed on each occasion, so that the prince had to enter negotiations with his subjects whenever his projects required the raising of funds beyond the means at his immediate disposal.[2] The way in which this acted upon the course of religious policy adopted by the dukes of Inner Austria in the sixteenth and seventeenth centuries will be discussed in detail at a later stage of this work. It should be said in advance that the precarious state of ducal finances at the accession of Karl II in 1564 was further aggravated by the persistence of the Turkish threat to the duchies' borders up to the peace treaty of Zsitvatorok in 1606 and, later on, by the outbreak of the Thirty Years War, so that financial dependence remained the rule in the period under consideration. Constant financial pressure and the changing fortunes of the Imperial party until the peace of 1648 exerted a strong influence on the course of the Counter-Reformation in Inner Austria, as will be exemplified by the case of Styria.

It is argued in the following that the outcome of the confessional struggle was above all determined by Ferdinand II's energetic and ultimately successful attempt to realize the political potential of his constitutional position. While there is no evidence of a headlong attack on the estates' right of taxation in this period, it can nevertheless be demonstrated that Ferdinand used the confessional issue to reduce the political momentum of this residue of noble autonomy by subjecting the assemblies and executive committees of the three duchies' estates to a rigorous control which effectively prevented co-ordinated opposition. The reshaping of the provincial diets along lines of confessional loyalty further supported the process of subjection.

---

[2] On the medieval constitutional settlement see H. Pirchegger, *Geschichte der Steiermark*, i: *1282–1740* (Graz, 1931), esp. 138–44, 238, and the relevant chapters in A. Mell, *Grundriß der Verfassungs- und Verwaltungsgeschichte des Landes Steiermark* (Graz, 1929). In the elective kingdoms of Bohemia and Hungary, the estates laid claim to a share in the legislative process and espoused concepts of corporate sovereignty that are reminiscent of the English notion of king-in-parliament, see W. Eberhard, 'The Political System and the Intellectual Traditions of the Bohemian *Ständestaat* from the Thirteenth to the Sixteenth Century', in Evans and Thomas, *Crown, Church and Estates*, 23–47. Parallels to the English situation are pointed out in L. Makkai, 'The Crown and the Diets of Hungary and Transylvania in the Sixteenth Century', ibid. 80–91, here 81–2.

If Ferdinand II's religious policy is discussed primarily in terms of a broader contest for political power, this is not to dispute the importance of genuine religious conviction as a driving force behind the prince's actions. The latter were not at all times subject to considerations of political expediency, as for example when the young Archduke Ferdinand antagonized the Inner Austrian estates at the height of the Turkish War in 1599–1600 by his sweeping measures against urban Protestantism. Contemporary reports testifying to Ferdinand's extraordinary piety and unwavering belief in his responsibility as Catholic prince abound. A combination of missionary fervour and dynastic hankering after past Imperial glories seems to have been behind the over-ambitious Edict of Restitution in 1629, which effectively shattered any prospects of a short-term confessional settlement with the moderate Protestant party in the Empire.[3]

In the following, it is argued that the close-knit alliance of Church and dynasty which emerged in the course of the Counter-Reformation was sustained by a coincidence of interests, and that the intellectual foundations of the resulting symbiosis were not challenged before the 'enlightened' reforms of the second half of the eighteenth century. As will become clear from the following account of the early and largely futile quest for a reform of the Church and religious practice, there was nothing ineluctable about this outcome. Indeed a brief look at the first decade of Charles V's reign during which political tensions culminated in the military excesses of the 'Sacco di Roma' in 1527 should suffice to bring to mind the degree of friction and disagreement which had characterized the state of relations between the Habsburgs and the head of the Catholic Church in the early stages of the Protestant Reformation.

With regard to the part played by the largely Protestantized provincial nobility, I shall seek to demonstrate that they in fact contributed to the strengthening of monarchical power and the creation of a confessionally homogeneous state by adopting a conciliatory and defensive attitude at

---

[3] A. Coreth, *Pietas Austriaca* (2nd edn., Vienna, 1982), 50–7. For a contemporary view see the eulogy composed by Ferdinand II's confessor, the former rector of the Jesuit college in Graz, Guilelmo Lamormaini, 'Ferdinandi II Romanorum Imperatoris Virtutes' (Vienna, 1638), ÖNB, MS 7378. This text was reprinted by the Catholic Georg Widmanstetter press in Graz in 1687 as an annual gift (*Xenie*) for the *sodales* of the university's largest Marian confraternity, of which Ferdinand had been a member. A copy of this text can be found in the collection of Widmanstetter prints in the manuscript department of the Karl-Franzens University in Graz, no. I 14235. The origins of the Edict of Restitution are traced back to the contentious interpretation of the religious settlement in 1555 in M. Ritter, 'Der Ursprung des Restitutionsediktes', *HZ* 76 (1895), 62–102.

crucial stages of the conflict with the prince. It is nevertheless argued here that in the late sixteenth century and during the domestic crisis of the Monarchy at the beginning of the seventeenth century, there was a small group of Styrian noblemen who possessed the acumen to grasp the larger political issues behind the seemingly negotiable confessional conflict. As will be shown, the evidence extant suggests that these political dissenters advocated a confrontational policy, supported by suitable alliances with the Protestant party in the Empire. However, for reasons discussed in the following, the majority of the provincial nobility acting as a corporate body in the Styrian and Inner Austrian estates opted for a conciliatory approach that ultimately led to their defeat and subjection as a confessional party, which, in turn, prepared the ground for a significant shift in the balance of power in favour of the prince.

The political dimension and religious implications of the Counter-Reformation as directed and executed by the prince and his local executives are but one side of the process under consideration. Of greater importance for the diffusion of the Tridentine spirit of the Counter-Reformation in Inner Austria were the missionary and reforming initiatives of the clergy, though the (arch)bishops and diocesan clergy were initially mostly opposed to the nuncio and the new religious orders among whom the Jesuits were of pre-eminent importance. The clerical reformers' efforts in the reign of Ferdinand II's predecessor Karl II were, according to the central argument in this part of the interpretation, not immediately successful. They were nevertheless preparatory to future governmental action. Their activity was complementary to Ferdinand's subsequent coercive policy, and became effective in terms of generating a self-sustained Catholic culture from about the mid-seventeenth century onwards, when the expulsion of the Inner Austrian Protestant nobility in 1628, rendered subsequently definitive by the relevant clauses of the Peace of Westphalia in 1648, had shattered any lingering hopes of a bi-confessional settlement for Inner Austria.

The present study is thus primarily concerned with the methods and achievements of the Counter-Reformation under the auspices of Habsburg policy in the above period. Supplementary to the interpretation developed in these chapters are two briefer sections of the text which trace the further fate of the Counter-Reformation once the immediate pressure of external political conflict in the Empire had relented. The chronological scope is extended to permit an assessment of the long-term effects on the Styrian Church and society in the seventeenth and eighteenth centuries. The thesis put forward here is that the duchy experienced a century of confessional consolidation from about 1630 to 1730, the achievements of which were eventually called into question by the resurfacing of crypto-Protestantism in the eighteenth century beyond the previously recorded individual cases. It will be demonstrated that the issue of crypto-heterodoxy served as a catalyst for the transformation of the intellectual climate in reaction to the last resurgence of systematic religious persecution in the decades of 1750 to 1780. Though a fuller discussion of the reform initiatives of this period is beyond the scope of the present study, it is suggested that this change prepared the ground for the definite termination of Counter-Reformation policies as manifested in the dismantling of the ecclesiastical substructure, both jurisdictional and financial, and the appropriation of the spoils by the 'enlightened' Josephinian state.

The methodical approach adopted in the present text combines analysis and interpretation with description and narrative. The latter is necessitated by the state of research on the subject, which is characterized by significant lacunae with regard to both the range of documents used and the chronological and thematic scope of their evaluation. Most striking is the absence of any account which would follow up the narrative of events until 1590 presented by the Styrian historian Johann Loserth in 1898. His study focused on the spread of Protestantism and the beginnings of the confrontation between the Catholic prince and the Protestant nobility in the reign of Karl II (1564–90), father and predecessor of Archduke Ferdinand.[4] Loserth's pioneering work is to some extent the product of nineteenth-century denominational controversy and is devoted to a vindication of the Inner Austrian Protestant estates against charges of disloyalty to the House of Habsburg. His account of events concludes with the year of Karl II's death, 1590, thus dismissing the decisive phase of the political Counter-Reformation under Ferdinand II (1596–1628). This curious abridgement is explained by Loserth's conviction that the Jesuit pupil Ferdinand was merely executing a policy that had been determined in detail by Karl II, Archduke Ferdinand of Tyrol, and Duke Wilhelm V of Bavaria in 1579.[5] Hence, Loserth did not concern himself with the details of the Ferdinandean Counter-Reformation, or the recatholicization of Inner Austria, though he provided an outline of the political conflict and governmental action that bore upon it in the prefaces to his edition of key documents. The material included reflects Loserth's intention of providing an underpinning to his earlier argument in favour of the

---

[4] J. Loserth, *Reformation und Gegenreformation in den innerösterreichischen Ländern im 16. Jahrhundert* (Stuttgart, 1898), henceforward quoted as Loserth, *Gegenreformation*.
[5] Ibid. 571.

estates' unswerving loyalty and political submissiveness throughout the confessional conflict.[6] Modern historiography has so far made no systematic use of the wealth of source material presented, and no attempt has been made to reassess Loserth's interpretation on this basis. A similar statement could be made for the evaluation of the nuncios' reports from Graz. This valuable source was unavailable to Loserth, but a substantial number of the widely scattered reports has now been edited by Johann Rainer.[7] To date, the chronological and thematic framework of Loserth's interpretation has remained the largely unchallenged paradigm for the discussion of the Inner Austrian Counter-Reformation, though some of its defects have recently been pointed out by the participants in a conference on the subject. On this occasion, it was noted that most of the published documents, including Loserth's own voluminous collection as well as the published nuncios' reports from Graz, still await their systematic evaluation. The contributors further stated the desideratum of a confessionally unbiased and methodologically 'modernized' account covering all aspects of the Counter-Reformation and Catholic reform in the sixteenth and seventeenth centuries.[8]

No express mention was made in this context of the concept of 'confessionalization' as developed chiefly by the German historians Heinz

---

[6] J. Loserth (ed.), *Acten und Correspondenzen zur Geschichte der Gegenreformation in Innerösterreich unter Erzherzog Karl II. (1578–1590)* (Vienna, 1898). Id., *Akten und Korrespondenzen zur Geschichte der Gegenreformation in Innerösterreich unter Ferdinand II. (1590–1600)*, pt. i (Vienna, 1906), and id., *Akten . . . (1600–1637)*, pt. ii (Vienna, 1907). The volumes appeared in the series Fontes rerum Austriacarum, vols. 50, 58, and 60, and are henceforth cited as *FRA/50*, *FRA/58*, and *FRA/60*. The imbalance in Loserth's account is not redressed by H.-B. Neumann, 'The Styrian Estates during the Counter-Reformation, 1578–1628' (unpublished doctoral thesis at the Faculty of History, University of Toronto, 1976?). The author gives a curiously reduced account of his subject—the development of the duchy's estates in the period of the Counter-Reformation—which seems rather unconnected to its setting in time and geographical space. His account furthermore needs modification on several points such as the characterization of the clergy as the 'third estate or social class of Styrian society', 'Styrian Estates', 23, or the alleged uniqueness of Styria's two-tier division of the noble estate, ibid. 17.

[7] J. Rainer (ed.), *Nuntiaturberichte. Sonderreihe: Grazer Nuntiatur*, i: *1580–2* (Vienna, 1973); ii: *1582–7* (Vienna, 1981). Henceforward cited as *Nb i* and *Nb ii*. Rainer has drawn on a selection of them to clarify various aspects of the founding history of the Styrian nunciature, see id., 'Die Grazer Nuntiatur', in F. M. Dolinar, M. Liebmann, and H. Rumpler (eds.), *Katholische Reform und Gegenreformation in Innerösterreich 1564–1628* (Graz, 1994), 289–94.

[8] See the editors' introduction in Dolinar et al., *Katholische Reform*, 11–18. The same point is also made briefly in H. J. Mezler-Andelberg, 'Erneuerung des Katholizismus und Gegenreformation in Innerösterreich', in H. J. Mezler-Andelberg, *Kirche in der Steiermark* (Vienna, 1994), at 176.

Schilling and Wolfgang Reinhard in a series of essays over the past two decades, but the question of its applicability to the issues under discussion merits further consideration. The scholarly interest aroused by this concept has sparked a debate which has by now become thematically fissiparous at the expense of conceptual precision. Some of the main points which bear on the issues of the present study can nevertheless be identified. 'Confessionalization' was conceived as a broad term of reference denoting the process and ensemble of mechanisms by which confessional, i.e. denominational, awareness was created through the precepts of the Catholic and Protestant theologians, which were in turn transmitted to the mass of the population by the agents or institutions of clerical and secular governmental authority.[9] The idea of Schilling and Reinhard was to invent a theoretical device for interdenominational comparative research into the relations between the institutional and ideological expressions of Christian religion on the one hand, and the nascent modern society and bureaucratic state on the other. Working from a background of field studies on the development of the 'modern' state in the principalities of the Empire, the authors drew attention to the common ground shared by Protestant princes and their Catholic counterparts with regard to the technique of expanding their power over their subjects through a skilful handling of the confessional issue. In the process of enforcing confessional uniformity, the princes imposed a measure of 'social discipline' which effectively increased their control of every aspect of their subjects' life.[10] The authors likewise stressed that there were common features to the spiritual side of 'confessionalization' as directed

---

[9] For the positions outlined here see the seminal articles by W. Reinhard, 'Zwang zur Konfessionalisierung? Prolegomena zu einer Theorie des konfessionellen Zeitalters', *ZHF* 10/3 (1983), 257–77, and H. Schilling, 'Die Konfessionalisierung im Reich', *HZ* 246 (1988), 1–45. The present state of research is documented in H. R. Schmidt, *Konfessionalisierung im 16. Jahrhundert* (Munich, 1992). Cases of Calvinist, Lutheran, and Catholic confessionalization in the Empire are discussed in the conference volumes edited by H. Schilling, *Die reformierte Konfessionalisierung in Deutschland: Das Problem der 'Zweiten Reformation'* (Gütersloh, 1986), H.-C. Rublack (ed.), *Die lutherische Konfessionalisierung in Deutschland* (Gütersloh, 1992), and W. Reinhard and H. Schilling (eds.), *Die katholische Konfessionalisierung* (Gütersloh, 1995). The most recent discussions of the aspect of statebuilding are H. R. Schmidt, 'Sozialdisziplinierung? Ein Plädoyer für das Ende des Etatismus in der Konfessionalisierungsforschung', *HZ* 265 (1997), 639–82, and for the Catholic context H. Klueting, ' "Quidquid est in territorio: etiam est de territorio". Josephinisches Staatskirchentum als rationaler Territorialismus', *Der Staat*, 37/3 (1998), 417–34.

[10] The tightening of social control as a result of confessionalization is discussed in H. Schilling, *Kirchenzucht und Sozialdisziplinierung im frühneuzeitlichen Europa* (Berlin, 1994). See also the comparative study by R. Po-Chia Hsia, *Social Discipline in the Reformation: Central Europe, 1550–1750* (London, 1989).

by the Churches. Among these, doctrinal clarification formed the starting
point for the development of new norms of conduct that were henceforth
to regulate the religious life of the confessionally homogeneous community. The strategy adopted combined positive encouragement by propaganda, education, and reform of religious practice with the use of
coercion to suppress 'counter-propaganda' and to punish deviant behaviour.[11]

'Confessionalization' as defined above obviously covers important
aspects of the subject discussed in the present work, but the term needs
to be applied in its comprehensive sense in order to avoid overemphasiz-
ing the spiritual side of this process. Such an interpretation would run the
risk of misreading the evidence for the level of ideological penetration
both envisaged and achieved. The main thesis put forward here is that
Habsburg religious policy was generally a kind of resultant of the forces
of political necessity, dynastic interest, and individual piety. For most of
the period under discussion, this meant that its objectives fell in practice
considerably short of the ideal of a fully 'confessionalized' society characterized by a notably increased level of doctrinal awareness and religious
activity of its members. Governmental interest in the control of the noble
and civic elites and their offspring was in fact lively and unflagging. As for
the broad populace, however, a tendency to rest content with outward
conformity, manifested by the performance of a prescribed minimum of
obligatory religious acts, became the prevailing attitude of the secular
authorities in Graz and Vienna as indeed of a substantial part of the clerical authorities prior to the inquisition into and campaign against crypto-
heterodoxy in the eighteenth century. The present text argues that the
survival of Protestant enclaves as well as the uneven educational development of the different groups of Styrian society should be seen as resulting from these as well as from structural shortcomings.[12]

The debate about the impact of the Reformation and Counter-
Reformation on the patterns of religious and social life at the local level
of early modern German society has so far produced a number of
instructive field studies which illuminate the ways in which secular and
ecclesiastical authorities in early modern central Europe contributed to
the emergence of institutionally and intellectually transformed or
'modernized', confessionally aware states.[13] Regrettably, the hazards of

---

[11] See Reinhard, 'Zwang zur Konfessionalisierung', 263.
[12] The importance of clerical exemptions is discussed below, Ch. 2, last section.
[13] A sample of significant recent contributions for central Europe would include B.
Nischan, *Prince, People and Confession: The Second Reformation in Brandenburg*

archival survival have in the case of Styria resulted in a dearth of relevant documentation of urban and parochial provenance, though such fragmentary evidence as could be traced in ecclesiastical and state archives has been scrutinized for information of micro-historical interest. By contrast, ample documentation for the activity of the ecclesiastical authorities is provided by the records of the episcopal archive of the bishopric of Seckau, seat of the suffragan bishop and vicar general of the archbishop of Salzburg.

Among the documentation consulted, mention must be made of the various and initially somewhat steoreotype visitation records from 1585 to 1752, the episcopal correspondence with Salzburg, as well as the instructions and reports of the bishop and his subordinate Styrian clergy. The information gathered from these sources frequently proved an important supplement to the official records of the Inner Austrian government, especially for the eighteenth century. It likewise complemented the relevant municipal documentation of the Styrian State Archive in Graz. It should be noted, though, that hopes of restoring the local perspective from the parish records in the episcopal archive were frustrated by the scarcity and low informational value of most of the surviving material. More promising documentation in the shape of the Jesuits' annual reports as well as the letters to and from the General of the Society was found in the Austrian National Library and in the General Archive in Rome. This material proved especially useful in shedding light on problems arising from conflicting concepts of the Counter-Reformation mission, with important implications for understanding the Jesuits' attitude towards the government and the different social groups of Styrian society.

Regrettably, even the most perceptive use of such troves cannot make up entirely for the loss of the bulk of first-hand material from the dissolved or secularized colleges and monasteries of the Styrian Jesuits

(Philadelphia, 1994), A. Herzig, *Reformatorische Bewegung und Konfessionalisierung: Die habsburgische Rekatholisierung in der Grafschaft Glatz 1530–1730* (Hamburg, 1996), M. G. Müller, *Zweite Reformation und städtische Autonomie im königlichen Preußen: Danzig, Elbing und Thorn in der Epoche der Konfessionalisierung (1557–1660)* (Berlin, 1997), as well as the series edited by Anton Schindling and Walter Ziegler, *Die Territorien des Reichs im Zeitalter der Reformation und Konfessionalisierung* (Münster, 1989–93), and the contributions to an international conference held in 1997 in J. Bahlcke and A. Strohmeyer (eds.), *Konfessionalisierung in Ostmitteleuropa* (Stuttgart, 1999). Some limitations of the concept are pointed out in a contribution to this volume by A. Pettegree, in which the author argues that the religious history of the British Isles, France, and the United Provinces does not conform to the patterns assumed by confessionalization theory, see A. Pettegree, 'Confessionalization in North Western Europe', ibid. 105–20.

and Capuchins. It is, however, hoped that the broadening of the documentary basis to include evidence from scarcely less involved religious orders like the Augustinians, and the use of miscellaneous sources bearing on the issue of characteristic religious practices of the seventeenth and eighteenth centuries, can make up for some of these defects and help capture the spirit of Catholic piety, both reformed and revived. Finally, the collections of manuscripts and rare documents in the Styrian State Library and in the manuscript department of the University of Graz have supplied ample information for the analysis of contemporary confessional propaganda and education.

2

Protestantism Ascendant (1525–1578)

I. THE HABSBURG MONARCHY AND THE REFORMATION IN SIXTEENTH-CENTURY CENTRAL EUROPE

To recount the story of the rise of Styrian Protestantism as indeed of Austrian Protestantism in general is to some extent to relate the spiritual turmoil which attended the formation of the Austrian Habsburg Monarchy in the sixteenth century. The spread of heterodoxy stood at the beginnings and accompanied the early stages of dynastic 'state-building' policy by which the Austrian duchies of Upper, Lower, and Inner Austria were slowly but inexorably drawn away from the Empire to become part of an increasingly eastern-based composite Monarchy.[1]

While it is argued here that the Austrian Monarchy received its distinct intellectual identity during the Counter-Reformation of the sixteenth and seventeenth centuries, this is not to dispute the fact that the dynasty had hitched its fortune to the Catholic faith well before this date in important ways which effectively precluded members of the Austrian branch from open confessional deviance.[2] It is important to remember that the latter's political standing and scope for action in the Empire and the recently acquired eastern kingdoms rested on the dynasty's firm grip on the Imperial office and the resultant power of disposition over Imperial honours and privileges. It further depended on the Spanish Habsburgs' military and economic power and their capacity for intervention on behalf of their Austrian relatives.[3] Both sources of authority had important implications for the course of religious policy adopted. The

---

[1] The 'eastern' and 'western' strands in Habsburg (foreign) policy are set out in Evans, *Making of the Habsburg Monarchy* and C. Ingrao, *The Habsburg Monarchy 1618–1815* (Cambridge, 1994).

[2] For an assessment of Maximilian II's religious views and ambivalent confessional policy see below, second section of this chapter. H. Louthan, *The Quest for Compromise* (Cambridge, 1997), argues for the existence of a different, 'eirenicist' Habsburg tradition linked to the quest for a 'via media', which he sees represented mainly by Ferdinand I and Maximilian II, see ibid. 1–10, and the references on pp. 123, 127, 143, 152, 163.

[3] For the changing pattern of interdependence of Habsburg military fortunes during the Thirty Years War, see G. Parker (ed.), *The Thirty Years' War* (2nd edn., 1987), esp. 108–9, 170 ff.

combat of heresy and hence the preservation of the spiritual integrity of
the Imperial Church had been a pre-eminent obligation of the German
emperors in the Middle Ages, and had originally served to underwrite the
assumed sacral properties of that office.[4] The Habsburgs were to add
ideological weight to their aspirations for a permanent, hereditary possession of the Imperial title by a carefully cultivated and displayed devotional tradition, the 'Pietas Austriaca', which was celebrated as the
spiritual foundation of the dynasty's political rise.[5] As for the Spanish
Monarchy, its very existence, like its claims to overseas expansion, was
based on the accomplishments of the fifteenth-century Catholic
Reconquista in the Iberian peninsula. Against this background,
Protestantism was bound to become identified with the centrifugal forces
of noble power and regional particularism as represented by the
Protestant territorial estates of the Austrian Habsburgs' dominions, an
assumption that became a self-fulfilling prophecy in the seventeenth
century.[6]

For a contemporary Catholic observer, such apprehensions would have
been fully borne out by the progress and political implications of the
spread of the new faith in the Empire and the adjoining eastern kingdoms
of Hungary, Bohemia, and Poland before the onset of the Counter-
Reformation at the end of the sixteenth century. Among the nobility and
urban elites of the German principalities, the Lutheran faith had spread
rapidly in spite of the Imperial ban imposed by the Edict of Worms in
1521. This declaration was countered by demands for a national synod
and redress of grievances concerning clerical abuses. Such demands were
voiced most emphatically by a group of Imperial princes led by Elector
Johann of Saxony (1525–32), his successor Johann Friedrich (1532–47),
and Landgrave Philipp of Hessen (1518–67) at successive assemblies of
the Imperial diet in Nuremberg (1522–4), Speyer (1526/9), and afterwards. Most of these grievances concerned the clergy's disposition over
ecclesiastical benefices and property, e.g. the malpractice of cumulation of
benefices and the related problems of nepotism, simony, and clerical
absenteeism. Secular discontent as expressed by the sixteenth-century
gravamina movement had in fact antecedents dating back to the mid-

---

[4] F. Kern, *Gottesgnadentum und Widerstandsrecht im früheren Mittelalter: Zur
Entwicklungsgeschichte der Monarchie* (6th edn., Darmstadt, 1973), at 46–121: 'Der
theokratische Amtsgedanke'.
[5] See Coreth, *Pietas Austriaca*, esp. 9–18.
[6] The views of Ferdinand II and his advisers on this subject will be discussed in Ch. 4
below.

fifteenth century, but was now gaining fresh impetus from the theological advance of Luther's critique. Failure to come to an agreement with the Emperor at a further diet in Augsburg in 1530 led to the formation of the Schmalkaldic League, a defensive alliance of those princes and Upper German towns who had already committed themselves fully to the Protestant faith.[7] At the same time, divergent doctrinal formulas which effectively provided the theological foundations for the subsequent organization of Protestant school and church ministries were fixed in the 'Confessio Augustana', devised by Philipp Melanchthon (1497–1560), in the somewhat misleadingly named 'Confessio Tetrapolitana' drafted by Martin Bucer (1491–1551) and Wolfgang Capito (1478–1541) for Strasbourg, Konstanz, Memmingen, and Lindau, and in Huldrych Zwingli's (1484–1531) 'Fidei ratio'.

The outbreak of hostilities between the League and the Emperor and the latter's victory in the Schmalkaldic War of 1546–7 led to Imperial reprisals against the political heads of the confederation and a confessional purge of the recalcitrant town magistrates. However, the precariousness of this victory was revealed by the volte-face of the Emperor's most important ally, Maurice of Saxony (1521–53, elector since 1547), and the ensuing revolt of the Protestant princes which forced the Emperor into retreat. On 25 September 1555, a religious peace was agreed through the mediation of Ferdinand (I), archduke of Austria, king of Hungary and Bohemia, and designated successor of Charles V. The openly defensive terms of the Peace of Augsburg effectively sanctioned the favourable status quo of Protestant expansion, leaving most of the German fiefs and principalities from the duchy of Holstein in the north to the duchy of Württemberg in the south-west as well as a number of bishoprics under Protestant control, though reserving a right of emigration to subjects who would not conform. Modest successes were scored for the Catholic cause by the requirement for Protestant towns to continue Catholic services where they had been reintroduced after 1548. More important were the terms of the 'ecclesiastical reservation' which sought to check further secularizations by laying down that clerical

---

[7] Members of the Schmalkaldic League were Electoral Saxony, Hessen, Anhalt, Mansfeld, Braunschweig-Lüneburg, Braunschweig-Grubenhagen, and the towns of Magdeburg and Bremen, Strasbourg, and a number of Upper German towns, with the notable exception of Nuremberg, which remained neutral, see W. P. Fuchs, *Das Zeitalter der Reformation* (8th edn., Munich, 1986), 167. For a fuller discussion of the origins and aims of the League see E. Fabian, *Die Entstehung des Schmalkaldischen Bundes und seiner Verfassung 1529 bis 1531/33*, Schriften zur Kirchen- und Rechtsgeschichte 1 (Tübingen, 1962). The text of the confederal constitution is reprinted on pp. 357–76.

members of the Imperial estates, i.e. bishops and prelates, would forfeit both their office and Imperial fief on converting to the new faith. Cathedral chapters were entitled, though significantly not obliged, to elect a Catholic successor. Off record, the secret 'Declaratio Ferdinandea' further weakened the immediate effect of this regulation by granting freedom of worship to Protestant subjects of Catholic ecclesiastical princes if the former had adopted the Lutheran faith before 1555.[8]

In the end, the attempted settlement proved unacceptable to both sides, and clashes over the interpretation of the ecclesiastical clause were repeatedly threatening to turn into conflict on a major and potentially European scale, beginning with the conflict over the attempted secularization of the archbishopric of Cologne in 1582–3, which was prevented by joint Bavarian and Spanish action, to the Bavarian annexation of the Imperial town of Donauwörth in 1607–9 on the pretext of defending the Catholic minority and executing the Imperial ban (*Reichsacht*) incurred for a minor transgression in 1605.[9] More immediately, the Peace of Augsburg succeeded in limiting toleration to adherents of the Lutheran 'Confessio Augustana', thus excluding radical sects like the anabaptists as well as the multiple variants of the 'reformed faith'. Among the latter, Calvinism, as will be seen, was to play a key role as a prop to aristocratic self-assertion in Poland and Transylvania in the sixteenth century, and the ideological rallying point for the discontented nobility of Habsburg Hungary in the seventeenth century.

By contrast, radical popular Protestantism resumed the tradition of late fifteenth-century anti-feudal revolt which couched its demands in religious terms. Prior to the great Peasant War of 1525, the most recent and most threatening example had been the large-scale peasant uprising led by Joß Fritz, a bondsman of the bishop of Speyer, which spread from that bishopric to the Breisgau and thence across the Upper Rhine region in the years 1502 to 1517. To contemporary Catholic observers, it seemed that the apostate monk Martin Luther had passed the torch of rebellion to the revolu-

---

[8] Losses of ecclesiastical territory after 1555 included the bishoprics of Bremen, Verden, Magdeburg, Halberstadt, and Kammin. A map indicating the dates of Protestant acquisition can be found in R. Stupperich, *Die Reformation in Deutschland* (2nd rev. edn., Gütersloh, 1980), appendix. It should be noted that the northern border of the Holy Roman Empire in this map is erroneously drawn along the northern border of Schleswig instead of Holstein and Dithmarschen. For the turnabout of Elector Maurice of Saxony and the revolt of the Imperial princes in 1552–5, see K. E. Born, 'Moritz von Sachsen und die Fürstenverschwörung gegen Karl V.', *HZ* 191 (1966), 18–66.

[9] See G. von Lojewski, 'Bayerns Kampf um Köln', in H. Glaser (ed.), *Um Glauben und Reich* (Munich, 1980), 40–7, at 43–5, and for Donauwörth Parker, *Thirty Years War*, 23–4.

tionary evangelical preacher Thomas Müntzer, his erstwhile protégé.
Müntzer took upon himself the task of *spiritus rector* of the rebellious
German peasants who based their protests against the extension of princely
jurisdiction and the expansion of the feudal tithes and dues on an egalitar-
ian interpretation of the Bible and unwritten or customary as opposed to
Imperial civil law.[10] Spurred on by Luther's scathing denunciation of the
rebellious peasants, Lutheran princes like Landgrave Philipp of Hessen
played a prominent part in the savage noble reaction that stamped out the
revolt. The rebellion spread to the archbishopric of Salzburg in 1525–6,
and from thence to the neighbouring area of Upper Styria, where the population of the mining settlements, most notably of the town of Schladming,
had joined the opposition of the archbishop's subjects. The uprising was
squashed by a levy under the Lutheran head of the Styrian estates
(*Landeshauptmann*), Siegmund von Dietrichstein, who at one stage fell into
the hands of the rebels and narrowly escaped execution.

At a meeting of the deputies of the five Austrian lands in December
1525, an attempt was made to turn the peasants' anticlerical grievances to
good use by demanding admission of the Lutheran faith. At the same
time, however, the estates persuaded Ferdinand (I) to issue an 'Order for
the suppression of unrest' (*Empörungsordnung*), which strengthened the
penal authority of the estates at the expense of the government. The cases
in which recourse could be had directly to the prince, not the
Landeshauptmann, were strictly limited. Moreover, rebellious subjects'
life and property was to be forfeit and at the mercy of the feudal lord.[11]

---

[10] The origins of the *Bundschuh* movement dated back to the mid-15th century, see A.
Laube, 'Precursors of the Peasant War: *Bundschuh* and *Armer Konrad*—Movements at the
Eve of the Reformation', in J. Bak (ed.), *The German Peasant War of 1525* (London, 1976),
49–53. There is now an extensive literature on the great German Peasant War of 1525
(which in fact started in 1524). For comprehensive interpretations see P. Blickle, *Die
Revolution von 1525* (2nd rev. and enlarged edn., Munich, 1981) and H. Buszello, *Der
deutsche Bauernkrieg von 1525 als politische Bewegung* (Berlin, 1969), and, for specific aspects,
the collection of articles in B. Scribner and G. Benecke (eds.), *The German Peasant War
1525: New Viewpoints* (London, 1979), esp. J. Bücking, 'The Peasant War in the Habsburg
Lands as a Social Systems-Conflict', 160–73. A detailed account of regional events as well
as an analysis of the roots and ideological strands of the revolts can be found in H. Buszello,
P. Blickle, and R. Endres (eds.), *Der deutsche Bauernkrieg* (Paderborn, 1984). For Thomas
Müntzer, the radical Reformation, and anabaptism see H.-J.Goertz, *Religiöse Bewegungen in
der frühen Neuzeit* (Munich, 1993), 11–15(ff), 75–89, 114–34.

[11] Pirchegger, *Geschichte der Steiermark*, i. 353–64 for the Peasant War and 364, nn. 417
and 418, and 365 for the terms of the new order. The Habsburgs, of course, reserved their
power of intervention on behalf of oppressed subjects, as was demonstrated on the occasion
of the Táhy uprising in Lower Styria in 1572–3, see below, this chapter. Contrary to the
estates' wishes, direct appeals from their subjects to the prince were not outlawed wholesale,
see Pirchegger, *Geschichte der Steiermark*.

By revealing the revolutionary potential of a radical reading of the Protestant doctrine, the events of 1525 arguably exerted a formative influence on the theological and political outlook of the Styrian elite, who adopted in their majority a pacific stance in the subsequent confessional conflict with the prince.[12] The same could be said for the influence of anabaptism. This sect had made its appearance with some success among the rural population of Tyrol and in a few Styrian towns in the 1520s. Again, the Lutheran estates and magistrates of Styria were no less ruthless than their Catholic counterparts in Tyrol in persecuting these conventicles, culminating in the summary execution of nine anabaptists at the town of Bruck in 1528 in compliance with Ferdinand (I)'s religious decrees. As a result of the joint efforts of the prince and estates, anabaptism seems to have become extinct in Styria and the adjacent Inner Austrian duchies of Carinthia and Carniola by the end of the 1530s.[13]

The Peace of Augsburg had similarly stigmatized the Calvinist faith, which was, in consequence, slow to make headway among the Imperial princes. In 1560, it was, however, gaining a foothold of some importance by the conversion of Friedrich III, Count Palatine, and after some confessional shifts until 1583, the Palatinate with its capital at Heidelberg was becoming a stronghold of the reformed faith.[14] If the beginnings of the

---

[12] For a similiar assessment of the impact of the Peasant War of 1525 on the Styrian nobility see the statements in G. Scholz's *Habilitation* thesis, *Ständefreiheit und Gotteswort. Studien zum Anteil der Landstände an Glaubensspaltung und Konfessionsbildung in Innerösterreich (1517–1564)* (Frankfurt am Main, 1994), 91–9. The Styrian uprisings are treated summarily in G. Pferschy, 'Die steirischen Bauernaufstände', in F. Posch (ed.), *Das Bauerntum in der Steiermark* (Graz, 1963), 50–4. For the early 16th-century revolts see F. Mayer, 'Materialien und kritische Bemerkungen zur Geschichte der ersten Bauernunruhen in Steiermark und den angrenzenden Ländern', *BKSTGQ* 13 (1876), 1–32. The peasant uprising of 1525–6 is the subject of studies by M. Rabenlechner, *Der Bauernkrieg in Steiermark* (Freiburg, 1901), and more recently by R. Schäffer, *Der obersteirische Bauern- und Knappenaufstand und der Überfall auf Schladming 1525* (Vienna, 1989). For the radical Protestant movements in the Empire see R. van Dülmen, *Reformation als Revolution* (2nd edn., Frankfurt am Main, 1987).

[13] Anabaptism in Bruck an der Mur and other towns of the duchy is discussed in J. Loserth, 'Wiedertäufer in Steiermark', *MHVST* 42 (1894), 118–45, as well as P. Dedic, 'Reformation und Gegenreformation in Bruck an der Mur und im Mürztal', *JGGPÖ* 63–4 (1942–3), 16–23, and more recently R. Höfer, 'Die kirchlichen Zustände in Bruck an der Mur und seiner Umgebung nach den Visitationsprotokollen von 1524, 1528 und 1544' (graduate thesis at the Faculty of Theology, University of Graz, 1977), 60. A similar situation prevailed in the archduchy of Austria, where the anabaptist preacher Balthasar Hubmaier was captured and burnt in 1528, see W. Ziegler, 'Nieder- und Oberösterreich', in Schindling and Ziegler, *Die Territorien des Reichs*, i. 118–33, at 124.

[14] See V. Press, *Kriege und Krisen* (Munich, 1991), 107–8. A Calvinist reformation occurred towards the end of the 16th century and affected mainly the western territories of

Calvinist party in the Empire were numerically modest, they were all the more significant in securing the support of a prince who by virtue of his dignities as both prince elector and member of the regency government in the case of an Imperial vacancy was of sufficient standing and political influence to become a plausible candidate for any organized political opposition in need of a leader. This was to be the case in 1619, when Elector Friedrich V responded to the Bohemian estates' appeal to challenge Ferdinand II over the Bohemian crown. It should be noted that the Imperial constitution stated that the Elector of Saxony, by 1560 invariably a Lutheran, was to act as the other Imperial governor or *Reichsverweser* in case of a crown vacancy. As a result, only one of the three highest Imperial dignities—the office of imperial chancellor (*Reichserzkanzler*)—remained in the hands of a Catholic, that is, of the archbishop elector of Mainz.[15]

No less ominous for the future of the Catholic faith seemed to be the joint progress of Lutheranism and Calvinism in the adjoining eastern kingdoms of Hungary, Bohemia, and Poland.[16] In the last, the reformed faith had been disseminated by the proselytizing of Jan Laski

---

the Empire, see the contributions in Schilling, *Reformierte Konfessionalisierung*, and M. Schaab (ed.), *Territorialstaat und Calvinismus* (Stuttgart, 1993). For the related processes of reformed confessionalization and state-building see V. Press, 'Die "Zweite Reformation" in der Kurpfalz', in Schilling, *Reformierte Konfessionalisierung*, 104–29, as well as V. Press, *Calvinismus und Territorialstaat: Regierung und Zentralbehörden der Kurpfalz 1559–1619* (Stuttgart, 1970).

[15] See Press, *Kriege und Krisen*, 84–5. In Mainz, Archbishop Elector Cardinal Albrecht of Brandenburg (1514–45), Luther's main adversary at the outset of the Reformation controversy, headed the Catholic party in the Empire and initiated wide-ranging reforms in the vast and dispersed territories of the archdiocese. The suffragan bishoprics of Magdeburg and Halberstadt were, however, lost to Protestant expansion, see F. Jürgensmeier, 'Kurmainz', in Schindling and Amon, *Die Territorien des Reichs*, iv. 60–95.

[16] For a survey see R. R. Betts, 'Poland, Bohemia and Hungary', in G. R. Elton (ed.), *The Reformation 1520–1559, New Cambridge Modern History*, vol. ii (2nd edn., Cambridge, 1990), 198–222. A comparative 'functionalist' approach to Protestantization in the eastern kingdoms is offered by W. Eberhard, 'Reformatorische Gegensätze, reformatorischer Konsens, reformatorische Formierung in Böhmen, Mähren und Polen', in J. Bahlcke (ed.), *Ständefreiheit und Staatsgestaltung in Ostmitteleuropa: Übernationale Gemeinsamkeiten in der politischen Kultur vom 16.–18. Jahrhundert* (Leipzig, 1996), 187–215. Modern historiography has paid less attention to the adjoining lands, but see the previously quoted study by A. Herzig for the Reformation and Counter-Reformation in the county of Glatz. A brief but instructive survey of the Silesian Reformation can be found in O. Wagner, 'Der Einfluß von Reformation, Gegenreformation und Barock auf die Nationsbildung in Schlesien', in R. Riemenschneider (ed.), *Schlesien und Pommern in den deutsch-polnischen Beziehungen vom 16. bis 18, Jahrhundert* (Braunschweig, 1982), 119–45. The article also provides a helpful account of the political and ecclesiastical organization which structured the conglomerate of Silesian territories, at 119–20.

(1499–1560), the erstwhile Lutheran preacher turned Calvinist after an encounter with the Genevan reformer. Calvinism's remarkable success with the Polish nobility of Małopolska and Lithuania, among whom it. had won a majority by the 1550s, arguably resulted from the appeal of its elitist and self-assertive elements as expressed in the concept of the 'elect' and the right of resistance of magistrates, which chimed with the self-perception of the Polish nobility regarding their relations with the monarch.[17]

By contrast, Lutheranism was making headway among the urban population, though its sweeping progress in ducal Prussia remained unparalleled. Here, the entire territory was brought into the Lutheran fold by the conversion of its ruler, the former Grandmaster of the Teutonic Order, Prince Albrecht of Hohenzollern (1490–1568), who received the secularized duchy as a fief from the Polish king in 1525. Though himself a Catholic, the weakness of the Polish monarch's power over his noble subjects ensured that further heterodox groups could thrive under their protection, like, for example, the Hussite Bohemian Brethren who had been evicted from Bohemia after lending support to an abortive anti-Habsburg uprising in support of the Schmalkaldic League in 1547. These groups further diversified the kingdom's confessional composition, and by 1560, *de facto* toleration had been established which received further sanction, though no constitutional safeguards, by the declarations of the estates' assemblies of Sandomierz (1570) and Warsaw (1573).[18]

A similar situation developed in Hungary, which was subject to a tripartite political division after 1541, leaving the central plains of Hungary and Slavonia as the new 'Pashalik' of Buda under direct Turkish rule, while the principality of Transylvania came under Turkish suzerainty. Hence, the Habsburg kingdom of Hungary, prior to the military successes in 1683–9, comprised no more than the remnants of territory of so-called 'Upper Hungary' mainly in the north, and part of the kingdom of Croatia. The emerging patterns of confessional allegiance

[17] For Laski see Betts, 'Poland, Bohemia and Hungary', 217. The beginnings of the Reformation in Poland are related briefly in J. Tazbir, 'The fate of Polish Protestantism in the Seventeenth Century', in J. K. Fedorowicz (ed.), *A Republic of Nobles: Studies in Polish History to 1864* (Cambridge, 1982), 198–217, at 198–200. For a detailed discussion of the nobility's religious affinities in the different parts of Poland-Lithuania see G. Schramm, *Der polnische Adel und die Reformation, 1548–1607* (Wiesbaden, 1965). On the introduction of Lutheranism and the secularization of the lands of the Teutonic Order by Albrecht of Hohenzollern see ibid. 116–36.

[18] Tazbir, 'Polish Protestantism'.

were similar to those prevailing in Poland, except that the military cata-
strophe of Mohács in 1526 had helped prepare the ground for the diffusion of heresy by nearly annihilating the native episcopate. Protestantism
in the shape of Lutheranism spread mainly in Upper Hungary, and
among the German-speaking urban population.[19]
  Like their Polish peers, the magnates of royal Hungary were mostly
drawn to the Calvinist doctrine, persuasively expounded by the humanist
preacher Mátyás Dévai Bíró (1500–45), an apostate Catholic priest who
had first turned Lutheran and then Calvinist. Largely as a result of his
proselytizing, the town of Debrecen became the territorial focus and
stronghold of Hungarian Calvinism.[20] However, while far-reaching toleration laws protected religious liberty for the Turkish vassals of the
Catholic princes of Transylvania, there were no comparable binding
statements from the Habsburg rulers of Hungary before the agreement
between Archduke Mathias and the Hungarian estates in 1608.[21]
  Again, parallels could be drawn to the state of Protestantism in the
Habsburg kingdom of Bohemia, which was subject to the same legal
vagaries until Rudolf II's so-called 'Letter of Majesty' in 1609. The situation was, however, complicated by the Hussite legacy of 'Utraquism',
which had incorporated the demands of the aristocratic and civic elites
for a strengthening of lay participation in the mass (communion in both
kinds and lay preaching), and control over church property. The different
varieties of this faith in a sense took the place of contemporary Calvinism
in Hungary and Poland in underwriting the distinct identity of the noble
elite in its relations with the Catholic monarch. Lutheranism in its pristine form had found a following among the German population of the
towns and had also transformed the outlook of the Bohemian Brethren.
More importantly, it had blended with the anti-Catholic tradition of
Utraquism to become the acknowledged faith of the Bohemian nobility.[22]

---

[19] Evans, *Making of the Habsburg Monarchy*, 235–6, Betts, 'Poland, Bohemia and
Hungary', 217–18. The military and spiritual reconquest of Hungary in the later 17th
century is outlined in Ingrao, *Habsburg Monarchy 1618–1815*, 64–104.
[20] Betts, 'Poland, Bohemia and Hungary', 218. For a fuller discussion of Dévai's theological views in relation to the doctrines of Luther and the Helvetic reformers see the
biographical article by D. P. Daniel in J. Hillerbrand (ed.), *The Oxford Encyclopedia of the
Reformation*, 4 vols. (Oxford, 1996), i. 475–6.
[21] See K. Péter, 'Tolerance and intolerance in Sixteenth-Century Hungary', in O. P.
Grell and R. Scribner (eds.), *Tolerance and Intolerance in the European Reformation*
(Cambridge, 1996), 249–61.
[22] For the above see F. Machilek, 'Böhmen', in Schindling and Ziegler, *Die Territorien des
Reichs*, i. 136–46. Bohemia's confessional development in the 15th and 16th centuries is
analysed closely by W. Eberhard, *Konfessionsbildung und Stände in Böhmen 1478–1530*

Since 1567, the non-Catholic estates had fought for a religious concession, and in 1575 they agreed on a formula of compromise. The so-called
'Confessio Bohemica' was modelled on the 'Confessio Augustana' to render
acceptance more palatable to Emperor Maximilian II, who had previously
granted religious liberty to the Lutheran nobility of Upper and Lower
Austria in 1568 and 1571. In the case of Bohemia, however, formal recognition was prevented by the intervention of the papal nuncio Giovanni
Delfino (1571–8), one of the signs of change which were to multiply over
the final decades of the sixteenth century from 1570 onwards to announce
the beginning of the Counter-Reformation and a confessional turnabout in
the Habsburg Monarchy and the adjoining eastern kingdoms.[23] For the
moment, however, Catholicism was on the defensive, and relied for its
survival on the staying power of the ecclesiastical princes and the two most
powerful Catholic dynasties of the Empire, the Austrian Habsburgs and the
Bavarian Wittelsbachs, who acted as the Church's secular arm.

2. THE ADVANCE OF LUTHERANISM IN THE AUSTRIAN
HEREDITARY LANDS, 1525–1578: FROM PERSECUTION
TO LIMITED LEGAL TOLERATION

For the Habsburgs, the threat of heresy rose even closer to the centre of
their political power, in the hereditary lands.[24] Demands for the admis-

(Munich, 1981). The author repudiates the term 'Neo-Utraquism' as blurring theological
distinctions and overstating the influence of Lutheranism. Instead, he stresses its continuity with the radical Hussites and its affinities with the Bohemian Brethren and suggests
using the terms 'radical' or 'left-wing Utraquism' as more appropriate, 144–9, 280–92. The
political dimension of Utraquism as the estates' creed in their arguments with Ferdinand I
is discussed ibid. 289–92. The same point is made more forcefully in id., *Monarchie und
Widerstand: Zur ständischen Oppositionsbildung im Herrschaftssystem Ferdinands I. in Böhmen*
(Munich, 1985), 82–97.

[23] The negotiations with Maximilian II are related in J. Pánek, 'Maximilian II. als König
von Böhmen', in F. Edelmayer and A. Kohler (eds.), *Kaiser Maximilian II.: Kultur und
Politik im 16. Jahrhundert* (Vienna, 1992), 55–69, at 63 ff. The importance of papal intervention emerges from secretary Ptolomeo Gallio's instructions for the Imperial nuncio,
Giovanni Delfino, of 8 and 9 Apr. 1575, see D. Neri (ed.), *Nuntiaturberichte aus Deutschland,*
viii: *Nuntiatur Giovanni Dolfins (1575–1585)* (Tübingen, 1997), 119–23. Further signs of
change were the raising of Catholic priests at the Jesuits' German seminary in Rome for the
recatholicization of Hungary in 1580, the series of Imperial Counter-Reformation decrees
for Bohemia, issued between 1584 and 1602, and the gradual recatholicization of royal
offices, see I. Bitskey, 'The Collegium Germanicum in Rome and the Beginning of Counter-
Reformation in Hungary', in Evans and Thomas, *Crown, Church and Estates*, 110–22, and I.
Auerbach, *Stände in Ostmitteleuropa: Alternativen zum monarchischen Prinzip in der frühen
Neuzeit* (Munich, 1997), 89–118.

[24] After 1627, the term was frequently understood to include Bohemia, but prior to this

sion of Protestant preaching were voiced first by an executive committee of the Upper Austrian estates in 1525, who made a shrewd bid for toleration by predicting the further spread of the present peasant rebellion into Habsburg territory if their requests were denied.[25] Admission of the Protestant faith was demanded by the Upper and Lower Austrian nobility in its own right in 1525/6 at a general assembly of the estates of the five Austrian lands of Upper and Lower Austria, jointly referred to as the 'archduchy', and the three Inner Austrian duchies. The estates of Inner Austria held back on this occasion, though showing sympathy for the reform demands of the Lutheran party, and their statements acquired recognizable Protestant overtones only at the 'post-Augsburg' diets from the late 1530s onwards.[26]

The more rapid progress of the new faith in the archduchy seems to have been the result of a coincidence of favourable circumstances, not the least important of which was an enduring dispute between the secular and ecclesiastical authorities over administrative and jurisdictional issues. Almost the entire territory was subject to the spiritual authority and ecclesiastical jurisdiction of the bishop of Passau. This bishopric was wedged in between the duchy of Bavaria and Upper Austria, with a northern border to Bohemia, and remained at least until the election of Archduke Leopold as bishop (1598, 1605–25) firmly outside Habsburg control. Moreover, the prince's rights of presentation in the archduchy were limited to the proposing of suitable clergy for visitations and the nomination of candidates for 300 benefices. In the past, Habsburg attempts to counter foreign interference had included the creation of the bishoprics of Vienna in 1469, incorporating the town and its surroundings, and Wiener Neustadt (1477), a slightly less diminutive diocese which covered the south-eastern tip of Lower Austria. The jurisdictional issue remained a bone of contention between the bishop of Passau and the Habsburgs, including Ferdinand I, and the archduchy's estates skilfully played off

---

date it denoted the five Austrian duchies, see Evans, *Making of the Habsburg Monarchy*, 157, n. 1. While Vienna remained the seat of the Austrian government, the Imperial court of Rudolf II (and with it the Imperial nunciature) was transferred to Prague in 1583, see Machilek, 'Böhmen', 146.

[25] See Ziegler, 'Nieder- und Oberösterreich', 123.

[26] For Inner Austria see Loserth, *Gegenreformation*, 56–77 and the instructive account in Scholz, *Ständefreiheit und Gotteswort*, esp. 39–64 for the early Reformation. For the archduchy see Ziegler, 'Nieder- und Oberösterreich', 120–4, and K. Gutkas, *Geschichte des Landes Niederösterreich* (St Pölten, 1973), 158, as well as S. Haider, *Geschichte Oberösterreichs* (Vienna, 1987), 164 ff. For the following account of the ecclesiastical structure and religious development of the archduchy see Ziegler, 'Nieder- und Oberösterreich', 120–4.

both sides to prevent the extradition of Protestant preachers, so that heresy was able to spread clandestinely in the shadow of this conflict. Lutheranism had been fast in acquiring a wide following especially among the Upper Austrian estates through their close contacts with the German nobility of the rest of the Empire, the most notable example being the communications between Luther and the Upper Austrian family of Jörger of Tollet, who were subsequently to play a conspicuous part among the rebels of the archduchy in 1619.[27]

The nobility's conversion was fast becoming effective in terms of the establishment of the new faith at parish level by virtue of the laity's rights of patronage. In Upper Austria, the nobility held the right of presentation (*ius patronatus*) over one in seven parishes and exerted jurisdictional powers as well as adminstrative control over ecclesiastical property (*ius advocatiae* or *Vogtei*) on behalf of one in two parishes, thus giving them power to support obliging incumbents and to trouble recalcitrants.[28]

At a general meeting of the executives of the estates of Upper, Lower, and Inner Austria in Vienna in 1556, an attempt was made to claim freedom of worship for the nobility by virtue of the terms of the Imperial religious Peace of Augsburg agreed in the previous year. In this, the delegates were presumably acting on the assumption that the abdication of Charles V and the accession of the prince who had negotiated the settlement would usher in a new and more auspicious era of Habsburg religious policy. These hopes, however, proved deceptive and the ensuing exchange of arguments between Ferdinand I and the estates' executives foreshadowed an almost identical confrontation between Ferdinand II and his subjects in 1628, though with markedly different results. In his answer of 8 February 1556, Ferdinand I firmly rejected the demands of the Protestant estates who could not claim official recognition before 1555, a precondition for the applicability of the agreement. Moreover, he pointed to the clauses which invested him as a Catholic prince with discretionary power for the settlement of the confessional status of his dominions, though he would cede his subjects the right of emigration. By way of reply to the delegates' objection that this would in the present state mean

---

[27] See H. Wurm, *Die Jörger von Tollet* (Linz, 1955), 138–64, 178–90. The Jörger intermarried with the Tschernembl family. They likewise acquired links with the Inner Austrian nobility like the Stubenberg, Rattmanstorf, Herberstein, Breuner, Praunfalk, see genealogical tables ibid. 252, 293.

[28] Fifty per cent of all parishes in Upper Austria belonged to monasteries which held a right of representation at the diet, a fact that was to become relevant for the progress of the Counter-Reformation in the later 16th century, see Ziegler, 'Nieder- und Oberösterreich', 121–2.

the depopulation of his lands, Ferdinand prudently qualified his first statement by indicating his willingness to refrain from a strict exertion of his rights. Apart from this, however, he was as averse as his predecessor to the granting of any formal concessions beyond the repeal of an earlier decree of 20 February 1554, by which he had tried to stop the practice of communion in both kinds.[29] Financial needs, however, acted as a constraint upon his religious policy. Prior to the conclusion of the Peace of Adrianople by Maximilian II in 1568, the fiscal and military demands of defence against the Turks remained such as to rule out any attempt to enforce Ferdinand I's orthodox views at the risk of a confrontation with the estates. The Emperor was hence unable to effect a reversal of the Protestant gains of the past decade among the nobility and in such larger towns as Linz and Steyr in Upper Austria or the Lower Austrian capital of Vienna.

In the end, Ferdinand's opposition could not stop the advance of Protestantism in the archduchy. Formal recognition was eventually obtained from the Emperor's more approachable successor Maximilian II (1564–76), who accepted the doctrinal formula devised by Lutheran theologians from Rostock and the Palatinate, David Chytraeus (1531–1600), and Christoph Reuter (1547–81), as the basis of his religious concessions for the estates of Upper and Lower Austria in 1568 and 1571. Maximilian's Erasmian claims seemed to cloak more straightforward heretical Lutheran views, which made him the object of Protestants' hopes as much as Catholics' fears for a bi-confessional solution for the Monarchy. In practice, however, the Emperor's religious policy remained committed to a moderate but nevertheless orthodox course of ecclesiastical and religious reform where it was feasible. Toleration in Upper and Lower Austria was limited to the nobility. At the same time, a government board was created to encourage and supervise monastic reform, and on 18 February 1572, Maximilian admonished the prelates to evict heretical clergy from their parishes and make sure that any vacancies were filled with Catholic candidates only.[30] As previously mentioned, the long-drawn-out quarrel

[29] Loserth, *Gegenreformation*, 101–4.
[30] See Haider, *Oberösterreich*, 170–1. The church agendas for Upper and Inner Austria are reprinted in G. Loesche, 'Die reformatorischen Kirchenordnungen Ober- und Innerösterreichs', *Archiv für Reformationsgeschichte*, 18 (1921), 3–4, 35–55, 121–54. For the monastic council and the decree of 1572 see T. Wiedemann, *Geschichte der Reformation und Gegenreformation im Lande unter der Enns*, vol. i (Prague, 1879), 195–202. Maximilian's views were the subject of contemporary conjecture and clerical concern: in 1555, the rector of the Jesuit college in Vienna, Nicolaus de Lanoy, reported that Maximilian attended the sermons of the Protestant preacher Stephan Phauser, see *Epistolae Mixtae . . .*, vol. v (Madrid, 1901),

over admission of the Lutheran confession in his Bohemian kingdom remained inconclusive to 1576, so that the religious settlement was in abeyance at the accession of Rudolf II.

Before discussing the course adopted by the Inner Austrian estates, who, after initial hesitation, followed their co-religionists in the archduchy and scored what seemed at the time a sweeping success on the constitutional issue in 1578, we must briefly consider the case of Tyrol. Developments here took a very different turn, with important implications for the launching of the Counter-Reformation in Inner Austria in the late sixteenth century.[31]

For various reasons, Protestantism failed to attract a significant following among the Tyrolean nobility and the urban elites. The most plausible explanation put forward argues that the strength of Catholic orthodoxy reflected an elite reaction to the experience of religiously motivated social unrest in the Peasant War of 1525–6. In the same way, it could be related to the remarkable success of anabaptism among the rural and urban population in the 1520s and 1530s.[32] The campaign against anabaptism was thus crucial in creating a Catholic alliance among the archduke, the nobility, higher clergy, and the members of the urban elite who were represented in the government at Innsbruck and among the prelates and cathedral chapters of the Tyrolean dioceses.

Of equal importance was the vigorous religious policy pursued by Emperor Ferdinand I and Archduke Ferdinand II of Tyrol (1564–95). In compliance with Ferdinand I's partition plan for his lands, collateral branches for the government of Tyrol, Inner Austria, and the archduchy were created on his death in 1564, and the government of Tyrol fell to Ferdinand's son of the same name, who had sought to stem the tide of Protestantism and supported a defensive Catholic policy as royal govern-

Lanoy to General Ignatius of Loyola, 3 Nov. 1555, 73–9. Fears on account of Emperor Maximilian II's religious views were expressed in the nuncio's letters, e.g. Giovanni Delfino's letter of 26 May 1576 in Neri, *Nuntiaturberichte*, viii. 585–6. On his deathbed, Maximilian refused to take the sacraments of confession and communion according to the Catholic rite, although stating his adherence to the Catholic faith, see Delfino's report of 12 Oct.1576, in Neri, *Nuntiaturberichte*, viii. 639–40.

[31] The following account is based on H. Noflatscher, 'Tirol, Brixen, Trient', in Schindling and Ziegler, *Die Territorien des Reichs*, i. 86–101, and J. Gelmi, *Kirchengeschichte Tirols* (Innsbruck, 1986), 88–125.

[32] The argument for Catholicism as elite reaction is made by Noflatscher, 'Tirol, Brixen, Trient', 92. See ibid. p. 91 for the early successes of anabaptism. A different explanation links the failure of Protestantism to the absence of a politically strong and separate estate of lords (*Herrenstand*), see G. Burkert, 'Protestantism and Defence of Liberties in the Austrian Lands under Ferdinand I', in Evans and Thomas, *Crown, Church and Estates*, 58–69, at 59.

or in Bohemia from 1548 to 1567. In spite of grave and extended conflicts over the competing jurisdictions of the exempt Imperial sees of Trent and Brixen, Ferdinand co-operated with both bishops to secure the swift and systematic extirpation of heresy. A Catholic printing press was established in Innsbruck in 1548 to supply the literate population with Catholic devotional literature and the clergy with homiletic works when extensive searches for heretical propaganda had revealed the considerable extent to which Lutheran books were circulating in the duchy. The prince's educational effort was boosted by foundations of Jesuit schools in Innsbruck (1560), Hall (1574), and Trent (1625) and a school ordinance in 1586, which made provisions for a modicum of elementary schooling and religious instruction under the supervision of the parish clergy. As for the pressing issue of clerical reform and education, episcopal plans for a seminary in Brixen foundered on the opposition of the archduke, who feared educational competition to the Jesuit college at Innsbruck, and the cathedral chapters, who dreaded the financial burden involved. Seminaries were eventually opened in Trent in 1579 and Brixen in 1607, but prior to this date, the dioceses relied on the support of foreign clergy, among whom the former alumni of Pope Gregory XIII's German seminary, the Germanicum in Rome, formed a small but distinguished group.[33]

A modicum of heretical activity, such as the reading of Protestant literature, was detected among the rural population in the sixteenth century, and Lutheranism prevailed among the miners of Schwaz and Hall into the first half of the seventeenth century. At the beginning of the 1630s, declining rates of productivity of the local ore mines encouraged Emperor Ferdinand II's brother Archduke Leopold V to issue sweeping decrees which led to the eviction of the Lutheran miners in 1630–2.[34]

Setting aside the unresolved question of the extent and theological hue of popular Protestantism as opposed to elite orthodoxy, it could thus be stated that Tyrol remained a Catholic stronghold throughout the period under consideration. As will be shown, co-operation between the dukes of Tyrol and Bavaria was crucial for the formation of a Counter-Reformation alliance in the Habsburg lands in 1579.

If the estates of the archduchy of Upper and Lower Austria, on the one hand, had taken the lead while Tyrol stayed outside the Protestant

[33] For the papal alumni at the Germanicum and the foundation of new seminaries see Noflatscher, 'Tirol, Brixen, Trient', 94–5.
[34] Ibid. 99.

fray, the question arises how Inner Austria and more precisely Styrian Protestantism fitted into the overall context of central European confessional change. The main stages which marked the visible progress of Protestantism as the avowed faith of the majority of the estates could be sketched out as follows: like their co-religionists in the archduchy, though on a more modest scale, Styrian noblemen maintained contacts with their peers in the German principalities of the Empire and were thus in touch with the Lutheran movement from an early stage.[35] Following up their tentative support of the reform party at the general diet of 1525–6 in Augsburg, the estates of Inner Austria began to express their requests for the preaching of the uncorrupted gospel and the suppression of superstitious cults in terms that acquired a distinctly Protestant flavour without, however, exposing themselves to sanctions by unambivalent declarations.[36] At the meeting of delegates of the five Austrian lands in Vienna in November 1536, the Styrian deputies demanded, ostensibly on behalf of the common illiterate folk, that able clergy be appointed for the preaching of the 'purified' gospel in the vernacular. Decisions on the eviction of 'suspect', meaning non-Catholic, clerics should be subject to joint examination by the clerical and lay authorities. The same strategy of formulating thinly veiled Protestant 'reform' proposals was adopted at the general diet of the five Austrian and the Bohemian lands in Prague in 1544 and individually by the Inner Austrian estates in 1549, when Ferdinand I demanded their opinion on the reform statutes decreed by a recent diocesan synod at Salzburg.[37]

Despite official prohibitions and occasional episcopal action, Protestant preachers from the Empire made their way into office as private instructors to the nobility and preachers to the estates. Through the channels of noble patronage, they began to infiltrate the Inner Austrian parish clergy. In his efforts to stem this tide, Ferdinand's ban on Lutheran literature in 1551 proved as ineffectual as the previously mentioned decree of 20 February 1554, by which he tried to prohibit the use of the lay chalice and sought to enforce the obligation of annual confession and communion. The same applied to his Catholic church

---

[35] For some of these links see the example of the Jörger family quoted above. The scope and precise nature of these links would merit further inquiry.

[36] For the estates' tactics up to 1556 see Loserth, *Gegenreformation*, 56–105.

[37] The exchange of arguments between the clergy, the Upper and Lower Austrian government, and the deputies of the estates of the five Austrian lands are related in detail in J. Loserth, 'Die Salzburger Provinzialsynode von 1549', *AÖG* 85 (1898), 131–357. The deliberations and decrees of this synod are further discussed below.

ordinance for the five Austrian lands, issued in 1560. The decree on compulsory annual communion was revoked in 1556, but this conciliatory gesture failed to placate the Styrian estates, who had protested in vain against the deposition of their Lutheran leader, the *Landeshauptmann* Hans von Ungnad, in the previous year. Over the next decade, Protestantism came into the open with ever fewer restraints. While Ferdinand's successor Emperor Maximilian II was struggling to limit toleration to the nobility of Upper and Lower Austria and successfully fended off the Bohemian estates' attempt to obtain similar safeguards, events took a different turn in Inner Austria. As will become clear from the following, Karl II, who in 1564 acceded as duke to the Inner Austrian part of Ferdinand's heritage, was confronted with a number of adverse circumstances which left him in a weak position to confront the estates' religious demands at the beginning of his reign and subsequently obstructed the policy of recatholicization which he tried to implement during the last years of his life.

Among the determinants of Protestant progress, Ferdinand I's financial legacy was crucial in severely circumscribing the young archduke's scope of action in negotions with his heretical subjects. At his accession in 1564, Karl II was obliged to accept a share of 1,000,000 fl. of the dynasty's debts, against which he could muster a mere 100,000 fl. annual revenue from his various sources of income. Among these, customs and tolls formed the single most important item.[38] The Inner Austrian estates were quick to perceive the strategic advantages to be derived from the archduke's financial straits. Under Styrian leadership, the Inner Austrian estates from the beginning of his reign countered Karl II's demands for adequate financial support with petitions for the admission of the Protestant faith as defined by the Confession of Augsburg. Following years of quibbling on the side of the prince and unsatisfactory negotiations with the full assembly of the estates of the nobility, clergy, and ducal towns, Karl eventually tried to obtain a tax grant from an assembly of the Protestant ducal municipalities in Styria. Contrary to custom, they were convoked separate from the rest of the estates to assemble in Bruck an der Mur in 1571. The idea was to render the urban Protestants more tractable by depriving them of aristocratic support. This, however, backfired by

---

[38] Pirchegger, *Geschichte der Steiermark*, i. 415. The author gives the following figures for the distribution of the dynastic debts in 1564: Upper and Lower Austria: 887,961 fl.; Tyrol and Further Austria: 2,103, 484 fl.; Inner Austria: 1,057, 277 fl.

provoking vociferous protest from the Styrian nobility, who now pressed for a comprehensive declaration granting religious freedom to the estates and the towns in general before continuing negotiations on the settling of the debts and military expenditure. After further futile prevarication, Karl II eventually made a statement to the diet of the Styrian estates assembled in the capital in 1572 which became known as the religious 'Pacification of Graz'.

Far from being clear and unequivocal in its meaning, this concession was elusive on important points and had built-in weaknesses. Essentially, it amounted to acceptance of the religious status quo regarding the spread of the new faith among the nobility. Freedom of conscience was granted to the estates and, after further haggling, to their rural and urban subjects, but the duke succeeded in attaching several strings, the most notable of which was the omission of safeguards for the Protestant ducal towns. Echoing the terms of the religious Peace of Augsburg, it was stated that the concession was to last until a definite and general agreement had been reached. Its conditional nature was further stressed by clauses that stated the nobility's dual obligation to use their liberty 'with modesty and all due obedience to the prince' and to punish offenders who in any way molested the Catholic party, thus effectively making its validity dependent on ducal grace. It was likewise deliberately vague in confirming the 'customary and traditional' rights of the nobility as church patrons without any reference to the presentation of Protestant candidates, though a strictly secret verbal 'amendment' assured the estates of a favourable decision in cases of dispute with the clergy. Karl also avoided any reference to the future which would have elevated this concession to permanent constitutional rank. In contrast, his reticence on this question was calculated to leave his successor free to adopt a different policy.

Nevertheless, the estates were sufficiently placated for the moment to proceed with a scheme for the settlement of the ducal debts, but they were soon disabused of their hopes for lasting confessional peace by the impact of two decisions of major consequence, taken in the same and the preceding year. In 1571, negotiations between the Habsburg and Wittelsbach dynasties procured the marriage of Duke Karl of Inner Austria with Maria of Bavaria, daughter of the fervently Catholic Duke Albrecht V (1550–79). As will be shown, this dynastic match was instrumental in paving the way for a Counter-Reformation alliance of Habsburg and Wittelsbach princes in 1579. The no less momentous decision to invite the notorious shock-troops of the Counter-Reformation, the Society of Jesus, to Graz, where they opened a college and a school in

1572–3, was an early example of Bavarian influence bearing upon the Inner Austrian duke's religious policy.[39] The educational and polemical activity of the Jesuits among the population of the duchy's capital of Graz, and the arrival of the Dominican Felician Ninguarda as papal emissary and itinerant nuncio in 1578, spurred the alarmed estates into defensive action. Again, financial exigency provided the estates with a lever for the exaction of further safeguards for their religious liberty. The occasion arose in the same year, 1578, when Emperor Maximilian's son and successor Rudolf II (1576–1612) entrusted Karl formally with the maintenance and defence of the Hungarian–Croatian border of his dominions, which formed the Empire's south-eastern military frontier against the Turks. Although the Peace of Adrianople concluded by Maximilian II in 1568 gave a brief respite at that stage and was successively renewed in 1576 and in 1584, Turkish border raids continued until full-blown war for the Hungarian fortifications broke out in 1593.[40]

To cover the additional costs of military expenditure which fell to the Inner Austrian duke, a system of regular proportional contributions by the estates of the three duchies had to be implemented. A general diet was therefore convoked for 1 January 1578 to the ducal town of Bruck to deliberate on military defence measures and the details of the financial scheme.[41] The moment would hence have seemed auspicious for a redress

---

[39] For the campaign that led to the 'Pacification' of 1572 see Loserth, *Gegenreformation*, 126–204 and id., 'Die steirische Religionspazifikation und die Fälschung des Vizekanzlers Dr. Wolfgang Schranz', *JGGPÖ* 48 (1927), 1–57, at 5–11. The negotiations between Archduke Karl II and the General of the Society, Francis Borgia, for a Jesuit settlement in Graz began in 1569 and are related in detail in A. Socher, SJ, *Historia Provinciae Austriae Societatis Jesu* (Vienna, 1740), 168–75. A college and a grammar school were founded for the express purpose of raising the nobility's youth in the Catholic faith and for the training of priests to fill the depleted ranks of the native orthodox clergy, see Socher, *Historia*, 172–3, and Karl II's letter to General Borgia of 21 May 1571, which is reprinted in R. Peinlich, *Geschichte des Gymnasiums in Graz*, i (Graz, 1869), 7. The above aims are also stated in the founding deed for the Jesuit college and gymnasium, dated 12 Nov. 1573. The text is printed in full in Peinlich, *Geschichte*, i. 8–10.

[40] For Ninguarda's mission see below, Ch. 3. For the military situation in the 16th century see L. Toifl and H. Leitgeb, *Die Türkeneinfälle in der Steiermark und in Kärnten vom 15. bis zum 17. Jahrhundert* (Vienna, 1991). These hostilities gained unforeseen political momentum in 1604, when they fused with a Hungarian uprising under the leadership of the Transylvanian prince Stephen Bocskay during the 'Long Turkish War' of 1593–1606. The repudiation of the Peace of Vienna (1606) by Rudolf II caused a crisis in dynastic government in the years 1606–11 which threatened domestic collapse and the loss of the Monarchy's Hungarian kingdom in 1606–11/12, see below, Ch. 4.

[41] For the distribution of fiscal contributions see S. Vilfan, 'Crown, Estates and the Financing of Defence in Inner Austria, 1500–1630', in Evans and Thomas, *Crown, Church*

of the defects of the 'Pacification' of 1572, and the estates' subsequent publication of the terms indeed conveyed a sense of sweeping victory to contemporaries in both confessional camps of the Empire. On closer inspection, however, the supposed amendments turn out to be curiously limited if measured by the strength of the Protestants' negotiating position. They are also inconclusive as to the central question of the concession's constitutional status and duration. Worse still, the version registered in the estates' records received no official sanction by ducal signature, though with a view to the settling of the financial issue, Karl refrained from publicly denying its authenticity for the time being and hence confirmed the estates' interpretation of tacit approval. According to their account, a ducal promise to abide by the terms of the concession of 1572 had been made by secret, oral declaration of his Catholic privy counsellors in 1576.

At the beginning of the negotiations, in a petition of 4 February 1578, the estates formulated a demand of unprecedented scope that would by virtue of its inclusion of all rural and urban subjects have established confessional parity well beyond the terms granted by the concession of Augsburg. Thus they urged a written 'Assecuration' of general religious toleration, excluding no Protestant in the country, regardless of his estate, who voluntarily adopted the Augsburg faith. This might have been a strategic measure, designed to strengthen their bargaining position at the outset by deliberately aiming too high. In any case, the estates quickly climbed down when confronted with firm ducal opposition and concentrated on demanding safeguards for their urban co-religionists and provisos for the nascent Protestant school and church ministry, the formal organization of which was already under way in Styria. As previously mentioned, no authenticated document of the ducal reply of 9 February 1578 existed. Instead, two versions were drafted, one recorded and subsequently published in essence by the Inner Austrian estates, the other prepared secretly by Karl II's Catholic vice-chancellor and councillor, the lawyer Wolfgang Schranz, for future political use. In the circumstances, it seems plausible to assume that a fair amount of equivocation was resorted

<hr/>

and Estates, 70–9. The figures on pp. 73–6 show that by the system established in 1578, Styria continued to pay the largest share, but while the duchy had covered between 56 and 59% in the years 1530–78, its contribution was reduced to 45% in the period 1607–18. The organization of Inner Austria's defence system is discussed in detail in W. Schulze, *Landesdefension und Staatsbildung: Studien zum Kriegswesen des innerösterreichischen Territorialstaates 1564–1619* (Vienna, 1973). For the following account see Loserth, *Gegenreformation*, 255–83. The diet was held at Bruck an der Mur, as an outbreak of plague had reached Graz, where the diet would normally have assembled, ibid. 255.

to by both parties in their verbal dealings, and that 'adjustments' were subsequently made in the written versions, so that the truth of the matter must be gauged from the likelihood of the claims.

The main point in the estates' rendering was a confirmation of the Pacification of 1572, applied expressly to the assembled estates of the three duchies and the ducal towns, and 'any other adherents of the Augsburg Confession'. This, however, does not square with the following admission of a ducal proviso for Karl's right of disposition over his municipalities and estates—as opposed to the nobility's subjects—nor with his refusal to grant the right of unrestricted admission of Protestant preachers to every urban community in his lands, even if the promise not to trouble or 'burden the conscience' of the Protestant burghers is accepted as authentic. Given Karl II's previous firm insistence on the exemption of his towns and demesne from any formal concessions, the added clause that this was not to be misread as an intention to suppress the nascent Protestant school and church ministry in the duchies' capitals of Graz, Laibach, and Klagenfurt—which was incidentally no ducal municipality but a *patrimonium* of the Carinthian estates—as well as Judenburg in Upper Styria appears to have been glued on for rather obvious purposes. In contrast, the estates faithfully recorded Karl II's ominous declaration that he intended to uphold the Catholic faith for himself and his family, thus inserting his earlier safeguards for his successor's freedom of action in religious matters.

The ducal version was drafted after the event, with the clear objective of providing arguments to counter Protestant claims arising from Counter-Reforming action. It is hence more rigorous in stressing the voluntary and conditional nature of the concession, omitting any but a passing reference to freedom of conscience for the burghers while expressly prohibiting the acceptance of Protestant preachers in future. Further, the activity of Lutheran preachers and teachers already present in the above four towns was limited to services to the nobility and their entourage or households, on condition of the preachers' good behaviour.[42]

It seems implausible to assume that the estates acquiesced in a concession that would effectively have outlawed the incipient organization of a Protestant institutional network. However, their willingness to accept an

---

[42] A cogent reconstruction of the negotiations and the drafting of the different versions can be found in Loserth, 'Religionspazifikation', 12–21, 30–57, with a synopsis of both texts on pp. 22–30. Supplementary information mainly on the estates' document is provided by id., 'Zur Geschichte des Brucker Libells', *JGGPÖ* 53 (1932), 7–23.

equivocal verbal commitment in place of a plainly worded written document is striking and stands in need of explanation.[43] The most plausible reason for this apparent lack of judgement or determination would seem to lie in the 'primacy of foreign policy' and, linked to this, a peculiar legalistic notion of political relations between prince and subject which formed the guiding principle of the Inner Austrian estates' action. This outlook received an ideological underpinning from the doctrine of 'passive obedience' that was propagated by the estates' theologians and became the accepted position of the majority of the nobility, with significant consequences for the outcome of the confessional conflict.[44]

Historians have followed contemporary Catholic critics in asserting that military exigency worked overwhelmingly in favour of the Protestant party, limiting as it undoubtedly did the prince's scope of action.[45] However, given the geographical proximity and frequent destructive border raids of the Turkish troops which threatened the estates of the nobility and the lives of their subjects, the same could be claimed with equal plausibility for the position of the Protestants. Considerations of military exigency were arguably uppermost in their minds when they accepted repeated postponement of a religious concession after the accession of Karl II in 1564. This situation was changed to some degree, though not, the present evidence suggests, radically, when the beginning of Counter-Reformation activity in the wake of the archduke's Bavarian marriage disturbed the tacit confessional agreement. 'Primacy of foreign policy' in the shape of defence against the permanent Turkish threat had gained fresh strength in 1578 from the imposition of joint responsibility for the administrative and financial upkeep of the Empire's south-eastern borders. Financial support was voted formally at the Imperial diets, but for most of the period, the military threat seemed too remote to the

---

[43] The apologetic tone of the concluding sentences in the estates' document is striking: 'Dieweil sie dann E[urer] F[ürstlichen] D[urchlauch]t jetzige mündtliche erclerung und vertröstung anderst nicht verstehen künnen dann daß es iro, der lande, negst übergebnen schriftlichen erclärung nichts durchaus zuwider, sonder eine gn[ädigste] ratification derselben sei, wiewol sie an E[urer] F[ürstlichen] D[urchlauch]t gn[ädigstem] wolmeinen hievor gn[ädigst] nie gezweifelt, allein was sie sich der mißgünner und unruehigen leut [meaning the Jesuits] halber besorgen müeßen, so wolte inen doch keineswegs gebüren in E[urer] F[ürstlichen] D[urchlauch]t fürstliche gnedigiste wort ainichen zweifl zu stellen.' Quoted from the text in Loserth, 'Religionspazifikation', 25.
[44] The doctrine of passive or 'suffering' obedience is discussed below.
[45] This position was allegedly first voiced by one of Karl II's (Jesuit) court clergy in 1578, see the quotation in Loserth, *Gegenreformation*, 247. The same point is made forcefully by Mezler-Andelberg, 'Erneuerung des Katholizismus und Gegenreformation in Innerösterreich', 183.

majority of the Imperial estates to induce prompt payment, so that their contributions were notoriously in arrears.[46]

Although the Inner Austrian estates did seek to harness necessity to their cause when pressing for constitutional safeguards, they did so without disputing in principle their duty to render financial and military support, and in the contest with Archduke Ferdinand at the end of the century, it was the prince who was able to press the religious issue in spite of imminent military disaster. Until then, the almost permanent exigency of military defence against the Turks, and, in 1614 against their Transylvanian vassal Gabriel Bethlen, exacerbated the persistent struggle to secure financial aid from the Emperor and the Imperial estates. Throughout the period of the Counter-Reformation under Archduke Karl and Ferdinand II, the Protestant estates were therefore in the awkward position of petitioning the Imperial Protestants for intercession with the prince in the religious matter while at the same time putting up a united front with the Catholic ruler and his episcopal envoy on the issue of financial aid from the Imperial diet.[47]

It could be further argued that the notion of overriding necessity creating a bond between the Catholic prince and the Protestant estates regardless of confessional differences formed part of a broader concept of relations between ruler and subject which assumed a state of harmony achieved through negotiation of interests as the normal state of affairs. In this, the estates would have shared common ground with any of the

---

[46] See J. Loserth, *Innerösterreich und die militärischen Maßnahmen gegen die Türken im 16. Jahrhundert: Studien zur Geschichte der Landesdefension und der Reichshilfe* (Graz, 1934), esp. 113–17, 149–68.

[47] See the illuminating account in Loserth, *Innerösterreich und die militärischen Maßnahmen*. The envoy to the Imperial court in 1597/8 was Bishop Martin Brenner of Seckau, whose zeal in this mission was praised by the Styrian estates, see ibid. 166–7. In spite of his endeavours, the Imperial contribution was not forthcoming and the estates were frequently forced to borrow from Viennese and foreign merchants and noblemen, ibid. 171. The (selective) list of 1591 recording arrears in Imperial aid granted by the diet in 1587 is revealing: thus, the outstanding Imperial contribution amounted to no less than 825,409 fl. from the *Reichspfennigmeisteramt*, while the (electoral) bishoprics of Cologne, Münster, and Trier owed a total of nearly 130,000 fl. Unpaid contributions from Burgundy and Lorraine amounted to *c*.200,000 fl. In 1605, arrears from Württemberg totalled another 70,000 fl., see p. 115 n. 1, p. 171, and the figures for 1611 and 1623 on pp. 171–8. In 1614, a unique situation was created when the most general of all Habsburg assemblies convened in Linz to deliberate on the situation in the principality of Transylvania. With Turkish connivance, the Habsburg protégé Sigmund Báthory had been evicted by Gabriel Béthlen, recognition of whom was now demanded by the sultan. The assembly was summoned by Emperor Matthias and attended by delegates from Spain, the Spanish Netherlands, Hungary, Bohemia, Moravia, Silesia, Lausitz, the archduchy of Upper and Lower Austria, and Inner Austria, see ibid. 175 n. 2.

contemporary representative assemblies, regardless of the actual allot-
ment of power among the different parts which together were thought to
form the 'body politic'.[48] However, faith in the feasibility of consensus
did not imply blindness to the existence of important divisive issues, most
notably the prince's attempts to extend his fiscal powers.[49] In the reign of
Karl II, the protests of the Inner Austrian estates concentrated on the
interference of 'foreign troublemakers', i.e. the Jesuits and the nuncio,
who were charged with undermining the peace between the prince and
his loyal Protestant subjects, and this would seem to have been a genuine
rendering of their perception of the Counter-Reformation as an extrane-
ous threat. In this assumption, they were not entirely mistaken, as Karl
II's temporary public withdrawal of support for the belligerent approach
of the Catholic reformers at his court in 1581 would suggest.[50] Nor did
the Protestant nobility's conciliatory approach to the question of written
safeguards form a deviation from the pattern of estates' politics in the rest
of the Austrian duchies. While negotiations on the religious issue went on
at the diet of Bruck, the estates of Lower Austria were assembled in
Vienna to take the oath of allegiance to the recently elected Emperor
Rudolf II (1576–1612). Like their Inner Austrian co-religionists, the
assembly demanded a written confirmation of their religious liberties,
referring to Emperor Maximilian II's concessions of 1568 and 1571.
Anticipating the Counter-Reformation alliance that came into being in
the following year, Rudolf II turned to the dukes of Tyrol and Bavaria for
advice on the best way to achieve his aims without ceding ground in
matters of religion. Duke Albrecht V urged the Emperor to embark on a
policy of gradual but steady retrenchment, starting with the burghers and
the Protestant school and church ministry in the capital and proceeding
step by step to a complete repeal of the religious concessions. While
aiming in the same direction, Archduke Ferdinand's memorandum
concentrated on the importance of preventing further loss of constitutional ground to the Protestants. Taking this advice to heart, Rudolf II

---

[48] Revisionist critique of conflict-centred Whig interpretations of British 17th-century
history has led in turn to an overemphasis on the prevalence of consensus-oriented parlia-
mentary politics. The theoretical assumptions of 17th-century politico-legal language are
examined in G. Burgess, *The Politics of the Ancient Constitution* (Pennsylvania, 1993), esp.
115–211.

[49] See Burkert, 'Protestantism and Defence of Liberties in the Austrian Lands under
Ferdinand I', 58–69, esp. 59, and more fully id., *Landesfürst und Stände: Karl V., Ferdinand
I. und die österreichischen Erbländer im Ringen um Gesamtstaat und Landesinteressen* (Graz,
1987).

[50] See below, Ch. 3.

resorted to equivocation and eventually managed to coax the nobility to proceed with the taking of the oath against a merely verbal promise not to revoke the concession. Such commitments notwithstanding, Rudolf immediately embarked on an attempt to put the Bavarian advice into practice and a decree of 6 May 1578 sought to abolish the Protestant church and school ministry in Vienna with one blow.

This example served as a warning to the Upper Austrian estates' assembly in Linz, who made a solemn declaration of their determination to abide by the Protestant faith before taking the required oath of obedience. Moreover, they unflinchingly defended the Protestant burghers of the duchy against a similar attack to that in Lower Austria. On this as on later occasions, they stood by their avowed support for the towns, a policy that was considerably to strengthen the Protestant cause in the future conflicts with the Emperor. In spite of these significant differences, however, the Upper Austrian estates dared not refuse taking the oath of allegiance to extort a more binding declaration from Rudolf II.[51] Hence, if future events were to prove the Inner Austrian estates' judgement misguided, they were at this stage not out of step with the approach adopted by the political elite of the rest of the Austrian Protestants.

3. PATTERNS OF PROTESTANTIZATION: LEGAL, ECONOMIC, GEOGRAPHIC

A balance sheet of the achievements and shortcomings of Inner Austrian Protestantism in 1578 would first and foremost have to note its success in winning over the vast majority of the nobility who, together with the prelates' *curia* of the estates, formed the political elite. In October 1580, the recently appointed nuncio in Graz, Germanico Malaspina (1580–4), estimated that there were not more than five Catholic noblemen to be found in Inner Austria.[52] Of potential importance was the attempt to

---

[51] The negotiations attending the taking of the oath in Vienna and Linz and the beginnings of the Counter-Reformation in both parts of the archduchy are related in V. Bibl, *Die Einführung der katholischen Gegenreformation in Niederösterreich durch Kaiser Rudolf II. (1576–1580)* (Innsbruck, 1900), id., 'Erzherzog Ernst und die Gegenreformation in Niederösterreich (1576–1590)', *MIÖG*, supplementary vol. 6 (1901), 575–96, and for Upper Austria id., *Die Religionsreformation Kaiser Rudolfs II. in Oberösterreich*, offprint from *AÖG* 109 (Vienna, 1921).

[52] Malaspina's letter of 28 Sept. 1580 is reprinted in *Nb I*, at 26–8. A contemporary alphabetical register of those Styrian noblemen whose names appeared in the estates' records relating to religious affairs in the years 1581–2 lists no fewer than 130 members of the nobility by name as adherents of the Augsburg Confession, see appendix no. 9 to Loserth, *Gegenreformation*, 597–8.

form a union of Protestant estates of the three duchies in 1578 to co-ordinate their actions where matters of religion were concerned. In the negotiations with Archduke Ferdinand, the select committee which usually conducted the estates' business between the diets (*Verordnetenausschuß*) now acted as its messenger and executive 'in religious affairs'. Apart from this tenuous link, however, the envisaged Protestant union remained rather insubstantial. Such autonomous estate action as did come about nevertheless became the butt of the prince's charges of disobedience after 1600.[53]

As for the share of the estates' power at parish level, it would seem that the nobility's right of presentation to full parish benefices was a negligible quantity, though such fragmentary evidence as has survived suggests that this statement has to be slightly qualified for Lower Styria. Below this level, however, where rights of presentation to curacies and other lesser-endowed benefices were concerned, the nobility exerted influence in 50 per cent of all recorded cases. As for the jurisdictional representation and economic control of the parishes by right of *Vogtei*, estimates suggest that the nobility owned this right in one-third of all parishes. Powerful estate owners like Hans Hoffmann von Grünbüchel and Strechau, who held the *Vogtei* to such parishes as Irdning, Liezen, Rottenmann, and Oppenberg in Upper Styria, were able to exert pressure on the choice of the incumbent as well. Lay expansionism reached a peak at the Styrian diet in 1569, when an appeal for the official cession of this right was made to the episcopal powers concerned.[54] In general, however, the impact of this right arguably did not match the importance of the clergy's and prince's more direct control through presentation of candidates as parish priests.

Hence, if Protestantism was nevertheless spreading at parish level, it was helped by clerical neglect and inconsistent princely policy rather than resulting from any inherent structural flaw.[55] This is not to deny that in

---

[53] The wording of the estates' vow to proceed jointly in matters affecting religion is quoted in Loserth, *Gegenreformation*, 278. For the conflict with Ferdinand see the account in Ch. 4 below.

[54] The proposition of 1569 is mentioned by K. Amon, *Die Steiermark vor der Glaubensspaltung: Kirchliche Zustände 1490–1520* (Graz, 1960), 138–40. This right was never ceded, and Amon's generalizing inferences from this example and from Hans Hoffmann's exceptional case are debatable. In particular, his claim that the *Vogtei* in this period conferred the right of presentation *de facto*, though not *de jure*, would need substantiation.

[55] For the above information on the legal situation see the fragmentary evidence of the visitation record edited by R. Höfer, *Die landesfürstliche Visitation der Pfarren und Klöster in*

those instances in which the nobility *did* exert patronage, Protestant intervention could have a direct impact on parish life, as, for example, in the wealthy Upper Styrian parish of Pöls, which Ferdinand I had mortgaged to the most influential Protestant estate owner in the region, Hans Hoffmann, who subsequently procured the appointment of Protestant incumbents.[56] The proselytizing efforts of substantial estate owners like Hoffmann, who founded Protestant schools for his subjects, preached to them in person, and encouraged them to attend religious instruction at his castle, constituted a formative influence in this region and initiated a lasting change in its confessional complexion. On the whole, however, the frequent recurrence of the same names in the documentary evidence on such activity which mentions the Stadl and Hoffmann in Upper Styria and the families of Stubenberg, Herberstein, Herberstorff, or Windischgrätz in other parts of the duchy, suggests that the number of noblemen in Styria and Inner Austria at large who envisaged a comprehensive and thorough Protestantization at parish level was limited.

In terms of quantity, the nobility's control of a substantial part of the municipalities in Styria was of far greater importance. While two-thirds or fifteen of the duchy's twenty-one towns were directly subject to the prince, this applied to only seventeen of the ninety-five market towns (*Märkte*) that dotted Styrian territory in the sixteenth century. A very

---

der Steiermark in den Jahren 1544/1545 (Graz, 1992), 79–86 and Amon, *Steiermark vor der Glaubensspaltung*, 114–25, 225–44.

[56] Höfer, *Landesfürstliche Visitation*, 84, and W. Huber, 'Hanns Friedrich Hoffmann, Freiherr von Grünbüchel und Strechau, der bedeutendste Vertreter des Protestantismus in Innerösterreich im 16. Jahrhundert', *JGGPÖ* 48 (1927), 58–165, at 90–4 for his proselytizing activity in Styria and, through his office as bailiff of the bishop of Bamberg, on the latter's estates in Carinthia. Hoffmann's family were comparative 'newcomers' among the Styrian lords' estate and had risen through services to the emperor and archduke as late as the 15th century. Hans Friedrich (1530/5–89) rounded off his inherited estates with further acquisitions in Upper Styria which made him the foremost estate owner in this region, nicknamed the 'king of the Enns valley'. The family was related to the Upper Austrian Jörger von Tollet, and Hans Friedrich himself married into the Starhemberg family after the death of his first wife from the likewise Protestant Styrian Windischgrätz. Like his father and his son, Hans Friedrich was *Landmarschall* or president of the Styrian estates' diet (1564–89). In this function, he mediated in negotiations between the ducal government and the estates and presented the ducal propositions. Together with the Styrian estates' secretary Matthes Amman, Hoffmann served as commissioner to the board of the school and church ministry and was in charge of the recruitment of clergy from abroad. He also had a hand in the drafting of the estates' version of the religious concession of 1578. A Catholic campaign to charge Hoffmann with high treason in connection with an anti-Catholic uprising by his subjects in the Upper Styrian parishes of Lassing, Liezen, and Oppenberg in 1587 resulted in Hoffmann's withdrawal from active involvement in estates' politics, though he nominally remained in office until 1589. For the biographical information see the above article by Huber. The uprising and its results are discussed below, Ch. 5.

few of these were subject to episcopal rule, but it was the Lutheran nobility who exerted temporal power over the vast majority of these settlements. Throughout the sixteenth century, members of the estates can be shown to have connived at and even supported the spread of Protestantism among the burghers and populace not only of these places, but of the neighbouring ducal or episcopal municipalities as well.[57] This growth of urban Protestantism in Styria and the rest of the Inner Austrian duchies constitutes a no less remarkable triumph of the new faith than its sweeping success among the nobility. As in the case of the estates, links with the Imperial Protestants were instrumental in acquainting Styria's commoners with the new faith. Economic contacts through trade and commerce between the duchy's merchants and the Imperial towns and fairs were crucial, though the adverse effects of war acted as a constraining factor.

By the end of the fifteenth century, the combined impact of Turkish raids (1471–80), outbreaks of plague, and, above all, the Hungarian war (1479–90) had led to a general economic crisis. The inflation caused by the minting of debased coins, the notorious *Schinderlinge*, during the Hungarian war wiped out Styrian merchant capital if it was not rescued by timely transfer to the Imperial cities in the form of permanent bonds (*Ewiggeldrenten*) or by the acquisition of landed property. After 1490, south German and Italian merchants took over a significant share of Styrian trade with Hungary and Italy. This period witnessed in fact very few if spectacular careers of Styrian merchants in the south German towns, e.g. the rise of the Eggenberg family from Radkersburg in Lower Styria, who made their fortune in Augsburg, and Heinrich Ernst, a former citizen of Graz, who rose to be one of the wealthiest members of the Nuremberg merchant elite.

In general, Styrian merchants continued their trade as agents of one of the prominent south German houses. During the first half of the sixteenth century, links with the German fairs and the cities of Augsburg, Memmingen, Nördlingen, Frankfurt, and, most conspicuously, Nuremberg were thus supported. Contacts established through these routes of commerce were arguably the reason behind the fact that the larger Styrian towns like Graz, Bruck, or Radkersburg figured among the

---

[57] Figures are taken from O. Pickl, 'Die wirtschaftliche Lage der Städte und Märkte der Steiermark im 16. Jahrhundert', in W. Rausch (ed.), *Die Stadt an der Schwelle zur Neuzeit* (Linz, 1980), 93–128, at 94. The examples of Georg von Stubenberg's support for his patrimonial town of Mureck and the ducal town of Bruck, and the case of Karl von Herberstorff's support for Radkersburg, which was subject to the bishop of Seckau, will be discussed below, Chs. 3 and 5.

earliest Protestant towns on record. The fact that the wealthy arms manu-
facturer and fervent Lutheran Sebald Pögl received news of the fateful
diet at Worms in 1521 through his correspondence with this town is a case
in point.[58] The diffusion of the new doctrine among the urban population was subsequently furthered by the wealthier burghers' emulation of
the Inner Austrian nobility in having their sons educated at one of the
Protestant universities of the Empire, among which Tübingen, Jena,
Wittenberg, and Rostock were preferred.[59] In spite of the prince's determination to exempt his towns from any conceivable concession, a declaration of faith was made by the representatives of the ducal towns at the
diet of 1572 on behalf of sixteen mostly ducal towns and markets, including the duchy's capital Graz and the economically most important mining
and trading towns of Upper and Lower Styria.[60]

Joint forces should have formed the basis of a strong alliance between
the Protestant burghers and the nobility, as was realized by the Upper
Austrian estates when they came to the aid of their co-religionists in the
towns in 1578. However, although the Styrian estates' sympathetic efforts
and petitions on behalf of the duke's urban subjects continued until the
end of the century, there were divisive issues that prevented an effective
alliance in this duchy. Pre-eminent among these was the question of taxation and political representation at the diet. As in Lower Austria and in

---

[58] See O. Pickl, 'Grazer Finanzkaufleute und Fernhändler im 15. und 16. Jahrhundert',
in *850 Jahre Graz* (Graz, 1978), 147–65 and F. Tremel, 'Die oberdeutschen Kaufleute in der
Steiermark im 15. und 16. Jahrhundert', *ZHVST* 40 (1949), 13–35, and id., 'Der öster-
reichische Kaufmann im 16. Jahrhundert', in H. J. Mezler-Andelberg (ed.), *Festschrift Karl
Eder* (Innsbruck, 1959), 119–40. For Pögl's contacts see M. Liebmann, 'Die Anfänge der
Reformation in der Steiermark', in *Evangelisch in der Steiermark*, catalogue of the exhibition
(Graz, 1981), 7–15, at 9–10.
[59] See L. Achberger, 'Die innere Entwicklung der evangelischen Kirche in der
Steiermark im 16. Jahrhundert', in *Evangelisch in der Steiermark*, 25. For a close analysis
revealing the marked attraction of the University of Tübingen, where Jakob Andreae's
conciliatory theology was taught, see A. Kohler, 'Bildung und Konfession: Zum Studium
der Studenten aus den habsburgischen Ländern an Hochschulen im Reich (1560–1620)', in
G. Klingenstein, H. Lutz, and G. Stourzh (eds.), *Bildung, Politik und Gesellschaft: Studien
zur Geschichte des europäischen Bildungswesens vom 16. bis zum 20. Jahrhundert* (Munich,
1978), 64–123, at 75. The subordinate importance of Wittenberg emerges also from Johann
Loserth's broader discussion of Styrian contacts with the Imperial academies, see id., *Die
Beziehungen der steiermärkischen Landschaft zu den Universitäten Wittenberg, Rostock,
Heidelberg, Tübingen, Straßburg und anderen in der zweiten Hälfte des 16. Jahrhunderts* (Graz,
1899).
[60] These sixteen municipalities were: Graz, Marburg, Leoben, Judenburg, Radkersburg,
Fürstenfeld, Rottenmann, Voitsberg, Aussee, Neumarkt, upper and lower Eisenerz (counted
individually), Weißkirchen, Feldbach, Oberzeiring, Obdach, see J. Loserth, 'Die
Gegenreformation in Innerösterreich und der innerösterreichische Herren- und
Ritterstand', offprint from *MIÖG*, supplementary volume 6 (1901), 599.

Bohemia after 1547, the towns' say in political deliberations was a negligible quantity. Among the Styrian municipalities, only the ducal towns possessed the right of representation, amounting to the casting of a single collective vote by their elected delegate, the so-called *Städtemarschall*. Confessional affinities notwithstanding, the estates remained adamant in turning down as an unacceptable 'novelty' ('neuerung') the towns' petition in 1568 for the granting of individual votes to each ducal municipality.[61]

Hierarchic concerns thus outweighed considerations of expediency with regard to a strengthening of the Protestant party, however desirable. While emphasizing in their dealings with the prince the tripartite constitution of the estates as composed of the nobility, prelates, and commoners, the nobility in fact espoused a more limited concept of the diet as an aristocratic and clerical redoubt. This concept survived the forcible settlement of the confessional issue in 1628 to form the political complement of re-established elite consensus, Catholic hegemony constituting the other part of its ideological foundations.[62]

The nobility's stance on the question of political participation was in line with their attitude towards economic points of friction. In stark contrast to the token representation of their interests, the towns were obliged to raise one-quarter of the total tax granted at the diet in 1510, regardless of the fact that the crisis of trade in the south German towns and the Turkish advance in the east had severe repercussions on Inner Austria's trade and commercial prosperity.[63] To aggravate matters, the estates' towns which engaged in trade were nevertheless exempt from general taxation. Likewise, noblemen and prelates used their tax privileges for urban residences to engage in the local wine trade. A quarrel over this issue broke out in 1535 and dragged on until the end of the sixteenth century. Eventually, at the beginning of the seventeenth century, the estates acknowledged the fact of urban decline by agreeing to

---

[61] Mell, *Verfassungs- und Verwaltungsgeschichte*, 330.

[62] For relations between the estates of the lords and knights (*Herren- und Ritterstand*) and the towns see Mell, *Verfassungs- und Verwaltungsgeschichte*, 329–31.

[63] See Pickl, 'Städte und Märkte', 100–8. Tremel argues that the 'age of the merchant' in Austria gave way to the 'age of the nobility' from about the mid-16th century onwards, see id., 'Der österreichische Kaufmann im 16. Jahrhundert', 135. For the argument about the town's economic and political grievances in the 16th century see Pickl, 'Städte und Märkte', 97–8 and F. Mensi, *Geschichte der direkten Steuern in Steiermark bis zum Regierungsantritte Maria Theresias*, vol. iii, pt. 3 (Graz, 1936), 40–6. In 1542, there were 72 exempt houses in Graz. The ratio of tax-exempt noble households to civic houses liable to taxation was 114 to 286 in 1612, and 174 to 196 in 1710, see Mensi, *Geschichte*, 48.

a reduction of the towns' contribution to one-twelfth of the ordinary taxes. However, these gains were almost nullified by the nobility's success in having the largely ineffectual ducal decrees of 1574 and 1601 against unlicensed trade in the countryside formally repealed. Henceforth, rural competition based on their estates could channel away the towns' and markets' local trade with impunity.[64]

In spite of the nobility's patronage of their urban co-religionists, there were thus contentious issues that beset and eventually obstructed the process of Protestant unification as envisaged by the church ordinance and plans for a union of the three duchies in religious matters in 1578. As will be seen later on, it was precisely this flaw which encouraged the adoption of a skilful dividing strategy by their Catholic adversaries towards the end of the sixteenth century.

So far, the progress of Protestantism has been discussed in terms of time rather than space. However, a brief sketch of Styria's geographic and demographic make-up should help provide a sense of place to locate the relations between noblemen, burghers, and rural populace on the one hand, and trade links with Styria's neighbours on the other, as factors which contributed to the shaping of the confessional landscape of Styria.

For administrative purposes, Styria had in the fifteenth and sixteenth centuries been divided into five districts, confusingly termed *Viertel* (quarters). The first of these was made up of the town and area of Judenburg, while the second comprised the rural and mining settlements of the Enns and Mürz valleys. Together, these two districts covered most of the region of Upper Styria. Next to these was the district of Vorau, which in turn bordered on the Lower Styrian quarter 'between the rivers of Mur and Drau'. The *Viertel* of Vorau essentially comprised present-day east Styria, but in the early modern period stretched into Upper, Lower, and west Styria as well and included the capital and its surroundings, thus covering, so to speak, middle Styria. Lastly, there was the south-eastern Slovenian district or 'windisches Viertel' which consisted of the formerly independent county of Cilli and bordered on the duchy of Carniola in the south.[65]

---

[64] Pickl, 'Städte und Märkte', 96–8.
[65] See P. Dedic, *Der Protestantismus in Steiermark im Zeitalter der Reformation und Gegenreformation* (Leipzig, 1930), 1–4. The term middle Styria had no currency and is used here for purposes of description only. Contemporary sources incidentally refer to Graz, for example, as being situated in Lower Styria, whereas it belonged administratively to the district of Vorau.

Estimated population figures on the basis of registers of communicants and more reliable eighteenth-century censuses suggest that the population of the duchy grew from *c*.278,000 in 1528 to *c*.543,000 in 1650, 614,000 in 1700, 707,000 in 1750, and 798,000 in 1782. In absolute figures, population growth occurred in each of the duchy's regions, but there was a relative decline for Upper Styria throughout the period. Thus, Upper Styria's share of one-third of the population total (33.4 per cent) during the first half of the sixteenth century steadily declined to *c*.21 per cent by the end of the eighteenth century, while the population in the central and eastern parts of the duchy increased from *c*.41 per cent to 45–6 per cent in the decades 1644 to 1690. Presumably as a result of the outbreaks of plague in the late seventeenth century and the destruction of the border raids from Hungary during the 'Kuruc wars' in 1704–9, this region experienced a loss of *c*.2–2.5 per cent of its population to remain at a level of *c*.43 per cent from about 1710 onwards till the end of the century. The population of Lower Styria increased in the same period from 27 per cent (1528) to *c*.31 per cent (1700–10), to 36 per cent in 1770, with minor variations explained mainly by plague casualties.[66]

Regional disparities were the outcome of differences in economic patterns: population growth in the central part of the duchy and in Lower Styria resulted from an economy based on labour-intensive viticulture and small farming units that were run by individual families and were subject to division among heirs. By contrast, the often large farming units in Upper Styria were passed on undivided at a late stage in the life of the tenant, with the tenant's unmarried siblings and servants staying on as members of the household who constituted the main labour force.[67] The smaller farmers and cottagers of this mountainous region relied on seasonal work as farmhands and day labourers in the south German towns and principalities to supplement their meagre incomes from dairy farming (*Almwirtschaft*). Through their contacts with towns like Nuremberg and Regensburg, Upper Styrian farmers would often become acquainted with and pedlars in Lutheran literature, an exchange

---

[66] Rounded figures on the basis of M. Straka, 'Die Bevölkerungsentwicklung der Steiermark von 1528 bis 1782 auf Grund der Kommunikantenzählungen', *ZHVST* 52 (1961), 3–53, tables on 14–15, 16–17, 26, 40, 43. For the impact of the 'Kuruc' raids see F. Posch, *Flammende Grenze: Die Steiermark in den Kuruzzenstürmen* (Graz, 1968).

[67] K. Klein, 'Die Bevölkerung Österreichs vom Beginn des 16. bis zur Mitte des 18. Jahrhunderts', in H. Helczmanovszki (ed.), *Beiträge zur Bevölkerungs- und Sozialgeschichte Österreichs* (Munich, 1973), 47–112, at 79. The population figures for Styria on p. 77 are based on the previously quoted article by Straka, 'Bevölkerungsentwicklung der Steiermark'.

which turned into a regular clandestine trade in the seventeenth and eighteenth centuries.[68]

The stated population figures for the region are further explained by the government's policy of forcible emigration of the crypto-Protestant population, and by the gradual decline of Styria's regionally based mining industry in the seventeenth century. The mines of Upper Styria and its production of iron and ironware nevertheless remained Styria's industrial mainstay throughout the period and even attracted foreign traders, so that in 1542, for example, there were no fewer than eighteen Upper German firms using the entrepôt at Murau as a depot (*Niederlage*). The Styrian mining and iron industries traditionally had to recruit their labour force largely from the skilled workers of the Salzkammergut, Saxony, and Thuringia, and employment of this mobile and volatile workforce remained a constant throughout the early modern period. Lutheranism had spread from an early stage among these groups, who had played an important part in the great Peasant War of 1525–6 and were again conspicuous among the pugnacious Protestants who defied the roving Counter-Reformation commissions in Upper Styria in the 1590s.[69] Patterns of labour recruitment and modes of production thus contributed to the shaping of a confessional landscape.

Diverging regional economic patterns affected not only the size, but also the distribution of the population. The economic pattern of mining industry and trade in the valleys and *Almwirtschaft* in the mountainous part of Upper Styria led to a greater concentration of the local population in the larger municipalities, such as Judenburg, Bruck, Murau, and Oberwölz, whereas the Lower Styrian mixture of viticulture, small trade,

[68] The means and paths of the clandestine book trade, which was carried out by seasonal workers and professional book peddlars in disguise in the 18th century, was essentially a continuation of the earlier tradition, see P. Dedic, 'Besitz und Beschaffung evangelischen Schrifttums in Steiermark und Kärnten in der Zeit des Kryptoprotestantismus', offprint from *Zeitschrift für Kirchengeschichte*, 3rd ser., 9/58, 3–4 (1939), 476–95. The practice of seasonal migration was the subject of ducal and Imperial regulations from the 16th century onwards, for example the ducal statutes for rural servants and day labourers issued by Karl II in 1577. An Imperial decree of 24 July 1688 prohibited the migration of peasants from Upper Styria and the district of Vorau who worked as farmhands during the spring and summer in the Austrian archduchy, Salzburg, Bavaria, Württemberg, and Hungary. The relevant documents are cited in D. Kreuziger, 'Rechts- und sozialhistorische Entwicklung des ländlichen Dienstboten- und Gesindewesens in der Steiermark . . .' (doctoral thesis at the Faculty of Law, University of Graz, 1969), 55–6, 61–2.

[69] On the national composition and political importance of the Upper Styrian miners see F. Tremel, *Der Frühkapitalismus in Innerösterreich* (Graz, 1954), 36, and H. Pirchegger, *Geschichte der Steiermark*, i. 64. For their resistance against the 16th-century Counter-Reformation commissions see below, Ch. 5. For Murau see Pickl, 'Städte und Märkte', 103.

and agriculture entailed the spreading of the population over a dense net of small settlements, villages, and market towns. While the vast majority of Styrian municipalities in the sixteenth century had up to 500 inhabitants, most rural markets (*Bauernmärkte*) in Lower Styria numbered on the average less than 200, for example the town of Friedau with a population of 150.[70] Most of these Lower Styrian settlements were exceedingly poor, so that there was often only a small group of thirty inhabitants or less who were at all subject to taxation, and the total of urban capital was in some cases equal to the value of a single larger Upper Styrian farm. There were, however, notable exceptions to this rule, namely the towns of Radkersburg, Pettau (*Ptuj*), Marburg (*Maribor*), and Cilli (*Celje*), whose wealth from the cattle and wine trade placed them among the richest Styrian towns. Together with the smaller and poorer Lower Styrian municipalities of Windischgraz, Windischfeistritz, and Rann, they belonged to the prince's demesne, unlike the overwhelming majority of the surrounding patrimonial market towns.[71]

These places formed German or mostly German-speaking enclaves. Their neighbouring settlements were often linguistically mixed, as were the *Windischbühlen* in the south-west, and the valley along the Drau up to Marburg. The smaller rural settlements were largely Slovenian in this period, and entirely so by the end of the eighteenth century.[72] From an early stage, Lutheranism made an inroad among the larger German towns as opposed to the rural communities and the smaller municipalities of Lower Styria, and the difference between the towns of Radkersburg and Marburg, where heretical books were confiscated and burnt as early as 1528, and the unaffected Slovenian parishes of the surrounding countryside was commented upon by the members of the visitation commission staged in that year.[73]

[70] See Pickl, 'Städte und Märkte', 98–100, especially map 1, p. 95, showing the Styrian towns and markets in the 16th century, and map 2, p. 99, which indicates the geographical distribution of the population.

[71] Ibid. 106–8, and 95, map 1.

[72] See G. Werner, *Sprache und Volkstum in der Untersteiermark* (Stuttgart, 1935), 53–5. As the title would suggest, this work is marred by its ideological drift. It nevertheless contains usable bits of information on Josephinian cartography as well as a good geographical description of linguistic boundaries.

[73] See E. Winkelmann, 'Geschichte des Luthertums im untersteirischen Mur- und Draugebiet', pts. i–iv, *JGGPÖ* 54–7 (1933–6), and G. Dirnberger, 'Geschichte der landesfürstlichen Stadt Radkersburg . . .' (doctoral thesis at the Faculty of History, University of Graz, 1973), 192–4. For the commission's findings see K. Eder, 'Die Visitation und Inquisition von 1528 in der Steiermark', *MIÖG* 63 (1955) 318–19. For Marburg see M. Rupel, *Primus Truber*, German trans. by B. Saria (Munich, 1965), 35.

It seems that the development of confessional divergences between town and countryside in Lower Styria on the one hand and a parallel evolution of regional differences between Upper Styrian Protestantism and Lower Styrian orthodoxy was furthered by a considerable imbalance in the legal and economic situation of the rural population of the respective regions. As shown above, the ducal towns' quest for adequate political representation, a more equitable distribution of the tax burden, and a stop to illicit rural trade formed divisive issues which at times pitted the towns against their co-religionists, the Protestant estates, and prevented a close alliance. The nobility's efforts to entrench the new faith more firmly and secure a supply of native staff for its school and church ministry had nevertheless extended by 1578 to the provision of Protestant services for the German towns and the constitutional safeguard of the Pacification of Bruck.

By contrast, economic and legal issues formed a source of permanent trouble and sporadic violent clashes between the Lower Styrian Protestant estates and their rural subjects throughout the sixteenth and the first half of the seventeenth centuries. A series of uprisings, the last of which was quelled in 1635, marked the Slovenian peasants' response to the massive increase in feudal dues and labour services (*Robot*). In 1572–3, this led to an eventually brutally crushed uprising in Carniola and Lower Styria sparked off by the outrages of the particularly rapacious Croatian estate owner Franz Táhy, which fuelled the estates' fears of a large-scale peasant uprising in the duchy. Opposition was likewise directed against alternative attempts to replace traditional leases for life with heritable contracts. Given the fact that tenant farms had by this time mostly become quasi-heritable as leases were renewed with the tenant's heir as a matter of course, these enforced sales seemed no more than a pretext for extorting the payment of a large lump sum of money instead of the customary fee that was due on renewal of the lease for a lifetime. Against this, recourse could be had to the duke only as highest feudal lord.[74]

[74] The situation of the wine-growing *Bergholden*, who likewise strongly opposed commutation of leases, differed from that of the peasants in so far as the former were obliged to render dues in cash and kind only, but were exempt from *Robot* services. The general increase in dues in the 16th and 17th centuries was nevertheless burdensome, see A. Kern, *Ein Kampf ums Recht* (Graz, 1941), 13. The different types of leasehold are described in A. Mell, *Die Lage des steirischen Unterthanenstandes* . . . (Weimar, 1896), 4–6. The deterioration in the Styrian peasants' legal and economic situation is discussed by F. Posch, 'Bauer und Grundherrschaft', in id., *Bauerntum in der Steiermark*, 11–16, and in F. Tremel, 'Grundzins, Robot und Zehnt', ibid. 35–42. For the Táhy uprising see F. von Krones,

Economic interests were thus affecting the process of Protestantization: on the one hand, they caused friction among the Protestant nobility, towns, and the rural population, to the detriment of the Protestant party; on the other, they strengthened the bond between the Slovenian Catholic peasants of Lower Styria and the Catholic prince. As regards the border settlements of east Styria and some of Lower Styria's towns, like the markets of Neudau, Friedau, Burgau, and the towns of Radkersburg and Pettau, it could be argued that they possessed an equivalent to Upper Styria's Protestant connection with the German towns. By virtue of their cattle and wine trade with neighbouring Hungary and through contacts made in cross-border trade at local markets, Lower Styrian merchants and farmers maintained relations with the Lutheran population of their neighbours to the east which affected their religious views.[75]

4. THE IDEOLOGICAL FOUNDATIONS AND INSTITUTIONAL STRUCTURES OF INNER AUSTRIAN PROTESTANTISM

Economic interests could also fuse with social concerns to affect the religious outlook of the elites. It has previously been suggested with reference to Upper Styria's part in the German peasants' revolt of 1525–6 and fears of large-scale unrest in 1572–3 that a combination of political and economic motives informed the nobility's concern for the suppression of potentially radical autonomous popular Protestantism. These arguments resurfaced in Hans Hoffmann's warnings in the 1580s that the Catholic government's attempt to root out Lutheranism in Upper Styria would invite Calvinism and rebellion in its stead. Again, during the domestic crisis of the dynasty in 1606–9, the Inner Austrian estates asserted that outbreaks of rural rebellion in support of the Hungarian Protestants were imminent. The propagandistic value and strategic use of this argument

'Aktenmäßige Beiträge zur Geschichte des windischen Bauernaufstandes vom Jahre 1573', *BKSTGQ* 5 (1868), 3–34. The Lower Styrian uprising in 1635 is discussed in A. Mell, 'Der windische Bauernaufstand des Jahres 1635 und dessen Nachwehen', *MHVST* 44 (1896), 205–87. That Ferdinand II's response to peasant appeals against extortionate seigneurial demands depended on the estate owners' confessional outlook is demonstrated by a case study for the Herrschaft Schönstein in Lower Styria, which in 1590 had come into the possession of the Catholic convert and court favourite Balthasar Wagen von Wagensperg, see H. Valentinitsch, 'Willkür und Widerstand. Die wirtschaftliche und rechtliche Lage der Untertanen der untersteirischen Herrschaft Schönstein in der frühen Neuzeit', in *Grafenauerjev Zbornik* (Ljubljana, 1996), 469–82, at 474–5.

[75] This link is commented upon by the government's reformation commissioners, see below, Ch. 5.

notwithstanding, there were nevertheless genuine apprehensions that mounting tax pressure to cover defence costs might eventually cause a large-scale peasant uprising, and these fears were to have palpable consequences for the estates' attitude in the confessional conflict.[76] This political premiss had implications for the complexion of Inner Austrian Protestantism. Its basic theological content was fixed since all of the concessions obtained from Austrian princes required the drafting of binding church ordinances on the basis of the Confessio Augustana of 1530. Hand in hand with the adoption of the Lutheran faith went acceptance of Luther's early position of non-resistance to tyrannical but legitimate temporal authority which he formulated in 1523.[77] At the height of the Counter-Reformation, the doctrine of passive or 'suffering obedience' ('leidender Gehorsam') as expounded in the memoranda of the Württemberg theologian Jakob Andreae (1528–90) was resorted to by the Styrian estates, who had approached him for advice on their political conduct in 1582. The decision to adopt his argument in favour of strict abidance by the law and political submissiveness in case of conflict is all the more significant in view of the fact that dissenting voices among the estates and their local clergy pointed out conceivable alternatives in the early stages of the conflict.

One of these was formulated by the superintendent of the Styrian church ministry in Graz, the Hessian theologian Jeremias Homberger (1529–93), in 1584, though he prudently left its political implications to be spelt out by his listeners. At the height of Karl II's campaign against the Protestant *exercitium* of the capital's burghers, the latter had approached the superintendent for advice on their conduct in this precarious situation. While acknowledging the ducal prerogative in general, Homberger had indirectly appealed to the estates to support the burghers' resistance. Thus, his verbal reply stressed the contractual nature of the relations between the prince and the estates, whom he described as the 'lawful hereditary lords or heirs of the country' ('die

---

[76] In 1605, the Styrian estates' executives reported that there was unrest among the peasants in Gleisdorf in east Styria, who had given word that 'things would not get better until the noblemen (*Edelleute*) were slain', quoted in Loserth, *Innerösterreich und die militärischen Maßnahmen*, 171. The Styrians' response to the dynastic conflict of 1606–11/12 will be discussed in Ch. 4. Scholz, *Ständefreiheit und Gotteswort*, 96–9, briefly discusses the social objectives of Lutheran proselytizing among the nobility's subjects in the earlier period, see ibid. 98, for the 'Indienstnahme des Evangeliums für Disziplinierungsabsichten im Zuge frühneuzeitlicher Herrschaftsbildung'.

[77] This position was adopted in Luther's treatise on 'Temporal Authority: To What Extent it should be Obeyed' (1523), see the discussion in Q. Skinner, *The Foundations of Modern Political Thought*, vol. ii (4th edn., Cambridge, 1988), 14–17.

rechten erblandherren, oder die erbnemenden im lande'). Contrary to Andreae's position, he therefore disapproved of the 'passive' solution of emigration, but stressed the estates' obligation to defend the 'liberties of the country' ('das liebe vatterlandt bey seiner [sic] gerechtigkheiten und Freyheiten zuerhalten').

Charges of high treason were immediately levelled against Homberger, and although he succeeded, with great difficulty, in placating for the moment both the prince and the terrified estates by a long-winded apology, the incident rendered him a liability to the Styrian Protestants that was ended only with his eviction from the archduke's lands in the following year. As will be shown, the estates adopted his advice neither then to aid the burghers of Graz, nor later to defend their own religious privileges against Ferdinand II's onslaught.

The second challenge to acquiescence came from within, by a member of the Styrian estates. The author of a fragmentary memorandum entitled 'Ratio Dubitandi' (1580–1) deals with charges that could be conceived against the legitimacy of the Protestant estates' case. He begins by stating Inner Austria's membership of the Empire against any privileges of the House of Austria, and hence the applicability of the Imperial religious Peace of 1555 to the duchies and their right to appeal to the protection of the Protestant estates of the Empire. The limitation of the prince's power by the regulations of the Imperial constitution and the ancient (fiscal) privileges of the estates are then mentioned. A brief conciliatory paragraph, which puts forth arguments developed by the eirenic Catholic theologian Georg Cassander (1518?–66), is devoted to allaying Karl II's fears that by granting the concession of 1578, he had transgressed upon papal authority in spiritual matters. The author suggests that Karl refer his critics to ancient and recent examples of Imperial orders on questions of religion. He likewise somewhat unconvincingly points to the examples of the Netherlands, Hungary, Poland, and France, which the archduke might quote as cases in which monarchs had made religious concessions under duress. Having thus given the prince's objections short shrift, the author turns to a carefully argued defence of the primacy of obedience to God in matters of conscience and the magistrates', i.e. estates', right of active resistance against impious rulers. To support this as well as a more general right of self-preservation against violent acts of arbitrary rulers, biblical examples are adduced. He then stresses the Inner Austrian estates' authority as ancient and lawful *corpora* who were entitled to assemble at diets for the organization of (self-)defence and deliberation on any matters of common concern, a claim that was directed against their Catholic adversaries' attempts to outlaw such congregations as treasonable conspiracy. In the same vein, the 'union u[nd] confoederatio' in religious matters which the Inner Austrian estates had concluded in 1578 is declared a lawful act.[78] Although 'passive obedience' eventually prevailed, the estates' option for the moderate Lutheran doctrine as taught by the Württemberg theologians like Jakob Andreae was not a foregone conclusion by the mid-sixteenth century. Initially, the Flacian variant with its strong crypto-Calvinist emphasis on innate human corruption had won a large following among the Carinthian and Carniolan nobility. In the later sixteenth century, it was even discovered to linger on among some of the remote parish communities of Upper Styria and Carinthia.[79] However, when the Inner Austrian estates entrusted David Chytraeus with the drafting of a church ordinance to give an institutional underpinning to the confessional settlement of 1578, they took care to renounce Flacian views, though in this, the tone was markedly more moderate than in their

[78] The (biblical) theological origins of the doctrine of passive obedience are described in Kern, *Gottesgnadentum*, 175–212. For Luther's contribution to the 16th-century debate see E. Wolgast, *Die Religionsfrage als Problem des Widerstandsrechts im 16. Jahrhundert* (Heidelberg, 1980), at 17–21. For the early Lutheran position on passive obedience and Jakob Andreae's interpretation see T. Koops, *Die Lehre vom Widerstandsrecht des Volkes gegen die weltliche Obrigkeit in der lutherischen Theologie des 16. und 17. Jahrhunderts* (Kiel, 1968), 28–32, 148–54. On the Austrian debate see H. Sturmberger, 'Jakob Andreae und Achaz von Hohenfeld: Eine Diskussion über das Gehorsamsproblem zur Zeit der Rudolfinischen Gegenreformation in Österreich', in Mezler-Andelberg (ed.), *Festschrift Karl Eder* 381–94. Andreae's memorandum for the Styrians is discussed by H. J. Mezler-Andelberg, 'Der Obrigkeit gehorsam', in id., *Kirche in der Steiermark*, 211–30. The memorandum is reprinted in full length ibid. 225–42. The key passages for strict non-resistance can be found on pp. 226 and 227. For Homberger's memorandum see id., 'Diß ist der beste weg, den ich auß gottes wort in diser schweren sache zeigen khan', in id., *Kirche in der Steiermark*, 199–210. Quotations at pp. 206–7. Homberger had already been chastised by a ducal decree in 1580, see below, Ch. 3. The 'Ratio dubitandi' is reprinted in J. Loserth, 'Miscellen zur steiermärkischen Religionsgeschichte', *JGGPÖ* 20 (1899), 185–192, at 188–92. W. Schulze plausibly suggests the authorship of the estates' secretary, Matthes Amman, for this document, see id., 'Zur politischen Theorie des steirischen Ständetums der Gegenreformationszeit', *ZHVST* 62 (1971), 33–48, at 42. Amman was secretary to the bishop of Salzburg before entering the Styrians' service in 1564. He was well versed in the law and theological argument and, together with Hans Hoffmann, drew up the estates' version of the 'Pacification' of 1578. He also secured the services of David Chytraeus for the drafting of the church order of that year. As commissioner of the Styrian church and school ministry, he strongly backed Homberger's authority. He also supported the burghers' case in the 1580s and must hence be considered the head of the 'radical' party among the Styrian estates at this stage. Amman died in 1601. For the above biographical details see J. Loserth, 'Matthes Amman von Ammansegg, ein innerösterreichischer Staatsmann des 16. Jahrhunderts', *AÖG* 108 (1920), 1–68.

[79] See J. Loserth, 'Der Flacianismus in Steiermark und die Religionsgespräche von Schladming und Graz', *JGGPÖ* 20 (1899), 1–13, and O. Sakrausky, 'Der Flacianismus in Oberkärnten', *JGGPÖ* 76 (1960), 83–109.

denunciation of Calvinism and Zwinglianism. The text adopted was based on the provisional church and school ordinance which Chytraeus had devised for Styria in 1574.[80]

If the concessions of 1572 and 1578 were to be put into practice, the creation of institutional structures for a school and church ministry was of utmost importance.[81] In Styria, a rudimentary organization based in Graz did come into life in 1578, and proved surprisingly efficient in spite of its considerable inherent flaws, and in defiance of mounting Catholic pressure. As for educational facilities, their provision was an obvious necessity if the raising of a native clergy and the orthodox instruction of the young were to be achieved. Efforts concentrated on the improvement of the local grammar school in Graz, which had hitherto catered to the sons of the nobility only, but was opened by consent of the estates to the sons of the capital's burghers in 1569. After 1578, it consisted of a preparatory class as a kind of elementary school that was subdivided into three *decuriae*. Five further classes formed the grammar school proper, the fourth and final classes of which were intended to provide training in theology, law, and philosophy at university standard. Additional grammar schools of a more limited design, comprising four grammar school classes each, were opened in the Carinthian and Carniolan capitals of Klagenfurt and Laibach (in the 1560s), and a further institute was founded in the Upper Styrian town of Judenburg in 1578. As a result of its more limited size, the latter school turned out to be unable to compete with its counterpart in Graz, and pupils seeking higher education had to continue their studies in Graz after completing the fourth class. It would also seem that the educational needs of the province's nobility were already saturated with the availability of a reformed and extended grammar school in the capital. Moreover, the burghers of Judenburg showed a marked preference for the basic instruction obtained at the German schools which was considered more suitable as a preparation for subsequent vocational training in one of the town's professions. As a result, the new school was to suffer from chronic underfunding in spite of the known wealth of the Upper Styrian nobility and merchants of Judenburg.[82]

[80] See E. Doleschall, 'Die Kirchenordnung Innerösterreichs im 16. Jahrhundert', *JGGPÖ* 5 (1884), 163–83.

[81] For a comparative perspective of the aims and institutional structures of Protestant schooling in Lower and Inner Austria see G. Heiss, 'Konfession, Politik und Erziehung: Die Landschaftsschulen in den nieder- und innerösterreichischen Ländern vor dem Dreißigjährigen Krieg', in Klingenstein et al., *Bildung*, 13–63.

[82] For the problems besetting the development of this grammar school see J. Loserth, *Die protestantischen Schulen der Steiermark im 16. Jahrhundert* (Berlin, 1916), 83–7, and P.

In Graz, problems of procuring Lutheran teachers and preachers in sufficient numbers and of satisfactory quality persisted until the abolition of the Protestant school and church ministry in Inner Austria in 1598. Clergy and teachers were recruited from all over the Empire as well as from Hungary and Transylvania, provided that they passed the test of Lutheran orthodoxy. However, the appointment of Johannes Kepler, who taught in Graz from 1596 until the abolition of this school in 1598, was to remain the exception among an otherwise undistinguished staff. Low standards of teaching and consequently of the pupils' performance led to repeated reform efforts. From 1578, members of the Styrian estates and their deputies acted as commissioners (*Subinspektoren*), who visited and supervised the grammar schools and appointed teachers on the basis of nominations by the superintendent in Graz. The improving effect of these measures was partly offset by the restrictive decrees that were issued from December 1580 onwards. As will be shown, they formed part of a strategy gradually to abolish the Protestant school and church ministry by denying commoners access to the existing educational facilities, so that the line of supply of future native teachers and clergy would be cut. Although it was not before the implementation of the final edict of Archduke Ferdinand in 1598 that the relevant regulations were fully enforced, their disruptive effect was sufficient to stunt the growth of the Protestant ministry in the preceding decade.[83]

In spite of the stated defects, the estates' school in Graz held up well against its Catholic competitors. In 1573, the Jesuits opened a Catholic grammar school in the capital. The purpose of the latter was to divert the nobility from Protestant alternatives in the duchy and the Empire and create a Catholic supply to refill the depleted ranks of the parish clergy. However, in his letter of 8 July 1582 to the General of the Society, the rector of the college, Emmerich Forsler, was forced to describe the school's progress as 'rather modest' ('satis mediocriter'). He related this mainly to the heretics' 'abject perfidy' of providing tuition free of charge

---

Dedic, *Geschichte des Protestantismus in Judenburg* (Graz, 1932), 17, 43–89, and the survey and quotation from contemporary sources in J. Andritsch, *Unser Judenburg* (Judenburg, 1975), 83–4.

[83] On the organization, curriculum, and progress of the estates' school in Graz see Loserth, *Schulen*, 17–73, and 114 for Kepler. The list on 114–15 n. 1 of officially registered teachers in the duchy of Styria in 1597 reveals that the vast majority of them were foreigners. Candidates had to be examined and approved by the church ministry in Graz to ascertain their Lutheran orthodoxy. This was particularly important in view of the intake of teachers from Hungary and Transylvania, see ibid. 41–3.

rather than risk losing able commoners to the Catholics.[84] As previously mentioned, the wealthier nobility and burghers had the additional option of sending their sons abroad to study at one of the academically distinguished Protestant academies in the German principalities of the Empire, but the limited means of the less well-endowed knights and of the majority of burghers rendered the local institute the obvious choice. In spite of their dedicated efforts, the Jesuits were to find that superior educational facilities were insufficient to induce a change of confessional allegiance of the elites as long as heterodoxy remained the avowed faith of the province's nobility.

After 1578, a Protestant church ministry was set up in the capital, with extensions into the different parts of the duchy. An elementary local network was established by the appointment of preachers to all five 'quarters' of the duchy, who acted as the intermediate authority of the superintendence in Graz. The latter board of clergy was initially headed by Jeremias Homberger and was entrusted with the nomination of candidates for the clergy and teaching posts. As the highest ecclesiastical authority, they also examined and ordained prospective preachers, and settled doctrinal disputes.[85] A notable controversy occurred during the interregnum (1590–5), when the parishioners of Mitterndorff in the Upper Styrian Enns valley opposed the deposition of their Flacian preacher Christoph Schwaiger. Efforts to suppress residual Flacianism likewise aroused protest among the burghers of the mining town of Schladming. Its obstreperous population had a record of rebellion dating back to the community's participation in the Upper Styrian offshoot of the German Peasant War of 1525–6, resulting in the town's temporary loss of its municipal rights.[86]

---

[84] For the founding of the college and grammar school and its aims as defined by the founding deed see Socher, *Historia*, 172–3, and Peinlich, *Geschichte*, i. 7, 8–10. The Protestants' strategy and the modest progress of the Jesuits' school are related in the annual report for 1581, AGR, 'Austria 132', 'Litterae Annuae 1575–1599', fo. 36, and in rector Emmerich Forsler's letter to General Claudius Acquaviva, 8 July 1582, AGR, 'Epp. Germ., Germ. 160 (1582)', fo. 373.

[85] Loserth, *Gegenreformation*, 204–30, id., *Schulen*, 38–49.

[86] In 1577, the ministry in Graz twice cited the head of the Flacian faction in the region, the preacher Stefan Haßler from Schladming, for a theological disputation. Having failed to persuade Haßler formally to renounce his views, the theologians in Graz peremptorily demanded obedience and adopted a repressive stance towards residual Flacianism afterwards, see Dedic, *Protestantismus in Steiermark*, 50. For this and the Mitterndorf incident see Loserth, 'Flacianismus', 1–13 and the relevant documents in *FRA/58*, 6, 162, 175–80, 181–2, 186–8. Flacianism in Schladming is dicussed in F. Hutter, *Geschichte Schladmings und des steirisch-salzburgischen Ennstales* (Graz, 1906), 222–34, and for its rebellious tradition ibid. 150–79. For a fuller account of the Mitterndorff incident see below, Ch. 4.

These incidents are indicative of problems of control over remote
regions with a strong regional identity. In Upper Styria, this identity
derived from the described economic patterns of semi-autonomous farming communities with a tradition of seasonal migration, who supplied the
local mining settlements. The latter's labour force was recruited partly
from the local rural population, but also from the migratory Protestant
miners of Salzburg and the Empire, who traditionally formed a politically
volatile element. As will be seen later, problems of control were to present
themselves with even greater vigour to the Catholic secular and ecclesiastical authorities in Graz, Seckau, and Salzburg during the Counter-
Reformation campaigns of the seventeenth and eighteenth centuries.

During the last two decades of the sixteenth century, the superintendent's board of clergy in the capital also acted as theological advisers to
the estates and watched over the orthodoxy of those Protestant clergy
who ministered as preachers and tutors to the nobility. Charges of
deviance from the Augustan Confession were potentially subversive of
the estates' religious privilege and were hence forestalled by swift action
against offenders, as, for example, in the case of the Styrian nobleman
Georg Kleindienst, who was rebuked for keeping a Calvinist preacher.[87]

On acceptance of the church agenda by the estates of the three duchies
in 1578, it had also been agreed that the organization of the Protestant
school and church ministry in the duchies of Carinthia and Carniola and
the appointment of clergy and teachers would be subject to the authority
of the superintendent in Graz to ensure uniformity and orthodoxy.
However, only rudimentary structures came into existence, and a broader
comparison reveals that Protestantism was making uneven progress
among the population of the other two duchies at large. As in the Styrian
capital, Protestant grammar schools were set up in the capitals of
Klagenfurt (Carinthia) and Laibach (Carniola), and the estates' preachers
in these towns likewise provided the burghers with instruction in the new
doctrine, but it seems that no local network of clerical provision comparable to the system of district preachers established in Styria came into
existence.[88]

If Lutheranism was firmly established among the Carinthian and

[87] See Loserth, *Schulen*, 43.
[88] Loserth, *Gegenreformation*, 219–21. A Protestant press had been established by the
printer Hans Mannel in Laibach (Ljubljana) in 1575. He was expelled in 1580 for attempt-
ing to print a Slovenian translation of the Bible by the Protestant reformer and preacher of
the Carniolan estates Georg Dalmatin (1547–89), ibid. 397–8. The Slovenian mission is
discussed below.

Carniolan nobility, there were marked differences in the spread of the new faith among the urban and rural population of both duchies. The pattern for confessional change in Carinthia strongly resembled the Styrian example in making progress among the burghers, turning the most important towns of Klagenfurt, Villach, and Gmünd into Protestant strongholds. Moreover, the peasants and miners of the Upper Carinthian region which bordered on Styrian and Salzburg territory in the north and northwest resembled their Upper Styrian counterparts in possessing a sense of independence and a tradition of self-sufficiency which made them receptive to the community-centred views of the new faith. Significantly, this region was also found in the eighteenth century to be tainted with residual Protestant heresy.[89]

By contrast, the situation in Carniola resembled conditions in Lower Styria in so far as Protestantism had taken firm root only in the capital and in the larger market towns without having much impact on the majority of the rural parishes. In contrast to the situation in Styria, urban development in Carniola (with the exception of Laibach) was marked by the close integration of the market towns into the agrarian economy of the duchy, which seems to have had a levelling effect on their confessional development. As in Lower Styria, economic grievances pitted the Slovenian peasants against their Protestant lords, and ensured that Catholicism remained the prevalent faith. The eventually futile missionary efforts of the Styrian Hans Ungnad von Sonneck and the Carniolan preacher Primus Truber in the 1540s to 1560s testify to the social limitations of the Protestant vision espoused by the Carniolan nobility, who failed to lend their activities crucial support.

Ungnad, who had been deposed as head of the estates' administration (*Landeshauptmann*) by Ferdinand I's orders in 1556, left the duchy in the following year and settled in the Protestant principality of Württemberg. With the help of Truber and the apostate Istrian priests Stephan Consul

---

[89] Local resistance to the Counter-Reformation is discussed in K. Burgstaller, 'Zur Geschichte der Gegenreformation in Kärnten: Die Gegenreformation in Kärnten bis zum Tode Kaiser Ferdinands II.' (doctoral thesis, University of Vienna, 1910), esp. 81–142 for the progress of the Counter-Reformation after the end of the campaign at the turn of the century (1601–37). See also P. Dedic, 'Der Kärntner Protestantismus vom Abschluß der "Hauptreformation" bis zur Adelsemigration (1600–1629/30)', *JGGPÖ* 58 (1937), 70–108. Eighteenth-century crypto-Protestantism in the region and its 16th-century roots are discussed in I. Koller-Neumann, 'Zum Protestantismus unter der Jesuitenherrschaft Millstatt', *Carinthia* 1/178 (1988), 143–63, and more fully in P. Tropper, *Staatliche Kirchenpolitik, Geheimprotestantismus und katholische Mission in Kärnten (1752–1780)* (Klagenfurt, 1989), 140–61.

and Anton Dalmata as Croatian translators, he set up a printing press for the translation of the Bible and Lutheran devotional literature into the vernacular for the sake of the Slovenian and Croatian population of the Inner Austrian duchies and the Dalmatian coast. The enterprise was approved by Duke Christoph of Württemberg and received theological guidance from the duchy's Lutheran authorities in the person of their provost (*Landespropst*), the Reformer Johannes Brenz (1499–1570). Substantial donations to cover the costs of translation and printing were made, among others, by the future Emperor Maximilian II, and the Imperial princes Landgrave Philipp of Hessen (1518–67), Duke Johann Friedrich of Saxony (reigned 1554–67), Counts Wolfgang (1508–64) and Joachim (1516–61) of Anhalt, Elector August I of Saxony (reigned 1553–86), Elector Johann of Brandenburg (reigned 1535–71), Duke Albrecht of Prussia (1490–1568, duke since 1525), by the burghers and magistrates of Vienna, and by twelve Imperial towns, including Strasbourg, Nuremberg, Ulm, and Frankfurt. The quantitative scope of the press's production is not clear, but 200 copies of Consul's vernacular Croatian edition of the New Testament published in 1557 were subsequently distributed in Inner Austria. However, the enterprise at Urach came to an abrupt end when its patron Hans Ungnad died in 1564 and none of the Inner Austrian estates were willing to take on this task.[90]

A more direct attempt to influence the religious views of the Slovenian population was made by Primus Truber as preacher in the Carniolan parish of Lack (Loka) near Ratschach (Radece) and Tüffer (Laško) in Lower Styria in the first half of the sixteenth century. His account of the

---

[90] Georg Dalmatin seems to have received some support, though, and was able to publish his Slovenian translation of the Bible in 1584, see Amon, 'Innerösterreich', 110. For Carniolan Protestantism and its printed products in the Slovenian and Croatian vernacular in the years 1541 to 1564 see A. Dimitz, *Geschichte Krains*, ii: *1493–1564* (Laibach, 1875), 205–16, 227–49, 254–63, 277–88. Information on the Urach press and its contributors has been taken from C. F. Schnurrer, '*Slavischer Bücherdruck in Württemberg im 16. Jahrhundert* (Tübingen, 1799), 14, 43–4. The figure of 200 copies is mentioned ibid. 50. A list of the titles of the Urach press publications can be found on pp. 61–2. The names of contributors are mentioned ibid. It has been noted that the circle in Urach/Tübingen gave Croatian translations priority, but it is unclear whether this was done with an eye to making inroads among the thoroughly Catholic nobility of neighbouring Croatia, see Schnurrer, *Slavischer Bücherdruck*, 50 ff., G. Stökl, *Die deutsch-slavische Südostgrenze des Reiches im 16. Jahrhundert* (Breslau, 1940). The fact that the burghers and magistrates of Vienna were among the most generous supporters of the press testifies to their broad vision of Protestantization. The Carinthian estates donated 100 fl. at the request of the Viennese bookseller Ambrosius Frölich. For this and the part played by the Viennese burghers see B. Zimmermann, 'Die Bedeutung Wiens für die Reformation und Gegenreformation bei den Kroaten und Slowenen', *JGGPÖ* 65–6 (1944–5), 21–53, at 27 ff.

superstitious religious practices of his parishioners and his futile efforts at instructing them in the Lutheran doctrine bear testimony to an inherent weakness of the Protestant cause as disseminated by the written word and learned sermon. Truber's report of 1558 revealed that, among the Slovenian population of Lower Styria and Carniola, Catholic devotional practices, attendance at mass, and pilgrimages to places of Marian worship in Italy, Bavaria, and the Rhineland continued unaffected by the spread of the new faith. He was particularly dismayed by his encounter with an ecstatic visionary sect which mingled elements of Catholic saints' cult with pagan belief. The message proclaimed by these rural 'visionaries', who were on the fringes of parish society, usually amounted to an imperative order by the Virgin or else one of the saints for the building of a church or chapel on a specified place, and the instruction for certain offerings to be made there. These messages were usually coupled with a threat of retributive action in the shape of epidemics, hail, and storm if their orders were ignored. Frequent outbreaks of the plague and cattle epidemics in the sixteenth and seventeenth centuries, which threatened the lives and livestock especially of the border population of east and Lower Styria and Carniola, arguably provided the material background to these visions, which often centred on the cult of the plague saints St Sebastian and St Roch. The sect cropped up again in the second decade of the seventeenth century in spite of repeated government action.

While their Catholic successors embarked on systematic repression only after this so-called 'leaper' ('Springer') sect had lost its function as a tolerable safeguard against the spread of Lutheranism at popular level, the Protestant reformers responded from the start with uncomprehending dismay to the sect and related variants of the Catholic cult. Primus Truber's vigorous preaching against the 'superstitious practices' of the parishioners of Smarcna in Lower Styria outraged its adherents to the point of threatening physical violence against their pastor. His subsequent prevention of the construction of three 'leaper' churches in the region permanently impaired relations, and his retreat first to Laibach in 1536 and then to the Imperial town of Rothenburg ob der Tauber in Franconia epitomizes the overall failure to establish Scripture-based Protestant piety among the illiterate population of this region.[91]

---

[91] Rupel, *Truber*, 37. Truber's account of 1558 is quoted ibid. 38–44. The Catholic orthodoxy of the Slovenian population was noted by the commissioners in 1528, see B. Saria, 'Die slowenische Reformation und ihre Bedeutung für die kulturelle Entwicklung der Slowenen', in R. Trofenik (ed.), *Geschichte, Kultur und Geisteswelt der Slowenen*, vol. i (Munich, 1968), 23–49, at 25. The 'Springer' considered themselves orthodox and were not

To revert to the question of the achievement and possible shortcomings of the Protestant cause in Inner Austria *c.*1578, it could be said that, in terms of political importance, the most significant success was scored by the conversion of the noble and civic elites of the three duchies. At the institutional level, the Styrian estates were able to establish a basic organizational framework for the Protestant education of the nobility and selected commoners. But for the adverse current of late sixteenth-century Counter-Reformation politics, arguably the latter group would have in time supplied a native clergy and hence ended Styria's dependence on support from the Empire and Hungary. More elementary institutional structures were created in Carinthia and Carniola, and unification was aimed at by formal subjection to control by the superintendent in Graz.[92] On the other hand, there were constellations of economic interests and political concerns which could set the different groups of society at odds, to the detriment of Protestant progress, e.g. the conflicts between the Protestant estates and ducal towns in Styria, or the conflicting interests of Protestant feudal lords and their rural subjects in general.

It has also been demonstrated that the estates' approach to the question of constitutional safeguards was based on certain assumptions about the workings of provincial politics. The latter was understood to be regulated by negotiations towards the establishing of consensus, and by the

---

concerned with magic rites. Their Catholic identity is stressed by E. Winkelmann, 'Springersekte und Bergkirchen in der alten Südsteiermark', *JGGPÖ* 62 (1941), 33–7. For a full-length study see J. Till, 'Stifter und Springer' (doctoral thesis at the Faculty of Theology, University of Graz, 1977). Their visions and rites are described on p. 292. The different social and religious motives that underlay the haphazard occurrence of sectarian activity would need further investigation. For the Turkish threat and the outbreaks of cattle plague in Lower and east Styria see Pirchegger, *Geschichte der Steiermark*, i. 120–1, 515 n. 640. Truber's contribution to the Reformation in south-east Europe and to the shaping of vernacular literary traditions in particular has received much scholarly attention, see, for example, Saria, 'Slowenische Reformation', and O. Sakrausky, 'Der Einfluß der deutschen Theologie auf die südslawische Reformation', *Südostdeutsches Archiv*, 13 (1970), 86–7.

[92] K. Amon, 'Innerösterreich', in Schindling and Ziegler, *Die Territorien des Reichs*, i. 102–16, at 109–110, states that Truber was formally appointed superintendent of the Carniolan Protestant Church in 1561 and was succeeded by his son Felician in 1565, who held this office until 1594. Truber's authority and formative influence are beyond dispute, but the thesis that a formal Protestant Church (*Landeskirche*) existed in Carniola as early as 1561 and hence prior to the various religious agreements with Karl II in 1572 and 1578 would need further substantiation. The fact that the Carniolan estates referred a dispute with the headmaster of the Protestant school in Laibach, Nicodemus Frischlin, in 1584 to the Styrian and Carinthian estates for joint decision would suggest that there was no separate highest authority in ecclesiastical matters in Laibach. The Carniolans' letter of 12 May 1584 to the Styrian estates' executives is reprinted in Loserth, *Gegenreformation*, appendix 6, pp. 588–9.

unifying force of common, especially military concerns. However, these assumptions were soon to be called into question by Karl II's clerical advisers and by his successor Ferdinand. As previously noted, this concept of provincial politics was informed by the estates' sense of a precarious social peace which, in their view, was jeopardized by radical Protestantism on the one side and, after 1580, forcible recatholicization on the other. Finally, it has been argued that the estates' political outlook encouraged the adoption of the defensive theological doctrine of 'suffering' or 'passive' obedience, which expressly ruled out armed resistance to repressive religious policy and was hence to prove of direct relevance to the outcome of the confessional conflict in the reign of Ferdinand II. However, the apogee of Protestantism's political success which was reached with the religious concession of 1578 temporarily obscured these inherent weaknesses.

5. PROTESTANTIZATION AND THE FAILURE OF ECCLESIASTICAL REFORM

So far, the rise of the new faith in Inner Austria has been explained mainly in terms of Protestant expansion through Inner Austria's various links with the Lutheran party in the Empire and its cross-border exchanges with the province's Protestant neighbours in the east. Modern Reformation historiography is agreed on a rejection of simplistic explanations of rapid Protestant progress as resulting mainly from clerical corruption in the Roman Church and has come to acknowledge the capacity of the new doctrine to attract a following through its specific forms of self-governed and -controlled religiosity. The relevance of such explanations notwithstanding, there is a clear link between the failure of pre-Tridentine ecclesiastical reform and the concomitant spread of the new faith in Inner Austria. As the threads of reform were taken up by the party of clerical Counter-Reformers in the last decade of Karl II's reign, a brief summary of the preceding period might be helpful in stating the background to their activity.

During the first half of the sixteenth century, both King Ferdinand I and the archbishop of Salzburg as the highest ecclesiastical authority for most of Inner Austria's territory recognized the need to counter what was indisputably a moral and material decline of the Church. In 1528 and 1544–5, commissions of government and ecclesiastical officials jointly conducted visitations of the parishes and monasteries in Upper, Lower, and Inner Austria. As in the case of the Austrian archduchy, reports on the state of the faith and Church in Styria were gloomy.[93] Both records emphasized the poor economic situation of the parishes. Lay patrons were notoriously slack in reporting vacancies to the bishop. Instead, they used their administrative rights to despoil the property of vacant parishes. Moreover, parish revenues were frequently exiguous, and were further diminished by the parishioners' notable reluctance to pay tithes and dues. While the clergy lamented the resulting threat to their subsistence, there were countercharges of excessive ecclesiastical fees, so-called *Stolen* and *Taxen*. Reluctance to comply with financial obligations towards the incumbent was taken as evidence of heresy.

In this, the commissioners were probably not wide of the mark where Upper and central or 'middle' Styria as well as border towns like Radkersburg in Lower Styria were concerned, since further inquiry into the state of religion in 1528 revealed that attendance at mass and communion had often lapsed, and the cults of the Virgin and the saints as well as traditional devotional practices such as requests for special blessings on feast-days, the use of holy water, and participation in Corpus Christi processions were in decline. There had even been instances of blasphemy and iconoclasm in Graz. While the sacraments of baptism and marriage were generally accepted, confirmation was unknown and extreme unction remained unpopular, the latter, one presumes, because it was still considered the harbinger of death rather than an act of spiritual preparation which a devout Christian would request of his own volition. Among the utterances recorded, those indicating Christocentric belief and a depreciation of the Virgin are the most revealing, especially if seen against the background of the late medieval flowering of the Marian cult in the duchy, where notable places of worship existed, e.g. Mariazell in Upper Styria.[94]

---

[93] Critique of the clergy was less prominent in the record for 1528 and was directed mainly against the practice of clerical marriage, which seems to have been more frequent than concubinage. A further complaint concerned extortionate clerical fees, see Eder, 'Visitation', 320–1. For the findings of 1544/5 see Höfer, *Landesfürstliche Visitation*, as discussed in the following, see also Malaspina's observations discussed below, Ch. 3. For the findings of the commission in the archduchy in 1544 see Wiedemann, *Geschichte der Reformation und Gegenreformation*, i. 90–104. The government board or 'monastic council' which Maximilian II created in 1568 revealed that the regular clergy had accumulated debts amounting to more than 200,000 fl., see the list of debts ibid. 197–8.

[94] The economic situation of the lower clergy and the impact of secular interference at parish level is analysed in G. Scholz, 'Aspekte zur Situation des niederen Klerus in Innerösterreich während der Reformationszeit', in R. Bäumer (ed.), *Reformatio Ecclesiae* (Paderborn, 1980), 629–40. For Mariazell see G. Gugitz, *Österreichs Gnadenstätten in Kult und Brauch*, vol. iv (Vienna, 1956), 197–208. For the application of the term 'middle' Styria see the comment above, this chapter.

Again, regional differences can be observed, and the evidence for Lower Styria is in line with Truber's account of the state of religion in this part of the duchy. The visitation record for 1544–5 shows that the average parish had several confraternities, the actual vitality of which is suggested by the existence of wardens (*Zechpröpste*), the collection of money by the confraternities' members, and celebration of mass in the parish church.[95] There was arguably a connection between the denser network of parishes and the largely intact framework of Catholic parish life in Lower Styria. Thus, there were around seventy-one parishes with ninety-three affiliated churches in the two large administrative Upper Styrian districts of Judenburg and Ennstal. By contrast, the two smaller Lower Styrian districts 'between Mur and Drau' and Cilli had no less than 267 filial churches administered by the parish priests and their curates to supplement the cure of souls of their seventy-eight parishes.[96]

In this part of the duchy, it was poverty and clerical vacancies resulting from neglect and from want of suitably qualified clergy rather than the spread of heresy which threatened the foundation of the Catholic Church. The case of the parish of St Peter near Marburg in the Lower Styrian district between the rivers Mur and Drau was typical. The right of presentation as well as the secular administration or *Vogtei* to the parish and its four affiliated churches was held by the bishop of Gurk in Carinthia, and nominations were subject to confirmation by the archbishop of Salzburg. However, by 1545, the parish had been vacant for three years because the bishop had mortgaged the income to a layman, Mathias Weitzler, to pay off debts which the parish owed the latter. To provide for the cure of souls in the various churches, there had in the past been three ordained priests, but as a result of the above contract, there were now merely one 'laypriest' who had not been confirmed by the archbishop, and two subordinate clerics. The parishioners complained of this arrangement, and blamed Weitzler for neglecting the care of the parish's

[95] See for example the entries for the parishes of St Lorenzen near Landsberg, St Michael at Schönstein, St Nikolaus at Lichtenwald, St Georgen at Gonobitz, St Leonhard at Neukirchen near Cilli, St Martin in Gams and St Peter. The latter two were situated near the town of Marburg, Höfer, *Landesfürstliche Visitation*, 180–7, 226–30, 180–7, 249–50.

[96] These figures are based on an evaluation of the text of the protocol edited by Höfer, *Landesfürstliche Visitation*, 153 ff. The figures stated in the report are not complete because an unspecified number of small parishes and their dependencies in east and Lower Styria were omitted as too insignificant, see the commissioners' statement ibid. 163. The difference between the figures for Upper and Lower Styria and the total of Styrian parishes recorded as mentioned below suggests that there were at least eighty-six parishes that were situated in the mainly eastern district of Vorau, which is not included in the above discussion.

property and buildings. Excepting the problem of their unconfirmed status, there were no complaints against the clergy, who read mass three times a week as well as on feast-days, but had to eke out a living from a fragment of the parish's actual income. There is no indication of heretical influences; quite to the contrary, it is noted that the parish church and two of its filial churches had been burnt down by Turkish raiders in the late 1520s or 1532 and had since been rebuilt by the parish community.[97]

Officially, both commissions were entrusted with a full-scale inquisition into the spiritual and material state of the Church in Austria. However, as the above example suggests, the actual focus of the commissioners' attention shifted between 1528 and 1544–5. In the earlier case, they had been concerned mainly with detecting heretical influences, while the latter assessment focused on the material state of the parishes and monasteries in Styria, presumably with an eye to its taxable value for future contributions to Ferdinand I's war efforts. Significantly, the total number of parishes was unknown. All in all, the commissioners recorded 189 Styrian parishes and 406 affiliated churches (*Filialkirchen*). The latter were administered by a vicar on behalf of the incumbent of the parish, and usually had to be maintained from the same sources of income.[98]

More revealing of structural problems were gaps that resulted from claims of exemption to the prince's jurisdictional authority, which had a parallel in the limits of episcopal control. Thus, the commissioners were denied surveys of the Lower Styrian parishes near Windischgraz that were subject to the bishop of Laibach at Ober(n)burg. The parish of Marburg had to be omitted because of protests from the bishop of Gurk as patron, though this right was about to be transferred to the local burgher community. This change undoubtedly facilitated the subsequent introduction of Protestantism in the town, which appears in the list of municipalities which declared themselves Protestant in a petition to Karl II in 1572. Two of the vast majority of the duchy's parishes that were subject to the archbishop of Salzburg's ecclesiastical jurisdiction claimed exemption on this account, and four belonging to the suffragan bishopric of Seckau followed their example. The west Styrian town of Voitsberg was passed over because the abbot of the Benedictine monastery of

---

[97] For the above see entry in the visitation record, Höfer, *Landesfürstliche Visitation*, 165, 184–7. The source is not consistent on the duration of the vacancy of the parish benefice, which had by 1545 lasted either two or three years, see ibid. 184, 186.

[98] For the key instructions in 1528 see Eder, 'Visitation', 313–14. The instruction for the commissioners of 1544–5 is reprinted in Höfer, *Landesfürstliche Visitation*, 135–40. The above figures have been drawn from the published evidence.

Admont as patron of the incorporated parish had failed to install an incumbent to the vacancy, and also claimed exemption on this occasion. The spiritual void thus created was soon filled by the new faith, and in 1572, Voitsberg likewise figured in the list of Protestant towns.[99] If this example is indicative of the combined effects of clerical privilege and negligence, the cases of the Lower Styrian town of Friedau and the border market towns and villages of Neudau, Burgau, and Wörth in east Styria can serve to illustrate the problems resulting from Ferdinand I's chronic lack of funds to finance his campaigns against the Turks. These places had to be dropped from the commissioners' list on account of mortgages to Lucas Zäckl, a Protestant member of the estates, and the family of Polhaim. The latter had already announced their interest in the acquisition of the monastery of the Augustinian canons regular at Pöllau, and the case of this monastery is further evidence of the undesired side effects of Ferdinand's fiscal policy. The entry in the visitation record reveals that the monastery had originally been lavishly endowed, and had possessed extensive feudal rights and property. However, as a result of heavy financial contributions to the prince's war efforts, the monastery was forced to sell or mortgage a considerable part of its property to the nobility. No less than eight members of the Teuffenbach family—Andreas, Balthasar, Bernhard, Georg, Hans, Jakob, Polykarp, and Servatius—profited by these bargain sales. Several members of the Teuffenbach family, among them Servatius, were later actively involved in the Protestant estates' politics. To raise the contribution for 1529, Pöllau was forced to sell the bailiwicks (*Ämter*) of Waldbach and Ratten to the Lutheran estates' captain Siegmund von Dietrichstein, who lost no time in introducing Lutheranism by way of his patronage rights.[100] To varying degrees, this problem affected all of the nineteen Styrian monasteries that were visited in 1544–5.[101]

The general state of monasticism as expressed in numbers of clergy

---

[99] The commissioners added a list of those parishes and monasteries that had to be left out. The reason is stated in each instance, see Höfer, *Landesfürstliche Visitation*, 162–3. For Voitsberg's declaration together with fifteen further Styrian towns see Loserth, 'Gegenreformation und Herren- und Ritterstand', 599.

[100] Höfer, *Landesfürstliche Visitation*, 163, 464 n. 2. for Dietrichstein. For the Teuffenbach see ibid. 303, 305 f., 465, and *passim*. Their purchases are also mentioned in Loserth, *Gegenreformation*, 29–30 n. 3, and id., *Das Kirchengut in Steiermark im 16. und 17. Jahrhundert* (Graz, 1912), 28, 33. For Polhaim's designs on Pöllau see Loserth, *Gegenreformation*, 70–1. Servatius von Teuffenbach's name is mentioned in the list of Protestant estate members engaged in religious affairs, ibid. 597.

[101] See the commissioners' register of sold or mortgaged monastic property in Höfer, *Landesfürstliche Visitation*, 294–311.

shows that some of the wealthier and more highly reputed monasteries and convents continued to hold some attraction for the elites, although monasticism in general was notably in decline. Thus, there was little difference between the situation encountered in 1528 at the Benedictine convent of St Lambrecht and at the Augustinian canons regular of Pöllau, at which time they had twenty-two (St Lambrecht) and fifteen (Pöllau) members, and in 1544–5, when there were twenty-one and sixteen religious. The evidence for the social significance of these institutions is even stronger in the case of the Benedictine nunnery of Göss. In 1544–5, the community consisted of twenty-five pupils and twenty-nine nuns from noble families. Throughout the period, this convent retained its attraction as a suitable place for the education and lodging of younger daughters of the nobility, regardless of the latter's Protestant convictions. By contrast, monasteries like Rein (Reun), Seckau, and Stainz lost half of their original number of religious, and the convent of the Augustinian canons at Vorau in east Styria was by 1544–5 reduced to a single religious as compared to fifteen in 1528. In general, a decline in the overall number of parish and regular clergy can be observed for the first half of the sixteenth century, amounting to almost a halving of their number between 1528 and 1544–5.[102]

The implications for the future of the Catholic Church were obvious to contemporaries, and the commissioners pointed to the various reasons which lay at the root of this evil. Next to the spread of Protestantism and the resulting loss of prestige of the clerical office, the commissioners considered the devastating effects of economic maladministration and the resulting debt burden of the parishes of prime importance, since they not only oppressed the present incumbents but also deterred possible candidates for the clergy.[103] However, it was not before the accession of Archduke Ferdinand, the future Emperor Ferdinand II, that the recommended remedy of pressurizing the estates into a general remission of the debts of the lower clergy was enforced. In many cases parish income was in fact insufficient for the maintenance of the number of clergy that had been maintained in previous years, and the commissioners suggested backing up funding by the reincorporation of affiliated churches. Parish priests should be allowed to impropriate the endowments for additional clergy for their own subsistence. The visitation records suggest that the

---

[102] Höfer, *Landesfürstliche Visitation*, 107–10, 117–18.

[103] 'Der commissarien guet beduncken, belangendt die general anliegen und beschwarungen der clöster und pfarren 1546', reprinted in Höfer, *Landesfürstliche Visitation*, 587–602, at 599–600 for the present conduct of the clergy.

latter strategy had in many cases already been adopted. In the case of Upper Styria, this meant the further stretching of an already thin parish network.[104]

If clerical grievances were acknowledged in the commission's report, they were nevertheless followed by sharp criticism of the clergy's short-comings. The lower clergy were castigated for their frivolous conduct which was giving offence to the laity and put off more suitable candidates. Ferdinand I was therefore urged to plead with the bishops for a reform of the clergy as prerequisite to the restoration of the impaired reputation of the clerical estate.[105]

A combination of these adverse circumstances was at the root of the widespread problem of parish vacancies, which contributed to a further aggravation of matters by laying the Church open to charges of neglect and providing an opportunity for the appropriation of parish property by laymen. The spoliation of ecclesiastical property by secular patrons (*Vögte*) was denounced by the commissioners in their final report, and again by the assembly of the church province's clergy (*Metropolitan-synode*) in Salzburg in 1549. In recognition of the spiritual dangers that could follow from this erosion, Ferdinand I issued a decree in 1548 which ordered lay patrons to appoint candidates to vacant benefices and restore usurped church property forthwith, threatening forfeiture of patronage rights to defaulters.[106]

Any improvements which might have been achieved by these measures were in fact nullified by the long-term effects of Ferdinand's earlier tax policy. Backed by papal consent, he had proceeded to collect

---

[104] Commissioners' memorandum of 1546, ibid. 598. Contrary to this advice, the diocesan synod of 1569 decreed that a sufficient number of parish clergy was to be maintained everywhere. If the affiliated churches were too remote from the main parish, it was suggested that they be linked to a nearer parish or else become independent, see K. Hübner, 'Die salzburgischen Provinzialsynoden im XVI. Jahrhundert', *Deutsche Geschichtsblätter*, 12/4 (1911), 97–126, at 115. However, as the synod offered no solution to the funding problem, cumulation of benefices or neglect of the outlying parish communities continued into the 18th century.

[105] Höfer, *Landesfürstliche Visitation*, 599–600. No reference is made to the conduct of the religious of the visited monasteries. This is probably explained by the stated major concern with the material situation of the Church. The secular commissioners were accompanied by the archbishop's (arch-)deacons (*Erzpriester*) for Upper and Lower Styria, but an inquisition 'in spiritualibus' among the regular clergy claiming exemption from the archbishop's juris-diction would have involved participation of the superiors of the respective orders or else direct papal intervention through a nuncio, as was to be the case in 1581, see J. Rainer and S. Weiß, *Die Visitation steirischer Klöster und Pfarren im Jahre 1581* (Graz, 1977).

[106] For Ferdinand's decree of 20 Mar. 1548 and a mandate on 30 May 1551 against simony and spoliation of ecclesiastical property see Loserth, *Kirchengut*, 139–40.

heavy contributions from the clergy in the years 1523–4, 1526, and 1529 to meet the costs of military defence against the Turks. Fiscal pressure resulted in the sale and massive change of ownership of church property, as revealed by the entries in the Styrian tax register for the years 1528 to 1540. The precarious economic situation of the Styrian gentry ruled out any significant purchases by this group, but large-scale acquisitions were made by members of the elite of government and estates' officials, often by families who had adopted Lutheranism at an early stage, like the Hoffmann, Ungnad, Teuffenbach, or Windischgrätz. On the other hand, Ferdinand's attempt to top this with a clerical contribution in support of the University of Vienna in 1539 brought about a temporary coalition of the confessionally opposed estates. As a corporate body, they protested against the imposition of an extraordinary levy on the clergy as an attempt at separating the *curias*. They likewise criticized the implied denial of the voluntary nature of the estates' contributions and the related right to negotiate the terms of acceptance. The constitutional argument thus offered a measure of protection to the clergy, and this helps explain the prelates' reluctance to close ranks with the foreign Catholic party, meaning the Jesuits and the nuncio, at the beginning of the Counter-Reformation.[107]

Adding to the pressures which caused the material and spiritual erosion of the Catholic Church were the effects of structural flaws in the ecclesiastical administration of the duchy.[108] Styria's ecclesiastical structure was shaped by the rights of the archbishop of Salzburg and his suffragan bishops of Seckau, Lavant, and (to a negligible extent) Passau, by the patriarch of Aquileia and the bishop of Laibach. While small fringes and enclaves were subject to Passau (the northernmost tip of the duchy), and Laibach (two enclaves in the south-west, bordering on Carinthia and overlapping with Aquileian territory, and in the south-east), the southernmost strip of territory up to the river Drau was under the patriarch's jurisdiction. In the late sixteenth century, the Styrian diocese of Seckau consisted of thirty-one parish districts of multiple parishes, filial churches, and curacies. In addition, thirty-nine parishes of

---

[107] For Ferdinand's fiscal measures see ibid. 1–39, and pp. 39–67 for the acquisition of property by the nobility and commoners. The Styrian estates' petition on behalf of the clergy, dated 18 Jan. 1539, is reprinted ibid. 139.

[108] The following account is limited to Styria. In neighbouring Carinthia and Carniola, matters were aggravated by the effects of highly fragmented jurisdictional authority. The duchy of Carniola and part of Carinthia were outside the church province of Salzburg and were subject to the *Patriarchat* of Aquileia as well as to a number of Imperial sees. For a brief survey of the duchies' ecclesiastical organization see Amon, 'Innerösterreich', 104–5.

the archdiocese were subject to Seckau through incorporation and the bishop's right of presentation. During the first half of the sixteenth century, the bishopric was administered by coadjutors who had been appointed by the prince, sometimes against the explicit will of the archbishop, as in the case of Christoph Rauber (1512–36), and they therefore failed to obtain episcopal approbation. While notably slack in meeting the spiritual obligations of their office, among which the attack on clerical concubinage and heresy should have had first priority, they were very active both in the Imperial service and, as members of the estates, in negotiations on the defence issue. Neglect of spiritual duties had a parallel in the coadjutors' economic maladministration of their office, which drained the modest resources of the bishopric and led to a vacancy in 1551–5. Until the end of the century, the see's main sources of revenue had to be farmed out or pawned to pay off its heavy debts.

To aggravate matters for the cause of religious reform, the suffragan's jurisdictional power and right of visitation in his diocese was limited by numerous rights of exemption of the diocesan clergy, such as were held by the provost and canons of the cathedral chapter of Seckau, the wealthy Benedictine monasteries of Admont and St Lambrecht, and, later in the century, the houses of the Jesuits. These mostly Upper Styrian convents and their incorporated parishes formed blank spots on the map of episcopal supervision, a shortcoming that contributed to the rapid spread of heresy in this region. The eighteenth-century inquisitions were to reveal the degree to which jurisdictional and crypto-Protestant enclaves overlapped.[109]

No less important for the rise of Protestantism was the circumstance that, prior to the authorization of the bishop of Seckau as archiepiscopal vicar general in 1591, more than 182,000 of the estimated 271,000 of the duchy's population in 1544–5 were directly subject to and hence dependent on the directions of the archbishop of Salzburg. There were first tentative reform efforts under Cardinal Matthäus Lang (1517–40), but with such worldly minded incumbents as Duke Ernst of Bavaria

---

[109] For a survey of the administrative structure and size of the diocese of Seckau see Amon, 'Innerösterreich', 102–5, and L. Schuster, *Fürstbischof Martin Brenner* (Graz, 1898), 104–9. On the administrators and bishops of Seckau and the problem of maladministration see the biographical sketches in K. Amon (ed.), *Die Bischöfe von Graz-Seckau, 1218–1968* (Graz, 1969). A survey of clerical exemptions prior to 1520 can be found in Amon, *Steiermark vor der Glaubensspaltung*, 109–13, which should be supplemented with the list of such privileges held in the early 17th century in D. Cwienk, 'Kirchliche Zustände in den Salzburger Pfarren . . .' (doctoral thesis at the Faculty of Theology, University of Graz, 1966), 36–40. The problem of crypto-Protestantism is discussed below, Ch. 7.

(1540–54) at the helm of the archiepiscopal government, there was little hope of ecclesiastical reform. Although prospects seemed to improve with the issuing of Counter-Reformation decrees for Salzburg by Archbishop Michael von Khuenburg (1554–60), a further setback occurred when agreement on a reform programme drafted at the provincial synod in 1549 foundered on mutual recriminations of the secular and ecclesiastical authorities concerned.[110]

The struggle for a comprehensive reform of the Church and religious practice was resumed after the conclusion of the Council of Trent (1545–63), the development of which had a parallel in the course of events in the church province of Salzburg in being disrupted by disagreement among the secular and ecclesiastical authorities, that is Emperor Charles V and his successor Ferdinand I and the successive popes who presided over the Council. With a view to the settling of the religious schism in the Empire, Charles V urged the clerical delegates at Trent to address the question of ecclesiastical reform before settling the theological dispute, whereas the latter issue was of primary importance to the assembled theologians.[111]

On 14–18 March 1569, a synod of the church province's clergy assembled in Salzburg to consult on the ways and means of putting the decrees of the Tridentine Council into practice.[112] Its deliberations resulted in the drafting and proclamation of sixty-four statutes which dealt with the problems of heresy and lay interference, but also addressed the need for a

---

[110] For Salzburg see below, Ch. 6. The eventual failure of the synod in 1549 on account of mutual recriminations is the subject of Loserth, 'Salzburger Provinzialsynode', 131–357, at 235–59. The secular and clerical *gravamina* are listed in detail, and an appendix on pp. 264–356 reprints the relevant correspondence. For the Styrian estates' reply of 6 (?) Sept. 1549 see pp. 302–27. By decree of 14 Oct. 1549, Ferdinand instructed the Lower Austrian government to suspend (as it turned out, permanently) the publication of the decrees, see ibid. 137.

[111] The twenty-five intermittent sessions of the Council witnessed the pontificates of five popes, beginning with Paul III (Alessandro Farnese, 1534–49), followed by Julius III (Giovanni Maria Ciocchi del Monte, 1550–5), Marcellus II (Marcello Cervini, 1555), Paul IV (Gian Pietro Carafa, 1555–9), and, finally, Pius IV (Giovanni Angelo de' Medici, 1559–65). A summary account of the Council's proceedings can be found in R. Po-Chia Hsia, *The World of Catholic Renewal, 1540–1770* (Cambridge, 1998), 10–25, see also the useful bibliographical survey of relevant studies and translated documents ibid. 212. R. Bäumer (ed.), *Concilium Tridentinum* (Darmstadt, 1979) is a collection of studies which deal with the aims and issues discussed by the Council, with the impact of its decrees and the historiography of research into the subject.

[112] For the following see Hübner, 'Provinzialsynoden', 112–26. The impact of the Tridentine decrees on the life of parishioners in Catholic Europe is discussed in the then ground-breaking article by J. Bossy, 'The Counter-Reformation and the People of Catholic Europe', *P&P* 47 (1970), 51–70.

reform of the clergy and the improvement of parochial administration in line with the prescriptions of the Council. To put an end to the diffusion of heretical literature, the bishops were exhorted to exert close supervision over the local book trade and printing presses. Instructions were given for the regular administration of the sacrament of confirmation. At the same time, the Tridentine prohibition of intermarriage between the family of the baptized or confirmed and the family of his godfather was proclaimed. The intention of this measure was to give visible expression to the separation of the spheres of the sacred and the profane, and these regulations directly affected marriage patterns in the parish community. The statutes then proceeded to admonish the parish clergy to keep an eye on the activity of persons from suspect parishes, and to suppress heretic conventicles. Admission to Easter communion according to the Catholic rite was to be subject to prior confession and absolution. Parish priests were admonished to fulfil their spiritual obligations, instructed in the Council's reform of ceremony and liturgy, and ordered to enhance parish administration by the keeping of separate registers for the recording of baptisms, marriages, and deaths in their parishes. To mitigate the effects of the present want of clergy, the synod adopted the proposal of the visitation commission of 1544–5 for the reunion of parishes and affiliated churches as a temporary administrative measure. In accordance with the importance of this matter, a separate set of regulations was drawn up to deal with the related issues of clerical recruitment, education, and discipline. By the terms of this official document, the suppression of clerical concubinage should have been a particular concern of the assembly. However, these statements must be set against a background of increasing pressure by the laity and secular authorities on the one hand, and a widespread practice of concubinage among members of all ranks of the clergy on the other. The enforcement of Tridentine standards of conduct remained a problem to be solved by future generations of Counter-Reformers. The same applied to the synod's plans for the creation of educational facilities for the raising of a reformed clergy. It was decided to open a seminary in Salzburg for candidates from all parts of the church province. However, as with the plans for a detailed provincial church ordinance, this turned out to be a long-term project that was eventually realized in the seventeenth century.

The synodal statutes of 1569 received papal approval in 1572, and were repeated by a further provincial synod in the following year. In spite of these auspicious beginnings, the episcopal reform initiative came to naught because it proved impossible to settle the mutual grievances. As in

1549, the synod touched upon issues which affected the rights of the secular rulers, most notably the clergy's claim to jurisdictional immunity. Likewise, the prince's power of taxation of church property remained disputed as was his wider claim that this property formed part of the dynasty's demesne (*Kammergut*). Through the mediation of the papal nuncio Germanico Malaspina, an agreement was reached for Inner Austria between Karl II and the archbishop which removed this obstacle to a joint proceeding for the reform of the clergy and the extermination of the Protestant heresy in the archduke's lands. Until then, however, clerical resistance against internal reform initiatives combined with the prince's intransigence on the questions of jurisdictional and fiscal authority to obstruct the progress of ecclesiastical reform.[113] It was not until the formation of the secular Counter-Reformation alliance in 1579 and the appointment of Jesuit-educated clergy as suffragan bishops and vicars general that the basis for a decisive change was laid.

By 1578, the state of religion and society in Styria and the adjoining Inner Austrian duchies was therefore characterized by the political predominance of the Protestantized noble elite, who shared common ground with the clergy in their opposition to extraordinary taxation and in their support of repressive action against radical Protestant sects that might pose a threat to the social order. On the other hand, there were divisive issues of major importance, most notably the infringements of the clergy's jurisdictional and property rights by lay parish patrons and the nobility's support of the further diffusion of the Protestant faith among the urban and rural population of the duchies. These offences rendered the established confessional coexistence increasingly irksome as well as politically awkward to the estate of prelates as the political representative of the clergy. However, the tentative ecclesiastical reforms of this period were doomed to failure because of administrative flaws, internal resistance, and lack of consensus among the secular and ecclesiastical authorities involved.

Meanwhile, the new faith continued to spread among the urban and rural population of the duchy, though regionally different economic and legal patterns produced uneven results. Lutheranism was firmly entrenched in Upper Styria and the major Lower Styrian towns, whereas the smaller municipalities and the Slovenian population remained mostly impervious to the teachings of the new doctrine, and, indeed, were rarely exposed to proselytizing efforts by their Protestant feudal lords. As

[113] For the above see Hübner, 'Provinzialsynoden', 112–26.

previously demonstrated, the political success which the Inner Austrian estates achieved with the religious concession of Bruck in 1578 proved to lack real constitutional substance. Moreover, the estates' legalistic notion of politics as regulated by negotiations directed at the establishing of consensus and binding agreements was translated into the theological concept of passive obedience, which rendered them ill equipped to meet the challenge of princely confessional absolutism.

Towards the end of the 1570s, the forces of the Counter-Reformation were already rallying at the courts of Munich, Innsbruck, Vienna, and Graz, reflecting a more general though gradual Catholic recovery in central and eastern Europe towards the end of the sixteenth century. To the eyes of contemporary observers, however, the Inner Austrian nobility seemed to have achieved a success that spelt religious toleration for the Austrian lands at large. As will be shown below, 1578 proved a turning point in bringing the opposed Catholic forces together in an effort to stem the tide of heresy.

3

The Catholic Alliance and the Beginning of the Counter-Reformation under Karl II

News of the Inner Austrian Protestants' success in obtaining what seemed to be a religious concession of unprecedented scope spread rapidly among the princes of the Empire.[1] By apparently confirming the confessional status quo in the towns, the published version of the 'Pacification' went considerably beyond the terms of the Maximilian privilege for the nobility of the Austrian archduchy and seemed to signal a change of policy in the direction of general religious toleration in Inner Austria. Karl II had hoped to keep the agreement secret, and the publication of the unauthorized text confronted him with an awkward choice between immediate revocation at the risk of further confrontations with the estates and financial deadlock, or else tacit consent, which would undermine his political standing as a Catholic prince and member of the dynasty. The news of the concession alarmed the Habsburg and Wittelsbach princes, and caused sharp protests from Rome. At a conference in Munich in October 1579, a detailed programme for the gradual recatholicization of Inner Austria was worked out by Dukes Wilhelm V of Bavaria, Ferdinand II of Tyrol, and Karl II of Inner Austria. The subsequent campaign for the implementation of this agenda was to some extent directed from Rome through the activity of papal nuncios and Jesuit missionaries in Graz. While the Munich programme served as a guideline for the policy of Karl II and his more self-assured and determined successor Ferdinand, it remained for the ecclesiastical reformers to commit the clergy to the Tridentine cause, and to create or sharpen confessional awareness among the Catholic laity as the basis for the reconversion of the province.[2]

---

[1] For the reaction to the 'Pacification' see Loserth, *Gegenreformation*, 287–99.
[2] Cf. the assessment of the Jesuits' task by the rector of the college P. Emmerich Forsler in his letter of 8 July 1582 to General Claudius Acquaviva, AGR, 'Epp. Germaniae, Germ. 160 (1582)', fo. 373.

In the following, it will be shown that the Catholic counter-attack during the second half of Karl II's reign could not effect a complete reversal, but was able to discourage the further spread and institutional consolidation of the new faith by restrictive legal and political measures against urban Protestantism and the Lutheran school and church ministry. The resulting conflicts revealed the heterogeneity of forces in the Protestant camp, meaning that Styria frequently had to fight single-handed for the common cause of the Inner Austrian Protestants. Moreover, the estates' attitude towards the Counter-Reformation in Gorizia as discussed in the following was indicative of the formation of a loyal and non-belligerent majority which increasingly marginalized radical and potentially rebellious noblemen.

As soon as the news of the 'Pacification' reached Rome, it was decided to dispatch the Dominican Felician Ninguarda to Graz to ascertain whether the rumours concerning the terms and the scope of the concession were correct, and to present the papal brief of 7 May 1578, which excommunicated Karl II for his surrender to the heretical party and urged immediate revocation of the edict. The papal reaction was above all motivated by fears of a further spread of the Lutheran heresy to Gorizia, Trieste, and Fiume and thence to Venetian territory.[3] In his reply to the nuncio, Karl II defended his action by pointing to the financial, political, and confessional problems he had encountered since the beginning of his reign. Responding to the main drift of Gregory XIII's appeal, he assured the Pope that the controverted territories and towns were excluded from the terms of the concession, and expressed his determination to preserve them in their allegedly pristine orthodox state.[4]

Karl's optimism, however, turned out to be ill founded where the Gorizian nobility and the towns, most notably Trieste, were concerned. Earlier curial inquiries like the visitation of Gorizia and Aquileia by the nuncio Bartolomeo Porcia in 1570 had revealed that practically half of the Gorizian noble families had converted to Lutheranism.[5] It seems likely that Gregory XIII's appeal to Karl II for rigorous action to prevent any

[3] K. Schellhass, *Der Dominikaner Felician Ninguarda und die Gegenreformation in Süddeutschland und Österreich 1560–1583*, vol. ii (Rome, 1939), 1–4.

[4] *FRA/50*, 2–4.

[5] S. Cavazza, 'La controriforma nella contea di Gorizia', in Dolinar et al., *Katholische Reform*, 143–53, at 144. The religious situation in Gorizia and Trieste is discussed further by F. Tassin, 'La situazione religiosa ed ecclesiastica del Goriziano negli atti della curia patriarcale (1570–1616)', ibid. 123–31, G. Paolin, 'La visita apostolica di Bartolomeo da Porcia nel Goriziano nel 1570', ibid. 133–42, and P. Zovatto, 'La controriforma a Trieste', ibid. 171–89.

further Protestant inroads into Catholic territory was actually prompted by Venice, which hoped to annex Gorizian territory. In February 1579, Gregory demanded a ducal decree by which only the Catholic faith would be tolerated in the county of Gorizia. Lutherans were to emigrate immediately. To lend weight to this demand, it was added that Venice and Rome would declare war on the county if the duke should refuse to comply.[6] The warning did not go unheeded, and in May 1579, the desired decree prohibiting the new faith was issued. Lutherans, including those holding government offices, were to be expelled, and were to be replaced by Catholics. The bishop of Salzburg's archdeacon (*Erzpriester*) in Graz was instructed to report on suspects. To prove his determination, Karl made an example of seven Protestant noblemen from distinguished Gorizian families who were ordered to leave the county within a month.[7] Early Catholic reform efforts in Gorizia were thus directly related to the initial focus of papal concern and were equally closely linked to Venetian attempts to exploit the confessional situation for further territorial gains, a fact that suggests the extent to which concerns of foreign policy influenced the course of the Counter-Reformation in Inner Austria.

Considering the Inner Austrian estates' attitude towards the Gorizian campaign, it would at first sight seem surprising that there is no evidence of any intercession on behalf of their co-religionists. The list of religious grievances of the Styrian estates presented at the diet in December 1580 makes no mention at all of the recent measures, although a petition from the Protestant Gorizian nobility submitted in August 1579 had urged the estates of the three duchies to raise this issue.[8] Instead, the Styrians merely expressed their sympathy in a letter to the exiled Gorizian noblemen and advised them to bear their cross patiently.[9]

The key to this apparently inconsistent attitude arguably lies in the estates' legalistic definition of their relationship with the prince, which had its spiritual equivalent in the adoption of the politically submissive early Lutheran doctrine of passive obedience ('leidender Gehorsam'). As the estates considered the terms of the religious concession binding on both parties, they willingly acknowledged its express limitation to the nobility of the three duchies. Moreover the estates' earlier opposition to

---

[6] Summary of the report by the *Landeshauptmann* Count Georg von Thurn, 2 Feb. 1579, *FRA/50*, 41. Venice's long-standing designs on Habsburg Gorizia and the possibility of an annexation under the pretext of a pre-emptive strike against the heretics were discussed at the Conference of Munich in Oct. 1579, see ibid. 32.

[7] Summary of the decree of 8 May 1579, ibid. 46.   [8] Ibid. 49, 70–5.

[9] Summary ibid. 48.

the radical Reformation, and their option for the more accommodating forces in the Protestant camp had implications for their course of action when religious persecution set in. Though the doctrine of passive obedience was not undisputed, it eventually prevailed as the logical consequence of these earlier decisions, which rendered the estates defenceless against Ferdinand II's Counter-Reformation onslaught. Hitching their fortune to a legalistic interpretation of relations with the prince effectively meant that the Protestant estates exposed themselves to ostensibly legal attacks on their position. At the same time, the political implications of the religious doctrine they espoused limited their choice regarding political and military means of defence. In the long run, this approach became a self-prepared trap which definitely closed in 1628, after the estates had fought a long-drawn-out battle of retreat. In 1578, however, the political implications of this disposition were obscured by the fact that a dazzling Protestant success seemed to have been achieved purely by a combination of perseverance and the skilful conduct of negotiations with the prince.

Although Ninguarda's mission in that year was first of all concerned with the implementation of 'emergency measures' to prevent further erosion of the Catholic position in Inner Austria, plans for an active reforming and Counter-Reformation policy in this region dated back to the 1560s. The nuncio's involvement in an earlier abortive reform initiative from Salzburg and the concomitant deliberations on the German situation in Rome formed the background to his mission. In 1559, Ninguarda had been commissioned to visit the Dominican convents in the ecclesiastical province of Salzburg.[10] Together with its suffragan bishoprics of Passau, Regensburg, Freising, Brixen, and Chiemsee and the Inner Austrian suffragan bishoprics of Seckau, Gurk, and Lavant, the ecclesiastical province of Salzburg united most of the Bavarian, Austrian, and Tyrolean duchies' territory under the spiritual rule of the archbishop. His archbishopric, the *Erzstift*, formed an enclave almost at the geographic centre of this complex under Habsburg and Wittelsbach rule.[11] During the following years, Ninguarda acted as the archbishop's court theologian, councillor, and representative at the Tridentine Council. The summoning of the reform synod in Salzburg in 1569, and the subsequent drafting of synodal decrees which sought to adapt the

[10] Schellhass, *Ninguarda*, vol. i (Rome, 1930), 6.
[11] Details are shown in the map of the archbishopric and church province of Salzburg in E. W. Zeeden's article 'Salzburg' in Schindling and Ziegler, *Die Territorien des Reichs*, i. 72–85.

Tridentine programme to the local situation, were largely his work.[12] As previously shown, this effort essentially shared the fate of its precursor in 1549, and although the decrees were authorized by Gregory XIII at the beginning of his pontificate in 1572, discord with the Wittelsbach and Habsburg princes who wielded temporal power over most of the territories of the Salzburg province rendered this reform programme for the moment ineffectual.[13]

The subsequent synod and deliberation in 1573 and 1576 were intended as a demonstration of episcopal will to abide by the reform programme of 1569, but turned out to be a complete fiasco for the archbishop. On the first occasion, only the bishops of Passau and Chiemsee deigned to participate. The second meeting in 1576 was initially convened as a synod, and the abolition of clerical concubinage was the main issue on the agenda. However, the bishop of Chiemsee was the only member of the episcopate who attended in person, so that no effective work was possible. On both occasions, the Inner Austrian suffragans sent neither the archdeacons for the Salzburg districts of their dioceses, nor any other delegates. Evidently, the party of reformers among the prelates was too small, and its influence too limited, to effect substantial reforms without the coercive power of the secular rulers.[14] In view of the Protestant successes, culminating in the concession of 1578, the urgency of a settlement of mutual grievances was recognized by both secular and ecclesiastical authorities, and in 1583 and 1592 concordats between Salzburg and Munich, and between Passau and Vienna, paved the way for more effective co-operation on reform issues in the church province.[15]

Meanwhile, Ninguarda's activity helped to give a geographical focus to the discussion of the 'German problem' in Rome. In the 1560s, deliberations for the creation of a cardinals' congregation which should deal exclusively with German affairs had remained inconclusive. At the instigation of Peter Canisius and Cardinal Otto von Truchseß, a cardinals' deputation for the conversion 'delli heretici oltramontani' was called into

---

[12] Schellhass, *Ninguarda*, i. 26–65.

[13] Hübner, 'Provinzialsynoden', 112–26, and 126 n. 5, his quotation from Florianus Dalham, *Concilia Salisburgensia . . .* (1788), 586.

[14] The account by Hübner, 'Provinzialsynoden', 125–6, misrepresents the character of the 'synods' in 1573 and 1576, but see G. B. Winkler, *Die nachtridentinischen Synoden im Reich: Salzburger Provinzialkonzilien 1569, 1573, 1576* (Vienna, 1988), esp. 287–8, 326–7.

[15] D. Albrecht, 'Wilhelm V. (1579–1598)', in *HbBG* ii. 351–63. The terms of the two agreements are listed by P. Gradauer, 'Vom "Münchner Konkordat" (1583) zum "Wiener Rezeß" (1675)', 363–6, in K. Amon an, B. Primetshofer (eds.), *Ecclesia Peregrinans: Josef Lenzenweger zum 70. Geburtstag* (Vienna, 1986), 361–70.

life by a papal decree of 23 July 1568. However, its existence is recorded for the space of a few months only, and the project was tacitly dropped.[16]

By contrast, Pope Pius V's successor, Gregory XIII, was more responsive to the suggestions of reformers who possessed first-hand knowledge of the situation in the Empire. A 'Congregatio Germanica' was set up by the end of 1572 to examine reports and petitions for help from Germany, and to develop suitable remedies.[17] In 1585, the *Congregatio* fell victim to the changes of policy and the reshuffle of personnel at the beginning of Sixtus V's pontificate.[18] Its creation was thus part of the new approach which characterized Gregory XIII's German policy, and during the brief span of its existence, it helped elaborate and sustain this course. In 1573, a member of this committee, Cardinal Zaccaria Delfino, presented a memorandum in which he discussed the confessional situation in Germany in the light of the Peace of Augsburg.[19] As the *ius reformandi* granted to the territorial rulers had weakened the Emperor's power in religious matters, direct negotiations with the Catholic princes were to be entered on. His basic idea was to use a safely Catholic enclave surrounded by Protestant neighbours as an outpost from which to launch the spiritual reconquest.[20]

While the necessity of direct negotiations was acknowledged, the 'outpost' strategy was modified by Ninguarda's alternative. He urged the new Pope to choose the confessionally mixed province of Salzburg as a starting point, a complex of territories that had the advantage of being politically subordinate to Catholic princes.[21] The new Pope had already discussed the situation in the south German lands with Ninguarda shortly before his accession, and subsequently accepted the nuncio's advice.[22] Ninguarda's calculation proved correct once the mutual grievances had been settled by a series of compromises and agreements.[23] For the progress of the Counter-Reformation in Inner Austria, the co-oper-

---

[16] J. Krasenbrink, *Die Congregatio Germanica und die katholische Reform in Deutschland nach dem Tridentinum* (Münster, 1972), 2–69.

[17] Ibid. 77–96. The founding document was issued a few months later, on 5 May 1573, see ibid 127.   [18] Ibid. 249–60.

[19] Krasenbrink, *Congregatio Germanica*, 82–94, describes the structure and composition of the *Congregatio*. Delfino had been, with brief interruptions, nuncio to the Emperor since 1553. From 1556 to 1559, he acted as papal adviser on German questions. As *Reichsprotektor* from 1573–4 to 1584, he supervised the examination and election of candidates for higher ecclesiastical offices and as such had considerable insight into and influence on the progress of clerical reform in Germany. For a biographical sketch see Krasenbrink, ibid. 86–9.

[20] The content of Delfino's 'Discorso' of 7 Jan. 1573 is related ibid. 98–106.

[21] Ibid. 114–17.   [22] Schellhass, *Ninguarda*, i. 91.

[23] Gradauer, 'Münchner Konkordat', 363–6. For Inner Austria see the discussion below.

ation of the Wittelsbach and Habsburg princes turned out to be of vital importance.

Delfino's advice on the use of direct negotiations chimed with Gregory XIII's policy of establishing a network of permanent nunciatures in Europe.[24] The decision to create a permanent 'south German' nunciature in Graz was laid down already in the founding document for the *Congregatio* in 1573.[25] Additional support for this strategy came from the Jesuit authors of three memoranda for the *Congregatio* in January 1573, and from Archduke Ferdinand of Tyrol, who had likewise been asked for his advice. By contrast, the reply of Duke Albrecht V of Bavaria focused on the need for a thorough reform of the clergy.[26] On the basis of these memoranda, the *Congregatio* decided to dispatch Kaspar Gropper as nuncio for the north-west of the Empire, and Bartolomeo Porcia for the south. As south German nuncio, Porcia was accredited at the courts of Graz, Innsbruck, Munich, and Salzburg, and the ensuing multitude of tasks prevented him from making any lasting and effective intervention in Inner Austria. In 1576, Porcia succeeded Gropper in Cologne, and the nominal nunciature at Graz was left vacant.[27]

The events of 1578 brought Graz back into focus. It was recognized that the presence of a papal representative was needed to achieve the revocation of the recent concession. However, the appointment of Ninguarda did not bring a decisive change since he was charged with the continuation of Porcia's work in south Germany in addition to his obligations as resident nuncio in Graz for a term of six months of the year.[28] At the conference in Munich in October 1579, Karl II, Ferdinand of Tyrol, and Wilhelm V of Bavaria therefore demanded the creation of a permanent nunciature in Graz as part of their far-reaching Counter-Reformation programme for Inner Austria.[29] Rome complied with this

[24] K. Jaitner, 'Die päpstliche Kirchenreformpolitik von Gregor XIII. bis Gregor XV. (1572–1623)', 280–1, in Dolinar et al., *Katholische Reform*, 279–88.

[25] Krasenbrink, *Congregatio Germanica*, 127.

[26] The Jesuit authors were Petrus Canisius (Vienna), the provincial of the Rhenish province Hermann Thyraeus (Mainz), and Johannes Rethius (Cologne). For details of their memoranda see Krasenbrink, *Congregatio Germanica*, 107–12 and B. Duhr, *Geschichte der Jesuiten in den Ländern deutscher Zunge*, vol. i (Freiburg im Breisgau, 1907), 766–7. The princes' memoranda are summarized by Krasenbrink, *Congregatio Germanica*, 112–13.

[27] J. Rainer, 'Die Grazer Nuntiatur 1580–1622', 291, in Dolinar et al., *Katholische Reform*, 289–94.

[28] Ibid. 291. For Ninguarda's activity in south Germany and in the Swiss cantons in the years 1578–80 see Schellhass, *Ninguarda*, ii, chs. 4–10.

[29] 'Consultation', 13 Oct. 1579, *FRA/50*, 36. Wilhelm V 'the Pious' (1548–1626) succeeded his father Albrecht V as duke of Bavaria in 1579.

request in the following year, and in September 1580, Germanico Malaspina was accredited as permanent papal nuncio to the archduke's court in Graz.[30]

In spite of the multitude of his tasks, Ninguarda's expertise regarding the affairs of the church province of Salzburg and his diplomatic skill enabled him to further the reform process in Inner Austria. His mediation in 1578–9 helped to bring about the subsequent close co-operation between the permanent nuncio and the Catholic forces in the three duchies and south Germany. After his initial conference with Karl II, Ninguarda discussed matters further with the archduke's Catholic councillors: the chancellor Bernhard Walther and his vice-chancellor Wolfgang Schranz, the bishop of Seckau Georg Agricola, and the ducal vicegerent (*Statthalter*), the bishop of Gurk in Carinthia, Christoph von Spaur. It seems that Schranz took the opportunity to prepare the ground for the spread of his version of the concession, an important step for the restoration of the archduke's understanding with the Catholic princes and the Pope. Schranz eventually had his version registered in the government records as the authentic text.[31] He claimed that he had convened the privy counsellors immediately after the decisive ducal statement of 9 February 1578, and had made them sign a declaration that the concession had been granted exclusively to the estates, not the towns.[32] This would have meant that the Catholic side possessed the Catholic and Protestant councillors' written testimony for their version, and hence most powerful evidence to controvert the estates' claims. However, such a document was produced neither on this nor on a later occasion.

Schranz's statement is in line with the defensive strategy pursued by the ducal advisers in the following years when dealing with Ninguarda's successor Germanico Malaspina. The latter had reason to suspect that he was being deliberately misinformed about the nature and extent of the

[30] Rainer, 'Grazer Nuntiatur', 292. Germanico Malaspina (*c*.1550–1604) had attended the electoral diet in Regensburg as papal legate in 1575 and took up his office as permanent nuncio in Graz in Sept. 1580. After a mission to Cologne in 1583, he was appointed nuncio at the Imperial court in Prague in 1584. He returned to his episcopal see of San Severo in Apulia in 1586, see Rainer, *Nb i*, pp. xv–xx.

[31] On Schranz's forged document see Loserth, 'Religionspazifikation' and id., 'Eine Fälschung des Vizekanzlers Wolfgang Schranz: Kritische Untersuchung über die Entstehung der Brucker Pazifikation von 1578', *MIÖG* 18 (1897), 341–61. My account follows Loserth's argument. A divergent view in favour of the 'official' version is put forward by K. Schellhass, 'Zum richtigen Verständnis der Brucker Religionspacification vom 9. Februar 1578', *QF* 17 (1924), 266–77.

[32] Schellhass, *Ninguarda*, ii. 9–10.

Catholic dilemma.[33] In any event, the archduke was quick to catch at the straw which his vice-chancellor offered, and his protestations persuaded the nuncio that the estates' version did not present the authentic terms of the concession.[34] Ninguarda subsequently presented the terms of Schranz's draft in his negotiations with Archduke Ferdinand of Tyrol and Duke Albrecht of Bavaria, and the surviving evidence proves that it gained currency among the Catholic princes. It was decided that Schranz should consult with Archduke Ferdinand on a practicable way to achieve a revocation and secure Karl II's absolution. He also accompanied Ninguarda to Munich in October 1578, where he presented the registered version of the concession.[35]

In December, Ninguarda reported the results of his conferences with Archduke Ferdinand of Tyrol and Duke Albrecht of Bavaria in Innsbruck and Munich.[36] The nuncio hoped to canvass support for a joint effort to bring about the revocation of the 'Pacification'. Both princes agreed on this general aim, and promised to take steps to further it, but they considered a straightforward revocation as politically too hazardous, and detrimental to the reputation of the dynasty.[37] In view of the recent developments in Lower Austria, where the expulsion of the estates' preacher Josua Opitz from Vienna had worsened the relations between the Emperor and the nobility, the duke of Bavaria feared that a measure as drastic as a complete revocation of the Inner Austrian concession would cause a general Protestant uprising in the Austrian lands. Presumably with an eye to Palatine and Saxon plans in 1576 for a Protestant Imperial regency,[38] he dreaded even further-reaching consequences. Undoubtedly, the rebels would be aided by the Elector of Saxony and other Protestant princes in the Empire.[39] Ferdinand and Albrecht agreed that, for the time being, Karl had no choice but to tolerate the estates' religious liberty under the terms of the concession. The unfounded claims of the burghers, however, were to be firmly rejected.[40]

---

[33] Malaspina to Cardinal Secretary Tolomeo Gallio, 4 Oct. 1580, *Nb i*, 29–30, and Malaspina to Gallio, 9/10 Oct. 1580, ibid. 35.

[34] This emerges from the synopsis of the two versions in Ninguarda's letter to Archduke Ferdinand, n.d. [1578], *FRA/50*, 4–21, synopsis on pp. 14–15.

[35] Schellhass, *Ninguarda*, ii. 50–62.

[36] For the following see Ninguarda's reports on his negotiations in Innsbruck and Munich and Ferdinand's and Albrecht's advice, 18 Dec. 1578, *FRA/50*, 22–5.

[37] Ibid. 23–5.

[38] Bibl, *Rudolf II*, 1–2. For the long-drawn-out struggle and the eventual eviction of Opitz, following the Imperial decree of 23 June 1578, see ibid. 16–19, 50–3, 88–97.

[39] *FRA/50*, 25. [40] Ibid. 22–5.

The Bavarian duke likewise responded to Ninguarda's call for support, but characteristically, the following negotiations for a meeting with the Habsburg archdukes were kept secret.[41] The development in Inner Austria with its possible repercussions on the confessional situation in the Empire in general, and its conceivable consequences for the safety of the military frontier along the province's border, belonged to the sphere of Imperial politics (*Reichspolitik*).[42] Hence, the appropriate political measures could only be decided on by the secular authorities, the leading Catholic princes of the Empire. Duke Albrecht V of Bavaria seemed predestined to head such an alliance. Since the accession of Rudolf II, he had been kept informed on the confessional struggle in the archduchy, and had repeatedly been asked for his advice. In July 1577, he drafted a provisional Counter-Reformation agenda for Vienna, in which he demanded the expulsion of Opitz as a warning to the estates. The duke's programme rested on the assumption that the concession had to be tolerated for the moment, but that any transgressions by the nobility's preachers should be punished rigorously, and possibly be used as a pretext for a legal campaign against the Protestant church and school ministry in general. His advice anticipated the eventual proceeding in Inner Austria, with its focus on the Counter-Reformation in the capital, the recatholicization of the court as well as the magistrates in the prince's towns, its military precautions to forestall a revolt, and, finally, its emphasis on the need for a thorough reform of the clergy.[43]

The Emperor's headlong attack on the Viennese church and school ministry in May 1578 and the eviction of Opitz in June threatened a revolt of the town's citizens and exacerbated the conflict with the estates. Rudolf retreated to Prague, and left his vicegerent Archduke Ernst with the difficult task of achieving a reconciliation without abandoning the Counter-Reformation course set out in the Emperor's recent decrees.[44] Rudolf subsequently chose not to respond to Duke Albrecht of Bavaria's repeated appeals for a conference on the religious situation in the Habsburg lands.

[41] Schellhass, *Ninguarda*, ii. 61.

[42] Duke Albrecht of Bavaria's message to Schranz as ducal emissary on 5 Oct. 1578 is summarized ibid. 57–8.

[43] Bibl, *Rudolf II*, 11–24, 56–71, 119–33, 152–4. The content of Albrecht's programme, dated 24 July 1577, is paraphrased on pp. 21–3. His second memorandum, dated 24 Jan. 1578, is much sharper in its tone and demands resolute measures against transgressions. It especially urges the recovery of (confessional) control over the prince's towns by means of heavy fines and expulsions. Paraphrased content ibid. 39–41.

[44] Bibl, 'Erzherzog Ernst', 578–9.

On 24 May, Albrecht V had suggested a meeting of Habsburg and Wittelsbach delegates in Innsbruck. Presumably as a result of Ninguarda's appeal for support in the Inner Austrian matter, he extended this plan in his further advice of 11 May 1579, suggesting a conference in Salzburg or Innsbruck attended by himself, the nuncio, the Emperor or an Imperial representative, and the archdukes of Tyrol and Inner Austria as well as the archbishop of Salzburg.[45] Whether Rudolf rejected the Bavarian plans as too ambitious, or too hazardous, or simply disliked the idea of a conference on 'domestic affairs' under Bavarian auspices, remains unclear.[46] In any case, such a meeting was never held. The opportunity to join forces and to co-ordinate religious policy in the Austrian duchies was thus waived in spite of the acknowledged fact that the confessional development in either part had repercussions on the other and rendered co-operation indispensable.

Nevertheless, in October 1579, Wilhelm V of Bavaria, Ferdinand of Tyrol, and Archduke Karl met in Munich to discuss the situation in Inner Austria.[47] The Bavarian duke's advice on this as on later occasions stands out for its rigour and its willingness in principle to resort to military means, which is explicable only if seen in the context of the successful consolidation of princely power and confessional unity in Bavaria. Wilhelm's Inner Austrian initiative signalled the new duke's will to continue his father's religious and dynastic policy. During his reign (1579–97), the House of Wittelsbach confirmed its reputation as protector of the Catholic faith in the Empire by its Counter-Reforming activity in the duchy and its support for the reform policy of the south German bishops. Like his father, Wilhelm 'the Pious' was a generous patron of the Jesuits, but the concordat with Salzburg in 1583 and the Bavarian intervention in Cologne in the same year showed that he was just as determined to reap the political fruits of his commitment to the Catholic

[45] Bibl, *Rudolf II*, 57, 130.

[46] It seems likely that Albrecht's repeated offer of military intervention in Vienna by the Catholic Landsberg Confederation of Imperial towns and princes had a more ambivalent effect on the Austrian government than the 'wesentliche Beruhigung' which Bibl, *Rudolf II*, 57, suggests. The *Landsberger Bund* (1556–98) was initially a confessionally mixed, though predominantly Catholic, confederation for the maintenance of confessional peace in the Empire and was directed jointly by the duke of Bavaria and the Emperor. However, the Bavarian dukes' attempt to transform it into an anti-Protestant alliance under Bavarian leadership met with the opposition of Rudolf II and Archduke Ferdinand of Tyrol, which in turn caused the withdrawal of the clerical electors' support. The Confederation was dissolved in 1598, see *HbBG* ii. 339–40, 357–8.

[47] Loserth, *Gegenreformation*, 299–308.

cause.[48] His support for Archduke Karl II was therefore in line with the general course of Wittelsbach dynastic policy.

The results of the conference in Munich were summed up in two documents, the first of which was a draft version and record of the preliminary stage of the discussion, dated 13 October 1579.[49] The second document, dated 14 October 1579, incorporates those schemes that were eventually agreed upon, and was intended as a practical guideline for the archduke's further religious policy.[50] In both cases, the question of authorship cannot be settled with absolute certainty, but the proposals especially of the second text essentially repeat and adapt Albrecht V's advice for the Emperor's operation in Upper and Lower Austria, so that their adaptation arguably originated with the Bavarian duke's son and successor Wilhelm V. Plans for Karl II's accession to the Landsberg Confederation and the project of a Habsburg–Wittelsbach union, to be joined by the archbishop of Salzburg, point in the same direction.[51]

In the final version of the programme, however, legal and political means are preferred to a military solution to effect a confessional purge, a shift of emphasis which resulted from Habsburg fears of a general revolt of the nobility in the Austrian duchies. A more circumspect strategy was therefore devised. Instead of a formal revocation at the next diet, a gradual proceeding amounting to a *de facto* 'annulment' was suggested.[52] First of all, the archduke was to restore his control over the printing press and thus wrest this influential means of heretical propaganda from the estates. He should then put a stop to any Protestant activities that were not covered by the terms of the concession, so that the burghers of the Inner Austrian municipalities would be excluded from the estates' Protestant services in Graz, Judenburg, Klagenfurt, and Laibach. Polemical sermons were to be prohibited. Likewise, the preachers were to abstain from ministering to the burghers and from similar encroachments on the parish priests' rights. New ordinations and the building of additional Protestant churches by the nobility were to be declared illegal.[53] Resorting to the legal argument to counter possible charges of breach of faith, the archduke was to make a declaration to the effect that his measures were

---

[48] Albrecht, 'Wilhelm V.', *HbBG* ii. 351–63.

[49] *FRA/50*, 31–6.

[50] 'Beschluss der Consultation, 1579 October 14', printed ibid. 36–40.

[51] For the reference to the Landsberg Confederation see the draft version, ibid. 35. The 'erbainung' is proposed in the final 'Beschluss' of 14 Oct., ibid. 38–9.

[52] See the 'Beschluss' of 14 Oct. 1579, printed ibid. 36.

[53] 'Beschluss', 14 Oct. 1579, ibid. 37.

directed exclusively against any unwarranted extension of the concession. He should contrast the estates' loyalty in the past with their present disobedience as instigated by their seditious, unruly preachers.

This speech would conveniently prepare the ground for the next measure, the expulsion of the estates' preachers from all of the prince's towns. Further resistance from the estates is taken for granted and, indeed, is counted upon to provide the pretext for finishing this gradual abolition with a final blow.[54] Next, the archduke should make use of his *ius reformandi*. In this, he would be supported by the constant advice and financial aid of the Emperor, the princes of Tyrol and Bavaria, the king of Spain, and the Pope. In case of a tax strike, the archduke should raise a contribution from the prelates separately, borrow from the Catholic princes, and increase the salt tax to be financially independent for at least one year. Eventually, he would retrieve these expenses from the rebellious estates. With an eye to a possible clash of arms, a reinforcement of the archduke's guards at his castle in Graz was recommended.

To effect a recatholicization of the court and government in Graz, the princes of Tyrol and Bavaria offered to supply Karl with Catholic councillors, officials, and servants. In fact, the 'purge' of the Privy Council ranked first among the successive 'praeparatoria' for the revocation. Henceforth, Catholics only should enjoy the archduke's favour and should be preferred to Protestant supplicants for vacant posts, a piece of advice that has more than just a tinge of reproach with an eye to the policy hitherto pursued by Karl II. He was furthermore urged to give financial support to Catholic candidates who had completed their studies and might be used as government officials once they were better versed in the 'laws of the land'. Reflecting especially Bavarian concern with clerical improvement, the necessity of a general religious and ecclesiastical reform was also taken into account. Gregory XIII was called upon to remind the bishops of their pastoral obligations such as the visitation and reform of their dioceses, the appointment of able archdeacons (*Erzpriester*), and the founding of seminaries according to the Tridentine prescriptions.[55] The creation of a permanent nunciature in Graz was likewise urged.[56]

---

[54] Ibid. 37–8.

[55] Ibid. 38–40. For the centrality of the issues of clerical reform and education to the religious policy of the Bavarian dukes see A. Seifert, 'Die "Seminarpolitik" der bayerischen Herzöge im 16. Jahrhundert und die Begründung des jesuitischen Schulwesens', in Glaser, *Um Glauben und Reich*, 125–32.

[56] Draft version, 13 Oct. 1579, *FRA/50*, 36.

Over the following decade, Karl II adjusted his religious policy to this programme. From May 1580 onwards, he issued a series of decrees to cut back any extensions of the Protestant school and church ministry. The first decrees were directed against the building of new churches by the estates, and against the burghers' attendance at Protestant services. Frequent repetition of these prohibitions indicates that they were mostly ineffective, but the constant legal pressure on transgressors nevertheless stunted the growth of the Lutheran Church.[57]

The impact of these restrictive measures was felt very soon, and relations between the prince and the Inner Austrian estates further deteriorated when Karl began to abolish the Protestant printing presses in the duchies' capitals. In 1579, he imprisoned the Styrian estates' printer, Zacharias Bartsch, who had refused to print the lecture list of the Jesuits' school. This attack was followed up by a decree against the press in the Carniolan capital in May 1580.[58] At the same time, a campaign was started against the new head of the Protestant school in Graz, Caspar Kratzer. The estates' choice of this candidate for such a weighty and conspicuous office seemed a deliberate provocation of their confessional adversaries and competitors in the field of education, the Styrian Jesuits, since Kratzer was an apostate Jesuit who had recently graduated from the Protestant theological faculty of Tübingen in Württemberg. Retaliation was swift, and Kratzer was banned from the three duchies by a ducal decree in June 1580, in spite of the estates' vociferous protest. In the same month, the archduke prohibited the superintendent of the Inner Austrian school and church ministry, Jeremias Homberger, from preaching in Graz.[59]

By the time the diet convened in November 1580, a considerable number of *gravamina* had therefore accumulated, and were promptly listed in the estates' petition to the archduke. Recognizing the responsibility of foreign Catholic powers for the archduke's change of policy, the estates concentrated their attack on the Jesuits and the recently arrived nuncio Malaspina, so that a direct confrontation with the archduke was

[57] For the ineffectualness of the decrees see the evidence from contemporary sources quoted by Loserth, *Gegenreformation*, 346–7. However, the fourteen orders issued from Mar. 1580 to June 1587 to stop the building of a new Lutheran church in Sachsenfeld near Cilli also document the persistence of these efforts, see *FRA/50*, 54.

[58] Peinlich, *Geschichte*, i. 17–18. K. Amon, 'Die geistige Auseinandersetzung', 41, in *Evangelisch in der Steiermark*, 39–43, and *FRA/50*, 59.

[59] For the Kratzer affair and the decree against Homberger see Loserth, *Gegenreformation*, 309–25, 468.

avoided.[60] There was an obvious strategic dimension to this statement, which aimed at driving a wedge between the provinces' clergy, who formed part of the corporate body of estates, and the foreign party of Catholic reformers. Nevertheless, there can be no doubt that the charge against the 'foreign nations' and 'unruly people' who disrupted the confessional peace in the province also reflected the estates' actual assessment of the situation and testified to their mistaken belief that a return to consensus politics on the religious question was still feasible.[61]

In the face of continuing attacks on their position, they were nevertheless determined to employ their means of power to force the revocation of the archduke's most recent and drastic Counter-Reformation measure. Brushing aside the Munich conference's regulations for a cautious and gradual proceeding, Karl had attempted to abolish the Protestant *exercitium* of the burghers in his municipalities at one stroke by a general edict of 10 December 1580.[62] His rash move not only failed to achieve its objective, but even temporarily strengthened the link between the Protestant elite and the towns. The nobility immediately sided with the commoners and retaliated by refusing to grant any taxes and contributions for the maintenance of the border troops.[63] Outraged by this affront to his authority, Karl threatened to avail himself of his *ius reformandi* against his disobedient subjects, an effective rhetorical device which he repeated after the estates' unsuccessful appeals to the Emperor and the Protestant Imperial princes in 1582 and 1584.[64] In March 1581, he dispatched his vicegerent, Bishop Christoph Spaur of Gurk, to Rome to ask for 'substantial help'. This grant would be used exclusively for the military defence against the Turks, and for the suppression and extinction of heresy. Karl even suggested that the nuncio in Graz should supervise the application of this contribution, so as to assure the Pope of its proper use.[65] However, the papal response and subsequent appeals to the allies of

---

[60] For the estates' complaint of 2 Dec. 1580 see *FRA/50*, 70–5. For their criticism of the Jesuits' and the nuncio's activity see ibid. 72–4.

[61] Ibid. 73, 74.

[62] 'Resolution' of 10 Dec. 1580, ibid. 78–83.

[63] For a detailed account of the conflict at the diet of 1580–1 see Loserth, *Gegenreformation*, 325–61. The relevant documents are printed in *FRA/50*, 69–234. The estates' personal intercession is mentioned in the nuncio's letter of 4 Jan. 1581, Malaspina to Gallio, *Nb i*, 173–5.

[64] Reply to the estates, 16 Jan. 1581, *FRA/50*, 190–2. For the failure of the estates' attempt to utilize Inner Austria's constitutional links with the Empire see A. Luttenberger, 'Innerösterreich und das Reich im Zeitalter der Gegenreformation', in Dolinar et al., *Katholische Reform*, 372–87.

[65] 'Instruction' for Christoph von Spaur, 18 Mar. 1581, *FRA/50*, 235–43.

1579 revealed that the financial issue was in fact a grave flaw in the ambitious Counter-Reformation scheme. Gregory XIII thus promised to contribute to the costs of additional ducal guards in the capital only. Papal letters urging immediate help for Karl II were sent to the Emperor, Archduke Ferdinand of Tyrol, Duke Wilhelm of Bavaria, and to the archbishop of Salzburg, but in the end none of the financial support promised at the conference of Munich was forthcoming.[66]

At the recommendation of his councillors, Karl therefore decided to show himself conciliatory. His orders to suspend the execution of his December decree, however, failed to persuade the Styrian estates to proceed with the granting of taxes. On the other hand, an ominous rift in the front of Protestant opposition became visible in the course of the negotiations which ran counter to a previous agreement in 1578 for mutual consultation and joint action in religious matters. Fearing an escalation of the crisis, the estates of Carniola relented and proceeded to grant the requested contribution.[67] The rest of the estates, led by the Styrian diet, held out, and on 3 February 1581, Karl issued a declaration by which he promised to stop the execution of the decree completely and 'to leave everything in its previous state'.[68]

Predictably, Karl's surrender was sharply criticized in the Catholic camp. The nuncio, who had castigated the archduke's lack of determination before,[69] now gave vent to his frustration in a meeting with Karl II and his Catholic councillors. He demanded that the archduke give proof of his will to extinguish the Protestant heresy in his lands. The importance of recovering key government offices from the Protestants had been given first priority in the Munich programme, and Malaspina now urged Karl to make a start by wresting the financial administration from the control of the thoroughly heretical ducal chamberlain (*Hofkammerrat*).

Against this were ranged the forces of established practices of appointment and the strength of Protestantism in the province itself. At

---

[66] 'Relation' of Christoph of Spaur, 20 July 1581, ibid. 268–9. In a letter to Archduke Ernst, dated 7 Mar. 1581, Malaspina described the prospects for financial help as bleak. The miserliness of the Bavarian duke was sharply criticized by Karl II's advisers. For an excerpt and summary of this letter see *Nb i*, 199–200. The papal briefs are mentioned by Rainer, ibid. n. 9, p. 189. See also Gallio's letter to Malaspina, dated 19 Feb. 1581, ibid. 194–5.

[67] The text of the agreement ('Vergleichung') of 14 Feb. 1578 is quoted in Loserth, *Gegenreformation*, 278.

[68] 'so wellen doch I. F. Dt. . . . bemelts decret hiemit gn. einstellen und alles wesen in dem standt, wie es vor dato ermelts decrets gewesen, gn. noch verbleiben lassen, treulich und ungeferlichen.' Decree of 3 Feb 1581, *FRA/50*, 217.

[69] See his second report to Gallio, 4 Oct. 1580, *Nb i*, 29–31, and also his report of 8 Dec. 1580, ibid. 138–41.

the accession of Karl II in 1564, a tripartite governmental apparatus had been established on the model of Ferdinand I's Lower Austrian government, consisting of a Privy Council and further executive offices at the core, a ducal chamber (*Hofkammer*) in charge of the ducal finances, and a war council (*Hofkriegsrat*). Supplementing and to some extent confronting this structure were the estates' administration and executive agencies, most notably the diet and the nobility's court (*Landschranne*), which had been created for the collection of taxes and the dispensing of justice respectively. The tax-granting power of the diet ensured that no prince could dispense entirely with this assembly, but it was nevertheless convoked and dissolved at the archduke's convenience. In the intervals, executive committees (*ständische Ausschüsse*) could be formed to handle any affairs that had been left unsettled by the diet.

The highest office of estates' captain (*Landeshauptmann*) formed a link between the ducal and the estates' executive apparatus by virtue of being a ducal appointment. Potentially, this office constituted a bridgehead of princely power into the political organization of the nobility, but custom had rendered the archduke's right of appointment to this office purely nominal, while the near-collective apostasy of the duchies' aristocratic elites left him with few Catholic candidates from which to fill government and court offices. However, when the post of *Landeshauptmann* became vacant in December 1580, Malaspina urged the archduke to assert his ancient rights by promoting a Catholic. At the same time, he pressed Karl II for a wholesale 'purge' of the rank and file of government and court officials, pointing to offers by the dukes of Bavaria and Tyrol to supply suitable candidates.[70] Karl was evidently impressed by the nuncio's remonstrance, though he shrank from the political risks involved in a collective deposition of Protestant officebearers. His Jesuit confessor Heinrich Blyssem could at least report to the General that the archduke had promised to appoint a Catholic *Landeshauptmann* against the estates' assumed right to nominate one of their number 'iuxta morem antiquum'.

Some steps were indeed taken to initiate a change in the confessional composition of the body of officials, for example, by the dismissal of the Protestant *Obersthofmeister* and *Kammerprokurator*, two high-ranking officers of the court and chamber. Karl further instructed the head of his court staff, the *Obersthofmarschall*, to employ henceforth no heretics. In 1581, Blyssem reported that vacant posts on the Privy Council were now

---

[70] Malaspina to Gallio, 23 Feb. 1581, *Nb i*, 195–8.

exclusively given to Catholics, and that the archduke had increased the
number of his Catholic servants and court officials.[71]

In fact, Karl proceeded more cautiously than these claims would
suggest. His decree of 25 May 1582 ordered the recatholicization of the
lower ranks of court officials and servants.[72] This measure was carried
through with the support of the duke of Bavaria, who promised to supply
candidates for the vacant offices.[73] With higher officials, Karl in general
sought to delay important appointments to avoid or at least postpone
further conflicts with the estates. Thus, he filled the office of
Landeshauptmann after a vacancy of six years, when he appointed the
Catholic Count Johann von Montfort in 1586.[74] Blyssem's information
concerning the dismissal of the Protestant *Obersthofmeister* and privy
counsellor Georg von Khevenhüller and the *Kammerprokurator* Johann
Linsmayr in 1580 was correct, but while the latter was followed by a
Catholic,[75] the office of the former went to an 'administrator' whose
orthodoxy was disputed.[76] The office was left vacant from 1590 until the
official accession of Ferdinand as duke in 1596, who appointed his own
Obersthofmeister, the Catholic Balthasar von Schrattenbach, as successor
in the following year.[77] Until the appointment of Wolfgang Schranz in
1576, even the vice-chancellor, Hans Kobenzl, was, as the nuncio put it, a
'politico', if not a heretic. The *Oberstkämmerer*, Wolf von Stubenberg,
was one of the Protestant leaders, but a close friend of the archduke, and
frequently acted as a go-between in the negotiations with the estates. He
therefore remained in office until Karl's death. This time, almost twenty-
five years lapsed before a successor, the convert Balthasar von
Thanhausen, was appointed.

---

[71] AGR, 'Epp. Germ., Germ. 159 (1581–1582)', fo. 113, Blyssem to Acquaviva, 18 Mar.
1581.

[72] *FRA/50*, 310.

[73] G. Cerwinka, 'Die politischen Beziehungen der Fürstenhöfe zu Graz und München
im Zeitalter des konfessionellen Absolutismus 1564–1619' (doctoral thesis at the Faculty of
History, University of Graz, 1966), 112.

[74] See Rainer, *Nb i*, 341, n. 4.

[75] For the following information on court and government officials see V. Thiel, 'Die
innerösterreichische Zentralverwaltung, 1564–1749', I, 203–9, in *AÖG* 105 (1916), 1–210.
The new *Kammerprokurator* was Dr Wolfgang Jöchlinger (1581–9), subsequently
Hofvizekanzler (1591–1602).

[76] Hans Ambros von Thurn, 'Verwalter des Obersthofmeisteramtes' and privy counsellor (1580–90). For a characterization see nuncio Caligari's letter of 11 Jan. 1585, *Nb i*, 351.

[77] For this and the following information from the government records see Thiel,
'Zentralverwaltung', I, 203–9. A relative of Balthasar, the likewise Catholic Maximilian von
Schrattenbach, was later made privy counsellor and Obersthofmeister of the widowed
Archduchess Maria of Bavaria during the regency, see below, Ch. 6.

A similar situation existed where most of the major government offices were concerned. If Karl could excuse himself with a reference to the thoroughly heretical chamber (*Hofkammer*) in 1580, it seems surprising that the president of this body was nevertheless allowed to stay in office until 1591. For the rest of the regency, no successor is listed in the government records. The fact that the War Council remained the domain of the Protestants almost until the general edict of 1628 was potentially of the greatest consequence. The offices of chancellor of the Inner Austrian government (*Regierungskanzler*) and vicegerent (*Statthalter*), however, were held exclusively by Catholics throughout the reign of Karl II.[78]

Blyssem's claim that the archduke increased the number of Catholic privy counsellors must therefore be modified. It seems that he was referring to the group of privy counsellors without special commission who were increasingly consulted as advisers on religious matters.[79] They were mostly lawyers, usually commoners, and above all good Catholics. The archduke's Catholic advisers soon formed an unofficial body which met separately and deliberated on the religious issue, so that in fact, though not in name, they constituted a kind of inner council of the larger Privy Council. This change of policy did not go unnoticed by the Protestant estates, who realized its confessional drift. In 1583 and 1584, they unsuccessfully petitioned the archduke against this practice and the preferment of Catholics in general.[80]

This outcry should, however, not divert from the fact that the archduke had in most cases to be content to reserve his right of appointment in principle, and to weaken the Protestant party by gradual changes and delay as envisaged by the plan devised in 1579. A slow shift of balance was brought about by Catholic appointments, but important offices, most notably in the military administration, remained in Protestant hands, and in December 1584, the new nuncio Giovanni Caligari regretted that Karl II's means of power did not match his good will.[81]

---

[78] *Regierungskanzler*: Dr Bernhard Walther (1564–86), Dr Elias Grienberg (1586–1602). *Statthalter*: the bishops of Gurk Urban von Trenbach (1569–74) and Christoph Andreas von Spaur (1577–84), Bishop Johann Tautscher of Laibach (1585–96).

[79] For a list of such councillors see Thiel, 'Zentralverwaltung', I, 206.

[80] J. Loserth, *Erzherzog Karl II. und die Frage der Errichtung eines Klosterrathes für Innerösterreich* (Vienna, 1897), ch. 1, 'Die katholischen Regimentsräthe', 3–14. For the estates' petitions of 18 Feb. and 1 Mar. 1583 and the ducal reply of 21 Mar. 1584 see ibid. 9–11.

[81] Caligari to Gallio, 10 Dec. 1584, in *Nb ii*, 340–2. Giovanni Andrea Caligari (1527–1613) was a protégé of Charles Borromeo. He acted as papal legate in various political missions in

Meanwhile, the Catholic princes and the nuncio had not ceased to urge the resumption of the Counter-Reformation in the archduke's municipalities. Karl's decision to suspend the decree of 10 December 1580 was taken as a sign that further joint action was needed to proceed with the realization of the October programme. In 1581, Malaspina began to consult with the Austrian and Bavarian princes and the Spanish ambassador in Vienna, Juan de Borgia, on the situation in Styria. Though backward in supplying financial support to tide Karl II over the consequences of a confrontational religious policy, Wilhelm V fervently pleaded for a rigorous proceeding, if need be by force of arms. As on the earlier occasion, this solution was firmly rejected by Rudolf II as too hazardous.[82]

Nevertheless, the criticism of his Catholic allies spurred Karl once more into action. The struggle for the recatholicization of his towns was resumed with a decree of 9 March 1582, which essentially repeated the orders of December 1580.[83] The Protestant towns appealed collectively to the estates, who immediately took up the battle with an intercession at the diet in 1582.[84] The ensuing conflict soon focused on Karl's proceeding in Graz. It seems that the advice of the Bavarian memoranda of 1577 and 1578 for the Emperor and the subsequent attack on urban Protestantism in the Lower Austrian capital of Vienna persuaded Karl II to choose the capital of his province as a starting point for his urban campaign.[85] The decree of 23 April 1582 prohibited attendance at the estates' church and school to the town magistrates, and ordered them to enforce the recent decrees against the burghers' Protestant *exercitium*.[86]

Italy and Poland and was entrusted with the implementation of the Tridentine decrees in the latter kingdom in 1577. After a spell of residence in his bishopric of Bertinoro in the Romagna in 1579–84, he became Malaspina's successor in Graz in Oct. 1584. Relations with the local Jesuits were tense from the start and steadily deteriorated as a result of constant quarrels over authority. In 1587, Caligari was recalled from Graz at his own request and subsequently had a career as papal secretary in Rome, see Rainer, ibid., pp. xii–xvii.

[82] Malaspina to Gallio, 27 Sept. 1581, *Nb i*, 327–30, and 16 Jan. 1582, pp. 367–70. The pros and cons are weighed—inconclusively—by an anonymous Jesuit author, probably Heinrich Blyssem, in a memorandum of 18 Mar. 1582, entitled 'Consultatio, Utrum expediat ut Archidux Carolus hoc tempore in arce et civitate Graecensi constituat militare p(rae)sidium, quo subditos ad Obedientiam compellat'. The Emperor's opposition to such a solution is emphasized. AGR, 'Epp. Germ., Germ. 160 (1582)', fos. 377–80.

[83] The decree and its confirmation by the archduke's 'further explanation' of 14 Mar. 1582 are printed in *FRA/50*, 274–9 and 287–8.

[84] Petition of nineteen towns and markets in Styria, 17 Mar. 1582, ibid. 288–91. The text of the estates' intercession of 17 Mar. 1582 is printed ibid. 291–3.

[85] This had been suggested by the papal secretary Gallio and by Duke Wilhelm V of Bavaria, see Gallio's letter to Malaspina, 29 Dec. 1581, *Nb i*, 363–4, and Duke Wilhelm V's letter to Karl II, 16 Oct. 1582, *Nb ii*, 47–53.

[86] *FRA/50*, 296–7.

Karl ignored the repeated protests and pleadings of the magistrates and the estates' representatives, and confirmed his orders on 7 and 10 May 1582.[87] When the mayor, the judge, and the leading municipal clerk (*Stadtschreiber*) refused to give up their Protestant *exercitium* and revoked their earlier promises to obey, they were arrested. Eventually, they conformed outwardly and were allowed to stay in Graz, although they lost their offices.[88]

In spite of the fact that the diet of 1583 had given weight to its protests against the recent measures by refusing to grant the military contribution, Karl now broadened his attack. In March and April 1584 he confronted the Protestant burghers of Graz with the alternative of compliance with his earlier decrees or emigration.[89] It has been seen that the Catholic princes who drafted the Munich programme in 1579 had considered it almost inevitable that a revolt of the nobility would break out at an early stage of the envisaged Counter-Reformation. This fear was now extended to the urban elite in the capital, who had allegedly formed an armed confederation and had taken an oath that they would rather die with the Protestant estates than give up their faith.[90] Karl set up a commission in Graz to inquire into these rumours, and examined the leading Protestant burghers. The advice of the Lutheran superintendent, Jeremias Homberger, not to take the prescribed oath by which they were bound to denounce their co-religionists was used as a pretext for his eventual expulsion from the archduke's lands. In June 1584, the Catholic party began to hope that the execution of Karl's decrees concerning Graz would cause neither an economically disastrous mass emigration of burghers nor an urban revolt as the estates had predicted.[91]

Karl nevertheless discussed these possible consequences at a meeting with the archduke of Tyrol and duke of Bavaria in Innsbruck. Archduke Ferdinand once more urged Karl to dismiss Protestants who held important offices, especially in the military administration. To make up for the

---

[87] Petitions of the magistrate and burghers of Graz, 27 Apr. 1582, ibid. 297–9, and n.d. [Apr.1582], ibid. 299. For the confirmations of 7 and 10 May 1582 see ibid. 302, 304.

[88] Ibid. 303–4, 329–31, 336–7.

[89] 'Resolution' of 18 Mar. 1582, ibid. 524, decree of 21 Mar. 1584, ibid. 527, and Malaspina to Gallio, 2 Apr. 1584, *Nb ii*, 253–4.

[90] AGR, 'Epp. Germ., Germ. 159 (1581–1582)', fos. 108–9, Blyssem to Acquaviva, 6 Feb. 1581.

[91] Loserth, *Gegenreformation*, 377–478. Homberger's memorandum of 18 June 1584 is discussed by Mezler-Andelberg, ' "Diß ist der beste weg" ', 199–210. For the Catholic assessment of the situation see the letters of Gallio to Malaspina, 2 June 1584, *Nb ii*, 268–9, and Malaspina to Gallio, 29 Aug. 1584, ibid. 304–6 and 6 June 1584, ibid. 269.

expected loss of Lutheran burghers, he had already selected a number of wealthy Tyrolean artisans who were eager to come to Graz if they were given burgher status. The duke of Bavaria had suggested a similar measure earlier on when he advised Karl to privilege Catholic artisans from Gorizia. The decision on the question of military and financial support, however, was postponed again.[92] Meanwhile, Karl's vice-chancellor Schranz and the Jesuits demanded a rigorous enforcement of the recent decrees against the burghers, and favoured the use of troops to ensure compliance.[93]

In the end, however, the problem dissolved after a crisis in the Protestant camp. The burghers of Graz had not only appealed to the estates as their patrons, but, as the nuncio reported, had also threatened open resistance to the government. Nobody was to answer the summons issued by the archduke's commission. Anybody who nevertheless complied would be banned by the burghers and turned over to the urban population for punishment. The evidence for the later riot in 1590 would suggest that the urban artisans at least were willing to resort to violence.[94] In any case, the threat of a popular revolt seemed as real to the Protestant estates and the urban elite as to their religious adversaries. Neither the capital's elite nor the Protestant nobility were to be pushed into rebellious action on behalf of the assumed confessional liberties of the unruly urban populace. The government contributed to the confusion by deliberately misdirecting its reply to the burghers' protests in a commissioners' letter to the estates. In this document, they related the threat of joint armed resistance which the burghers had allegedly uttered with the support of the nobility. At the same time, the letter confirmed the prince's determination to continue his religious policy. This coup had the desired effect. The estates withdrew their support from the burghers and publicly urged them to obey the commission and refrain from rebellious action. Predictably, the commissioners seized on this declaration for their propaganda, thus widening the breach among the different groups in the Protestant camp.[95]

The estates' legalism was arguably not the sole driving force behind their reaction to this crisis. As previously demonstrated, there was little common ground between the estates and the municipalities apart from

---

[92] Malaspina to Gallio, 9 Aug. 1584, *Nb i*, 300–2.
[93] Malaspina to Gallio, 29 Aug. 1584, *Nb ii*, 304–6.
[94] Malaspina to Gallio, 6 July 1584, ibid. 280–2. For the revolt in 1590 see below.
[95] That this was indeed a planned coup by the Catholic councillors emerges from Malaspina's letter to Gallio, dated 14 July 1584, *Nb ii*, 285.

the confessional question. On the contrary, dividing issues such as tax-ation and competition between urban and rural trade dominated their relationship in general, effectively strengthening the ties between the nobility and the prelates as the two leading political estates.

Faced with the prospect of large-scale urban unrest and confronted with the estates' repudiation of their cause, the urban elite of the capital publicly disowned any rebellious intentions. However, when a group of citizens was arrested and cross-examined, they named seven burghers who had allegedly drafted a plan for armed resistance if the archduke should proceed with the summoning of burghers before the commission. In view of this charge, the ducal verdict appears rather mild: the seven culprits were imprisoned, but the rest of the suspects were released. The commission resumed its activity, and those who were summoned had to take an oath to refrain from armed resistance if they were arrested, and to leave the duchy peacefully if they were expelled. Those ordered to emigrate would be outlawed if they returned clandestinely, and their property should belong to the person who arrested or killed them. Eager to make up for past offences, the magistrates hastened to co-operate with the commission. Those burghers who were subsequently interrogated promised to abstain from the Lutheran *exercitium* and to abide by the terms of the oath. By decree of 22 July 1584, the Catholic Julius von Sara, former captain of the ducal guards, was appointed 'town advocate' (*Stadtanwalt*) to exert close control over the conduct of municipal affairs.[96]

The ducal response to this crisis reveals that Karl was aware of the dangerous political tension that his new religious policy was causing among the population of the capital. On 22 January 1585, he permitted the burghers of Graz to attend Protestant services outside the capital.[97] While briefly relaxing pressure on Graz, Karl at the same time reinforced his activity in the rest of the ducal municipalities. In 1587–9, he issued decrees against the preachers and the Protestant *exercitium* in Upper Styria and in the Lower Styrian towns of Marburg, Radkersburg, Pettau, and Windischgraz. In the municipalities, specially appointed 'reformation commissions' tried to depose the Protestant magistrates and replace them with Catholics. Henceforth, no Protestants should be allowed to settle and obtain burgher status in these places. However, it soon became clear that Karl was unable to subject the Protestant urban and rural population when

[96] Malaspina to Gallio, 29 July 1584, 5 Aug. 1584, ibid. 289–91, 296–7. The decree of 22 July 1584 is printed in *FRA/50*, 554–5.
[97] Decree of 22 Jan. 1585, *FRA/50*, 571–2.

they received the full support of the nobility. In the case of the estates' rural subjects and the population of the patrimonial municipalities, he lacked effective means to cut this close bond.[98] It was therefore the main achievement of Karl II's urban campaign in the final decade of his reign to have brought Protestant growth at least to a standstill, and to have started the confessional 'purge' of the municipal administration in the ducal towns.

With regard to the future development of the confessional confrontation, the estates' position in the conflict between the ducal government and the burghers of Graz in 1584 was of considerable importance. While the estates' support of the burghers had forced the archduke to modify his decree of 10 December 1580, they publicly backed away from the militant urban opposition in the subsequent crisis over the Counter-Reformation in the capital. Dissenting voices of radical noblemen notwithstanding, it became increasingly clear that the estates as a corporate body were unwilling to risk an open confrontation over the issue of religious liberty for their non-noble co-religionists. The importance of this fact was temporarily obscured by the outbreak of concomitant but in fact unconnected incidents of religious unrest at the end of Karl II's reign, i.e. a large-scale riot in Graz in 1590 and a clash between the government and some east Styrian estate owners over the attempted destruction of a Protestant church. Karl II's recent Counter-Reformation measures were at the root of the revolt in the capital. His earlier steps for the disciplining of the obstreperous town council were followed by a confessional purge, involving the imposition of Catholic magistrates and an attempt to introduce a Catholic burgher oath in April 1590, a measure that was in line with his orders of 1588 for the rest of his municipalities. At the same time, he repeated an earlier decree of 25 October 1580 against the attendance of commoners at Protestant schools and services.[99] The estates protested, but this time their intercession had no effect on the ducal policy and could not prevent the outbreak of serious urban unrest on 4–6 June 1590.[100] A Catholic source of 1606 even speaks of a 'conspir-

---

[98] Decrees against the preachers in Schladming and Oeblarn and against Hoffmann's introduction of preachers in his Upper Styrian parishes, ibid. 605, 608–14, and Hoffmann's complaint of 21 May and 29 Aug. 1587, pp. 615–21, 623–31. For the Lower Styrian towns and the activity of the reformation commissions see ibid. 647–52, 658–9, 673–4, 683.

[99] For the decree of 25 Oct. 1580 see *Nb i*, 70. For the Catholic oath see the burghers' petition of Apr. 1590, *FRA/50*, 676–9. A copy of Karl's decree of 17 Dec. 1588 and the text of the oath can be found in STMLA, 'Archiv Leoben', Sch. 177, H. 1015a. For the introduction of Catholic magistrates and the uprising of 1590 see Schuster, *Martin Brenner*, 306–7.

[100] For the estates' protest see *FRA/50*, 683.

acy' among the burghers, and of attacks on the nuncio as well as the bishops of Gurk and Seckau.[101] While these reports would require substantiation, the facts of the urban revolt seem clear. On 4 June 1590, a riot broke out when the town magistrate tried to arrest a student of the estates' school, the son of a local artisan.[102] Over the next three days, between 400 and 500 artisans, led by a small group of young journeymen, forced the release of the student and took possession of the town. The vicegerent's and town magistrate's reports repeatedly mention that the rebels were armed with swords and halberds, so that the question arises whether they broke into the arsenal or were actively helped by sympathetic noblemen. The latter assumption cannot be dismissed out of hand, given the fact that relations between the prince and leading Protestant noblemen had been strained since Karl had attempted to extend the Counter-Reformation to parishes under their patronage, as was the case with Hans Hoffmann's parishes in Upper Styria. The ducal orders for the destruction of the Herberstorff church on the family's estates in May 1590 antagonized the local estate owners and temporarily raised the spectre of a violent reaction by a group of armed east Styrian noblemen in the district of Vorau.[103]

On 6 June, the town magistrate and the mayor of Graz succeeded in placating the crowd, whose leaders had threatened a 'Parisianische pluetige hochzeit', a Protestant Bartholomew's night, if the student was not released.[104] Whether divine intervention in the shape of a thunderstorm was responsible for the dispersal of the intimidated rebels, as the Catholic sources claim, or whether the crowd was simply content with its achievement, the revolt had come to an end. For the future course of the Counter-Reformation, it was important that punitive action to restore ducal authority was suspended, effectively for good, as a result of Karl II's death and the subsequent quarrel over the regency government. The archduke had been absent from Graz during these events. In May 1590, he had fallen seriously ill and had transferred his court to Laxenburg, where he died on 10 July 1590.[105] Details of the events, however, were

[101] 'Gründlicher Gegenbericht auf den falschen Bericht und vermeinte Erinnerung Davids Rungii . . . von Jacob Rosolenz, Propst von Stainz' (Graz, 1606), STMLA, MS 31, fos. 52–4.
[102] The following account is based on the eyewitness reports printed in *FRA/50*, 685–93 and Rosolenz, 'Gegenbericht', fos. 55–62.
[103] Loserth, *Gegenreformation*, 568–70. For a detailed discussion of this incident see below, Ch. 5.
[104] Anonymous eyewitness report, printed in *FRA/50*, 687.
[105] Loserth, *Gegenreformation*, 571.

faithfully related to Archduchess Maria of Bavaria, mother of Karl II's son and successor Ferdinand.[106] No eyewitness report exists to document the latter's reaction on receiving this news. There can, however, be little doubt that his Bavarian relatives and his Jesuit teachers impressed the crucial political lesson of Protestant rebelliousness and the concomitant humiliation of princely power on the young archduke.

The progress of Karl's Counter-Reformation policy had thus led to a crisis towards the end of his reign. Karl had stopped the spread of Protestantism by his proceeding against the burghers, and by his attacks on the Protestant school and church ministry. Using the proviso of the 'Pacification', he had begun to resume control over his municipalities. Beyond this, he had made forays into the Protestant estates' sphere of power and had questioned their religious privileges. Under this constant pressure, the Protestant coalition among the Inner Austrian estates threatened to disintegrate, and the frail links between the groups in the Styrian Protestant camp were beginning to give way.

The development of the 'political' Counter-Reformation raises a number of questions regarding the activity and influence of the 'foreign party', i.e. the nuncio and the Jesuits, and their relations with the local clergy. It soon became clear that, on the Catholic side, the attitude adopted by the prelates and the lower clergy formed the gravest obstacle to a genuine Catholic reform of the clergy and laity as envisaged by the authors of the Tridentine decrees. A month after his arrival in Graz, Malaspina suspected that the archduke's secular councillors and the prelates were withholding important information concerning the nature of the religious concession and the state of the Catholic religion in the province. Moreover, both parties refused to acknowledge their share of responsibility for the present state of affairs by pointing to the shortcomings of the other side 'because none of them wanted a domestic reformation (*la riformatione a casa sua*) if not of religion—because I take them to be Catholics—but to introduce pious and decorous customs'.[107] The nuncio soon found out that the estates successfully utilized the prelates'

---

[106] The relevant documents relating to the origins and course of the tumults in Graz and Vorau are reprinted in *FRA/50*, 680–93. Maria forwarded these reports to her brother Duke Wilhelm V of Bavaria, who in turn informed Archduke Ferdinand of Tyrol, see *FRA/50*, 693 and Loserth, *Gegenreformation*, 570.

[107] '. . . perché niuno di loro vorebbe la riformatione a casa sua, non diro già di religione, tenendoli per catholici, ma di buoni et santi costumi.' Malaspina to Gallio, 9–10 October 1580, *Nb i*, 36. For a more sceptical assessment of the secular councillors' orthodoxy see Malaspina's letter of 4 Oct. 1580, *Nb i*, 29–31, and his successor's report, Caligari to Gallio, 11 Jan. 1585, *Nb ii*, 351.

fear of a thorough papal investigation into their past conduct and administration of their offices. Details of the Munich programme had been leaked to the estates,[108] who used this information for a political manœuvre. Suggestions for a clerical reform and separate taxation of the clergy as envisaged by the various memoranda of the conference in Munich were used to persuade the prelates of the necessity to side with the secular estates. As has been seen, the issue of extraordinary taxation had played into the hands of the secular estates at an earlier stage, when Ferdinand I's fiscal policy had forced the prelates to seek their support. In November 1580, Malaspina informed the papal secretary that the nobility's representatives had persuaded the prelates that he had papal orders to subject them to a strict reformation and to punish them severely for their past misconduct. Once they had agreed to the separation of the estates, they would be asked to pay the total amount of taxes which they at present paid jointly with the secular estates. The nuncio noted that, as a result, the prelates had appealed for help and protection to the nobility. Although he had immediately convoked and rebuked them, and they had humbly promised to remain henceforth firmly on his side, Malaspina's faith in their reliability was profoundly shaken.[109]

Their co-operation was, however, essential for the realization of the Munich programme. It was important that Karl's Counter-Reforming legislation should appear as a response to the clergy's wishes. To achieve this, Malaspina used the co-operation of the small group of responsive prelates, most notably Bishop Christoph Spaur of Gurk and the somewhat less reliable bishop of Seckau, Georg Agricola, to launch a campaign which would force the clergy to take sides in the confessional argument. During the winter diet of 1580, Spaur submitted a petition which was drafted by the nuncio. Claiming to speak on behalf of the assembled clerical estate, it urged the archduke to make no further concessions to the heretics. In drawing a clear line between the Catholic party and its confessional adversaries among the estates, this petition prepared the ground for Karl II's legal campaign. Six days after the submission of this document, the battle against urban Protestantism was opened by the decree of 10 December.[110]

---

[108] Letter of the Imperial councillor Georg Eder to Duke Wilhelm V of Bavaria, 6 Feb. 1580, quoted in Cerwinka, 'Graz und München', 70.

[109] Malaspina to Gallio, 24 Nov. 1580, *Nb i*, 120–1.

[110] Malaspina to Gallio, 3 and 5 Dec. 1580, ibid. 131–6. In his letter of 14 Dec. 1580, Malaspina relates how the bishop of Seckau was temporarily alienated from the nuncio by an eloquent speech from a group of Protestant noblemen headed by Hans Hoffmann, ibid. 153. The episode showed the precariousness of Malaspina's achievement in separating the prelates from the rest of the (Protestant) estates.

Malaspina's campaign suffered a serious setback when the estates' threat of a tax-strike forced the archduke to suspend the most rigorous legal measures against urban Protestantism which he had issued between December 1580 and February 1581. Karl II and his councillors, who were joined by the faint-hearted Styrian prelates, hastened to shift the full burden of responsibility for the contentious measures onto the nuncio, in the hope of diverting the estates' protests.[111] In this situation, Malaspina fully relied on the support of a small group of clerical reformers, consisting of the bishop of Gurk, the archduke's confessor and Jesuit provincial Heinrich Blyssem, and the rector of the Jesuit college, Emmerich Forsler.[112] Their support was of utmost importance for the success of his efforts, which now concentrated on the issue of clerical reform.

To tackle this problem, Malaspina had urged a general reformation of the Styrian monasteries and the parish clergy since December 1580. His reports abound with comments on the moral defects of the prelates and the lower clergy, whose immorality had prepared the ground for the spread of heresy. As a result, he was convinced that a revocation of the religious concessions would only make sense if this measure were followed up by episcopal visitations from Salzburg and Aquileia. To achieve a thorough and lasting clerical reform, seminaries for the education of priests were likewise needed.[113]

In the following year, Malaspina began to visit the Styrian monasteries, and his subsequent description of the state of the province's clergy revealed the magnitude of the task of reform. According to Karl II, the generals of the religious orders had sent inept and rapacious superiors for the mendicant convents of the duchy, and had thus ruined their moral and material basis. This reproach was borne out by Malaspina's own observations. The number of regular clergy had declined to an average of two inmates per convent. In many cases, the monasteries were deserted and the buildings decayed.[114] The findings of his visitation of the most important Styrian parishes in 1581 persuaded the nuncio that drastic

---

[111] Malaspina to Gallio, 1 Feb. 1581, ibid. 185–6.

[112] Malaspina to Gallio, 14 Dec. 1580, ibid. 153.

[113] Malaspina to Gallio, 20 Dec. 1580, ibid. 161.

[114] Malaspina to Gallio, 30 Oct. 1580, ibid. 79–80. For evidence from Judenburg see Malaspina to Gallio, 1 June 1581, ibid. 282–6. Cases of clerical abuse by the Dominicans and Franciscans are reported in his letters of 30 Oct. 1580, ibid. 79–80, and 1 June 1581, ibid. 282–6. For especially crass examples, like the plunder of local convents by the Dominican provincial Castelnovo during his visitation of the province, see nuncio Andrea Caligari's report to secretary Rusticucci, *Nb ii*, 409–10. Malaspina's reports on the visitation of 1581 are published by Rainer and Weiß, *Die Visitation steirischer Klöster und Pfarren*.

measures against clerical concubinage were prerequisite to any effective
clerical reform. During his visitation of the Upper Styrian *Viertel* of
Judenburg, he evicted twenty 'concubines' from the parishes, and threatened grave ecclesiastical sanctions in the case of future transgressions.[115]
In a letter to the papal secretary, Malaspina complained that the decrees
of the Salzburg synod of 1569 were not observed by the provincial clergy,
and urged more determined papal support for his Salzburg-based reform
plans. Again, he castigated the immoral conduct of the secular and regular clergy. The diabolical doctrine would never have captured the nobility
and the population of the province if the previous moderate clerical
reform had borne fruit, 'but there has been no change in the clerical
conduct at all, so that it is no surprise that, while the cause persists, so
does the effect'.[116]

In April 1581, Malaspina reported on the recent synod in Salzburg.
Most of the sixty parish priests who attended had a wife or concubine,
and part of the clergy openly declared themselves Protestant. Among the
220 Styrian priests under the jurisdiction of Salzburg, there were not
even ten who did not live in concubinage or claim to be married. Worse
even, the latter group refused to send away their wives, and insisted that
their marriages were valid. They confirmed their determination to follow
the German Lutheran clergy, whom they considered 'as good as the
priests of other provinces'. Malaspina had, rather unrealistically,
demanded the collective arrest of the offenders, but the archbishop
thought it wiser to leave any attempt at wholesale reform to future visitation commissions. Meanwhile, he had issued a decree by which the secular clergy were ordered to send away their concubines on pain of loss of
their benefices, 'but they could not care less for this order'.[117]

Given this state of ecclesiastical affairs in the province, Malaspina was
confronted with the dual task of winning the prelates' confidence and
preparing the ground for an effective and lasting reform of the secular and
regular clergy. In the former, Malaspina was helped by his skilful handling
of a spectacular crisis in 1581. In furtherance of their attempt to cause
dissension among the Catholics, the estates had circulated a forged letter
according to which the nuncio had already deposed a number of the leading
Styrian prelates. As a result of this rumour, the abbots of the monasteries of

---

[115] Malaspina to Gallio, 7 Nov. 1581, *Nb i*, 347.
[116] 'Ma non essendo seguito mutatione alcuna de' costumi, non è maraviglia se durante la
causa dura ancora l'effeto d'essa.' Malaspina to Gallio, 4 July 1581, ibid. 290.
[117] 'Ma questo commandamento non sarà da loro stimato niente.' Malaspina to Gallio, 10
Apr. 1581, ibid. 224–6.

Vorau, Neuberg, and Pöllau sent an appeal for help to Karl II.[118] Shortly after this, the Jesuits warned the nuncio that the abbot of Neuberg planned to assassinate him. It seems that Malaspina's display of Christian magnanimity and his refusal to let the archduke take action against the malefactor were decisive in winning the prelates' confidence. In spite of temporary setbacks, they began to respond to the nuncio's appeals and at last joined forces with the foreign Counter-Reformers. In December 1581, Malaspina described the clerical representatives at the diet as united and 'ben animati' and noted that they had turned up, for the first time in years, in clerical dress. The implications of this act were not lost on the Protestant estates.[119]

Co-operation between the nuncio and the Jesuits also influenced the shaping and correction of the political Counter-Reformation. Malaspina frequently consulted with the leading Jesuits and the archduke's Catholic councillors, and conveyed the papal views through Karl's Jesuit confessor. Even more important was the Jesuits' support for his clerical reforms. However, it soon became clear that this could involve the Society in disciplinary actions against the local clergy which were bound to make them resented and could hence obstruct their efforts at clerical improvement by encouraging emulation of the Society's example. In 1581, Malaspina wrote to General Claudius Acquaviva to obtain his consent for the appointment of the Jesuit rector Emmerich Forsler as his assistant in the Styrian visitation. He pointed to the lack of zealous and suitably qualified clergy, and declared his intention to use Forsler as his messenger in communications with Salzburg.[120]

Malaspina's wishes were essentially in keeping with Counter-Reformation theory as devised by Peter Canisius in his important memorandum for Cardinal Morone in 1576. Canisius had strongly supported the creation of three permanent nunciatures with far-reaching powers, so that they should be able to spur on slack bishops and canons. To help them with their wide range of reforming activities, he had suggested the appointment of 'secreti Nuncii' who should further the regular nuncios' work and intensify communication with Rome. These agents should be picked from the German students of the papal college (Germanicum), and could in turn be appointed nuncios if they distinguished themselves as assistants.[121] Canisius' suggestion was taken up, but, given the impor-

---

[118] Malaspina to Gallio, 2 Oct. 1581, ibid. 121.

[119] Malaspina to Gallio, 6 Dec. 1581, ibid. 357–60.

[120] Malaspina to Acquaviva, 9 Aug. 1581, ibid. 312–13.

[121] B. Schneider, SJ, *Die Jesuiten als Gehilfen der päpstlichen Nuntien und Legaten in Deutschland zur Zeit der Gegenreformation* (Rome, 1959), 280–2.

tance of the Jesuits as teachers, theologians, and spiritual advisers of the Catholic princes, it was inevitable that not only their students, but members of the Society itself should be entrusted with special missions. Between 1550 and 1580, leading Jesuits, like Canisius, were frequently used as 'secret nuncios' by the Curia.[122]

As with the Jesuits' activity as councillors and confessors of the Catholic princes, it proved difficult to control the consequences of the Society's involvement in the full range of Counter-Reformation tasks.[123] Awareness of this problem was growing among the Jesuit directors of the German mission. From the later 1560s onwards, Canisius and the German provincial Paul Hoffaeus, for example, protested against the nuncios' habit of choosing Jesuits for their entourage on longer journeys. In a letter to Hoffaeus in January 1581, Canisius criticized the Imperial nuncio Bonomi for charging members of the Society with official and often troublesome commissions, and urged the provincial to effect a change of this policy in Rome.[124] Acquaviva was aware of the problem when he informed Forsler of his reply to Malaspina. With regard to the requested support for the visitation of Styrian monasteries, he had asked the nuncio not to involve the local Jesuits in affairs that would cause them trouble and render them odious to other religious orders.[125] In the end, however, Acquaviva complied with Malaspina's wishes, a change of mind that suggests papal intervention on behalf of the nuncio.

In view of the acknowledged shortage of adequately trained Catholic clergy for the Empire, the General found himself increasingly under pressure to grant dispensations from the Society's rules and give the local Jesuit superiors a free hand. The education of a sufficient number of provincial clergy and Catholic laity for the service of the prince was therefore of first priority not only in the view of Karl II's Catholic advisers in Graz, but also from the perspective of the General, who wished to extricate the Jesuits from burdensome additional tasks which undermined

[122] Ibid. 293–303.

[123] Conflicts occurred when the generals' decision to enforce the Society's regulations, especially the prescribed mobility of the members, clashed with the wishes of Catholic princes who refused to accept the removal of their spiritual and political advisers, see B. Duhr SJ, *Die Jesuiten an den deutschen Fürstenhöfen des 16. Jahrhunderts* (Freiburg im Breisgau, 1901), 31–6, and chs. 4 (Innsbruck) and 5 (Munich). After a brief argument, General Acquaviva obliged Karl II by revoking his orders for the exchange of the ducal confessor P. Nikolaus Coprivitz, AGR, 'Austr. Epp. Gen. (1573–1600)', i/1, fos. 301–2, Acquaviva to Karl II, 20 Sept. 1586, and Acquaviva to Emmerich Forsler, 30 Nov. 1586, 7 Feb. 1587, ibid. fos. 305–6, 326–8.

[124] Schneider, *Jesuiten*, 297.

[125] Acquaviva to Forsler, 30 Aug. 1581, AGR, 'Austr. Epp. Gen. (1573–1600)', i/1 fo. 160.

their centralized hierarchical structure and encumbered their spiritual mission.

In the Styrian context, this educational aim had already been laid down in the ducal foundation deed for the Jesuit college in 1573.[126] The Jesuits' grammar school was completed in 1578, when the fourth and fifth classes, the *Poesie* and *Rhetorik*, were added to the elementary school. In 1574, the archduke founded a seminary for poor students, later to be renamed the Ferdinandeum. The Convict, a seminary for the education of priests, opened in 1576, and was supplemented by Gregory XIII's foundation for papal alumni in 1577.[127] Both institutions were directed by the Jesuits. In 1585, the Jesuits' grammar school was extended by the addition of a theological and philosophical faculty and was elevated to the rank of a university, which opened at the beginning of 1586.[128]

The completion of the Jesuit school and the opening of the university in Graz in 1586 were complementary to the ducal policy of the preceding years. Karl II's decrees had aimed at the suppression of burgher attendance at the Protestant schools and his decree of 1 January 1587 tried to put a stop to the nobility's habit of sending their sons to Protestant universities. The Jesuit-directed schools, so it was hoped, would entice away the burghers' sons and the aristocratic youth from the heretics' schools. Until about 1620, however, the intake of students from the higher nobility of the province remained low, although *c*.45 per cent of all students came from the three duchies of Inner Austria, more than half of them being Styrians. At the beginning of the Counter-Reformation campaign, the total number of pupils at the Jesuits' school was very low, with an increasing proportion coming from the neighbouring eastern lands.[129] In 1584, 13 per cent of students in the Convict came from Hungary or Croatia. From the 1590s onwards, the University of Graz attracted students and candidates for priesthood from the (south-)east, a development that continued in the seventeenth and eighteenth centuries and therefore rendered Graz of considerable importance for the Counter-

---

[126] The document is printed in Peinlich, *Geschichte*, i. 8–10.

[127] Ibid. 11–14. The text of the papal deed is printed on pp. 14–17.

[128] For the text of the ducal and Imperial deeds and the papal bull see ibid. 25–31.

[129] See the annual report for 1581, AGR, 'Litterae Annuae (1575–1593), Austria (132)', fo. 36. For an estimate of the number and national composition of the student body see E. Engelbrecht, *Geschichte des österreichischen Bildungswesens*, vol. ii (Vienna, 1983), 293 n. 435. See ibid. for the above-quoted figures. For the intake of noble students see Peinlich, *Geschichte*, i. 109 and iii. 93–105. There is a more specific study for the Hungarian and Transylvanian Jesuits and students in Graz by J. Andritsch, *Studenten und Lehrer aus Ungarn und Siebenbürgen an der Universität Graz (1586–1782)* (Graz, 1965).

Reformation in its neighbouring territories.[130] For the moment, the social and national composition of the student body showed that more drastic political and legislative measures were required to make the scheme for the capturing of the Inner Austrian elites work. Lacking these aids for most of the reign of Karl II, the attraction of the Jesuits' institutions proved insufficient to lure the elite back to the Catholic fold. This meant that the elimination of a Protestant alternative in the field of higher education was indispensable, but it remained for Karl II's single-minded successor to take the necessary steps.

The reform process in the reign of Karl II was further hampered by divisions in the Catholic camp. Relations between the Society and the local clergy were adversely affected not only by the close co-operation between the Jesuits and the nuncio on the question of clerical reform, but also by the financial issue. The archduke's means were sufficient to provide a lump sum of money as well as tax-exempt income from landed property and vineyards in Styria for the foundation and maintenance of the Jesuit college. Like the institutions which were later founded under their direction, the college was to be permanently exempt from taxes and contributions. As the archduke's donation did not fully cover the expenses of the new foundation, however, a contribution was levied on the Styrian monasteries.[131] Given their often tight financial situation, the latter had to borrow the sums required, so that the Society's institutional expansion became a considerable burden on the local clergy. Worse even, these conspicuous favours were bestowed on the Society at a time when the archduke was forced to resort to similar financial expedients to Ferdinand I. In 1574—the year he founded the first Jesuit seminary in Graz—he demanded that the estates' executives draft a list of the clergy's taxable property (*Gülten*). The archduke subsequently obtained papal permission for the levying of a quinquennial contribution on the clergy to provide for the upkeep of the border defences. At the same time, he reinforced his predecessor's legislation against the sale of ecclesiastical property as a means of paying off the debts of the clergy, which further limited their financial means.[132]

[130] This aspect is discussed by J. Andritsch, 'Die Grazer Jesuitenuniversität und der Beginn der katholischen Restauration im Karpatenraum', in O. Pickl (ed.), *800 Jahre Steiermark und Österreich, 1192–1992* (Graz, 1992), 247–94, esp. the map on p. 251, indicating student numbers and places of birth of students from Hungary, Transylvania, Croatia, and Dalmatia in the years 1586 to 1782. The percentage of 'Convictisten' is stated ibid. 249.

[131] Peinlich, *Geschichte*, i. 7–10.

[132] Loserth, *Kirchengut*, 153–61.

The contrast between the privileged Jesuit order and the hard-pressed local clergy was hence glaring and predictably antagonized the latter. Even Bishop Georg Agricola of Seckau protested against this imbalance and referred the archduke to the Society for any future contributions.[133] Moreover, the Protestant nobility threatened to annul their ancestors' donations to local monasteries if Karl II insisted on furnishing the Jesuit college with monastic property. Again, they posed as protectors of the clerical estate by objecting to any extraordinary levies on the prelates. In the face of determined and united opposition, Karl had to give up his plan to endow the Jesuits with the property of the Carthusian monastery of Seitz near Cilli in Lower Styria, but the transfer of the property of two further convents, the Carthusian monastery of Geirach in Lower Styria and the Premonstratensians' house at Griffen in Carinthia, was confirmed by the Pope.[134]

A crisis occurred in the years 1585–7, resulting from the Society's strained relations with the papacy and its local representative, the permanent nuncio. Malaspina had been transferred to Bohemia in autumn 1584, and his successor, Giovanni Andrea Caligari, considered the Jesuits' notable influence at the ducal court as potentially subversive of his own superior authority. Even more serious was the change in the pontificate. The Jesuits' patron, Pope Gregory XIII, was succeeded by Sixtus V, whose aversion to the Society was well known.[135] In May 1585, Caligari reported that 'some unwise Friars'—presumably meaning Franciscans— had spread the rumour that the new Pope would never show any favour to the Jesuits because he shared the dislike which his order, the Franciscan conventuals, felt for the Society. The Jesuits were generally praised as the heretics' most formidable foe, but, so the general opinion ran, they were not very popular among the local Catholics 'on accout of a sort of craving for temporal goods . . . and a certain inclination to arrogate power over the rest [of the religious]' ('per una certa ansietà de le cose temporali . . . et un certo imperio, che volentieri si arogano sopra li altri'). Caligari added that this rumour had been generally applauded. As this state of affairs was obviously detrimental to the progress of the Catholic cause, he suggested that the Pope should order the Jesuits to remain strictly within

[133] Georg Agricola to archbishop Johann Jakob of Salzburg, 18 Mar. 1574, quoted in ibid. 51 n. 2.

[134] Peinlich, *Geschichte*, i. 13.

[135] Acquaviva apprised the provincial, Heinrich Blyssem, of the election and its possible adverse consequences for the Society, 3 May 1585, AGR, 'Austr. Epp. Gen. (1573–1600)', i/1, fos. 221–2. Sixtus V's pontificate began in Apr. 1585.

the boundaries of their constitutions, and submit to the nuncio's authority.[136]

As shown earlier, Jesuit involvement in papal visitations and disciplinary action against the regular clergy became a potential source of friction, and in 1585 an incident occurred which is revealing of the state of relations between the Jesuits and the local clergy. To oblige Karl II, Gregory XIII had consented to a rearrangement of spiritual functions and an exchange of buildings between the Jesuits and the parish of Graz which involved the almost completely deserted Dominican monastery in the town. Moreover, Gregory XIII had made over the property and all income pertaining to the Dominican church to the Jesuit college. In 1585, an attempt was made to put these arrangements into practice. Even Caligari supported this plan, mainly because the number of Dominicans in Graz had declined from eighteen or twenty to one or two, and the nuncio had to admit that he could not in good conscience intercede on behalf of these monks. Although he later on publicly confirmed that the Jesuits had never asked for this transfer and had no hand in the preceding negotiations, which had been entirely a result of ducal and papal favour, the plan foundered on the vigorous protest of the Dominican prior. Always mindful of the overriding importance of protecting the Society against charges of ambition and greed for temporal goods, Acquaviva realized that the Jesuits' reputation both in Rome and in Inner Austria was at stake. He therefore strictly prohibited any further negotiations.

The Jesuits' part in this affair was subjected to a close investigation, and the provincial was ordered to arrange for the immediate and complete restoration of the Dominicans' property and rights. As an act of obedience, he ordered this restitution to be made in the presence of the nuncio and the archduke.[137] In his letter to Caligari, Acquaviva expressed his concern at the local Jesuits' practices, which he had castigated before. The entire plan was 'difficult to stomach' ('di mal digestione'), because even if there were good reasons for a transfer, it meant in the last consequence the spoliation and eviction of a religious order from its place.[138] The General's letter to the rector of the college was written in the same

---

[136] Caligari to the papal secretary, Cardinal Rusticucci, 27 May 1585, *Nb ii*, 391–2.

[137] The relevant information can be found in the letters of nuncio Caligari to Cardinal Michael Bonelli, 13 Apr. 1585, ibid. 379–80, of the Dominican prior Fra Marco da Racanati to Cardinal Bonelli, 16 Apr. 1585, ibid. 380–1, Acquaviva to Caligari, 25 May 1585, ibid. 388–9, Caligari to Rusticucci, 17 June 1585, ibid. 394–7, and Acquaviva to Forsler, 15 Apr. 1585, 26 July 1585, 25 May 1585, AGR, 'Austr. Epp. Gen. (1573–1600)', i/1, fos. 214, 227–8, 239.

[138] Acquaviva to Caligari, 25 May 1585, *Nb i*, 388–9.

vein. The General of the Dominicans had complained to the Pope, and Acquaviva warned that great care had to be taken to prevent the new Pope from getting at the very beginning of his pontificate the impression that the Society was trying to deprive the established religious orders of their possessions.[139] Eventually, Karl's wishes were not rejected entirely, and a solution was found which permitted the extension of the Jesuits' pastoral activity. The General's decision on the property question, however, was definitive.[140]

For the remaining years of Karl's reign, the progress of the Catholic cause was hampered by these quarrels in the Catholic camp. In January 1587, Caligari asked to be transferred because of his abiding distrust of the Jesuits' influence on the archduke, which he continued to perceive as subversive of his own authority. He claimed that they were encouraging the archduke to pursue an independent religious policy, that they sought to obstruct the creation of a bishopric in Gorizia, and in general worked against him, undoubtedly because the authority of a bishop and a nuncio would put an end to their arrogated power over the clergy.[141]

The development of the Catholic mission and clerical reform in the reign of Karl II was therefore uneven. Initially, close links between the nuncio, the Jesuits, and the archduke's Catholic advisers helped lay the foundations for further progress, above all by separating the prelates from the Protestant estates. On the other hand, the results of the parish and monastic visitations showed that earlier reform initiatives, most notably the Salzburg synod of 1569, had failed, and that the determined effort of the Inner Austrian bishops and prelates would be needed to effect the implementation of the Tridentine decrees. During the final years of Karl's reign, the relation between the Jesuits and the nuncio underwent a profound crisis and change, with the result that the Jesuits were effectively drawn closer to the circle of the prince's advisers to secure support. This polarization in the Catholic camp temporarily hampered the nuncio's work. It also disproved the underlying assumption on which the permanent nunciature had been created, that is the expectation that instructions for the Inner Austrian Counter-Reformation could be developed in Rome and conveyed by the nuncio to the Jesuits and thence to the archduke who would proceed to implement them.

As has been shown, the Jesuits' privileged position was of ambivalent

[139] Acquaviva to Forsler, 15 Apr. 1585, AGR, 'Austr. Epp. Gen. (1573–1600)', i/1, fo. 214.
[140] Peinlich, *Geschichte*, i. 23.
[141] Caligari to Rusticucci, 10 Jan. 1587, *Nb ii*, 469.

value for the Society, and occasionally even jeopardized its spiritual mission. Although their educational work was slowly making progress, it became clear that more effective political pressure had to be exerted on the nobility and the urban elite to exclude Protestant competition in this field. The political framework within which the Counter-Reformation could operate successfully was to be provided by Karl II's successor, the future Emperor Ferdinand II.

4

The Ferdinandean Counter-Reformation and the Fall of the Protestant Cause

As seen earlier, Karl II's reign ended with a revolt in Graz against his Counter-Reformation policy. Further smaller-scale riots against his most recent measures occurred in the firmly Protestant Upper Styrian countryside as soon as the news of his death spread to the remoter parts of Styria. The intensity of Protestant feeling in this region, but also the complexity of religious dissent, were highlighted by an incident of local resistance to central control from Graz, involving the ducal parish of Mitterndorff. Shortly before the beginning of the personal rule of Archduke Ferdinand in 1595 (officially in 1596), the parishioners of this Upper Styrian village near Aussee forestalled the introduction of a Catholic candidate by 'electing' the son of the deceased priest of Aussee, Christoph Schwaiger. The ensuing conflict between the parish community and the church ministry in Graz revealed the latter's inability to enforce Lutheran orthodoxy effectively throughout the province. Since 1590, the parishioners had urged the superintendent to ordain and install Schwaiger, but the candidate had been rejected on account of his Flacian views. The ministry maintained this decision in 1595, and sharply criticized the forcible introduction of Schwaiger, which was bound to cause a conflict with the young archduke. However, the Mitterndorff parishioners abided by their decision and supported their preacher against both Catholic and Lutheran opposition from Graz.[1] Their case points to the persistence of a submerged theological current of Inner Austrian Protestantism. Flacianism had prevailed among the Carinthian nobility at an earlier stage, but was abandoned to secure the support of moderate co-religionists in the German principalities. The Formula of Concord was thus duly signed by the Inner Austrian nobility in 1580–2. However,

---

[1] Loserth, 'Flacianismus in Steiermark', 1–13. The relevant documents are printed in *FRA/58*, 6, 162, 175–80, 181–2, 186–8.

Flacian views were still widespread among the estates' rural subjects in Upper Carinthia and Upper Styria. Likewise, the mining town of Schladming had kept its Flacian preachers until 1577, and although orthodoxy was officially established in 1577/8, Flacian 'conventicles' and secret schools continued to exist in the town and its surrounding settlements, to the detriment of the local Lutheran school.[2]

Apart from its significance as evidence of the survival of Protestant dissent in the periphery of the duchy, the Mitterndorff incident was also indicative of a wider Protestant reaction by the rural population against Karl II's repressive religious policy. Where the impact of the Counter-Reformation was felt particularly keenly, a repeal of the most recent measures was now sought by appeals to the estates to act on behalf of their oppressed co-religionists, for example in the Upper Styrian parishes of Oberwölz and St Peter unter dem Kammersberg. These communities petitioned the diet in 1591 for redress of such grievances as resulted from the recent introduction of Catholic priests. The example of Oberwölz suggests that a sense of government-backed strength could inveigle Catholic priests into abusing their power. It emerged that the new incumbent had not been content to exert his rights as parish priest, but had actually intimidated and physically attacked his parishioners, who were mostly subjects of the Protestant Stubenberg and Teuffenbach families.[3] In general, however, the regency, necessitated by the fact that Karl's son and heir Ferdinand was in 1590 only 12 years old, meant a reprieve for the Protestant population of Inner Austria. Correspondingly, the number of Catholic baptisms in the capital, and in officially reconverted Catholic parishes such as Haus in Upper Styria, declined. It soon emerged that the undisputed authority of the legitimate prince would be necessary for the continuation of a policy of recatholicization.[4]

This task was facilitated by the outcome of the struggle for a constitutional guarantee of the major religious concessions. In this battle, the

[2] Hutter, *Geschichte Schladmings*, 222–34. Inner Austrian Flacianism is discussed in Loserth, 'Flacianismus in Steiermark', 1–13, and Sakrausky, 'Der Flacianismus in Oberkärnten', 83–109. The possible contribution of Flacianism to the crypto-Protestant tradition which evolved in the wake of the persecution under Ferdinand II would merit further inquiry.

[3] The petitions are printed in *FRA/58*, 13–18.

[4] The Catholic chronicler of the Counter-Reformation, Abbot Jacob Rosolenz of the Augustinian monastery of Stainz, briefly mentions the regency government's ineffectual attempts to sustain Karl's reform policy at local level and dismisses the regency years as a period of stagnation for the Catholic cause, see 'Gegenbericht', fo 64: 'es ist aber kein sonderbare Reformation fürgenommen, auch nichts namhaftes der Religion halben, verrichtet worden.'

estates' actions were directed by their secretary and theological adviser, the Lutheran Matthes Amman, who had ably defended the estates' cause on previous occasions.[5] It was therefore almost inevitable that he should lead the battle for an incorporation of this concession into the nobility's constitutional liberties. In view of Karl's change of policy, it was of crucial importance for the survival of Inner Austrian Protestantism that an effectively binding confirmation should be obtained from the regents on behalf of the archduke's successor.[6] At the beginning of the negotiations, the estates scored minor victories such as the dismissal of both the new Catholic *Landeshauptmann* and the notorious vice-chancellor Schranz. They even prevented a Wittelsbach regency government, in spite of the vigorous protest of the archduke's widow Maria, who considered herself the sole legitimate guardian of the future ruler's interests. After a brief spell of direct Imperial rule, the Archdukes Ernst (1592–3) and Maximilian (1593–5) were successively appointed regents of Inner Austria. However, their attempts to continue Karl II's course in religious matters were largely unsuccessful. A major cause of their failure was the government's preoccupation with the settling of the long-drawn-out struggle over the Inner Austrian estates' oath of allegiance. The pattern of the conflict remained constant: the new ruler's order for unconditional compliance was countered by the estates' demand that the Pacification of Bruck should be added to those laws and customs of the country which the prince swore to observe at his accession. Significantly, the diets of Carinthia and Carniola referred the regents to the traditional order by which the Styrians were to take the oath of loyalty first. By making their decision dependent on the attitude of the Styrian estates, they sought to avoid a direct confrontation with the Imperial governors.[7] Co-operation among the Protestant estates continued, though, and an Inner Austrian delegation was sent to Prague in 1591 to petition the Emperor.[8] Nevertheless, it became clear that the Carinthians' and Carniolans' fervent confirmations of the rather immaterial 'Protestant Union' of 1578 were made with the proviso that Styria would have to bear the brunt of the confessional battle.

[5] For Amman's biography and activities in the service of the Styrian estates see above, Ch. 2, and Loserth, 'Matthes Amman', 1–68.

[6] For the following, if not otherwise indicated, see J. Loserth, 'Der Huldigungsstreit nach dem Tode Erzherzog Karls II., 1590–1592', *FVVGST* ii/2 (Graz, 1898), and id. in *FRA/58*, pp. xi–xxv.

[7] Loserth, 'Huldigungsstreit', 95–100.

[8] *FRA/58*, 28–38.

In his response to the estates' petition for an explicit confirmation of the religious concession in 1591, the Emperor had to consider two objectives. First of all, a settlement of the Inner Austrian conflict was of considerable importance in view of the precarious military situation which soon deteriorated into the 'Long Turkish War' (1593–1606). On the other hand, however, the regent must under no circumstances make any concessions which would annul the modest achievements of the last years of Karl II's reign. He would have to take special care that the late archduke's reservations concerning the ducal municipalities as registered in Schranz's version of the 'Pacification' were preserved intact. Rudolf II therefore remained elusive on the subject of a confirmation by Imperial decree as requested by the Styrians, although a vague promise of future instructions to Archduke Ernst was made. After further futile pleading, the Inner Austrian estates eventually swallowed the bait and took the oath of allegiance to Archduke Ernst as regent in 1592, and again to Archduke Maximilian in 1593 without obtaining the desired amendment of the regent's oath that would have confirmed the incorporation of the religious concession of 1578 into the estates' constitutional liberties. On both occasions, they relied on the trustworthiness of a rather vaguely formulated promise that the regent would abide by the terms of the concession.[9] In spite of their experience during the last years of Karl II's reign, the majority of the estates thus seems to have been sanguinely dismissive of the fact that failure to secure a more tangible commitment from the prince rendered the 'Pacification' in practice useless as a legal safeguard.

Meanwhile, the tedious bargaining with the estates since the beginning of the regency and the complaints of the Habsburg princes and Karl II's widow Maria had at least the effect of persuading Rudolf II that it was advisable to hasten the transfer of government to the legitimate ruler. The young archduke was invested with governmental power in 1595, and his minority was terminated by the end of the following year, when he officially began his reign as duke of Inner Austria.[10]

The circumstances of Ferdinand's accession draw attention to those factors which determined the eventual success of the Ferdinandean Counter-Reformation: the outlook and political approach of the new ruler and the attitude of the Inner Austrian estates. Ferdinand not only rejected the estates' demand for an incorporation of the 'Pacification'; he

[9] Rudolf II to Archduke Ernst, 27 Sept. 1591, printed in Loserth, 'Huldigungsstreit', 205–6. Rudolf II to Archduke Ernst, 3 Dec. 1591, *FRA/58*, 27–8 n. 2.
[10] The relevant letters to Rudolf II are printed in *FRA/58*, 65, 78–84, 110–11, 153–4, 156–7.

even reverted to the old, strictly Catholic formula of the prince's oath, which had been modified in 1564 so as to be less offensive to the Protestant estates. Furthermore, he insisted that the estates' assemblies should take their oath of allegiance prior to any discussion of their religious grievances. Initially, the estates resisted this. The Styrians submitted a petition in which they listed their complaints and made their obedience dependent on Ferdinand's willingness to abide by the terms of the concession of 1578. However, Ferdinand passed over these protests in silence, and the Styrian Protestants characteristically chose to interpret this reaction as tacit approval. On 12 December 1596, they took the oath of allegiance to the duke; Carinthia and Carniola followed on 28 January and 13 February 1597.[11]

In their letter of 13 December 1596 to the estates of Carinthia and Carniola, the Styrians justified their action with a rather sweeping reference to the general state of affairs, which presumably meant primarily the military emergency.[12] If there were further political motives for the estates' surprising reversal, they have not gone on record, but the estates' conciliatory attitude is in line with their general reluctance to antagonize the legitimate ruler and risk an open confrontation. In this, they were arguably also motivated by fears of a spread of the peasant uprising in Upper Austria (1594–7), which served as a reminder of the need for united action for the maintenance of the social order.[13] As previously demonstrated, similar fears had influenced the confessional and political outlook of the majority of the nobility, which was essentially conciliatory and legalistic. Throughout the crisis of the 1580s, they had focused their attacks on the group of foreign 'troublemakers', most notably the nuncio and the Jesuits. These, it was asserted, were responsible for the disruption of the hitherto peaceful coexistence between the 'first estate' of prelates and the Protestant estates. Worse even, these foreigners sowed discord between the Catholic prince and his loyal Lutheran subjects, and advised him to break with the ancient customs of the land by promoting foreign Catholic protégés at the expense of his trusted servants and advisers from the duchies' Protestant nobility. The estates' perception and interpretation of Karl II's change of policy was to some extent misled as a result of the archduke's wavering attitude and his attempt to hide behind the papal

---

[11] Loserth, ibid., pp. xl–xlii.

[12] Letters of 13 and 29 Dec. 1596, ibid. 222–4.

[13] For the mixed religious and social motives of the second peasant uprising in the years 1594–7 and the vigorous governmental response see K. Eder, *Glaubensspaltung und Landstände in Österreich ob der Enns, 1525–1602* (Linz, 1936), 235–76.

authority as represented by the nuncio.[14] Moreover, the recent experience of a less active and confrontational religious policy during the regency seems to have given rise to hopes of a reversal of the course adopted in the final decade of Karl II's reign.

From the outset, however, Ferdinand proved himself a very different kind of ruler. Unlike his father, he refused to accept the estates' line of reasoning and become embroiled in a legalistic argument about the nature of the relations between the prince and the estates, between ducal rights and the estates' liberties, which they had tried to extend into the domain of religion. Instead, he cut through the Gordian knot by asserting his absolute power in the sphere of politics, and by repudiating any legal obligations which he considered incompatible with his duties as a Catholic prince. A public statement of his policy following a first series of far-reaching Counter-Reforming legislation in 1596–8 brushed aside the estates' claims for the constitutional basis of their protests. In his declaration of 28 September 1598, Ferdinand bluntly declared that he had received, but not accepted, their conditions for the act of homage at his accession. Furthermore, he stated that he knew of no concession that limited his power concerning religious reforms and forced him to protect or tolerate Protestant preachers in his lands.[15] In general, however, Ferdinand avoided a revelation of the aims and principles which underlay his policy. As will be shown in the following analysis, he achieved his ends by a combination of direct repressive measures with the manipulation of the administrative and legal instruments in his possession. The confrontation with the estates at the beginning of his reign in Inner Austria was the determinant of his political adolescence, and was crucial in shaping the views of the young prince and, as it turned out, future Emperor.

Any assessment of Ferdinand's religious policy in these years must take account of the influence of his clerical advisers, who either belonged to the Society or else to the new generation of Jesuit-trained clerics. On at least two occasions during the confrontation between the prince and

---

[14] See above, Ch. 3 These grievances were voiced at the Styrian diet in Dec. 1580, and in subsequent petitions in the years 1583–6, see *FRA/50*, 70–5, and Loserth, *Errichtung eines Klosterrathes*, 9–11.

[15] 'Resolution' of 28 Sept. 1598, *FRA/58*, 346–54, esp. 348 and 353. An anonymous memorandum entitled 'Deliberatio de modo, quo Religio Cath.ca a Ferd.o Archiduce Ser.mo restitui possit' and drafted before the accession of Ferdinand in 1596 characterized him as an obedient and zealous 'ecclesiae catholicae filius et ecclesiarum per suas provincias advocatus et protector', STMLA, 'Meillerakten', XIX-e (1–23).

the estates in September 1598 to April 1599, Ferdinand requested and implemented their political advice. This, however, is not to say that the young prince was a mere puppet of the papal reformers. Instead, their ideological support gave him the moral strength to overcome political obstacles on the course which he pursued with increasing self-assurance, that is, the assertion of his right to rule 'absolutely' and unrestrained by the estates' 'usurped' share of governmental power.

Prior to his accession as duke of Inner Austria, Ferdinand had been educated by Jesuit teachers at Ingolstadt. Throughout his reign, Ferdinand was to show his respect for the Society by conspicuous privileges and lavish donations for the Jesuits, often at the expense of the older religious orders.[16] From the beginning, his Jesuit confessors were among the most influential of his advisers, and papal support in general helped sustain this link. In December 1595, General Acquaviva informed the provincial Bartholomäus Viller of the Pope's request for intervention on behalf of the young archduke and his mother. Heretics and 'Politici' were allegedly gaining in influence at the court and were trying to prevent a restorative religious policy. It was therefore necessary that Viller should meet the archduke's confessor in Graz, P. Johann Reinel, and the nuncio, Girolamo Porcia, to deliberate on suitable countermeasures.[17]

At the insistence of the archduke, Viller remained his confessor and adviser until 1619. He was followed by P. Martin Beek (M. Becanus, 1620–4) and Guilelmo Lamormaini (1624–37). All three of them originated from the duchy of Luxemburg, and were educated in a period in which the Jesuits' Belgian province was of eminent importance for the progress of Catholic reform in the Spanish Netherlands. They also supplied the neighbouring archbishopric of Cologne with novices, some of whom became missionaries in the Habsburg lands of the Empire.[18] As

---

[16] R. Bireley lists fifteen Jesuit colleges in Austria, Bohemia, and Hungary/Croatia which were either founded or substantially supported by Ferdinand II, see R. Bireley, 'Ferdinand II: Founder of the Habsburg Monarchy', in Evans and Thomas, *Crown, Church and Estates*, 239. To these must be added the Inner Austrian houses in Graz and Leoben.

[17] Acquaviva to Viller, 2 Dec. 1595, AGR, 'Austr. Epp. Gen. (1573–1600)', i/1, fo. 709.

[18] Duhr, *Jesuiten an deutschen Fürstenhöfen*, 38–56. Viller was one of these novices, see ibid. 36. Other examples were Martin Stevordian from Brabant and his friend 'Arnoldus'. Martin had been a student at the college in Louvain, from whence he fled to Cologne in 1549 to become a member of the Society, against the wishes of his family, see *Litterae Quadrimestres . . .*, i: *1546–1552* (Madrid, 1894), 144–6. In 1556, Stevordian made a missionary incursion into Protestant Styria and preached in Bruck an der Mur, see Socher, *Historia Provinciae Austriae*, 60–1. For the activity of the Belgian Jesuits in the reign of Albert and Isabella see A. Pasture, *La Restauration religieuse aux Pays-Bas catholiques* (Louvain, 1925), esp. 312, 366–7.

was the case with his better-known successor Lamormaini, Viller's activity as adviser of the prince earned him a reputation as a politician. His anti-Bavarian stance during the Habsburg–Wittelsbach quarrel over the succession in the bishopric of Passau in 1597–8 was sharply criticized by the Society for aggravating the dissension between the leading Catholic dynasties.[19] That both Ferdinand II and his competitor for Catholic leadership in the Empire, Maximilian I of Bavaria, cherished spiritual advisers who had an equal reputation for Counter-Reforming zeal and political loyalty to the respective dynasty epitomizes the nature of the princes' relationship to the Tridentine cause. It was a symbiotic relationship, but its confessional aims were to be translated into terms conducive to *Hausmachtpolitik*, dynastic policy.[20]

In Inner Austria, the resumption of a vigorous Counter-Reformation policy was furthered by the succession of a new generation of Counter-Reformers to the suffragan bishoprics of Salzburg. The accession of the Swabian Martin Brenner to the bishopric of Seckau in 1585(–1615) ended the era of rather irresolute support for the reform party in Styria. His close links with the Society dated back to his education at the universities of Dillingen and Ingolstadt. In the first year of his office, Brenner proved his determination to pursue a firm Tridentine policy by starting a visitation of the Styrian parishes under his jurisdiction with the aim of subjecting them to a thorough Catholic reform, an effort he had to abandon for the time being in the face of massive protest from the estates.[21] Of even greater importance for the course of the Ferdinandean Counter-Reformation was the accession of Bishop Georg Stobaeus of Lavant, who acted as ducal vicegerent and councillor during the initial stages of the prince's reforms (1596–1609).[22] As will be shown, his memoranda gave the prince not only ideological support, but also important strategic advice.

[19] Duhr, *Jesuiten an deutschen Fürstenhöfen*, 45–6. For the conflict see M. Weitlauff, 'Die Reichskirchenpolitik des Hauses Bayern im Zeichen gegenreformatorischen Engagements und österreichisch-bayerischen Gegensatzes', in Glaser, *Um Glauben und Reich*, 58–9.
[20] On Maximilian I of Bavaria see now the monumental biography by D. Albrecht, *Maximilian I. von Bayern 1573–1651* (Munich, 1998), esp. ch. 10, pp. 285–337: 'Pietas Maximilianea'. Ferdinand of Inner Austria and Maximilian met for the period of a year as pupils at the Jesuits' school in Ingolstadt, see ibid. 108. For Maximilian's relationship with his Jesuit confessor Adam Contzen see R. Bireley, *Maximilian von Bayern, Adam Contzen S.J. und die Gegenreformation in Deutschland 1624–1635* (doctoral thesis, Harvard University, pub. Göttingen, 1975).
[21] For Brenner's education and the visitation of 1585 see Schuster, *Martin Brenner*, 21–51, 197–215, and *FRA/58*, 89–94.
[22] Stobaeus' career is discussed in J. Stepischneg, 'Georg III. Stobaeus von Palmburg, Fürstbischof von Lavant', *AÖG* 15 (1856), 71–132, and G. Wacha, 'Georg Stobäus, Pfarrer von Linz, Bischof von Lavant', *Carinthia*, 1/175 (1985), 215–28.

Ferdinand began his reign with a series of new appointments to government offices, including the vicegerent, the chancellor, and eleven Catholic noblemen or legally trained commoners for minor offices. His instructions of 1597 for the Inner Austrian government contain a clause by which its members were ordered to take action against heresies, an ambivalent term which the Protestants misinterpreted as referring to non-Lutheran heterodoxy. The ducal intention was clarified by an amendment in 1609, which prescribed a Catholic oath for office-holders. Nevertheless, Ferdinand did not risk a confrontation over a wholesale 'purge' of all government councils. Thus, the *Hofkriegsrat* continued to be dominated by Protestants until the early 1620s, and the decisive changes which determined the future composition of the *Hofkammer* came about under the presidency of Hans Ulrich von Eggenberg (1604–9), who followed the Protestant Ludwig von Dietrichstein. The line of Catholic governors or vicegerents was briefly interrupted in the years 1609–11, when Stobaeus abruptly withdrew from politics. His office was temporarily held by a Protestant, Hans Sigmund von Wagen (1609–11), until the bishop of Gurk, Johann Jakob von Lamberg, took over.[23]

Ferdinand sought to minimize the influence of Protestant presence among government officials by strengthening the Privy Council (*Geheimer Rat*), which he staffed with reliable Catholics, like Balthasar von Thanhausen, or with Catholic members of a Protestant family, like Hans Ulrich von Eggenberg, who married into the Thanhausen family in 1598.[24] To these should be added Andreas von Herberstorff, who had remained fervently Catholic while his brothers Karl and Otto belonged to the small group of radical Protestants among the estates. Andreas had arranged a mission by the Jesuits of Graz on his estates in 1580, and was to play an important role in the duchy's Counter-Reformation as principal reform commissioner during the next decade. At the accession of Archduke Ferdinand, he was appointed privy counsellor and *Obersthofmeister* of the archduke's brothers.[25]

---

[23] For Ferdinand's administrative reforms and early appointments until 1625 see Thiel, 'Zentralverwaltung', i. 64–71 and 203–9.

[24] R. Raab, 'Die Thannhausen', *Mittheilungen der Gesellschaft für Salzburger Landeskunde*, 12, (1872), 3–33. H. v. Zwiedineck-Südenhorst, *Hans Ulrich von Eggenberg* (Vienna, 1880), 10–11. Eggenberg's father had donated a building in Graz, the so-called 'Eggenberg-Stift', for the estates' Protestant school in Graz, ibid. 8.

[25] For Karl and Otto von Herberstorff see Loserth, *FRA/50*, 680–93, *FRA/58*, pp. xxxix, 4. The Jesuit mission is mentioned by Socher, *Historia Provinciae Austriae*, 243, who states that Andreas was almost the only Catholic member of the family. For the appointments in 1596 see Thiel, 'Zentralverwaltung', I, 206.

The impact of Ferdinand's policy can be gathered from a later petition by the Protestant estates, dated 31 March 1610. This letter was a reply to Bishop Martin Brenner of Seckau, who had criticized the Protestants for excluding the prelates from their deliberations at the diet and from all offices of the estates' administration. In his view, this went counter to the constitutional unity of the estates and therefore undermined the foundation of the *res publica*. By contrast, the estates claimed that they were now excluded from virtually all government, judicial, and court offices and had to ask the prelates for intercession with the archduke. The financial and personal sacrifices made in the service of the prince are stressed. Sons of the Protestant nobility often used up their patrimony to obtain legal training while government offices were in fact given to candidates who could boast no other qualification than adherence to the Catholic faith. Further, although the Protestants risked their fortunes and their lives by serving in the frontier militia, they were now systematically excluded from the higher ranks. They stated that twenty of their captains had been rejected solely on account of their confession. Instead, the archduke appointed his protégés, often Italians, who were—so the estates asserted—less qualified. By way of support, the petitioners quoted the judgement of the Catholic Croatian delegates who had come for a discussion of military affairs to Graz and had made no secret of their contempt for the utterly incompetent new officers.[26]

The estates' letter reveals the achievement of Ferdinand's reforms to this date. Considerable progress had been made on the way towards a complete purge of the government and administration, though Protestant interests were still strong. As the Styrians' complaint shows, Ferdinand made every effort to promote the numerically still weak Catholic party, which was augmented by Catholic foreigners, mostly Italians. The immigration of Italian merchants, artists, and engineers had begun with the setting-up of the court in Graz in 1564. Ferdinand subsequently adopted a policy of promoting this fresh supply of Catholics. Between *c*.1560 and 1620, forty Italian families obtained patents of nobility, thirty-three acquired estates, and sixteen of these landowners became members of the estates by obtaining the *Standschaft*.[27]

Regarding the more limited circle of his Catholic councillors,

---

[26] The Protestant Styrian estates to the bishop of Seckau, 31 Mar. 1610, DA, 'Religionsberichte Protestantismus', 1598–1730. The bishop's arguments are related in this letter.

[27] J. v. Zahn, *Styriaca. Gedrucktes und Ungedrucktes zur steiermärkischen Geschichte und Kulturgeschichte* (Graz, 1894), 158–204.

Ferdinand took care to bring his secular and clerical advisers together, as the composition of his entourage for his pilgrimage to Loreto and for his unfortunately unrecorded deliberations with Clement VIII in Rome in 1598 illustrates.[28] The beginning of Ferdinand's Counter-Reformation campaign in September that year bears witness to his close co-operation with these advisers and to the careful planning which characterizes the ducal religious policy. Eventually, the campaign was to result in the complete abolition of the Protestant school and church ministry in Inner Austria.

The archduke's protégé Lorenz Sonnabenter, a Jesuit pupil and former chaplain to the archduke during his Ingolstadt years, launched the initial attack. Sonnabenter had accompanied Ferdinand to Graz, where he became teacher to the archduke's brothers. As a sign of Ferdinand's special favour, he had invested Sonnabenter with the ducal parish of Hartberg, a benefice of considerable value.[29] In 1598, he was transferred to the parish of Graz, where he immediately disputed the authority of the Protestant ministry and denounced its local activities as an encroachment on his rights. Moreover, he ruled out the possibility of confessional coexistence, and thus attacked the basis of the religious concessions since 1572. In sum, Sonnabenter reclaimed the full jurisdictional and pastoral rights over the town's parish and threatened to turn to the archduke if the Protestant preachers continued their illegal *exercitium*.[30]

The relevant letter of 13 August 1598 was a piece of confessional polemic. Sonnabenter's attack alarmed the Protestant superintendent in Graz, Adam Venediger, who had been appointed after the eviction of Homberger, but it failed to provoke an imprudent reply which would have embarrassed the estates and supplied the priest with a pretext for addressing the archduke. Sonnabenter therefore pushed his argument further in a letter of 22 August 1598 to the estates' representatives (*Verordnete*), in which he demanded the dismissal of the estates' preachers in Graz. As these also taught at the estates' school, Sonnabenter's request was in fact tantamount to asking for a voluntary dissolution of the Protestant ministry in Graz. The estates' reply of the same day was still carefully worded, but it expressly warned against any further attack on the confes-

[28] Loserth, *FRA/58*, pp. xliii–xliv.

[29] According to the estates' tax register (*Gültbuch*), Hartberg (east Styria) followed close to the wealthiest parishes of Graz, Riegersburg (east Styria) and Voitsberg (west of Graz, now *Mittelsteiermark*), see Loserth, *Kirchengut*, 66.

[30] For biographical information see Loserth, *FRA/58*, p. xlvi. Sonnabenter was also in touch with General Acquaviva, who praised his zeal, Acquaviva to Archduchess Maria, 7 Nov. 1596, AGR, 'Austr. Epp. Gen. (1573–1600)', i/1, fo. 742. Sonnabenter's letters and the replies of the church ministry are printed in *FRA/58*, 292–5, 296–307.

sional peace. They were aware of his determination to undermine the settlement of 1578 and to involve the Protestant nobility in another confrontation with the archduke. With an eye to the imminent summoning of the diet, the estates also predicted, correctly, that a continuation of this quarrel would impede the negotiations over taxes and defence measures and would hence leave the duchy's frontier exposed to the Turkish enemy.[31]

The archduke was fully aware of this dilemma and turned to his *Statthalter* for advice. Stobaeus replied with a memorandum, the gist of which was to urge a shrewd and determined exercise of Ferdinand's right to restore confessional unity, in spite of the political risks involved.[32] Stobaeus was aware that this was a critical juncture which confronted the archduke with a choice between a return to dissimulation and largely ineffectual reform efforts, or a politically hazardous show of firmness. Stobaeus took account of this dilemma by dismissing the arguments of those who advised either violence or blandishments. The first approach would surely cause war, or else achieve merely external conversions, the second could hardly be taken seriously in view of the Protestants' determination. Instead, he emphasized the importance of reforms aimed at the public welfare, such as price control for the sale of grain and other basic commodities, public charity, firm action against usurers, etc., so that the archduke's subjects would submit more readily to his religious decrees. Similar measures had already been implemented by the archduke's reform commission in the ducal town of Leoben in April 1598, and comparable regulations were to become an integral part of the urban reform charters that were proclaimed in 1599–1600. As heresy had spread equally among the nobility, the burghers, and the rural population, Stobaeus thought it not advisable to attack the Protestants collectively. Instead, he took up the recommendations of the programme of Munich and urged a gradual but unrelenting advance, beginning with the abolition of the Protestant church ministry in Graz, to be followed up by the banning of Lutheran preachers from all ducal lands. Offenders would be

---

[31] *FRA/58*, 298–300 (Sonnabenter), 300–1 (*Verordnete*). The fortress of Kanizsa (Nagykanizsa), which was situated at a distance of *c*.50 km from the south-eastern tip of Styria, fell in 1600 and had to be left to the Turks in 1606, see A. Steinwenter, 'Der Friede von Zsitvatorok (1606)', *AÖG* 106 (1918), 162–70, 239.

[32] (Letter of 13 Sept. 1598), in 'Georgii Stobaei de Palmaburgo Episcopi Lavantini Epistolae ad diversos', n.p., n.d. 18th-century copy, STMLA, MS 506, fos. 14–16. The letter is probably identical with the document which Loserth partly summarizes in *FRA/58*, 297, for which he quotes three different editions. The date given here (21 Aug. 1598) is more plausible than that of the above MS copy.

liable to confiscation of property or even capital punishment. To prevent an uprising, he suggested that the number of Catholic troops quartered on the burghers of Graz should be increased. In a subsequent letter, Stobaeus rejected the nuncio's demand for the introduction of the Inquisition as too hazardous for the Catholic minority of the German lands, although he thought it suitable for the Italian territories of Inner Austria. In the three duchies, however, the Protestants would undoubtedly cause 'tragoedias' to the Catholic population. Besides, as Stobaeus added drily, there was nothing to inquire into because the Protestants practised their heresy publicly, and held all key posts in the military administration and the courts.[33]

Ferdinand's decree of 13 September 1598 must be understood as a response to the first memorandum. Sonnabenter had prepared a precedent by appealing to the archduke for support against the Protestant ministry. The archduke now issued an order to the *Landeshauptmann* and the *Verordnete* stating that the estates' reaction to Sonnabenter's just complaints had led Ferdinand to decide to abolish the ministry in Graz, Judenburg, and all of his municipalities. Ferdinand's declaration summarizes the driving forces that determined his policy: personal conviction, dynastic obligation, and an awareness of his power, deriving from his threefold authority as Imperial prince, member of the specially privileged house of Habsburg, and patron of the Church in his lands. Thus, the decree states that the archduke had taken this weighty decision 'of his own accord to save his conscience as a Catholic archduke of Austria, hereditary lord in Styria, also patron (*Vogt*) and liegelord of this local parish [i.e. Graz], and in general supreme patron of all ecclesiastical benefices in all his hereditary lands, by virtue of the special liberties (*specialfreyheit*) of the most excellent House of Austria, as well as by right of the terms of the religious pacification that is held and observed throughout the empire [i.e. the Peace of Augsburg]'.[34]

To weaken his adversaries, Ferdinand had picked the time between the sessions of the diet for his initiative. Likewise, he postponed the meeting of the courts (*Land- und Hofrechte*), which were due to assemble on 11 November 1598. As a result of Protestant dominance, this assembly

33 'Epp. Stob.', n.d. [1599], fo. 23.

34 'ex proprio motu zu salvierung ihres gewissens als ein catholischer erzherzog zu Österreich und erblandsfürst in Steyr auch vogt-und lehensherr der hieigen pfarr wie auch in gemain obrister vogt aller geistlichen stifften in ihren erblanden gelegen vermöge des hochl [öblichen] haus Österreich specialfreyheit als auch in kraft der im ganzen H[eiligen] R[ömischen] R[eich] statuierten und observierten allgemeinen religionspacification.' For Sonnabenter's 'Supplik' see *FRA/58*, 306–7. The decree is printed ibid. 309–10.

would undoubtedly have turned into a plenum of the opposition. The executive committee protested, in vain, that only the estates could declare such postponement.[35] Taking his confrontational policy even further, Ferdinand issued a decree on 23 September 1598 ordering the preachers and schoolteachers of Graz to leave within the next eight days. With an eye to the meeting of the diet in January 1599 he warned them that he would consider the withholding of taxes an act of rebellion. Furthermore, he prohibited a preliminary meeting of the Inner Austrian representatives which the Styrians had sought to bring about to deliberate on the recent ducal measures.[36] Henceforth, he was to take vigorous, though not always successful action to prevent such meetings, and in general to stop any autonomous and united action by the estates of his lands. He was thus applying the policy of separation of the orders as advised by the conference of Munich to isolate the estates of each duchy.

In 1596, the Carinthians and Carniolans had insisted on successive diets, ostensibly because the order of precedence prescribed this mode, in fact, however, to have more time to prepare their reaction. This lesson was not lost on Ferdinand, who henceforth limited the scope for negotiation and cooperation among the estates by summoning the Inner Austrian diets simultaneously but separately.[37] Moreover, to control their activity between the convocations of the assembly, he forced the estates to accept a prelate as a permanent additional member of their executive council (*Verordnetenausschuß*). On 15 January 1599, he responded to a petition by the bishop of Seckau and forced the Protestant committee to accept the determined Counter-Reformer Abbot Johann Jakob Hofmann of Admont.[38] Ferdinand's measure either rendered the committee useless as an instrument of communication among the Protestants or forced its Protestant members to exclude this fifth column by secret meetings which, however, would make them liable to the charge of conspiracy. The precariousness of the situation was proved in the same year (1599) by a trumped-up charge of high treason which the government brought against the estates' officials and messengers Hans Georg Kandelberger and Hans Adam Gabelkover. They were imprisoned and cross-examined under torture, and were eventually rescued by the estates' handing over of the *Stiftsschule* in Graz, a gesture that succeeded in placating the archduke.[39]

---

[35] Loserth, ibid. p. liii.   [36] Decree of 23 Sept. 1598, ibid. 321–4.
[37] Ibid. 542, and Loserth's interpretation of this policy ibid., lxvii.
[38] Loserth, ibid. pp. lx–lxi, 445.
[39] The case is discussed in J. Loserth, 'Ein Hochverratsprozeß aus der Zeit der Gegenreformation in Innerösterreich', *AÖG* 88 (1900), 315–65.

This episode was preceded by an unsuccessful attempt on the part of the estates to achieve a repeal of the September decrees, the last of which, dated 28 September 1598, was a peremptory order for the emigration of the preachers of Graz on the very same day. A final order was issued on 3 October that year. The ensuing peaceful exodus was completed by the emigration of Johannes Kepler in 1600.[40] The chronicler of the Ferdinandean Counter-Reformation, Abbot Jakob Rosolenz of Stainz, commented that the blow against the church ministry in Graz had been crucial because of this council's central importance for the survival of Protestantism at local level. The duchy's Protestants looked to Graz for encouragement and support, and the church ministry attracted and trained candidates for Protestant priesthood. In line with the decree of 13 March 1598, the Protestant preachers and schoolteachers of Judenburg and Laibach (Ljubljana) were expelled.[41] This attack on the provincial strongholds of Protestantism was subsequently broadened into a general Counter-Reformation campaign, carried out by roving reformation commissions in the municipalities and in the most recalcitrant rural parishes of Upper Styria.[42]

Predictably, Ferdinand's attack provoked the estates' refusal to grant financial support in January 1599. The diet was postponed on 12 March after an inconclusive session. In view of the development of the Turkish War, Ferdinand was forced to reconsider his decision against 'dissimulation'.[43] In their petition of 21 April, the estates had demanded the revocation of the recent decrees, and a confirmation of the religious concession of Bruck. Once more, Ferdinand consulted with his vicegerent. Taking up the political issue, Stobaeus forcefully argued for a demonstrable indissoluble link between the Catholic prince's obligation to defend the faith, and the political necessity to continue the Counter-Reformation:[44] he urgently warns Ferdinand against dissimulation or temporizing in this struggle. Instead, he encourages him to continue his religious policy, advice which he reiterates with the formula 'Imitare te ipsum' as the theme of his letter. As 'vicarius' and 'minister Dei', Ferdinand was called upon to execute the divine ordinances ('divina placita'), in this case the restoration of the Catholic faith as the true religion. Stobaeus plays down the danger of a large-scale uprising, while at

---

[40] Loserth, *Schulen*, 113–16.   [41] Rosolenz, 'Gegenbericht', fo. 107.
[42] Ibid. 115 ff. Their activity and achievement are discussed in Ch. 5.
[43] Loserth, *FRA/58*, pp. lxiv–lxviii.
[44] For the following see 'Epp. Stob.', n.d. [after 12 Mar. and before 30 Apr. 1599], fos. 57–63.

the same time pointing to the example set by the early Christian emperors. His reference to Emperor Constantine fuses the themes of divine and Imperial mission. The divine origin of the prince's power over his subjects is stressed. Disobedience to the prince is therefore resistance to the divine ordination, and hence doomed to failure. Stobaeus elaborates at length on the seditious nature of heresy, the arbitrary character of the 'sola fide' faith, and the resulting incompatibility of political stability with a plurality of faiths in one realm. He adduces the estates' refusal to pay the required contribution and their alleged willingness to surrender to the rule of the Turks as evidence of his argument. In sum, he advises Ferdinand to carry through his Counter-Reformation measures even if this entails granting obstinate Protestants permission to emigrate.

This powerful evocation of the Christian Imperial tradition chimed with the archduke's lofty notion of his obligations and authority as a member of the ruling dynasty. Neither was the main point of Stobaeus' political reasoning lost on the successor of a prince who had been blackmailed into tolerating heresy and whose authority had been scorned with impunity by a Protestant revolt in 1590. On the other hand, fears of continued noble obstructionism, or worse, were strong enough to cause a delay of almost three months before the archduke's answer was dispatched. Ferdinand's reply to the petition of the Inner Austrian estates is dated 30 April 1599, but a verso note reveals that he hesitated until 21 July 1599 before communicating it to the *Verordnete*.[45] In harsh words, he dismissed the estates' grievances as utterly unfounded and a sin against the God-given authority of the prince. In principle, their petition did not merit a reply. Their heretical religion had been rejected by the Emperor and the Council of Trent. Previous concessions had been merely temporary privileges. In fact, he was executing his father's will by his revocation of the 'Pacification'. Ferdinand then prohibited the estates' union in religious matters as proclaimed at Bruck in 1578 as damaging to the archduke's authority and directed against the Catholic religion.

Eventually, the military exigency aided the archduke's cause. The levying of troops from the nobility for the Turkish War became an issue of vital concern to both sides, and put a temporary stop to any further attempt to make contributions and reinforcements dependent on the redress of religious grievances. Apart from the emergency created by the rapid advance of the Turkish army, there were further reasons which persuaded the estates to give up their resistance. Thus, they feared that

45 'Haubt Resolution' of 30 Apr. [21 July] 1599, STMLA, 'Meillerakten', XIX-e (1–23).

strict opposition in the present situation would result in the complete loss
of military offices to foreigners. Moreover, as a compensation for the
nobility's military aid, the Inner Austrians had so far enjoyed the privilege
that foreign troops were not allowed to pass through their territory. The
estates suspected that the presence of foreign, mostly Italian, regiments
would be used to crush the Protestant movement if they refused to co-
operate with the archduke.[46]

In the event, the Turkish issue was not the sole force to strengthen
Ferdinand's position in the confessional battle. In Upper and Lower
Austria, a Counter-Reformation campaign was conducted after the
suppression of the major peasant uprising in the years 1594–7. The
Upper Austrian estates under their Calvinist leader Georg Erasmus von
Tschernembl (d. 1626) had already signalled their willingness to unite
with the Protestant population at large and resort to armed resistance.
They had also been in touch with the Calvinists in the Empire through
Count Christian von Anhalt (1568–1630). The government's subsequent
penal measures were implemented with the aid of foreign troops, a lesson
that was not lost on the Inner Austrian Protestants.[47]

An attempt was made to invoke the constitutional link with the
Empire. In a lengthy reply to Ferdinand's decree of 30 April (21 July)
1599, dated 24 February 1600, the Styrian Protestant estates pointed to
their unfailing loyalty to the dynasty. However, they accepted Ferdinand's
claim that he was a 'princeps absolutus' and not a 'princeps modificatus'
only in so far as this was compatible with their liberties and privileges.
They disputed the archduke's claim that the special privileges of the
Habsburgs rendered the estates immediately subject to him only. The
privilege of 1277 was adduced as evidence for the Styrians' assertion that
they were equally subject to the Habsburg duke and the Empire. The
authors then tried to prove the validity of these terms for Carinthia and
Carniola as well.[48] On the basis of this argument, the estates once more
approached Rudolf II and a number of Protestant princes of the Empire

[46] For the struggle over the 'conditionierte Bewilligung' see *FRA/58*, 560–1, 563–5,
571–81, 585–7.

[47] Gutkas, *Niederösterreich*, 219–21, Eder, *Glaubensspaltung*, 277–416, Haider,
Oberösterreich, 176–8. Christian von Anhalt was later to become the driving force of the
Protestant Union of 1608. He took service with the Elector Palatine in 1595, whence he
began organizing the anti-Habsburg opposition in the Empire. For the Calvinist leader of
the Upper Austrian estates see H. Sturmberger, *Georg Erasmus Tschernembl: Religion,
Libertät und Widerstand. Ein Beitrag zur Geschichte der Gegenreformation und des Landes ob
der Enns* (Graz, 1953).

[48] The 'Anbringen' is printed in *FRA/58*, 721–51. For the above argument see pp.
727–9.

for help. The delegation to Prague was headed by Georg von Stubenberg, who reported on its futile negotiations with the Emperor's councillor and *Obrist-Hofmarschall*, Karl von Liechtenstein, from September 1600 to March 1601.[49] A letter from the Styrian estates to this delegation in Prague, dated 13 December 1600, is revelatory of the estates' misjudgement of the situation: the war contribution was substantially increased as a sign of the estates' abiding loyalty and submissiveness in spite of the recent grievances ('Beschwerungen'). It was hoped that this would induce Rudolf II to intercede with Ferdinand for a 'moderation' ('Mäßigung') of his repressive religious policy.[50]

Exasperated by what he considered an attack on his authority, Ferdinand reacted with a formal prohibition of further appeals to the Emperor and the Empire. The estates' constitutional argument is dismissed as absurd and contrary to the well-known privileges of the dynasty.[51] Nevertheless, the estates approached their co-religionists among the Imperial princes several times during the following decades. This was facilitated by the activity of Ernreich von Saurau, who belonged to the small party of 'radical' noblemen, like Matthes Amman and Karl and Otto von Herberstorff. They viewed the Styrian and Inner Austrian events in the broader context of the fate of Protestantism in the Monarchy and the rest of the Empire. Protestant triumphs like the territorial gains of the Dutch in the years 1591–8, the successful defence of Swedish Protestantism against the attempted Catholic coup of the Polish King Sigismund III Vasa in 1598, and the wresting of a religious concession from the convert King Henri IV in the same year were offset by the rising tide of Catholicism in the Monarchy and among the Empire's north-western (Spanish Netherlands, France) and eastern (Poland) neighbours.

The radicals among the Styrian estates were therefore pessimistic about the chances of the majority's conciliatory approach, and alive to the need for a broader Protestant alliance. Saurau had warned the estates in 1595 against taking the oath of allegiance before receiving a confirmation of their political and religious liberties. By April 1599, he had established himself as the head of the Protestant opposition, so that the government

---

[49] STMLA, 'Stubenberg-Archiv', Sch. 95, H. 587, letters to the estates of Styria, dated 15 Sept. 1600, 31 Jan., 24 Mar. 1601, and from the Styrian estates to Stubenberg, 27 Feb., 21 Mar. 1601. The deputies failed to obtain an audience with the Emperor.

[50] Styrian estates' letter to Stubenberg, 13 Dec. 1500, STMLA, 'Stubenberg-Archiv', Sch. 95, H. 587.

[51] Decree of 3 Mar. 1601, *FRA/60*, 158–9.

demanded his dismissal as *Landmarschall*. In December 1601, he was a member of the 'council for religious affairs' which the Styrians had temporarily created to deliberate on appropriate measures to bring about a reversal of Ferdinand's religious policy. Saurau seems to have envisaged a closer co-operation with the Protestant princes of the Empire. In March 1602, the Styrians sent a letter of recommendation on his behalf to the Lutheran Margrave Georg Friedrich of Brandenburg. In November 1603, Saurau was acting as councillor of the Elector Joachim Friedrich of Brandenburg, but was also in touch with Wolfgang von Hofkirchen, whom the Lower Austrians had dispatched to canvass support among the Protestant princes. In August 1613, the Inner Austrians turned to Saurau as Imperial councillor as well as councillor of the recently acceded Calvinist Elector Johann Sigismund of Brandenburg in negotiations with the Count Palatine, Philipp Ludwig of Neuburg. However, their request was drowned out by the clamour of a confessional struggle of a different dimension.

By this time, the disputed succession in the north-western territories of Kleve, Jülich, and Berg had developed into a conflict that threatened to bring about a European war.[52] Moreover, the shifting confessional allegiances of Brandenburg and Pfalz-Neuburg were indicative of the secular agenda which increasingly dominated the territorial princes' religious policy. This rendered the Inner Austrians' diplomatic missions to the Empire even more difficult. It was hardly surprising that the Protestant princes were cautious enough to ignore the Styrians' invocation of the constitutional link with the Empire.[53] On receiving Hofkirchen's account of the latest developments in Inner Austria, the Councillors of the margrave of Brandenburg criticized the estates' fatal weakness: they should never have abandoned their links with the burghers and the Upper and Lower Austrian estates.[54]

Except for the patronage exerted over their subjects in the patrimonial towns, the Inner Austrian nobility had indeed sacrificed the third estate

---

[52] A brief modern account of the conflict over the succession in the principalities, supplemented by a map showing the disputed territories, is provided by H. Schmidt, 'Pfalz-Neuburgs Sprung zum Niederrhein: Wolfgang Wilhem von Pfalz-Neuburg und der Jülich-Klevische Erbfolgestreit', in Glaser, *Um Glauben und Reich*, 77–89.

[53] For Saurau see Loserth, *FRA/58*, pp. xxxi, xxxix, lxvii, *FRA/60*, 219, 317, and 622–3. For the war of succession see E. W. Zeeden, *Das Zeitalter der Glaubenskämpfe* (7th edn., Munich, 1986), 71–3. Examples of inconclusive missions by the estates and futile intercessions by Imperial princes are mentioned by Loserth, *FRA/60*, pp. xxii–xxvii, xxxii.

[54] Report by Wolfgang von Hofkirchen on his mission to the Protestant courts, 24 Nov. 1603, *FRA/60*, 318–23.

and thus had surrendered to Ferdinand's policy of separation. After the abolition of the Protestant church ministry, the archduke resumed Karl II's urban campaign and proceeded to purge the magistrates and civic communities in his municipalities. On 27 July 1600, a decree was issued by which all burghers of Graz, estates' officials, and recently ennobled persons were summoned before the government and confronted with the choice between conversion and emigration. Regardless of their rank, emigrants were to pay a tax on their property. This was called the 'tenth penny', a term which generally denoted the redemption (*Abfahrtsgeld*) which a subject had to pay to his overlord as compensation for his leaving.[55] The number of emigrants from Graz and the other ducal municipalities is difficult to establish, as there were frequently last-minute conversions of those who appear on the government's lists. Thus, only three of the forty burghers of Rottenmann in Upper Styria who were ordered to emigrate eventually left the duchy. In Graz, the Protestant magistrates and a number of distinguished commoners, among them Johannes Kepler, did leave. All in all, sixty-one burghers from the capital received such orders, but the actual number of emigrants remains unclear.[56]

In a petition to the Emperor in 1601, the estates complained of the economic consequences of these measures. As a result of the Counter-Reformation among the rural population, the nobility had lost many subjects, who often were unable to pay their tax debts before they had to leave. Undoubtedly, the estates sought to give weight to their petition by painting a picture of general economic decline, but their main point that both trade and agriculture were affected by these emigrations was certainly valid. Likewise, they pointed to the difficulty of finding adequate substitutes for arms manufacturers and craftsmen who were badly needed during the Turkish War. It is, however, difficult to assess the extent to which the change of ownership of the ironworks and the loss of miners and skilled workers contributed to the general decline of the Styrian iron industry which had set in during the last decades of the sixteenth century.[57] For the time being, Ferdinand was forced to 'purge'

---

[55] Ibid. 11–12.

[56] For Rottenmann see Loserth, *FRA/60*, p. xi. The figure for Graz is mentioned in a report of the Hofvizekanzler Wolfgang Jöchlinger, 3 Aug. 1600, STMLA, 'Meillerakten', XX-t-v.

[57] The petition is printed in *FRA/60*, 145–9. The decline of the Styrian iron trade and industry in these years is discussed in A. Pantz, *Beiträge zur Geschichte der Innerberger Hauptgewerkschaft 1625–1783* (Graz, 1903), 1, 15, 18 ff. A general discussion of this problem can be found in Pickl, 'Städte und Märkte', 108–15.

the iron trade gradually and grant temporary permissions to stay to those who were indispensable. In this, he followed the bishop of Salzburg's policy towards the Protestant miners of Gastein.[58]

More disquieting to the estates than the blow against the 'third estate' proper was the fact that Ferdinand had begun to attack the nobility, starting with its weakest link, the recently ennobled persons. The estates sharply criticized this step. They were especially upset at the indiscriminate charging of the 'tenth penny'.[59] The government proceeded to undermine the estates' position by disputing their right to grant membership of the estates to Protestants.[60] Henceforth, Ferdinand refused to authorize any admission of Protestants which had been made after the 'reformation' of 1600.[61]

On 1 March 1601, Ferdinand followed up his earlier decrees against the urban school and church ministry by a general edict ordering the eviction of all Protestant preachers and teachers from his lands.[62] The nobility responded by the creation of a church ministry in exile, across the border on Hungarian territory. With the help of Hungarian Protestants who owned estates close to the Styrian border, most notably the brothers Thomas and Ladislas Nádasdy, the estates dispatched a number of their preachers to these neighbouring territories, so that they could minister to the Inner Austrian nobility.[63] However, this stratagem failed to delude the archduke, and on 23 July 1603, a peremptory order strictly prohibited attendance at Protestant services abroad to all inhabitants of the duchies. Ferdinand was supported by the Emperor, who gave orders to the Hungarian noblemen to expel the Styrian preachers.[64]

In spite of these efforts, implementation at the local level turned out to be a long-drawn-out process, testifying to the resilience of Protestantism. In the end, it took several years and repeated intervention from Rudolf II to effect compliance. In November 1627, Ferdinand II was still forced to send similar Imperial instructions against the activity of Upper and Lower Austrian preachers in Hungary. The Styrian *Obrist* von

---

[58] The problem is indicated by the renewal of the decrees against the heretical 'Hammermeister' in Upper Styria in 1616 and 1617, *FRA/60*, 705, 712–13, who were nevertheless readmitted for briefer periods to prevent a disruption of the works, see ibid. 716. For Gastein see J. Loserth, 'Die Gegenreformation in Salzburg unter dem Erzbischof Marx Sittich, Grafen von Hohenembs (1612–1619)', *MIÖG* 19 (1898), 676–96.

[59] Petition of 1601, *FRA/60*, 146.   [60] 13 Mar. 1601, ibid. 164–5.

[61] Ibid. 629.

[62] The edict of 1 Mar. 1601 is printed ibid. 154–7.   [63] Ibid. 236–8.

[64] Ibid. 287. For Rudolf II's orders to Thomas and Ladislas Nádasdy, dated 8 Oct. 1603, see ibid. 296.

Herberstein had to answer a charge of sedition, among other things because he supported preachers in Varasdin.[65] Further help came from the Catholic Croatian estates, who promised to evict all heretical preachers from Styria who had taken refuge on their territory.[66]

By way of response to the recent measures, a council of Inner Austrian Protestant delegates met in 1603, in defiance of Ferdinand's orders, to draft and sign another petition to him. The authors indirectly attacked Ferdinand's breach of faith. Thus, they set his policy against the background of their past and present services for the dynasty. Abandoning hopes of a comprehensive religious toleration for the Protestants of the three duchies, they now claimed protection by the terms of the 'Pacification' exclusively for themselves. Thus, they maintained that 'religious reformations' in the Empire and elsewhere had always been limited to the burghers and rural population. The estates claimed exemption by virtue of their past military services to the dynasty, thus using the central feudal argument to justify their religious privilege. To lend weight to their argument, they concluded their petition with an 'offer' of voluntary collective emigration if Ferdinand should insist on his rigorous measures. This was combined with the request that the archduke should buy up their property as they were not aware of any other prospective buyers. Given the military emergency and the state of Ferdinand's finances, the estates' proposal was little more than a thinly veiled threat. The document was signed by ninety-one members of the Styrian *Herren- und Ritterstand*, seventy-nine Carinthians, and sixty-eight Carniolan noblemen.[67]

A further attempt was made to exploit the military and financial situation to exert pressure on Ferdinand. In September 1604, the Inner Austrian estates warned the archduke that he would receive little support from the Protestant princes of the Empire if he continued the present persecution, but in the absence of a more tangible commitment of the Imperial Protestants, this threat was in fact rather toothless.[68]

[65] For the orders of 1627 see ibid. 794. Herberstein's case is raised in Ferdinand's letter to Rudolf II, dated 5 May 1602, STMLA, 'Meillerakten', XIX-e (1–23).

[66] See the declaration of the Croatian diet to Matthias as designated king of Hungary, 6 Dec. 1608, *FRA/60*, 478–9.

[67] The petition of 20 Oct. 1603 is reprinted ibid. 299–314. For a last and abortive attempt in 1619 to effect a reversal of Ferdinand's religious policy via the intercession of the Imperial princes see below. Protestant hopes revived briefly as a result of Swedish successes, and again in connection with the Westphalian Peace, see Ch. 7.

[68] Petition of the Protestant estates of Inner Austria, 15 Sept. 1604, STMLA, 'Meillerakten', XIX-e (1–23). A paraphrase of its contents can be found in *FRA/60*, 371–2.

It seems that both petitions made some impression on Ferdinand, though not enough to cause a major change in his religious policy. On 20 September, he repeated his prohibition of unauthorized meetings of the Inner Austrian estates and threatened harsh punishment in case of further disobedience. The rest of the document is more conciliatory. Ferdinand praised the estates' loyalty and acknowledged their services to the Habsburgs. Evading the main point of the September petition, he stated that he had never expelled any nobleman on account of his religious views. Ferdinand expressed his hope that the estates would change their mind about emigration, but at the same time, he clarified that he would give no financial compensation through purchase.[69]

The estates' petition of 19 January 1605 essentially repeats their earlier arguments, including the now unconcealed threat to emigrate in spite of all considerations of loyalty and obligation.[70] More interesting is their account of the government's proceeding against members of the estate of the nobility, the *Herren- und Ritterstand*, which in fact annulled their religious privilege. As previously described, the decrees against the Protestant preachers and 'preceptors' and the subsequent prohibition of attendance at Protestant services abroad had tried to deprive them of their 'Religionsexercitium'. The estates now complained of crippling fines which the ducal procurator (*Kammerprokurator*) demanded from members of the estate of knights (*Ritterstand*) for offences against these decrees. The estates' petition to the Emperor in 1601 had already listed various grievances such as the destruction of Protestant churches, graveyards, and family vaults.[71] Furthermore, the case of the young barons of Windischgrätz, who had been summoned to Graz shortly after the arrest of their preceptor Paul Odontius in 1602, had proved that the archduke would make reprisals on the families of leading Protestant noblemen.[72]

Against this background, it would have been all the more important for the Inner Austrian estates to join forces with their co-religionists in the rest of the Habsburg lands. However, their irresolute attitude in the 'fraternal dispute' between the Emperor and his brother Matthias in the following years shattered their last chance of negotiating a new confes-

---

[69] *FRA/60*, 372–3.

[70] Petition of 19 Jan. 1605, STMLA, 'Meillerakten', XIX-e (1–23). A paraphrase can be found in *FRA/60*, 393–4.

[71] *FRA/60*, 145.

[72] The documents relating to this case are printed ibid. 232–6. The barons were heavily fined, but released as an act of grace after the Styrian estates had interceded on their behalf. See also the report of Paul Odontius, printed in R. Leidenfrost, 'Zur Geschichte der Gegenreformation in Steiermark', *JGGPÖ* 6 (1885) 51–80.

sional settlement. The conflict between Archduke Matthias and the Emperor in the years following the conclusion of peace with the Turks and Hungarians in 1606 was exploited by the Protestants of Hungary, Austria, Moravia, who supported the archduke, and Bohemia and Silesia on the Emperor's side to extort sweeping religious concessions in 1606, 1608, and 1609. The reasons which persuaded the Inner Austrian estates to remain, at least officially, neutral and thus to sacrifice the chance to obtain similar concessions must be gathered from the rather fragmentary evidence.[73] It emerges that the Inner Austrians were approached by the Hungarians and Matthias in April 1608, and urged to join the confederation which had been formed to ensure the enforcement of the Peace of Vienna (1606). However, the estates wished to avoid any suspicion of conspiracy.[74] Two sealed letters from the Hungarians and Matthias were handed over to Ferdinand's governor, Archduke Maximilian, in April 1608, together with a declaration that the Inner Austrian estates would not oppose the settlement with the Turks.[75]

The estates nevertheless expressed their concern at clauses nine and ten of the treaty, which prescribed the dismissal of all Germans from higher offices of the 'windisch'–Croatian frontier. By the terms of the treaty, these posts were to be held exclusively by Hungarians, in spite of the Inner Austrians' heavy financial contribution to the maintenance of the border fortifications and troops. Another contentious issue between the Inner Austrian estates and their Hungarian neighbours arose from the war damages inflicted on the province. The estates demanded that the Hungarians should give compensation for the border raids of Stephen Bocskay's troops, and make a declaration that they would help to effect the release of those Austrian peasants who had been carried off by the Turks and Tatars. Ferdinand and the Styrian estates agreed that the terms of the treaty had to include a safeguard from the Hungarians for the future.[76] On 22 April 1608, the Styrian deputies replied to Ferdinand's demand for their opinion on the political situation. The Styrians declared their wish to stay neutral in the dispute over the Peace

---

[73] The documents evaluated here are complementary to the material used by Steinwenter, 'Zsitvatorok', 194–215.

[74] The estates of Carniola to the estates of Styria, 17 Apr. 1608, STMLA, 'La. Arch.', IV. 3, Relations with Hungary, Sch. 705.

[75] This emerges from a 'Mandat' of Ferdinand, dated 22 Apr. 1608, in which he urges the Inner Austrians to refrain from any action which could be considered as rebellious, ibid.

[76] The Inner Austrian estates to the estates of Hungary, 8 May 1609, 'Memorandum' (of the Styrian government) of 29 July 1609, Instruction by Archduke Ferdinand for the Styrian deputies concerning the negotiations with Hungary, 25 Aug. 1606, ibid.

of 1606, but expressed fears of general disorder and a Venetian intervention if the present negotiations for the acceptance of the Peace should founder. They were willing to accept a compromise solution regarding military appointments, but threatened to withdraw their troops and financial support if the Hungarians continued to demand the undivided military command.

The Styrians' argument reveals the degree to which the contested issues now overshadowed the religious question in the Inner Austrian context and ruled out a united proceeding of the duchies' estates with their Hungarian neighbours. Quite to the contrary: it was not advisable, so the estates declared, to give money to an enemy which they had reason to fear as much as the Turks.[77] In January 1610, the Inner Austrians turned to the estates of Upper and Lower Austria with a request for intercession with King Matthias on their behalf. The Austrians obliged, but to no avail. Since the Inner Austrians had thought it prudent to decline his offer to join the confederation against the Emperor in 1608, it is hardly surprising that Matthias did not respond to their belated appeal for support.[78]

So far, the Ferdinandean Counter-Reformation had succeeded in suppressing the educational and ecclesiastical institutions which had furthered the dissemination of the Lutheran doctrine in Inner Austria. Likewise, Karl II's campaign of the 1580s against the burghers had been resumed and completed. The Protestant urban elite had been expelled, outward conformity had been imposed, and all public expressions of heresy were now liable to severe punishment. Moreover, the Counter-Reformers' strategy of separation had been applied successfully to the Inner Austrian estates. Lacking broader political vision, their opposition

---

[77] Styrian *Verordnete* to archduke Ferdinand, 22 Apr. 1608, ibid.

[78] Petition of the Austrian estates to King Matthias, 12 Jan. 1610, *FRA/60*, 552. Copy of Matthias's letter to the delegates of the Inner Austrian estates, 12 Jan. 1610, STMLA, 'Stubenberg-Archiv', Sch. 95, H. 587. Burgstaller, 'Geschichte der Gegenreformation in Kärnten', states that the archive of Count Lodron at Gmünd in Carinthia contains a copy of a contemporary newspaper which reproduced a letter by the executive committee of the Inner Austrian estates to the Hungarian Protestants in 1609, in which they asked the Hungarians to intercede with the Emperor and Archduke Ferdinand on their behalf. The simultaneous publication of this petition in a newsletter in Graz was presumably a precaution to forestall charges of conspiracy. It might also have been a safeguard against being blackmailed into joining Matthias's confederation. The letter and the fact of its publication are mentioned on pp. 134–5. See ibid. 135–6 n. 2 for the title of the newspaper article: 'Summarischer inhalt des ienigen Schreibens, welches die drei Ausschüsse in Steier, Kärnten und Krain an die akatholischen ungarischen Stände in causa religionis gerichtet haben' (Graz, 1609).

continued to be formulated in the language of legalism and loyalty, and had eventually succumbed to the coercive force of the military emergency. As a result, they found themselves excluded from the favourable religious terms of the bargain struck by their militant co-religionists. The subsequent Protestant revival was therefore limited to the archduchy, Hungary, and Bohemia, and brought no relief to the Inner Austrian Protestants.[79]

Ferdinand's refusal to acknowledge the constitutional character of the 'Pacification' at his accession had been the very first step to its revocation. Afterwards, the estates had fatefully admitted the drawing of ever narrower circles of 'legal' Protestantism, which excluded an increasing part of the Protestant party. On his side, Ferdinand had proceeded to regain control of the administration and the courts. Complementary to this was the restoration of jurisdictional rights and ecclesiastical property to the Catholic clergy. Further, he had promoted Catholics, and enhanced their number by granting patents of nobility to foreigners. Finally, he had disputed such elementary privileges as the right to confer estate membership, thus striking at the very root of the Protestant estates' power. That he would not stop here was made obvious by his arbitrary measures against estates' officials, newly ennobled persons, and members of the established nobility like the Barons Windischgrätz. The militant measures of the reform commissions did not spare the nobility's estates and churches, and the government sought to force their subjects back into the fold of the Catholic Church. By the eviction of most preachers and preceptors and the subsequent prohibition of attendance at Protestant services abroad, the estates were in fact deprived of their religious privilege, although Ferdinand persistently denied the validity of their complaints. Over the following years, heavy fines and summonses before the government were used massively to punish members of the nobility who defied these decrees. However, it proved impossible to put a complete stop to the nobility's evasive strategy of resorting to the services of Hungarian preachers.[80]

---

[79] For the Protestant revival in Upper and Lower Austria see G. Mecenseffy, *Geschichte des Protestantismus in Österreich* (Graz, 1956), 140–8.

[80] Loserth, *FRA/60*, p. xxxv, Ferdinand to Archbishop Marx Sittich of Salzburg, 6 June 1615, ibid. 649–50. In a letter to the bishop of Seckau, dated 2 June 1627, Ferdinand demanded that the diocesan clergy should report the names of those who received the sacraments from Protestant priests in Hungary, DA, 'Religionsberichte Protestantismus', 1598–1730.

Through the hazards of dynastic fortune, the example of the archduke's successful Counter-Reforming policy in Inner Austria turned into a direct menace to the Protestants of the rest of the Monarchy and Empire with the successive elections of Ferdinand as king of Bohemia (1617) and Hungary (1618), and his accession as Emperor in 1619. Archduke Albrecht of Austria, the youngest surviving son of Emperor Maximilian II, resigned his claims to the Imperial succession in favour of Ferdinand. This arrangement formed part of the dynastic settlement of 1617, which laid down Ferdinand's succession in the hereditary lands and his designation as king of Bohemia and future Emperor.[81] As a result, the five Austrian lands comprising the archduchy and Inner Austria would be reunited under the rule of the Styrian prince who had nearly crushed the Protestant movement in his patrimony Inner Austria. The Austrian estates therefore sought to foil the dynastic scheme by refusing to take the oath of allegiance to Ferdinand as archduke. A radical faction of Upper Austrian noblemen, led again by Georg Erasmus von Tschernembl, set up an interim government and on 16 August 1619 concluded a formal alliance with the Bohemian confederation which had been formed by Bohemia, Silesia, Lusatia, and Moravia—the latter having been coerced by Bohemian military intervention—for the defence of the estates' liberty. The same faction led the Upper Austrian estates and part of the Lower Austrian Protestants into open rebellion after the deposition of Ferdinand as Bohemian king, and his election as Emperor in August 1619. The rebels' defeat and submission in the following year (August 1620) was preceded by negotiations between Ferdinand II and the conciliatory majority of the Lower Austrian estates. They took the oath of allegiance to Ferdinand in April 1620, and received a guarded confirmation of their religious concession. The Protestant nobility's participation in the revolt was subsequently punished by large-scale confiscations. As a result, the Catholic Church recovered between 26 per cent and 47 per cent of the hitherto Protestant parishes in Lower Austria. Upper Austria fared even worse. In August 1620, the duchy was handed over as a pawn to Bavaria and was not redeemed before May 1628. It bears witness to the unbroken spirit of the Upper Austrian Protestants that the number of their communicants in the provincial capital of Linz reached an unprecedented high of 5,000 in 1623 before abruptly declining in the following year after the issuing of an Imperial decree against the heretic preceptors and preachers.[82]

[81] Haider, *Oberösterreich*, 181, Zeeden, *Zeitalter der Glaubenskämpfe*, 76.
[82] Haider, *Oberösterreich*, 181–5, Gutkas, *Niederösterreich*, 233–40. Mecenseffy,

For the Inner Austrian lands, Ferdinand's election as Emperor entailed their reduction to truly provincial status. Although the Styrian prince continued to take a special interest in the fate of the duchies, the transfer of his court to Vienna and the subsequent administrative reorganization meant that the nobility had lost its direct contact and most of its political influence. An Inner Austrian department (*Innerösterreichische Expeditur*) was added to the Austrian chancellery in Vienna. Communications between the Emperor and the Inner Austrian government (*Regierung und Kammer*) were henceforth to pass through this office and the Privy Council (*Geheimer Rat*), the prince's executive. The government was to be entrusted with the administration of justice and finance, and in general with the regulation of the province's affairs, most notably the religious question. Through the *Geheimer Rat*, it received the Emperor's directives and decrees. In 1625, Ferdinand appointed Hans Ulrich von Eggenberg governor of Inner Austria (*Oberst-Statthalter*) and head of the Privy Council in Graz. As the Emperor's closest adviser in these years, Eggenberg was also made director of the Imperial Privy Council, an arrangement which effectively ensured that the provincial interest would be represented, but subordinated to the general aims and considerations of Ferdinand's Imperial policy. The office of *Oberst-Statthalter* was abolished after Eggenberg's death in 1634, but the *Geheimer Rat* continued to gain in influence, at the expense of the Inner Austrian government. In 1639, Ferdinand III limited the latter's importance even further by granting extensive competences to the Privy Council as the prince's local representation and High Court, with the authority to decide those cases which the Emperor had reserved to himself. Throughout these years, the estates retained the right to deal directly with the Privy Council in financial matters such as the diet's tax grants and extraordinary contributions levied by the prince.[83]

During the years 1620–8, however, the emergence of this new pattern was obscured by the Inner Austrian government's importance for the implementation of the Emperor's Counter-Reformation policy. The progress of confessional reconquest was made possible by the series of

Protestantismus, 152–9. A list of those Upper and Lower Austrian noblemen who joined the confederation can be found in I. Hübel, 'Die Ächtung von Evangelischen und die Konfiskationen protestantischen Besitzes im Jahre 1620 in Nieder- und Oberösterreich', *JGGPÖ* 58 (1937), 17–28. For the Bavarian occupation regime see G. Heilingsetzer, 'Die Bayern in Oberösterreich (1620–1628)', in Glaser, *Um Glauben und Reich*, 416–23. The number of communicants is mentioned ibid. 419.

[83] Bireley, 'Ferdinand II', 227, Thiel, 'Zentralverwaltung', II, 513–20, Zwiedineck-Südenhorst, *Eggenberg*, 63, 70, 122.

military successes in the years 1620–7, following the victory over the Elector Palatine in 1620. These enabled Ferdinand to impose his religious programme in Bohemia and Austria. The draconian punishment meted out to the Bohemian rebels in 1621–7, the executions, large-scale confiscations, the forcible recatholicization or expulsion of the Protestant population, and the constitutional subjection to direct Habsburg rule by the revised constitution (*Verneuerte Landesordnung*) in 1627 should have shattered the illusions which the Inner Austrians still entertained regarding the safety of their religious liberty, which had already been reduced to a mere private freedom of conscience.

In August 1619, the Inner Austrian estates had planned to meet and draft a petition to the Imperial electors assembled in Frankfurt. They hoped to obtain the readmission of the Protestant religion in the three duchies and a safeguard for the future. Presumably, the electors would have been asked to demand this from Ferdinand as one of the preconditions of his election. However, Ferdinand was apprised of this scheme, which was dropped when he issued a strict prohibition of the preparatory meeting.[84]

From the beginning, the Inner Austrians had abstained from negotiations with the rebels which would have implicated them in treasonable activities.[85] As a result, they considered themselves safe from any direct attack. This illusion persisted in spite of the fact that Ferdinand began to reissue his earlier Counter-Reformation decrees which concerned the nobility as well, for example his decree of 26 April 1625, which prohibited attendance at foreign Protestant universities and visits to 'uncatholic' foreign places by noblemen and commoners alike.[86] At the same date, Ferdinand issued a sweeping general order (*Generalmandat*) to reinforce

[84] Letter of Ferdinand II to the Styrian estates, Frankfurt, 10 Aug. 1619, DA, 'Religionsberichte Protestantismus', 1598–1730. On 16 Aug., the day on which the Upper Austrians concluded the confederation with Bohemia in Prague, Ferdinand repeated his general prohibition of unauthorized meetings of the estates and sought to impose silence on the religious matter, STMLA, 'La. Arch., Religion und Kirche', Sch. 29. On 19 Aug., Ferdinand was declared dethroned as king of Bohemia; on 28 Aug., he was elected Emperor; see G. Schormann, *Der Dreißigjährige Krieg* (Göttingen, 1985), 28.

[85] A proviso must be made with regard to the possible activity of exiles like the former Styrian *Landmarschall* Ernreich von Saurau. He was probably the author of an anonymous leaflet which was circulated in the Empire in 1620 and which denounced Ferdinand's Counter-Reforming measures in Inner Austria in the years 1598 to 1609. The pamphlet repeats key statements and historical similes which Saurau employed in a speech held at an assembly of the estates in 1601. The text is printed in R. Leidenfrost, 'Religionsbeschwerden der evangelischen Stände von Steiermark, Kärnten und Krain', *JGGPÖ* 4 (1883), 26–30. For Saurau's earlier statement see *FRA/60*, 187.

[86] *FRA/60*, 756. For the reissuing of decrees see Loserth, ibid., xl.

his decrees of 1598 and 1599 concerning the investiture of candidates for vacant parishes and the protection of ecclesiastical property. Henceforth, the drafting of inventories of parish property and the administration of such property during vacancies were to be supervised by the bishop or a cleric who was authorized by him. Noblemen who exercised the *ius patronatus* were to present the bishop with suitable candidates for vacant parishes within two months. Alienation of church property by secular patrons or *Vögte* and any other abuses were liable to severe punishment. Ferdinand emphasized his determination to deprive offenders of their rights and exert these in his function as 'supreme protector of the clergy' in his lands.[87]

In August 1625, Eggenberg notified Bishop Jakob Eberlein of Seckau (1615–33) of the Emperor's decision to resume the religious reformation of Inner Austria, and to appoint special commissioners for this purpose. The bishop was requested to apprise these officials of abuses that needed redress. A year later, Ferdinand informed the bishop that he had suspended the campaign 'for certain reasons', but had now decided to resume it and complete the Catholic reformation in his lands. A closer look at the course of events in 1625–6 reveals that the chronology of the Counter-Reformation reflected every temporary change in the military field. Ferdinand's decision to postpone the completion of the religious reform in Inner Austria was probably due to the need to concentrate on more pressing foreign and 'domestic' issues, i.e. the campaign against Christian of Denmark, and, more important, the peace negotiations with the Transylvanian prince Gabriel Bethlen and the Turks in May 1625 and the election of Ferdinand (III) as king of Hungary in December that year. On 25 April 1626, Wallenstein defeated Mansfeld's army at Dessau, and temporarily stopped his dangerous march south-eastwards through Silesia. Duke Johann Ernst of Sachsen-Weimar and Mansfeld had hoped to meet Bethlen's troops in Upper Hungary and thus create a military front in the east, a plan that was resumed in the summer of 1626 after the diversion of Mansfeld's army to Brandenburg. Eventually, Wallenstein's campaign to foil this scheme lasted until December, but in May 1626, Ferdinand was as yet unaware of the momentous military threat to his lands.[88] The situation seemed to permit the settling of the Inner Austrian problem, and Ferdinand's decision was presumably intended as a measure

[87] 'obristen Schuzherrn der Geistligkhait', Decree of 26 Apr. 1625, STMLA, 'Stubenberg-Archiv', Sch. 95, H. 585. Decrees in the same sense were issued for Lower Austria on 14 and 24 Sept. 1627, see copy ibid., Sch. 96, H. 588.

[88] A. Gindely, *Geschichte des dreißigjährigen Krieges*, vol. ii (Leipzig, 1882), 79–91.

to isolate the Hungarian Protestants and prepare for the revocation of the recently confirmed religious concession.

As previously described, Ferdinand had from the beginning of his reign as archduke sought to suppress any unauthorized meetings of the Inner Austrian estates. In 1620, he denounced the 'pernicious union' ('hochschedliche union') of the Protestant estates, i.e. the Bohemian confederation, as the source of the rebellion ('der böhmischen rebellion mutter').[89] This experience fully confirmed earlier warnings of his spiritual advisers, and a lingering fear of Protestant conspiracy arguably hastened his decision to extirpate heresy in Inner Austria in spite of the estates' loyalty. In 1624, Ferdinand had begun to expel Protestant teachers and preachers in Upper Austria. In 1625–6, a campaign was led against the Protestant municipalities, comparable to Ferdinand's earlier measures in Inner Austria, and in September 1626, the Lutheran preceptors and teachers were ordered to emigrate. On 22 April 1627, Ferdinand issued a *Generalmandat* for Upper Austria which confronted the nobility with the choice between conversion and emigration. As a result of the concession granted to the loyal faction of the estates, the Lower Austrians fared better, though their religious liberty was now very narrowly circumscribed. In 1626, their preachers were expelled, and in September 1627, they were ordered to give up their Lutheran *exercitium*. However, no steps were taken to ensure the implementation of the September decree, and the status quo was confirmed later on by the Peace of Westphalia. Strict enforcement of the decree concerning 'ennobled persons' ('Nobilitierte', 23 April 1629) and regulations prescribing the Catholic education of Protestant wards (2 August 1631) ensured that the number of noblemen who enjoyed the privilege of 'religious liberty' remained limited.[90]

The blow against the Protestant nobility of Inner Austria who had remained loyal, but possessed no other safeguard than the 'Pacification' of 1578, was the ultimate proof that Ferdinand was determined to impose confessional conformity throughout his lands. On 27 March 1628, an Imperial decree constituted a general reform commission in Graz to organize and conduct a systematic inquisition and reform in Inner Austria, with the aim of thorough recatholicization.[91] On 6 May 1628, Ferdinand

[89] Quoted in Thiel, 'Zentralverwaltung', II, 511.

[90] Haider, *Oberösterreich*, 184–5, Gutkas, *Niederösterreich*, 132–4. Mecenseffy, *Protestantismus*, 164–5, 168–9.

[91] Eggenberg to bishop Jakob Eberlein, 29 Aug. 1625, Ferdinand II to the same, 14 May 1626, Imperial decree of 27 Mar. 1628, DA, 'Religionsberichte Protestantismus', 1598–1730.

issued a decree to all ennobled persons, as distinct from the 'ancient' established nobility. They were ordered to make their choice between conversion or emigration. Should they wish to claim exemption, they were to submit the documents which proved that they belonged to the established titled nobility ('alten herren und landleuth'). If they chose to emigrate, they were to pay the 'tenth penny' and submit a list of their estates and property in the Monarchy's lands.[92]

In view of Ferdinand's simultaneous proceeding against the Upper Austrian nobility, the Inner Austrian estates should have had few illusions about the next Counter-Reforming measures. However, over the next months, members of the old families, like the Khevenhüller, began to buy up the estates of noble emigrants.[93] It is unclear whether they wished to prevent these lands from falling into Catholic hands, possibly with an eye to resale once their co-religionists had been readmitted, or else seized the chance to round off their estates on the assumption that the members of the *Herren- und Ritterstand* were safe from a similar attack.

This, however, would have been a miscalculation. On 1 August 1628, Ferdinand fulfilled his promise to the bishop of Seckau and completed the Catholic reform in his lands with a general decree for the Protestant estates of Inner Austria.[94] Ferdinand acknowledged the estates' services to the House of Austria, and justified his decision to ban the Protestant nobility with his responsibility for the spiritual welfare of his subjects which ruled out connivance at the spread of heresy. The estates were to convert or to leave the Habsburg lands within the next six months, but they were spared the payment of the 'tenth penny'. They were granted an additional half-year for the sale of their estates by an authorized Catholic person. After the expiry of this term, remaining property would be sold by the government. Emigrants were allowed to retain the usufruct of entailed estates, which was to be paid out by Catholic mediators. Likewise, they received the permission to appoint Catholic representatives to settle their financial and legal affairs in the province. However, this might not be used as a pretext for their return, and offenders were threatened with severe punishment. All documents relating to their rights as patrons and *Vögte* as well as those pertaining to ecclesiastical foundations had to be handed over. The harshest clause of the decree concerned

[92] *FRA/60*, 804–5.

[93] W. W. Schnabel, *Österreichische Exulanten in oberdeutschen Reichsstädten* (Munich, 1992), 470.

[94] Copy in DA, 'Religionsberichte Protestantismus', 1598–1730. The text is also printed in *FRA/60*, 814–21.

the emigrants' children and wards, including those children and infants whose fathers had died, but whose mothers were still alive. These were to be entrusted to Catholic guardians and were not allowed to emigrate with their relatives or tutors.

The Inner Austrian emigration proved to be a long-drawn-out and complicated process, and the final sales of estates were made only by the middle of the seventeenth century.[95] This was partly due to the fact that emigrants were not prevented from inheriting landed property in the province, provided that they appointed a Catholic steward. The pressure exerted by the government nevertheless ensured that the majority of the emigrants sold their estates quickly and therefore at a low price. Frequently, property was transferred to those members of the family who had opted for conversion, or to Catholic cadet branches of the family, as in the case of the Stubenberg. These subsequently often failed to comply with the financial arrangements made and thus deprived the emigrants of their only means of subsistence. Likewise, it happened that the subjects of those emigrants who continued to derive an income from their estates refused to pay the dues and rents. In these cases, the sale of estates was the only way to obtain at least part of the property's actual value.

If the often ruinous consequences for the emigrants are obvious, it is much more difficult to assess the impact of this exodus on the province's economic life and social structure. Above all, it is not possible to ascertain the total number of emigrants.[96] Initially, Ferdinand had sought to establish control over the process of emigration by means of a register of the remaining Protestant nobility in the province. To facilitate this, the diocesan clergy were ordered to co-operate.[97] In 1641, the Styrian *Landeshauptmann* Karl von Saurau submitted a list of emigrants and their

---

[95] Schnabel, *Exulanten*, 472–3. The Styrian Hans Adam von Praunfalk, for example, sold his estates in 1657, ibid. 475.

[96] Schnabel, *Exulanten*, 70–4, speaks of a total of 'several hundred thousand' Austrian peasants, burghers, and noblemen who emigrated between 1598 and the middle of the 17th century. No less than 11,000 were said to have emigrated from Inner Austria by 1605. It should, however, be noted that Schnabel does not offer an assessment on the basis of his own findings, but derives this unrealistically high figure from the estimates of earlier 19th- and 20th-century studies, quoted ibid. 70–1. The sources consulted for the present study would suggest that for Inner Austria, a (maximum) figure in the range of *c*.3000–4000 emigrants for Styria, and perhaps a similar number for the neighbouring duchies of Carinthia and Carniola (jointly), are closer to the mark. There is no indication of large-scale desertion and depopulation of villages and municipalities, which would have been inevitable if Schnabel's figures were correct, regardless of the overall accelerated population growth in this period.

[97] Ferdinand II to *Landesverweser* Georg Galler, 26 Aug. 1628, STMLA, 'La. Arch., Religion und Kirche', Sch. 29.

dependants from the five Styrian districts. Saurau gave sixty-nine names, though admitting that his records were incomplete, and he was positive that the actual number of emigrants was much larger.[98]

A broader picture is given by contemporary estimates in the Upper German towns. It emerges that the majority of emigrants to the German lands turned to Regensburg, Nuremberg, Augsburg, Nördlingen, and Weißenburg.[99] The registers drafted by the Augsburg merchant Philipp Hainhofer and the Styrian emigrant Andreas Sötzinger are of particular interest. Hainhofer's 'Catalogus Exulum' for Inner Austria was drafted at the beginning of September 1629. His list counts 760 noble emigrants to the Empire and Hungary. Of these, 285 belonged to the *Herrenstand*, 429 were members of the *Ritterstand*, and 46 are described as ennobled persons. The author of the second register, Andreas Sötzinger, was a former secretary of the Styrian estates, and had been entrusted with the compilation of documents relating to the Ferdinandean reformation in the Austrian lands. It seems that he received this commission from members of the Inner Austrian nobility who intended to use his findings to further the emigrants' cause at the Imperial diet of 1653–4. The document was drafted in 1652 and gives a much lower figure than Hainhofer's estimate for Inner Austria alone would suggest. Sötzinger lists the names of 836 members of the established nobility of the five Austrian lands who had emigrated either to the Empire or to Hungary. This group was composed of 425 members of the *Herrenstand* and 411 knights.[100]

The Protestant elite did not invariably acquiesce in Ferdinand's policy, and a small proportion of the Inner Austrian emigrants joined the Swedish army. Though this contingent was not as large as the Upper Austrian,[101] the names of the leading families and exponents of the Protestant movement are not absent, for example the Dietrichstein, Khevenhüller, Herberstein, Kronegg, Teuffenbach, and Amman.[102] This development put Ferdinand II in a dilemma. If he stopped the drain of urgently needed emigrant capital from the province, as he tried to do by his decree of 21 June 1631 which ended the previous liberal practice of delivering emigrant capital, he risked impoverished exiled nobles joining

---

[98] Copy of Saurau's letter to Ferdinand III, 13 Aug. 1641, ibid.

[99] For a description of the most important catalogues of Inner Austrian and Austrian emigrants see Schnabel, *Exulanten*, 450–7. The geographic pattern of the Austrian emigration is dealt with by Mecenseffy, *Protestantismus*, 173, and the studies mentioned ibid. 184–5.

[100] Schnabel, *Exulanten*, 454.

[101] Ibid. 309, is vague on this point.

[102] Ibid. 299–303.

the Swedes in large numbers.[103] On the other hand, there were already spectacular examples of emigrants withdrawing capital from the province to support Ferdinand's enemies. The Carinthian Pal von Khevenhüller (1586–1655) and his brother Hans (1597–1632) joined Gustav Adolf's army and subsequently supported him with loans of 50,000 and 86,000 fl. Paul von Khevenhüller even recruited soldiers from his former Carinthian subjects who had been forced to emigrate to Nuremberg, and equipped a cavalry regiment of 1,500 for the Swedes. As for the Styrian Johann Friedrich von Teuffenbach (1594–1647), whom Bernhard of Sachsen-Weimar had installed in Regensburg as governor for the occupied Imperial territories (November 1633 to July 1634), he was later to plead that poverty had driven him to the Swedish side.[104]

There were, however, different careers for those emigrants who reverted to Catholicism. Rudolf von Teuffenbach rose to general's rank in the Imperial army and settled in Lower Austria, where he bought up confiscated estates.[105] Another convert, the Styrian Adam von Herberstorff, became notorious as head of the reformation commissions and governor of Upper Austria. In this function, he crushed the anti-Catholic peasant uprising of 1625–6.[106]

The majority of Inner Austrian noblemen, however, shrank from the prospect of emigration, just as they had shunned any radical opposition before 1628. This usually meant purely external conversion and hence the survival of heresy in the shape of crypto-Protestantism. It also meant that no large-scale change of the composition of the estates occurred in the aftermath of the emigration, although the cadet branches of established families and individual members of the nobility might profit from minor shifts. In 1668, the Catholic Wolf von Stubenberg, head of the younger line of the family, rejected the protests of his cousin Georg who had emigrated to Nuremberg. He admitted that the title and perquisites of the office of ducal cupbearer (*Erbschenk*) had always gone to the eldest member of the family as head of the house of Stubenberg, but referred him to Ferdinand III's declaration in 1648 that he would henceforth grant hereditary offices (*Erbämter*) only to the eldest Catholic members.

---

[103] Eggenberg to the Styrian estates, copy in STMLA, 'La. Arch., Religion und Kirche', Sch. 29. Saurau's report of 13 Aug. 1641 mentions thirty noblemen who derived interest from capital held by the Styrian *Landschaft*. The sum total amounted to 234,459 fl.

[104] Schnabel, *Exulanten*, 306, 311–15.

[105] Gutkas, *Niederösterreich*, 234.

[106] Mecenseffy, *Protestantismus*, 164–5, and in general H. Sturmberger, *Adam Graf Herberstorff: Herrschaft und Freiheit im konfessionellen Zeitalter* (Munich, 1976).

Stubenberg adduced the examples of the Khevenhüller and Windischgrätz families as evidence.[107]

Most conspicuous among the families who joined the leading provincial nobility after their conversion were the Saurau. The head of the family, Karl, had reverted to Catholicism in 1622 and claimed to have converted his wife, a member of the then Protestant Herberstorffs, in 1626. Saurau was appointed successively *Landmarschall* and *Landeshauptmann*, and sought to make up for his heretic past by a ruthless persecution of emigrants who dared return for a brief visit, of crypto-Protestants, and those he sought to denounce as such. In this, he spared neither his former friends nor relatives, and, as he proudly reported to the Emperor, made himself odious to the Styrian estates.[108] Although they were not able to surpass their rivals, the Stubenberg family, in either wealth or prestige, the Saurau were able to round off their estates in these years and continued torise among the Styrian nobility. In 1708 they ranked behind the Schwarzenberg, Stubenberg, and Eggenberg, but before the Herberstein.[109]

More important than the shifts among the secular estates was the impact on the material situation of the Church. Owing to the slump after 1628, the higher clergy, especially the wealthy monasteries, were able to acquire emigrant estates and recover the losses of the sixteenth century. During the second half of the seventeenth century, the increase of mortmain ecclesiastical property became a political issue that required Imperial regulation. As previously demonstrated, the precarious financial situation of a large part of the provincial clergy had contributed to the spiritual decline of the Church, and the material situation of the parish clergy especially in Lower Styria once more became an issue in the later seventeenth century. However, by the end of Ferdinand II's reign, at least the higher echelons of the Inner Austrian Church were moving from restoration and recovery to prosperity and in some cases abundance.[110] It remains to be examined whether this material recovery was matched by comparable achievements in the field of spiritual mission and ecclesiastical reform.

---

[107] Wolf von Stubenberg to Georg, 27 Nov. 1668, STMLA, 'Stubenberg-Archiv', Sch. 96, H. 588.

[108] Saurau to Ferdinand II, n.d. [1636], STMLA, 'Archiv Saurau', Sch. 230, H. 1601.

[109] J. Loserth, *Geschichte des altsteirischen Herren- und Grafenhauses Stubenberg* (Graz, 1911), 'Gülttabelle' for 1708, p. 289.

[110] Loserth, *Kirchengut*, 53–83.

5

The Counter-Reformation at Local Level

Ferdinand's facile political victory over the Inner Austrian estates was not matched by equally swift progress of the Counter-Reformation in the villages and municipalities. Above all, it was the experience of local resistance which shaped the governmental response over the three decades from the beginning of the urban campaign in 1598 to the general expulsion in 1628. The shortcomings of the systematic reformation campaign in 1599–1600 were revealed by subsequent reports testifying to the resilience of Protestantism in the remoter regions of Upper Styria, in the settlements along the Hungarian border, and, most conspicuously, in the patrimonial villages and municipalities of the nobility, which in turn hampered the progress of the Counter-Reformation in ducal towns such as Bruck an der Mur. A residue of Protestantism in Upper Styria survived the Catholic onslaught of Ferdinand II and his successors and became a political problem in the eighteenth century. As previously shown, Ferdinand did not waver in his determination to impose confessional conformity throughout the hereditary lands as soon as the military situation seemed auspicious. Hence, he did not spare the loyal Protestant estates of Inner Austria, whose expulsion removed the gravest obstacle to the completion of the Counter-Reformation at the local level.

In analysing the organizational side of this process, it should be noted that the origins of the reforming agencies can be traced back to the reign of Karl II. Ferdinand subsequently reorganized and co-ordinated these elements, and used them more systematically than his predecessor had done in the 1580s. This process was brought to a conclusion by the creation of a separate governmental commission for the general reformation of 1628. Its beginnings were closely linked to the prince's administrative reforms.

As already noted, Ferdinand increased the political importance of the Privy Council (*Geheimer Rat*) as his advisory body so that, from 1619–20 onwards, it acted as his executive council and highest court for Inner Austria. The execution of his religious policy, however, remained the task of the Inner Austrian government, which was staffed with a fresh supply of Catholic officials at his accession. The instructions of 1597 stated the government's duty to take steps against heresies, and the amendment of 1609 specified this religious obligation by introducing a Catholic oath for all government officials. Karl II's instructions of 1571 had already empowered the ducal procurator (*Kammerprokurator*) to institute proceedings against secular transgressors so as to safeguard clerical rights and protect or restore ecclesiastical property. Under the new archduke, the procurator was entrusted with the task of an inquisitor and prosecutor in religious matters. Ferdinand strengthened his control of this instrument of religious policy by appointing Catholic protégés who had no links with the duchies' Protestant elite, for example the Italians Angelo Costede (1595–9) and Johann Baptist Verda (1611–19). For the same reason, he appointed commoners, like the lawyer Christoph Prättinger (1599–1608), who persecuted noble offenders against the ducal decrees with particular rigour.[1]

If the Inner Austrian government and the *Kammerprokurator* provided permanent governmental institutions for the enforcement of Ferdinand's religious policy, a more flexible and mobile instrument was needed to exert pressure at the local level. To this end, reformation commissions were created which were composed of government officials who were in some cases accompanied by members of the clergy. The first of these commissions was appointed in 1586 at the request of the bishop of Seckau, Martin Brenner, to deal with the obstreperous Lutherans of Radkersburg. Brenner began his term of office in 1585 with a visitation of the parishes under his jurisdiction, among them the parish of Radkersburg in Lower Styria, close to the Hungarian border. Traces of Lutheranism there had been noted as early as 1528, and by 1541 most of the burghers professed the new faith. The growth of the Lutheran party was encouraged by Karl von Herberstorff, who provided the town with a preacher in 1581 and built a spacious Protestant church on his estate near Radkersburg in 1582 to cater for the urban community. Unsurprisingly, then, the town defied Brenner's orders to abandon their Protestant *exercitium* in 1585. In the following five years, Brenner's efforts to recover control of the local school and church were supported by the government

---

[1] The family of Verda had been invited as artists to the court in Graz by Karl II. Alexander de Verda drafted the design for the interior decoration of Karl II's mausoleum in Seckau in 1587–92, *Dehio: Handbuch der Kunstdenkmäler Österreichs. Steiermark* (Vienna, 1956), 271. For Prättinger's activity see the Styrian estates' complaint of 19 Jan. 1605, paraphrased in *FRA/58*, 393–4. Prättinger also brought a charge of high treason against Georg von Stubenberg in 1602, see below.

in Graz. Repeated reformation commissions attempted to enforce the ducal decrees for the eviction of Radkersburg's Protestant clergy and for a reversion of the community to the Catholic faith. However, since the community were admitted to the nearby church on Herberstorff's estates, they were able to continue their Protestant *exercitium*. Moreover, the government antagonized the urban Protestant elite by the attempt to depose the Lutheran councillors and replace them with 'low-born' local Catholics or Italians. The new government was swept away by riots in 1588 and 1589, and defiance continued although the ringleaders of these tumults, among them the town magistrate (*Stadtrichter*) Valentin Göbl and the clerk (*Stadtschreiber*), were arrested and sent to prison in Graz. The conflict over the implementation of the Catholic reformation charter was not settled at the time of Karl II's death in the following year.[2]

Initially, the Protestants of Radkersburg were supported by the estates.[3] However, the majority of this assembly had been anxious to dissociate themselves from the refractory burghers of Graz in 1584, and there is no evidence to suggest that they adopted a different attitude towards the rebellious actions of the Protestants of Radkersburg. As already noted, there were nevertheless 'dissenting voices' of radical noblemen who sympathized with their non-noble co-religionists and gave them active support, such as Karl von Herberstorff and his brother Otto. Although the course of the confessional struggle was determined by the loyalist majority of the estates, encouragement from the radical quarter was not a negligible factor for the Counter-Reformation 'on the ground' in these years. This emerges from the evidence for the 'Herberstorff affair' in the years 1585–90.[4] In 1585, the government had begun to contest Otto von Herberstorff's right of nomination (*ius patronatus*) to the parish of Ilz in east Styria. At the beginning of the contest, it seemed that Herberstorff would be able to defend his claim, but in 1589, the government tacitly dropped its earlier favourable decision, and a Catholic priest was installed by force. Herberstorff protested against this proceeding which in his view ran counter to the Pacification of 1578 and proved

---

[2] See Dirnberger, 'Radkersburg', 192–7, Schuster, *Martin Brenner*, 207, *FRA/50*, 584, and Winkelmann, 'Geschichte des Luthertums', i. 111–16. For Herberstorff's patronage see ibid. 107–8.

[3] Dirnberger, 'Radkersburg', 198, n. 2, also *FRA/50*, 641–5, petition of the Styrian estates on behalf of the persecuted Protestants of Marburg, Radkersburg, and Pettau, 4 Feb. 1588.

[4] For the following account see Loserth, *Gegenreformation*, 567–70.

the government's disregard for the estates' liberties. To ascertain his rights, and presumably to cater for the spiritual needs of his Protestant subjects, he began to build a church close to his castle at Kahlsdorf near Ilz. On 17 April 1590, the archduke ordered the destruction of this church by a dispatch of troops from the town guards. Anxious to avoid a confrontation, the estates urged Herberstorff to transfer the Protestant services to his castle, but he declined and began to levy troops from his subjects. Moreover, he issued warnings to the neighbouring municipality of Fürstenfeld, threatening reprisals if its burghers should decide to assist the government's troops. A number of noblemen from the mainly east Styrian *Viertel* of Vorau declared their support for Herberstorff in the case of a military confrontation, and urged the *Verordnete* to effect a revocation of the recent decree.

In view of the archduke's general abhorrence of hazardous measures, it remains unclear whether he would have accepted this challenge. In any case, he underestimated the determination of his opponents. The reformation commission which was eventually entrusted with the destruction of the church was not accompanied by troops, and was easily put to flight by a small levy of thirty mounted noblemen, supported by armed peasants. In the event, Karl II's death on 10 July 1590 brought the government's proceedings to a standstill, and the regents decided to drop the issue quietly, without bringing the rebels to account.[5]

As shown earlier, Karl II's Counter-Reformation policy was inconsistent for the greater part of his reign. For the resumption of the urban campaign by Ferdinand (II), it was nevertheless important that a beginning had been made by the earlier decrees and commissions. Special decrees (*Spezialmandate*) issued in the 1580s directly addressed the town councils of the municipalities, for example those of Kindberg, Bruck, Pöls, Mitterndorff, Obdach, and Neumarkt, and adapted Karl's general decrees against urban Protestantism to redress the prevailing 'abuses' in these towns.[6] Although the ducal instructions were not always enforced by the local authorities, they nevertheless forced the

---

[5] Loserth, *Gegenreformation*, 570. The attack on the commission is described by Rosolenz, 'Gegenbericht', fos. 40–1, who does not specify the number of peasant troops involved. Herberstorff's warning to the burghers of Fürstenfeld, who in fact belonged among the Protestant communities that were repeatedly chastised by ducal decrees and governmental reformation commissions (see below, this chapter), is further evidence of the previously described conflicts between the nobility and the municipalities, regardless of their confessional allegiances.

[6] See J. Loserth, 'Die Reformationsordnungen der Städte und Märkte Innerösterreichs aus den Jahren 1587–1628', *AÖG* 96 (1907), 99–190.

burghers to make their choice between obedience and confessional conformity or heterodoxy and open defiance.

The activity of Karl II's reformation commissions was also directed against Protestant activity in Lower and east Styria. Reform commissions consisting of the *Kammerprokurator* and a further government official were sent to municipalities like Marburg, Pettau, Windischgraz, Fürstenfeld, and Feldbach, and a series of decrees issued in 1588–90 repeated the orders that were proclaimed on these occasions. The commissions were especially concerned with the 'purge' of municipal offices. Protestant magistrates were to be replaced with Catholic burghers, and obstinate heretics were to be expelled from the archduke's lands.[7] As in Radkersburg, the earliest reformation commissions of 1587 and 1588 in Pettau and Marburg sought to replace Protestant magistrates with Catholic candidates from the lower ranks of the burghers. The burghers were ordered to abandon their Protestant *exercitium*, and had to take a Catholic oath.[8] The effect of these measures, however, was limited as a result of noble patronage. Like their co-religionists in Radkersburg, the Protestant communities of Marburg and Pettau benefited from the existence of a Protestant place of worship on the estates of the local nobility. In this case, Wolf Wilhelm von Herberstein built a Protestant church and school close to his castle in Windenau near Marburg, which was situated at a convenient distance from these towns and was kept open to the local population. Until the resumption of public worship during the regency of 1590–5, the burghers of Pettau and Marburg abstained from public Protestant worship within the precincts of their towns, but attended the Lutheran services at this church. Karl II tried to cut this link by issuing penal decrees in 1588–90, demanding fines of 10–30 fl. for each offence and threatening the expulsion of recalcitrants. In January 1589, thirty burghers of Marburg were arrested. The Protestant communities of Marburg and Pettau survived, in spite of these sanctions, thanks to their clandestine contacts with Windenau.[9]

Occasionally, the commissions met with violent opposition from the local Protestants, and the case of Feldbach in east Styria must have contributed to Ferdinand's decision to dispatch troops to assist and

---

[7] Loserth, *Gegenreformation*, 529–31, and *FRA/50*, 658–9, protest of the Styrian estates against the activity of the reformation commissions in the municipalities, 19 Mar. 1589.

[8] Loserth, 'Reformationsordnungen', 105, Winkelmann, 'Geschichte des Luthertums', ii. 89.

[9] Loserth, *Gegenreformation*, 530, and Winkelmann, 'Geschichte des Luthertums', ii. 88–9.

protect his roving commissions. In 1589, the *Kammerprokurator* Wolfgang Jöchlinger and a further commissioner had tried to institute a Catholic town council, but were hindered by a 'tumult' of the parishioners. The new head of the magistrates (*Stadtrichter*) who had already received the town's seal from the commissioners was subsequently threatened and attacked. Eventually he was badly wounded when a group of burghers stormed his house. A similar attack occurred in 1590, when a Catholic priest lodged with him. The Catholic incumbent was likewise exposed to attacks on his life, and resigned his parish after a particularly serious incident.[10]

Karl II's urban campaign also extended to the Protestant strongholds in Upper Styria. The operations of the first reformation commissions in May 1587 shed light on the confessional situation in this region, and provide further evidence of the important role which the new type of Catholic ducal official could play in advancing the Counter-Reformation in the periphery. In January 1587, the bailiff (*Landpfleger*) for the territory of the *Landgericht* Wolkenstein in the Enns valley, Primus Wanzl, had begun to take measures against the Protestants of the mining communities of Schladming and Oeblarn. Together with the miners of Eisenerz, they formed the backbone of Protestant opposition and potentially militant resistance in the region. In this, they were supported by the estates' preacher (*Viertelprediger*) for the Enns valley district (*Viertel*), Dionys Wiedemann, and his vicar, Vincenz Kumberger. Referring to the ducal instructions by which he was ordered to take steps against the spread of new doctrines and the summoning of conventicles, Wanzl demanded Kumberger's dismissal, and rejected a joint petition from the miners and the rural population of Schladming and Oeblarn in March that year. To suppress any Protestant activity in the Enns valley, he procured a ducal decree of 21 March 1587 by which Wiedemann was accused of proselytizing among the miners and peasants and was therefore ordered to leave the duchy.[11] This alarmed the Protestant lords in the region, Hans Friedrich Hoffmann and Hans Jakob von Stainach, who urged the estates' executive council to effect the revocation of this decree. Otherwise, they predicted a revolt of the local population. Thus, they warned the *Verordnete* that the miners and peasants possessed guns

---

[10] Rosolenz, 'Gegenbericht', fos. 47–51. The arrest of the culprits did not prevent further assaults, ibid. 51.

[11] This was not put into effect, as an entry in the register of the Styrian church ministry of 1590 proves, see appendix no. 8 in Loserth, *Gegenreformation*, 590–2.

and were determined to defend their preachers by force.[12] The commissioners who tried to introduce Catholic priests in the Upper Styrian parishes of Haus, Gröbming, and Oberwölz in the years 1587–9 were to find out that this was not a vain threat. Their attempts foundered on the resistance of the parishioners, who defended the Lutheran clergy by force of arms and put the new incumbents to flight.[13]

The conflict was exacerbated by the dispatch of a reformation commission, headed by Abbot Johann Jakob of Admont, to the Upper Styrian parishes of Lassing, Liezen, and Oppenberg in May 1587. These parishes were subject to the jurisdiction of the Augustinian canons of Rottenmann, but by this time, the Hoffmann exercised the right of presentation. From the past record of these parishes it was clear that the commission would encounter opposition, and the information produced in the course of the subsequent inquisition suggests that Wanzl and the party of clerical reformers in Graz deliberately dispatched this commission while Hoffmann was absent from the duchy and therefore unable to obey the government's orders to assist the commissioners. When the latter were resisted by force, Wanzl brought a legal charge against Hoffmann, whose absence was construed as defiance of the ducal authority. Moreover, the official claimed that Hoffmann had actually instigated the revolt. As a result, legal proceedings were instituted, and Hoffmann narrowly escaped trial for high treason. In a letter to the estates, he was able to draw on statements by Wanzl and the present nuncio's predecessor, Germanico Malaspina, to support his suspicion that the local conflict had been deliberately provoked and formed part of a wider political scheme of the Catholic reform party in Graz. Wanzl had previously demanded the execution of leading Protestant noblemen to terrorize their rural subjects into obedience, while Malaspina had uttered hopes of a general uprising that would provide the pretext for the dispossession of the Protestant nobility.[14] Against this background, Hoffmann plausibly argued that Wanzl and his clerical supporters had procured the recent

[12] See the quotation ibid. 523.

[13] Rosolenz, 'Gegenbericht', fos. 38–9, 42–5. The complaint of the parishioners of Oberwölz in 1591 (see above, Ch. 4) proves that the government eventually succeeded in instituting a Catholic priest. However, Rosolenz claims that the Catholic incumbent of Oberwölz was repeatedly attacked by his parishioners even after 1595, ibid. 46–7.

[14] For Hoffmann's account of the events see his letter to the archduke, dated 21 May 1587, and his report for the estates, 29 Aug. 1587, see FRA/50, 615–21 and 623–7. His argument for the existence of a Catholic design to overthrow the estates is stated in a separate (confidential) letter to the estates, also dated 29 Aug. 1587, see FRA/50, 628–31. See ibid. 616 and 628 for a quotation of Wanzl's and Malaspina's statements.

commission to force the archduke's hand by turning the local reaction into a large-scale 'conflagration' in the duchy.[15]

In any case, the legal proceedings had the effect of discrediting Hoffmann, who at this time held the office of *Landmarschall* of the Styrian estates (1564–89) and was the wealthiest and most influential estate owner in the region. Wanzl's attack thus continued Malaspina's efforts to dislodge the leader of the Protestant estates, a campaign which had already brought about the deposition of Hoffmann as administrator of the bishop of Bamberg's possessions in Carinthia in 1583/4.[16] Though the charge of high treason had to be dropped, the blow was sufficient to effect Hoffmann's withdrawal from politics. Initially, he had even pondered emigration for fear of further designs against his person.[17]

Apart from reflecting its primary purpose of exonerating him from the charge of rebellion, Hoffmann's defensive argument proves him a supporter of the loyalist stand for passive obedience.[18] This becomes particularly clear from his account for the *Verordnete*, which stresses the importance of the local Lutheran clergy for the maintenance of law and order among the unruly population of Upper Styria. The present revolts proved that Catholic incumbents stood no chance of acceptance by the peasants and miners, so that it was in the interest of the prince and the estates alike to support the activity of the local Lutheran preachers of the 'peaceful faith' ('raine prediger unserer fridfertigen confession zuegethan') as a guarantor of public peace. By contrast, further Counter-Reforming activities would disrupt the public peace in Upper Styria, and would prepare the ground for the spread of seditious Calvinistic propaganda.[19]

The main point of his account was to warn against the political consequences of the present reform campaign in Upper Styria. Existing social tensions in the region and throughout the duchy were such that a local anti-Catholic uprising could easily become the starting point for the outbreak of a series of (economically motivated) revolts which would be directed indiscriminately against Catholic and Protestant estate owners, and would sweep away the archduke's authority.[20] Hoffmann omitted this detailed assessment of the threat to social stability and political order in

[15] Letter to the *Verordnete*, 29 Aug. 1587, ibid. 628.
[16] Huber, 'Hanns Hoffmann', 147–8.
[17] See the above quoted letters to the archduke and the *Verordnete* in 1587.
[18] For the following see his letter to the *Verordnete*, 29 Aug. 1587, *FRA/50*, 623–7.
[19] Hoffmann's letter to the *Verordnete*, 29 Aug. 1587, quoted from ibid. 626.
[20] Ibid. 625–7.

his apologetic letter to Karl II, but he enlarged upon this issue in his presumably confidential report for the estates. In this, he resumed a line of reasoning which had been of crucial political importance during the formative years of Inner Austrian Protestantism. As previously demonstrated, there was a close link between the experience of socially subversive religious Radicalism in the Empire, most notably during the Peasant War of 1525–6, and the emergence of a politically submissive majority among the Protestant estates of Inner Austria. Persistent fiscal pressure by the archduke and the feudal lords caused rural unrest and uprisings in different parts of the duchies until 1635, so that a sense of precariousness was kept alive among the landed nobility. Hoffmann's warning must be seen against this background, which seemed to prove the permanent validity of the conciliatory argument in favour of co-operation with the prince. In Upper Styria, the problem of latent unrest was aggravated by the fact that communication and kinship ties had united the Protestant population of miners, woodcutters, day labourers, and farmers in a close-knit community. Hoffmann therefore feared that Counter-Reforming activities in one locality would cause a chain reaction of protest or even revolt in the region.[21]

The precarious situation in Upper Styria was also the subject of a 'discourse concerning possible ways of extinguishing Protestantism in the Enns valley', which was presented to the government shortly before the return of the young Archduke Ferdinand (1595), in December 1594.[22] It was submitted by Georg Mayr, a government official and protégé of the Archduchess Maria, in the hope that these proposals would secure him the vacant post of *Landpfleger* of Wolkenstein.[23] His memorandum is of interest not only for its confirmation of the earlier evidence for the militancy of Upper Styrian Protestantism, but also for its examination of the previous reformation commissions' shortcomings. Thus, he criticized the lack of a general plan which defined the objective of each commission. Likewise, he thought it detrimental that the commissioners had received no clear instructions for their operations. To forestall preparations for

---

[21] For a characterization of the Protestant network see Hoffmann's letter to the estates, ibid. 626.

[22] 'Mayrs discurs, wie die ketzerey im Embsthal auszureitten were', by Georg Mayr, 14 Dec. 1594, *FRA/58*, 120–8.

[23] Mayr based his treatise on information from the government records and was probably a *Hofkanzlei* official. He claimed that the archduchess had promised to invest him with the *Landpflege* as soon as possible, i.e. after Primus Wanzl's death, ibid. 123. Archduke Ferdinand indeed entrusted this Catholic zealot with the administration of Wolkenstein, see ibid. 650.

armed resistance in the parishes concerned, orders for the sending of commissions should be kept strictly secret. Furthermore, the commissioners were to move swiftly, and should arrange for support from Salzburg or Seckau to crush uprisings by joint forces. To increase the authority of reform commissions in Protestant municipalities like Schladming, he suggested the appointment of high-ranking officials or notables who might be able to check the rebels.[24] Hoffmann's death in 1589 removed the principal patron of the local Protestants, and Mayr misjudged the situation in assuming that this had discouraged the local opposition in Hoffmann's parishes. He had a stronger case in arguing that the outbreak of the Turkish War ruled out the use of force in domestic affairs for the time being. For the same reason, he recommended a prudent proceeding against such intractable parishes as Schladming, Oeblarn, or Gröbming. To prevent an uprising, Mayr thought it best to insinuate that the archduke wished to restore the Catholic parishes to orthodox incumbents, but would force nobody to reconvert. Likewise, the Catholic priests should be instructed to refrain from polemical preaching.[25]

As will be shown, Ferdinand adopted some of his official's advice, especially for the swift implementation of a general scheme and the gradual enforcement of the full Counter-Reformation measures in the restive parishes. On the other hand, Ferdinand was willing to take a greater risk in combining organizational improvement along the lines of the above memorandum with a show of military force which proved his determination to suppress the opposition of his lesser subjects.

While the situation permitted no similarly sweeping attack on the Protestant nobility, there were nevertheless incidents in connection with his reformation campaign at the turn of the century which foreshadowed Ferdinand's policy of the 1620s. With the decrees of 13 and 23 September 1598 against the exercise of the Lutheran religion in the ducal municipalities, Ferdinand intensified the battle against urban Protestantism. Even before his formal accession to power in December 1596, Ferdinand signalled his determination to resume his father's efforts. Special mandates of November and December 1595 demanded the dismissal of the Protestant teacher of Knittelfeld, ordered the burghers of Leoben to elect Catholic magistrates, and appointed reformation commissions for the parishes of Gottschee in Carniola and, in April 1596, for Neuberg in

---

[24] Ibid. 122–5. Mayr seems to have been unaware of the existence of a Flacian faction in Schladming, but see Hutter, *Geschichte Schladmings*, 228.

[25] *FRA/58*, 125–6.

Lower Styria. In February 1596, Ferdinand ordered the arrest and extradition of a preacher in Windischgraz who had been installed by the local
nobility.[26]

In spring 1598, Ferdinand began to issue more elaborate reformation
charters, beginning with the twenty-six points proclaimed by the reformation commissioners for Leoben on 27 April 1598.[27] This charter
became the model for the decrees that were issued for all municipalities
from February 1599 onwards, so that its contents deserve closer scrutiny.
As will be seen, Ferdinand combined strict Counter-Reforming measures
with orders for the restoration of 'good government' by the magistrates
to further acceptance of his religious policy by the urban population.
Moreover, the recatholicization of municipal offices and corporations was
supplemented by political reforms which strengthened the prince's power
at the expense of traditional municipal rights of self-government. The
statutes for his urban Counter-Reformation are therefore characteristic of
the dual aims which determined his policy of confessional absolutism, i.e.
the assertion of his political rights as a ruling member of the dynasty and
the fulfilment of his spiritual obligations as a Catholic prince.

The reform charter for Leoben stated that, henceforth, only
Catholics were to be admitted as burghers or might be elected to public
offices. Burghers who wished to emigrate were not to be given leave
without prior notification to the government. The function of this clause
was obviously to control such transactions, and ensure the payment of
the emigrants' 'tenth penny'. The next points are concerned with the
recatholicization of elementary education. Protestant teachers were to be
dismissed, and the Catholic parish priest was entrusted with the appointment of suitable successors. Further regulations deal with the Catholic
education of wards and repeat Karl II's decree of 1 January 1587
prescribing the recall of pupils who had hitherto studied abroad at
Protestant schools and universities. To restore the material basis of the
parishes, Ferdinand ordered the magistrates to reconstitute the ancient
guilds and confraternities. Likewise, the town councillors had to effect
the restoration of alienated ecclesiastical property. The next three points
concern the burghers' compulsory attendance at Catholic services and
the abolition of all forms of public or private Protestant worship, regulations which showed Ferdinand's determination to suppress any mani-

---

[26] *FRA/58*, 165, 174, 200–1, 192. For a list of further special decrees issued in these
years see Loserth, 'Reformationsordnungen', 112.

[27] Printed 'Reformationsordnungen', 136–42.

festation of the freedom of conscience which he allegedly was still willing to grant his subjects.[28]

The following points (10 and 11) prohibit trade and other work on
Sundays and feast-days and order the punishment of vagabondry, swearing, and blasphemy. These regulations lead over to the second, political
part of the charter. This consists of twelve points which deal exclusively
with matters of public order and welfare. Thus, Ferdinand urged the
magistrates to redress abuses such as the decline of the respectable inns
of the town. In this case, the archduke's economic interest is obvious. The
ducal town of Leoben was a centre of the Styrian iron trade, and its urban
economy should have profited from the increased demand for accommo-
dation and provisions. Instead, this valuable source of income had been
lost to the rural inns and thus indirectly to the nobility, to the detriment
of the ducal treasury.[29] Points 13 to 23 deal with various abuses, committed or at least tolerated by the magistrates and the privileged trades at the
expense of the majority of lesser burghers. The local innkeepers, bakers,
and butchers were ordered to stop the arbitrary fixing of prices and quan-
tities. Ferdinand's criticism then fastened on the magistrates' activity.
Taking up local grievances, Ferdinand reprimanded the town councillors
for their sluggish administration of justice and for their unfair distribution of the communal tax burden. The charge of corruption was implicitly repeated in the next regulation, by which the magistrates were
ordered to ensure the submission of exact accounts by all town officials.
Several additional regulations emphasized the magistrates' responsibility
for the community's health and safety, and for the improvement of the
local hospital and almshouse.[30] Finally, the town council was officially
subjected to the control of a Catholic magistrate (*Stadtanwalt*) who was
charged with the implementation and observance of these regulations
after the commission's departure. The new Catholic town councillors
were ordered to punish malcontents and were held responsible for the
safety of all Catholic officials.[31]

It seems that Ferdinand exploited existing tensions between the different social groups of the community to split the urban opposition to his

---

[28] Ibid. 136–9. For Karl II's decree of 1587 see *FRA/50*, 590–1.

[29] For this point and the following regulations see Loserth, 'Reformationsordnungen',
139–41. Leoben's importance for the Inner Austrian iron trade is discussed by F. Tremel,
'Beiträge zu einer Handelsgeschichte Leobens in der frühen Neuzeit', *ZHVST*, 60 (1969),
107–26.

[30] Loserth, 'Reformationsordnungen', points 19–22, pp. 140–1.

[31] Ibid. 141.

religious reforms. Thus, he took up grievances of the poorer population to pit the burghers against the magistrates. However, it was only in this exceptionally difficult situation that Ferdinand made use of social tensions as an instrument of his policy. As soon as the leading town offices had been restored to Catholics, Ferdinand and his successors took steps to suppress further inner-urban opposition and social unrest. The appointment of a *Stadtanwalt* as head of the town council and ducal representative meant that the local authorities were now subject to a more direct control of their activity. With the beginning of the urban reformation campaign in 1598, Ferdinand began to abolish the customary annual elections to town offices. Henceforth, appointments were for life. In the course of the Counter-Reformation, 'permanent councils' were created in Graz, Bruck, Leoben, and Fürstenfeld, while the burghers of Judenburg were able to defend the traditional electoral procedures at least until 1695.[32] Ferdinand thus ended the century-old struggle for the extension of the ruler's control of his municipalities.

Religious and political or economic motives were similarly closely linked in the case of the reorganization of the guilds. Initially, the Habsburg princes had tried to suppress any such associations, especially those of journeymen, as seditious. Ferdinand (I) issued a decree to this effect in 1527, but its implementation proved impossible. As a result, the prohibition was modified in 1554. The decisive change occurred with the accession of Ferdinand (II) as Inner Austrian duke. From the start, he pursued a policy of support combined with rigorous control. In 1596, he subjected the existing guilds to direct governmental or municipal control. Their statutes had to be submitted to the government for examination, and their orthodoxy had to be confirmed by the ecclesiastical authorities, e.g. the statutes of the guild of raftsmen (*Flößer*), which were approved by the Styrian archdeacons as the archbishop of Salzburg's local officials in 1616. With the beginning of the urban reformation, Ferdinand began to issue orders for the reform or creation of guilds. They provided for the tight organization of the urban trades, and the duke's support for compulsory membership should probably be seen as an attempt to settle the problem of illegal competition. However, this had little effect on rural competitors, who in general managed to elude ducal control.

Ferdinand was more successful in strengthening the guilds as a means of religious and social discipline. The example of the riot in Graz in 1590

---

[32] F. Popelka, 'Der "ewige" Rat: Eine Episode aus dem Kampf um die städtische Demokratie', *ZHVST* 46 (1955), 150–61.

had shown that the artisans could play a key role in urban confessional conflicts. The approved statutes therefore laid down a number of religious obligations which amounted to a public confession of faith. Such duties included attendance at the guild's Catholic services, communal prayer, and participation in the processions on feast-days. Swearing, blasphemy, and all kinds of misconduct in public were punished by the guild authorities. Compulsory membership in these corporations meant that they became valuable instruments for the imposition of strict social and religious discipline on a potentially unruly group of the urban population, for example in Radkersburg, where no less than eighteen guilds were created or reformed in this period.[33] In 1629, the guild of carpenters in the Upper Styrian *Viertel* of Judenburg petitioned Ferdinand II for a decree against their illegal rural competitors and sought to add weight to their request by a vow to further the Catholic religion in the region.[34]

Reformation charters which combined religious and political orders to effect a reform of various aspects of urban life were issued from 1599 onwards for most Styrian and some of the larger Carinthian municipalities. In each case, the burghers were ordered to return to the Catholic faith and abstain from their public and private Protestant *exercitium*. Offenders were threatened with rigorous punishment. As a rule, there was no explicit and general permission to choose between conversion or emigration, as was granted to the burghers of Graz and the burghers and miners of Upper Styria. Instead, it was attempted to limit the number of emigrants by transferring the decision from the local magistrates to the government in Graz.[35] The proclamation of such reformation charters, based on a draft version that was adapted to the special circumstances,

---

[33] For the changing Habsburg legislation and the traditional unruliness of the trades see O. Haberleitner, *Handwerk in Steiermark und Kärnten vom Mittelalter bis 1850* (Graz, 1962), 9–11, 114, 125. A survey of the development of the Styrian guilds can be found in J. v. Zahn, 'Über Materialien zur inneren Geschichte der Zünfte in Steiermark', *BKSTGQ* 14 (1877), 83–111. The sequel to this article in *BKSTGQ* 15 (1878), 74–128 reprints a number of guild statutes of the years 1600 to 1699, which concern the members' religious obligations and reflect the influence of the Counter-Reformation. For the statutes of the Radkersburg guilds see J. Gomilschak, 'Zünfte in Radkersburg und Materialien zu ihrer Geschichte', *BKSTGQ* 16 (1879), 51–82.

[34] Petition of the carpenters of Judenburg, Knittelfeld, Murau, Oberwölz, Weißkirchen, Obdach, Zeiring, Unzmarkt, Neumarkt, and the entire *Viertel* of Judenburg, 9 Feb. 1629, *FRA/60*, 835–6.

[35] Loserth, 'Reformationsordnungen', 121–33. The reformation charters for Judenburg (1587, 1600), St Veit (Carinthia, 1597), Villach (Carinthia, 1598), Leoben (1598, 1600), Radkersburg (1599), Marburg (Maribor, 1600), Unterdrauburg (1600), Fronleiten (1600), Vordernberg (1600), Gmünd (Carinthia, 1600), and for several of the smaller municipalities are printed in part on pp. 133–89.

concluded the proceedings of the roving reformation commissions which Ferdinand dispatched in the years 1599–1600.[36]

In his account of their activity, Abbot Rosolenz distinguished nine campaigns carried out by such commissions.[37] The abolition of the Lutheran church ministry in Graz, Judenburg, and Laibach in September 1598 is taken as the starting point of this campaign.[38] The second campaign concerned Eisenerz and the Enns valley (Upper Styria), the third the Lower Styrian towns, most notably Radkersburg and Marburg, the fourth reformed Judenburg, Murau, Bruck, Leoben, and a number of Upper Styrian parishes. The district of Vorau, covering 'middle' and east Styria, was visited by the fifth commission, to be followed by a further reform of Eisenerz and the parishes which were subject to Admont. The seventh to ninth commissions were sent to Carinthia and Carniola in the years 1602–4. They were led by the bishop of Laibach, Thomas Hren, and the bishop of Seckau, Martin Brenner, who devoted four months to an initially unsuccessful attempt to subdue the Protestant burghers of Klagenfurt.[39]

The Styrian reformation commissions which operated from 14 October 1599 until the end of July 1600 were closely supervised and directed by the archduke. In spite of the Turkish War, which made a concentration of forces and the preservation of domestic peace essential, Ferdinand had determined to punish those municipalities which had publicly defied ducal orders and had treated previous commissions with contempt. Foremost among these was the mining community of Eisenerz. A first reformation commission in 1597 had been put to flight by the miners, labourers, and woodcutters. To demonstrate their defiance of the ducal authority, they had subjected one of the ducal commissioners, the *Kammerrat* Peter Kuglmann, to a mock trial. Shortly after this incident, the nuncio Girolamo Porcia, who was on his way from Graz to Bavaria and spent the night in Eisenerz, had a very near escape when a group of armed burghers attacked his lodgings.[40] There is no evidence of

---

[36] The instructions are printed ibid. on pp. 151–7. For the different treatment of the rebellious Upper Styrian parishes and municipalities see below.

[37] Rosolenz, 'Gegenbericht', fos. 102–10, 115–275, Loserth, 'Reformationsordnungen', 116–33, and his list on pp. 116–17.   [38] Rosolenz, 'Gegenbericht', fos. 104–7.

[39] The following analysis concentrates on events in Styria. For the slow progress of the Counter-Reformation in the Carinthian capital of Klagenfurt see ibid. 172–5, 342–7. The initial difficulties which beset the otherwise successful educational work of the Jesuits there from their arrival in 1604 until the end of the Thirty Years War are discussed by L. Hertling, *Die Jesuiten in Kärnten* (Klagenfurt, 1975), 5–10.

[40] See Rosolenz, 'Gegenbericht', fos. 76–80.

a direct connection between these challenges to the ducal authority and the peasant uprising in the adjacent districts of Upper Austria (May 1594 to September 1597), but Ferdinand nevertheless feared that Austrian emissaries were fomenting unrest in Upper Styria.[41]

To punish the previous acts of rebellion and effect a Catholic reform of the community, Ferdinand appointed a commission consisting of the privy counsellor Andreas von Herberstorff, assisted by the abbot of Admont, the *Kammerat* Alban von Mos(ch)heim, and Ferdinand's protégé and companion Johann Friedrich von Paar as captain of the escort.[42] The commission met on 14 October 1599 in Leoben, where they deliberated on the ducal instructions and discussed the details of their planned advance on the nearby municipality of Eisenerz.[43] An unspecified number of troops were led to Leoben by night, where they joined forces with 126 Slovenian and German soldiers from the guards in Graz. The same night, the commission and its escort marched on Eisenerz and were able to forestall the rebels' attempt to barricade the way. A large number of miners, labourers, woodcutters, and some of the burghers were nevertheless apprised of the commission's coming and took position in and around the church and on the watchtower. Meanwhile, the local judge and three of the magistrates had changed sides and warned the commissioners that the rebels were armed with weapons from the burghers' arsenal. However, the commission had been reinforced with 316 armed peasants, recruited from the ducal subjects of the Aflenz valley near Bruck and from the subjects of the abbot of Neuberg. It seems that the sheer number of troops deterred the rebels from opening fire, and the commission was able to begin its proceedings. The keys to the local

---

[41] This emerges from a letter to Georg von Stubenberg, dated 18 Mar. 1597. Ferdinand speaks of mounted emissaries who might instigate an uprising in the region, STMLA, 'Stubenberg-Archiv', Sch. 12, H. 77. For the events in Upper Austria see Eder, *Glaubensspaltung*, 258–9.

[42] Mosheim had recently (re-)converted to Catholicism and became *Vizedom* of Styria on 29 Nov. 1599. He was subsequently involved in the process against the Protestant preacher and preceptor of the Windischgrätz family, Paul Odontius, see the latter's report in Leidenfrost, 'Geschichte der Gegenreformation', 51–80, esp. 59–60. For Mosheim's appointment and the case of Odontius see Schuster, *Martin Brenner*, 466 n. 1, and 505–8. Paar had accompanied Ferdinand to Rome in 1598, see Loserth, *FRA/58*, p. xliv. He was subsequently appointed ducal *Postmeister*, but was ill reputed among the population and his own troops on account of his misconduct, see the contemporary reports on the reform commissions in Gonobitz, Jan. 1600, *FRA/58*, 708–11, Cilli and Windischgraz, 21–5 Jan. 1600, ibid. 698–700.

[43] For the following account see the abbot of Admont's report as recorded by the commission's secretary, Adam Arnold, dated 22 Nov. 1599, *FRA/58*, 625–35, and Rosolenz, 'Gegenbericht', fos. 115–16.

church were confiscated, and a Catholic service was held in the presence of the miners' superiors, the *Radmeister*, who had connived at the rebels' activities. From the following inquisition, it emerged that the miners and labourers had elected a council to organize a strike for the readmission of the Protestant preachers. Some of the ringleaders, who had also been involved in the 1597 revolt, managed to escape. In their report, the commissioners suggested limiting the number of arrests and punishments so as to prevent a panic that could easily lead to the spread of the revolt.[44]

The commissioners' subsequent measures became the model for later inquisitions in Upper and Lower Styria. After the confiscation of the church and its restitution to a Catholic incumbent, the magistrates and the burghers were summoned. To punish their rebellion, the municipality's privileges were declared forfeit, thus reducing it to the legal status of a village. The burghers lost their civic rights, and the rural population had to submit the deeds of sale (*Kaufbriefe*) for their farms to indicate that they had forfeited their property. Moreover, the magistrates were deposed, and a *Stadtanwalt* was appointed as administrator. Those ringleaders who had failed to make good their escape were punished with a public whipping and were subsequently either banned from the duchy or sent to Graz for a long prison sentence. Gallows were erected in front of the town hall and the watchtower to 'commemorate' the rebellion. The houses were searched for heretical literature which was subsequently burnt under the gallows in a public ceremony.[45] Finally, 150 troops were billeted in the burghers' houses to ensure the community's future obedience to the ducal orders. Likewise, the burghers and the *Radmeister* of Eisenerz were charged with the costs of the commission, including pay and subsistence of the troops.[46]

The course of the subsequent reformation of the Enns valley was to prove the shrewdness of the commissioners' approach which combined a limited use of force, persuasion by the ecclesiastical commissioner, and symbolical punishments. As for the legal sanctions against the burghers and peasants, it was not in the archduke's interest to depopulate his municipalities or reduce them permanently to the status of villages. The commissioners were therefore instructed to demand for the time being merely an oath of obedience to the prince. It was stressed that this oath did not imply any religious obligation. Instead, it was hinted that the

44   Report of 22 Nov. 1599, *FRA/58*, 629–30.
45   Report of 22 Nov. 1599, ibid. 634.
46   Ibid. 634–5.

Protestants would later on be allowed to emigrate. As a result, there was no opposition.[47] For the time being, Ferdinand was content to accept this oath, together with the billeting of troops, as safeguards for the community's obedience. The formula of address used in later decrees reveals that Eisenerz, like all of the municipalities which were temporarily deprived of their privileges and liberties, was restored to its former status shortly afterwards.[48]

The strategy which had been used to subdue the rebels of Eisenerz proved equally successful in the case of the restive parishes and municipalities of the Enns valley. On 30 October 1599, the commission set out to punish and reform the communities of Aussee, Gröbming, Schladming, Wald, Neuhaus, Rottenmann, and Kalwang.[49] Previous reports such as Mayr's memorandum of 1594 suggested that resistance would be massive, so the number of troops was increased to 800. However, news of the commissions' activity in Eisenerz had already reached the miners of Aussee who had been involved in preparations for a strike. No attempt was made to oppose the commission's superior forces, and the population of Aussee submitted to the same orders as the rebels of Eisenerz, but the ringleaders had managed to escape before the arrival of the commission. In general, the mode of procedure in Aussee and the rest of the municipalities was the same as in Eisenerz. It should be added that Aussee was likewise punished for its rebellion by the billeting of troops, in this case fifty soldiers. The parishioners of Gröbming escaped the same treatment by submitting a written oath of obedience to the secular authorities and the Catholic parish priest.[50] Their preacher, the Flacian Christoph Schwaiger, had fled before the arrival of the commission. As previously mentioned, his installation in Mitterndorff had caused a conflict with the government and with the Lutheran church ministry in Graz in 1595. The support of the parishioners of Mitterndorff and Gröbming, and, it must be supposed, the approval of the Protestant Praunfalk family as local seigneurs, had nevertheless enabled him to remain in office until 1599. Schwaiger's farm was ransacked by the commission's troops, and his property and livestock

---

[47] Report of 22 Nov. 1599, ibid. 631.

[48] See also the estates' petition of 19 Jan. 1600 concerning the reformation in Eisenerz and the Enns valley, which mentions confiscations of property, but none of the legal sanctions, ibid. 678–89.

[49] The commissioners' report of 20 Nov. 1599 is printed ibid. 614–25.

[50] Ibid. 618–19.

were shared out to the soldiers and the new Catholic incumbent of Gröbming.[51] Traces of Flacianism were found among the population of the towns of Schladming and Rottenmann as well.[52] In Schladming, the miners' initial resistance to the commissioners was organized by Hans Stainberger, 'a wicked Flacian' ('ein böser Flacianer'), who had been banned from Salzburg for heresy.[53] As agent of one of the owners of the local mines, he belonged to the urban elite. In a letter to Rudolf II, he protested against his arrest and interrogation in Graz and referred to his privileges as Imperial councillor. Stainberger had become a conspicuous figure among the local Protestants, and the commissioners desribe him as 'as it were the hero of the whole community, and first among the ringleaders' ('gleichsamb der ganzen gemain abgott und haubträdlführer'). He was said to have instructed preachers in his heretical views, and the library which the commissioners consigned to the flames consisted of more than 3,000 books 'of all kinds of sects' ('von allerley secten').[54] Instead of creating a counterweight by increasing the number of Catholic clergy in the region, the commissioners entrusted the local parishioners to the care of the Catholic priest of Haus, a parish that was situated half a dozen miles away. This solution was probably devised with an eye to the relative geographic proximity of the parish, but was clearly insufficient to effect a recatholicization of the town, which would have demanded a sustained effort. A further mistake was made by focusing on the search for ringleaders. The subsequent survival of Protestantism in this region was to prove the strength of the Protestant communal and kinship networks which Hoffmann had characterized in his report to the estates in 1587.

An important and lasting success for the Catholic side was achieved by the eventual destruction of all public places of worship, which completed the dismantling of the Protestant school and church ministry. Thus, the commissions expelled the estates' preachers for the five districts of Styria (*Viertelprediger*), a measure that was in line with Ferdinand's abolition of the Protestant school and church ministry in September 1598. The destruction of churches, however, was a different matter. These had been

---

[51] Ibid. 618. The Upper Styrian noblemen Christoph Peter von Praunfalk and Hans Christoph von Stainach launched a futile complaint against the activity of the commissioners in the Enns valley, see p. 625.

[52] Rosolenz, 'Gegenbericht', fos. 131, 134–6.

[53] *FRA/58*, 620.

[54] Ibid. 620–1 and Rosolenz, 'Gegenbericht', fos. 132–3. Stainberger was released after his interrogation in Graz, perhaps as a result of his appeal to the Emperor.

built by members of the nobility on their own estates. Ferdinand never-theless considered the admission of the local population to these services a serious breach of the 'Pacification' which warranted the destruction of these places. As a result, the churches of the parish 'in der Au' and the building near Neuhaus in Upper Styria as well as the adjoining Protestant graveyards were destroyed by the commissions' troops.[55] Even more spectacular was the symbolical vengeance taken on the Hoffmann family. The heir of Hans Hoffmann, Ferdinand, had indicated his willingness to dismiss his preacher and abolish the entire Protestant *exercitium* in the parishes under his patronage if the church with the family vault near Rottenmann were spared. In spite of this, Herberstorff ordered the destruction of the church. Moreover, von Paar's soldiers desecrated the graves and despoiled the corpses. Two children of Hoffmann's peasants died in the fire which destroyed the building.[56]

Protestant graveyards and places of worship were systematically destroyed by the subsequent reformation commissions. They started with the reformation of the Lower Styrian parishes and municipalities (December 1599 to February 1600), proceeded from Graz to visit middle and Upper Styria (March–April 1600), and concluded with the reforma-tion of east Styria and, once more, some of the Upper Styrian parishes (May–July 1600). Their activity revealed the scope of the Protestant network which had developed since 1578. Churches and graveyards were destroyed in Windenau near Marburg (Herberstein), in Scharfenau near Cilli (Styrian estates), a graveyard in Arnfels (burghers of Arnfels), churches in Krottenhof near Leibnitz (Amman von Ammansegg) and in Schwanberg (Galler), a Lutheran 'chapel' in Peggau near Graz (burghers of Peggau), the church in Lind in Upper Styria (Jöbstl), the church and graveyard at Altenhof near Oberwölz in Upper Styria (burghers of Oberwölz), the church, school, and parsonage near Radkersburg (Karl von Herberstorff), the graveyard in Feldbach (burghers of Feldbach), and the Herberstorff church in Kahlsdorf, which had caused the spectacular confrontation between Otto von Herberstorff and the archduke in 1590. The Lutheran 'chapel' of the community of Eisenerz had been spared during the first visit in October 1599, but was blown up during the final

---

[55] Report of the commission, 20 Nov. 1599, *FRA/58*, 622. Rosolenz, 'Gegenbericht', fo. 134. For the destruction of graveyards and the expulsion of the *Viertelprediger* see the estates' complaint of 19 Jan. 1600, *FRA/58*, 678–89. The issue of crypto-Protestantism in this region is discussed more fully in Ch. 7 below.

[56] Account by Ferdinand Hoffmann (after Nov. 1599), *FRA/58*, 660–8.

round of reformation commissions in June 1600.[57] To these must be added the three churches mentioned before ('in der Au', near Neuhaus, and near Rottenmann in Upper Styria), so that a total of thirteen Lutheran churches or 'chapels' were destroyed, often together with the graveyard and adjoining buildings such as the parsonage.[58] Large numbers of troops were gathered to deter the local nobility and rural population from attempts to defend these places and buildings by force, for example the Herberstorff church at Kahlsdorf. More than 800 armed subjects were sent by the prelates of Vorau and Pöllau to assist the commissioners in the destruction of this building in June 1599.[59]

The reports on the destruction of the estates' church in Scharfenau near Cilli shed light on the attitude of the Slovenian rural population in Lower Styria, and are equally revealing of the strategy pursued by the commissioners.[60] Catholic and Protestant accounts describe the church as a spacious and singularly beautiful marble building of an estimated worth of 20,000 fl. Its material and artistic value led to a brief argument between the local Catholic burghers and the archdeacon (*Erzpriester*) of Lower Styria about the possibility of turning it into a Catholic church. However, the ducal instructions were unambivalent on this point, and the building had to be razed to the ground. While the burghers of Cilli were ordered by a ducal decree to take part in this work, there were several hundred Slovenian peasants who eagerly complied with the commissioners' orders, or even volunteered. Before the building in Scharfenau was blown up, it was ravaged by the Catholic peasants. Various acts of desecration were committed at the instigation of the archdeacon and a local government official. The archduke had granted the estates' petition to spare the nearby graveyard of the local nobility, but the peasants nevertheless took the chance to humiliate their heretical lords by destroying the family tombstones which were kept in the church.[61]

To explain the contrasting attitudes of the burghers and the rural population, it is important to recall the general economic situation of Lower Styria. As previously described, the spread of the reformation in Lower Styria had been strongly influenced by existing patterns of

[57] Rosolenz, 'Gegenbericht', fo. 252. Names in brackets refer to the owners of these places of worship.

[58] Ibid. 117–266.   [59] Ibid. 242–3.

[60] Eyewitness report of 1600, printed in *FRA/58*, 693–8. See also Rosolenz, 'Gegenbericht', fo. 197, who mentions the sum of 20,000 fl. and states that the local peasants rejoiced at the destruction of the church. For the estates' petition of 19 Jan. 1600 see *FRA/58*, 689–90.

[61] Report of 1600, *FRA/58*, 694.

economic, ethnic, and legal differences between the German or largely German-speaking municipalities and the Slovenian countryside. In the course of the sixteenth century, the material and legal situation of the peasants steadily deteriorated, and revolts like the Táhy uprising in 1572–3 occurred. By the end of the century, a constellation of interests and religious allegiances had emerged which was characterized by a considerable contrast between the majority of the Catholic Slovenian peasants on the one side and the Protestant nobility and larger municipalities on the other.

Ferdinand was able to take advantage of the ethnic and confessional contrast by employing Slovenian troops in Upper Styria, and this strategy proved no less successful during the subsequent campaign against the rebellious Lower Styrian towns. In December 1599, a commission under Bishop Martin Brenner of Seckau and Andreas von Herberstorff planned the subjection of Radkersburg. Rosolenz reports that the burghers threatened to oppose the commissioners by force and counted on help from their Hungarian neighbours and the Lutheran population of the border settlements.[62] The commissioners and troops, consisting of the ducal guards and 170 armed subjects of the bishop, therefore decided to march on Radkersburg during the night of 17–18 December 1599. They subsequently managed to keep the burghers in check until a reinforcement of 500 ducal troops and Slovenian subjects of Herberstorff arrived on 19 December. Most of the ringleaders like the town clerk Hans List were able to flee across the border to Hungary. Likewise, Rosolenz mentions the flight of preachers from the border markets of Burgau, Neudau, and Wörth into Hungarian territory. The Radkersburg preachers eventually found refuge on the Hungarian estates of the Lobkowitz family.[63]

Once the reinforcements had arrived, the burghers of Radkersburg were examined by the ecclesiastical commissioner, Bishop Martin Brenner, and were ordered to take an oath to observe from now on the religious obligations laid down by the reformation charter. The most refractory burghers were heavily fined, the arrested ringleaders were fined and banned. A date was fixed for those who wished to stay in the duchy and promised to convert. To ensure compliance, the commissioners gave a list of names to

---

[62] Rosolenz, 'Gegenbericht', fos. 138–9.

[63] For the Radkersburg commission from 17 Dec. 1599 to 5 Jan. 1600 see Rosolenz, 'Gegenbericht', fos. 138–65, and 'Verzeichnus der Rackelsburgischen Visitation', *FRA/58*, 652–4. The escape of the border parishes' preachers is described by Rosolenz, fos. 244–5. For the role of the Lobkowitz family see J. Loserth, 'Das Haus Lobkowitz und die Gegenreformation', *MVGDB* 43 (1905), 517–18.

the Catholic parish priest who was ordered to teach and examine these candidates before they were permitted to reconvert. The reformation was brought to a conclusion on 5 January 1600, after the public burning of heretical books on the previous day. As in Eisenerz, 150 soldiers were quartered on the town.[64]

A comparison of the commissioners' proceeding in Upper Styria and in Radkersburg raises the question whether uniform guidelines directed the operations of the commissions in 1599–1600. The fullest account of these campaigns, Rosolenz's chronicle, suggests an affirmative answer. Thus, the author states that reformation charters modelled on the general formula were issued for all Styrian municipalities.[65] According to his account, Ferdinand showed leniency towards commoners who promised to take the Catholic oath. They were frequently allowed to delay this formal act of conversion beyond the specified six terms for religious instruction by the parish priest.[66] On closer scrutiny, however, significant differences of approach can be discerned with regard to the proceeding in Upper Styria. It seems that reformation charters with binding religious obligations were not issued from the start, but from the Radkersburg commission in December 1599 onwards. The earlier commissions in Upper Styria demanded merely an oath of obedience to the archduke, and indicated that the local Protestants would be allowed to emigrate at a later stage. After the preliminary campaign had introduced Catholic incumbents and had begun to restore the material basis of the parishes, it remained for the second round of commissions to enforce obedience in religious matters. However, it will be seen that achievements in this respect were modest before the expulsion of the Protestant nobility in 1628.

Ferdinand's strategy becomes clearer if the subsequent reformation commissions until July 1600 are taken into account. Eisenerz, Schladming, and the smaller Protestant parishes of the Enns valley were subjected to so-called 'Super=Reformationen', meaning a second visit during which the full measure of religious obligations was announced.[67]

---

[64] Rosolenz, 'Gegenbericht', fos. 161–5 and 'Verzeichnus', *FRA/58*, 654. The substantial fines imposed on the burghers of Radkersburg amounted to *c*.12,000 fl., see the list in *FRA/58*, 656. Fines and contributions were used to finance the commissions, see Loserth, 'Reformationsordnungen', 118.

[65] Rosolenz, 'Gegenbericht', fo. 182.   [66] Ibid. 179–80.

[67] The commission returned to Eisenerz on 23 June 1600, ibid. 251–2, and operated in St Gallen and the district of Admont from 1 July onwards, ibid. 256–9. The commissioners then once more visited or summoned the parishioners of Schladming, Gröbming, Irdning, Aussee, Mitterndorff, Pürgg, Rottenmann, and of Hoffmann's parishes of Liezen,

Troops escorted the commissions and rounded up fugitives. The peasants and burghers were then summarily ordered to take the Catholic oath. 'Obstinate heretics' had to emigrate at short notice.

In general, these Counter-Reformation raids succeeded in keeping the number of emigrants very low. Thus, only eighteen overseers and joint owners of ironworks (*Radmeister*) and burghers of Eisenerz remained firm and received orders to emigrate. Of the 600 subjects whom the prelate of Admont summoned to his abbey on 2 July 1600, 307 confessed to Protestantism, but only four of them eventually refused to take the religious oath. The results for Schladming form an exception. About 700 burghers, miners, and peasants were summoned, and no less than 110 Protestant miners and peasants and twenty-three burghers, including two members of the town council, abided by their faith and were ordered to emigrate.[68] Still, it should be borne in mind that the number of actual emigrants was usually not identical with the number of those who received such orders. As previously mentioned, last-minute conversions were frequent, and temporary dispensations were granted to those emigrants whose knowledge and skills rendered them for the moment indispensable for the duchy's economy, e.g. the *Radmeister* of the ironworks in Upper Styria.

Predictably, the commissioners' tactics generated counter-strategies. On 7 July, the parishioners of Aussee, Mitterndorff, and the peasants of Pürgg were summoned to Irdning. All of these communities were notorious for their Lutheran or Flacian heresy. The parishioners of Irdning collectively confessed to Lutheranism. Nevertheless, all of the interrogated promised to receive the Catholic sacraments and took the prescribed oath with suspicious readiness.[69] By contrast, the burghers of Kapfenberg, a patrimonial market-town in Upper Styria which belonged to the Stubenberg family, collectively stated their determination to emigrate rather than abandon their Lutheran *exercitium*. The commissioners therefore limited their activity to the expulsion of the Protestant clergy, the burning of heretical literature, and the introduction of a Catholic parish priest. As will be shown, this did not mean that Kapfenberg was subsequently left to itself in religious matters.[70]

Oppenberg, and Lassing, whence they moved to the Mürz valley in Upper Styria. The attempted reform of Kapfenberg on 20 July 1600 and the subsequent reformation of Graz from 1 to 10 Aug. 1600 concluded the series of Styrian commissions, ibid. 260–75.

[68] Ibid. 251–2, 256–9, 260–2.   [69] Ibid. 179–80.

[70] Ibid. 270–1. The further reform campaign against Stubenberg's patrimonial markets is discussed below, this chapter.

In general, the reformation commissions were a complementary measure to support Ferdinand's legislation in the years 1598–1600. An attempt was made to restore the Catholic *exercitium* through the introduction of Catholic priests, although the number of appointments was in some cases insufficient. To restore the material basis of the Church, the commissioners took first steps for the recovery of the rights and property pertaining to the parish. Some of the tactics employed in 1599–1600, e.g. the manipulation of inner-urban conflicts and the gradual proceeding in Upper Styria, reflected the advice of Ferdinand's *Statthalter* Bishop Georg Stobaeus of Lavant and Georg Mayr's memorandum of 1594.[71]

The commissioners' approach to the special circumstances which prevailed in Upper Styria stands in marked contrast to the heavy-handed militant solution envisaged in 1587.[72] As previously stated, such a solution was not feasible in view of the demands of the Turkish War. It was also in the prince's interest to minimize the loss of subjects, especially where the urban elites, miners, and artisans were concerned, though in the last resort he was willing to suffer such losses for the sake of the true religion.

The scope of the Styrian campaign proves that it attempted to reach all of the parishes. From 14 October 1599 until the end of July 1600, more than 100 parishes were subjected to a reformation.[73] However, only the larger villages and municipalities were actually visited by commissions. The rural population of smaller and dispersed parishes was usually summoned to a more conveniently situated settlement. Such orders were also given to the burghers of towns at a distance of *c*.10 to 20 km from the temporary residence of the commission, e.g. in the case of the burghers of Vordernberg and Trofaiach, who were ordered to appear in Leoben in March 1600.[74] Occasionally, Rosolenz notes that parishes were reformed in passing.[75] By contrast, two or three weeks were spent on the reform of

[71] To complete the reformation in Upper Styria, Brenner and the government in Graz co-operated with Mayr as *Landpfleger* in the Enns valley, see the note to Brenner's memorandum of 2 July 1607, *FRA/60*, 440. For Stobaeus' memorandum of Sept. 1598 see above, Ch. 4.

[72] See the above discussion of Primus Wanzl's scheme.

[73] The maps by R. Höfer and K. Amon in R. Höfer, 'Bischof Martin Brenner als Gegenreformator und katholischer Reformer', in Dolinar et al., *Katholische Reform*, 26 and 31, show 111 parishes and municipalities (112 if Graz is included), but leave out some of the smaller parishes listed by Rosolenz, e.g. in the district of Admont, see Rosolenz, 'Gegenbericht', fo. 231.

[74] Rosolenz, 'Gegenbericht', fos. 176–8, 200, 212–14.

[75] Ibid. 130.

Protestant strongholds such as Eisenerz and Radkersburg, to be followed in some cases by a further visit for a 'Super=Reformation'.[76]

Ferdinand's effort was initially helped by the Emperor's policy in the neighbouring archduchy of Austria. From May 1597 onwards, Rudolf II followed up the suppression of the peasant revolt in Upper Austria with a thorough Catholic reform of the ducal municipalities (1597–1601).[77] In the following years, however, Ferdinand was forced to concentrate on the military issue, bound up with the Habsburg domestic conflict and its possible repercussions on Inner Austria. He nevertheless sought to maintain the pressure for confessional conformity, e.g. by the decree of 15 February 1603 which threatened capital punishment for the consumption of meat during Lent.[78]

To effect the implementation of his religious decrees, Ferdinand relied on the co-operation of the parish clergy whom the commissioners had ordered to supervise and instruct their parishioners and report on recalcitrants. Initially, however, there was little response.[79] Ferdinand generalized the commissioners' orders by a decree of 17 March 1604, which reminded the parish priests of their duty to report on the activity of Protestant preachers and the continuation of heretical practices among their parishioners. A charge of connivance or even complicity seems to be implied in the added warning that concealment of heretical practices would lead to the priest's deposition and further punishment.[80]

This threat had some effect, but it did not elicit a flood of denunciations. During the first decade of the seventeenth century, reports on heretical practices were sent from Pettau (1603, 1610), Mureck and Radkersburg (1604) in Lower Styria; Frauenberg near Liezen (1606), Kindberg (1606), Obdach (1607), Weißkirchen (1607), Murau (1607), and Pack (1607), all of these situated in Upper Styria.[81] To these reports should be added Bishop Brenner's memorandum of 1607, which focused on the problem of heresy in the district of Admont and in Georg von

---

[76] The first reformation of Eisenerz lasted from 14–15 Oct. to 3–4 Nov. 1599, ibid. 118–25, and *FRA/58*, 625–35, and the commissioners operated from 17 Dec. 1599 to 5 Jan. 1600 in Radkersburg, see 'Verzeichnus' in *FRA/58*, 652–4.

[77] Mecenseffy, *Protestantismus*, 96–108, Eder, *Glaubensspaltung*, 342–60.

[78] *FRA/60*, 267.

[79] The governmental records presented by Loserth mention only one denunciation by a Styrian parish priest for the years 1600–4. The document dates from June 1603 and refers to a Protestant school ('Winkelschule') in Pettau, see ibid. 284.

[80] *FRA/60*, 340–1.

[81] The documents are printed ibid. 284 and 590–1, 367, 412, 414–15, 433, 433–4, 464–5, 467.

Stubenberg's parishes of Mureck, Weiz, Kapfenberg, and Unzmarkt.[82] From 1608 to 1610, decrees were issued to enforce obedience in the Upper Styrian town of Leoben, whose burghers continued to frequent Protestant services abroad.[83]

The discovery of grave shortcomings of the Counter-Reformation after the campaign in the years 1598–1600 revealed that Ferdinand's scheme for a sweeping confessional 'purge' had been too ambitious. Its sheer geographical scope and the time allotted to the reform of each parish were in most cases at odds with the overall aim of a durable achievement. The use of coercion to bring about collective conversions had the same effect by encouraging evasive strategies and dissimulation. Moreover, the proximity of heretical neighbours in the north and east of the duchy militated against any attempt to deal with Inner Austrian Protestantism in isolation. Ferdinand's accession as Emperor and the outbreak of the Thirty Years War confronted him with the need to co-ordinate his religious policy in the different parts of the monarchy. Until then, however, he was reduced to appeals to Rudolf II and Matthias to limit this outside influence.

On the whole, the later evidence indicates that Protestantism was still widespread among the population of Upper and east Styria. Trade links and seasonal migration to the Protestant towns of the Empire arguably contributed to the survival of heresy in this region. The example of Leoben suggests that the revival of Protestantism in the archduchy of Austria from about 1608 onwards facilitated further adherence to Protestant practices in the neighbouring region of Styria. Similarly, it emerged that the proximity of Hungary accounted for most of the reported cases of heresy in the east and Lower Styrian municipalities. It will be noted that Pettau appeared twice in the reports. The results of subsequent investigations in 1610 and 1616 revealed that Protestantism still prevailed among the burghers of this town. By contrast, it seems that the repeated reforms of Radkersburg which had reorganized both its religious and economic life were slowly bearing fruit. The destruction of Herberstorff's church had deprived the burghers of important support,

---

[82] *FRA/60*, 437–9.

[83] Ibid. 475, 580. The geographical situation of Leoben suggests that they frequented Protestant services in Upper Austria, where Protestant life temporarily recovered after the death of the leading Counter-Reformer, Bishop Urban von Trenbach, in 1598. Protestant services were resumed in Linz in 1608. For the Protestant revival in the archduchy see Mecenseffy, *Protestantismus*, 140–8. In May 1610, a commission was sent to Leoben which fined or imprisoned thirty-five burghers, see *FRA/60*, 592–3.

and the reported cases of heresy refer to burghers who secretly resorted to the services of Hungarian preachers.[84] The resilience of Protestantism in Pettau is perhaps best explained by the town's economic links with Hungary. Pettau's share in the cattle trade between Hungary and Venice enabled the burghers to maintain close and legitimate contacts with the market towns of their co-religionists in the east.[85]

Ferdinand was fully aware of the problems posed by the geographical situation of the duchy. On 2 June 1627, he repeated his prohibition of attendance at foreign Protestant services and schools. The decree concluded by stating the duty of the Styrian parish clergy to keep an eye on anybody who crossed the border to Hungary, and this order was specifically directed to the parish priests of Radkersburg, Marburg, Cilli, and Sanntal in Lower Styria.[86] The importance of Styria's contacts with its heretical neighbours was also noted by the bishop of Seckau's reports in 1616 on the parishes of Upper Styria. He mentions several cases of obstinate heretics who confessed to attending Protestant services in Upper Austria.[87] In April 1617, Ferdinand issued a decree to the abbot of St Wolfgang in Upper Austria. It stated that the population of Schladming and the surrounding settlements frequently travelled to the archduchy under the pretext of a pilgrimage to the monastery. The abbot was ordered to demand the confessional slips from visitors and report on the results.[88] On the other hand, the case of Radkersburg demonstrates that urban Protestantism could be checked by a sustained effort of the secular and ecclesiastical authorities.[89]

---

[84] For the decline of Protestantism in Radkersburg see Winkelmann, 'Geschichte des Luthertums', *JGGPÖ* 58 (1937), 57–8. Cases testifying to the Hungarian link are related in *FRA/60*, 714, 716. For the commission in Pettau in 1610 and the parish priest's report in 1616 see ibid. 594–6, 670.

[85] For Pettau's (declining) importance in the transit trade see H. Valentinitsch, 'Die Bedeutung der steirischen Wirtschaft im Zeitalter des Absolutismus für Österreich', in *800 Jahre Steiermark*, 349. The importance of trade links for the survival of heresy was recognized by the commissioners in 1610, see *FRA/60*, 595.

[86] *FRA/60*, 783.

[87] Ducal decree to Bishop Jakob Eberlein of Seckau, 12 June 1616, and the examples quoted in Eberlein's reports for St Peter at Judenburg, 29 June 1616, Pöls, 1 July 1616, St Lorenzen at Scheifling, 5 July 1616, and Gröbming, 8 Feb. 1617, see DA, 'Religionsberichte Protestantismus', 1598–1730, XV-b-23.

[88] *FRA/60*, 717.

[89] It would seem that Radkersburg's trade with neighbouring Hungary and the presence of foreign merchants and cattle dealers at its fairs accounted for the persistence of residual Protestantism. On the other hand, the local Capuchins were able to turn these same circumstances to missionary uses by extending their efforts to both this itinerant group and the neighbouring population across the border. The attack on two Capuchins at Radkersburg in 1635 seems to have been an exception, see below, Ch. 7.

The Protestant nobility's influence constituted a further limiting factor which slowed down the pace of the Counter-Reformation without achieving a complete standstill or reversal. In his 'Religionis impedimentorum memoriale' of 1617, Bishop Jakob Eberlein of Seckau stated that the Lower Styrian Protestant lords, among them Stubenberg at his castle at Obermureck, continued to preach and read out Lutheran devotional literature to their subjects. He also claimed that they forced their subjects to attend the services of their Protestant preachers instead of Catholic mass at the local parish church. The occasional use of coercion seems likely if the regional confessional pattern and the peasants' share in the Counter-Reformation are taken into account.[90]

The important role of the nobility as patrons of a largely Protestant population was commented upon by the bishop of Seckau in 1607. Referring to the example of Georg von Stubenberg's patrimonial towns of Kapfenberg, Unzmarkt (both in Upper Styria), Mureck (Lower Styria), and Weiz (east Styria), he claimed that little or nothing had been achieved by the commissioners because there was no local authority to ensure the subsequent implementation of their decrees.[91] The latter task would have been incumbent upon the parish clergy and Stubenberg as the secular authority.[92] However, the Protestant Stubenberg and his like-minded bailiff (*Pfleger*) Remigius Ebner delayed a recatholicization and protected the Protestant subjects as long as possible. As previously mentioned, the first attempt to reform Kapfenberg on 20 July 1600 foundered on the collective opposition of the community, but it was Stubenberg's intercession which prevented immediate sanctions.[93] In March 1600, a commission visited Mureck and introduced a Catholic priest. In this case, Ebner surrendered the keys to the church and in general co-operated with the commissioners. He succeeded in persuading them that no special reform of the population was necessary, and they limited their activity to the confiscation and ceremonial burning of

[90] DA, 'Religionsberichte Protestantismus', 1598–1730', XV-b-23.

[91] *FRA/60*, 438.

[92] From 1597 onwards, Georg 'der Ältere' von Stubenberg zu Kapfenberg was the head of the House of Stubenberg, by far the wealthiest family in Styria. The family possessed estates in Bohemia and in 1610 Archduke Matthias pledged the *Herrschaft* and *Burggrafschaft* Steyr in Upper Austria to Georg von Stubenberg for a sum of 130,000 or 140,000 fl. Georg led the legation to Prague in 1600–1, and his correspondence proves him an important political figure who actively participated in the estates' affairs, see Loserth, *Stubenberg*, 218–36, and Stubenberg's correspondence in STMLA, 'Stubenberg-Archiv', Sch. 95, H. 587, Sch. 96, H. 588–90. For Matthias's *Pfandbrief* of 1610 see ibid., Sch. 11, H. 76.

[93] This emerges from Ebner's letter to Stubenberg, dated 3 Sept. 1603, see *FRA/60*, 37.

heretical books. Ebner proudly reported that not a single peasant or burgher had been examined. In fact, the commissioners had not concerned themselves with the religious issue at all ('[der] glaubens sach wenigist gedacht'). Likewise, Stubenberg remained the *Vogt* of the urban parish. By way of return, the commissioners demanded a promise that Stubenberg would protect the new incumbent, but Ebner indirectly declined any responsibility for the priest's safety.[94] Unsurprisingly, then, Brenner's memorandum of 1607 stated that Stubenberg's municipalities had become a refuge for heretics among the surrounding population.[95]

Among the reported cases, Kapfenberg's open opposition stands out. Ferdinand had no intention of depopulating the town by accepting the burghers' offer of collective emigration. He effectively barred this way by demanding the 'tenth penny' from all foreign property and capital administered by the local merchants on behalf of their partners in the Empire ('Gegenhändler').[96] Before Stubenberg resumed his legation to Prague in May 1601, he received a decree by which Ferdinand cancelled his previous concession for Stubenberg's preacher in Kapfenberg because he had encroached upon the office of the Catholic parish priest.[97] Confronted with Ferdinand's harsh terms for their emigration, the majority of burghers backed down from their decision, only to change their mind once more when ordered to take a Catholic oath.[98] A commission under the recently installed Catholic parish priest of Mureck, Aligius Grotta, began to examine the burghers of Kapfenberg and the local rural population in December 1603. Stubenberg was repeatedly ordered to assist and to summon his subjects before the commission, but he failed to comply. The commissioners' list of Protestants who were ordered to emigrate within a term of eight days is revealing. Seventeen of the twenty-seven peasants listed by name did not appear before the commission. Of the Protestant burghers eleven, including one magistrate, abided by their earlier decision but a further twelve burghers evaded the interrogations.[99]

---

[94] 'dan ich nit anderst vertrösten noch zuesagen künnen (dann) allain das er hoffentlich wie andere Pfaff da herumb sicher seyn werde.' Ebner's report to Stubenberg, 31 Mar. 1600, STMLA, 'Stubenberg-Archiv', Sch. 95, H. 587.   [95] *FRA/60*, 438.

[96] Petition of the burghers of Kapfenberg to Georg von Stubenberg, n.d. [prior to Feb. 1601], STMLA, 'Stubenberg-Archiv', Sch. 95, H. 587.

[97] Archduke Ferdinand to Stubenberg, 14 Feb. 1601, ibid., Sch. 95, H. 587. For the resumption of the Prague mission see the letter by the Styrian *Verordnete* to Stubenberg, 10 May 1601, ibid.

[98] This emerges from Ferdinand's decree of 18 Sept. 1603, ibid.

[99] For the repeated orders to Stubenberg see the decree of 18 Sept. 1603 and the commissioners' letters of 3, 9, and 10 Dec. 1603. The report of the commission is dated 10 Dec. 1603, ibid.

As a result of Stubenberg's delaying tactics, the reformation of Kapfenberg dragged on for another two decades.[100] In 1622, Ferdinand II instituted a commission, consisting of the parish priest of Bruck, Clemens Collin von Sternstein, and the ducal councillor Albinus Fabritius, to punish and reform the Protestant communities of Bruck and Kapfenberg. However, on 26 April, the commissioners informed the government that Stubenberg was unwilling to punish offenders against the prohibition of trade and work on Sundays. Likewise, he refused to force his subjects to appear before the commission. This example encouraged the burghers of Bruck, who declared that they would not obey the commissioners' orders as long as Kapfenberg remained unreformed. On 29 April 1622, Ferdinand ordered Stubenberg to stop obstructing the commissioners' work. Under the same date, he instructed the latter to continue their reform in Bruck and to institute similar proceedings in Kapfenberg.[101] Stubenberg's protests against the infringement of his jurisdictional authority over Kapfenberg further delayed the transfer from Bruck, and it was not before January 1623 that the commissioners were able to begin their inquisition in Kapfenberg.[102]

The evidence for Mureck is fragmentary, but the final document, dated 17 April 1626, suggests that the reform of this town was a similarly long-drawn-out process in spite of the installation of a Catholic parish priest. The burghers had only just received a reformation charter, and turned to Stubenberg for directions concerning their future behaviour. However, he refrained from commenting on the religious decrees of the charter, and the tone of his reply suggests that he had resigned himself to the inevitable.[103]

---

[100] The futility of the government's efforts is commented on in the correspondence between Stubenberg and his bailiff in Kapfenberg, Leonhard Niderl, in the years 1609–12. In his letter of 19 Feb. 1611, Stubenberg speaks mockingly of 'deformatio(n)s' commissioners, ibid.

[101] For the commissioners' report, 26 Apr. 1622, and copies of the letter from the *Hofkammer* to Stubenberg and the ducal decree, both dated 29 Apr. 1622, see STMLA, 'Meillerakten', Sch. XX-a-f. The original of the latter two documents can be found in STMLA, 'Stubenberg-Archiv', Sch. 96, H. 588.

[102] The content of Stubenberg's protests emerges from the ducal decree of 23 July 1622, which orders the summoning of his subjects. On 30 September 1622, Stubenberg informs his bailiff in Kapfenberg, 'that there is still no end to the [business of the] popish priests in Bruck' ('daß es mit den Pfaffen zu Brugg noch khein endt hat') and that he had been told to summon his subjects to the local parsonage. On 23 Jan. 1623, the commissioners notified Stubenberg that his subjects were to assemble there on 29 Jan., STMLA, 'Stubenberg-Archiv', Sch. 96, H. 588.

[103] Stubenberg to his market town Mureck, 17 Apr. 1626, STMLA, 'La. Arch. Religion und Kirche', Sch. 29. Georg von Stubenberg emigrated in July 1629 to Regensburg, see Loserth, *Stubenberg*, 236.

The reform of Stubenberg's towns proves that eminent members of the nobility exerted considerable influence on the course of the Counter-Reformation. However, it should be noted that Stubenberg's position was exceptional in many respects. He was not only the scion of the most ancient and wealthiest noble family in Styria, but also the son of Karl II's closest confidant, Wolf von Stubenberg, who, though himself a Protestant, had been a loyal servant and a mediator between the prince and the estates.[104] As a result of this relation, Georg became the protégé of Karl II's widow, Archduchess Maria of Bavaria.[105] Perhaps more important than all these assets was the fact that Ferdinand needed his co-operation for the organization of the border defences in the north and east.[106] In spite of such impressive safeguards, he was briefly accused of high treason as a result of his disobedience in religious matters. In 1598, Ferdinand had issued strict orders for the expulsion of Stubenberg's preacher who had administered to the parishioners of St Lorenzen in the Mürz valley in Upper Styria. Ferdinand assured Stubenberg of his favour in temporal matters, but warned him 'that we will by no means condone disobedience in matters affecting the honour of God and his holy Catholic religion'.[107] When Stubenberg failed to heed this warning, the archduke proved that this had not been a vain threat. On 8 June 1602, the ducal *Kammerprokurator* Christoph Prättinger brought a charge of high treason against Stubenberg for granting refuge to several burghers of Mureck who had been banned for heresy. Worse even, he had brought the outlawed preceptor of the Windischgrätzes, Paul Odontius, to administer the sacraments to these refugees. Prättinger urged exemplary punishment for Stubenberg's 'crimes'. Under the same date, Ferdinand ordered the institution of legal proceedings.[108] However, Archduchess Maria of Bavaria and Count George Zrinyi interceded for Stubenberg, and proceedings were stopped in the same month. Stubenberg was sentenced to the payment of 5,000 fl., subsequently reduced to 3,000 fl., and was restored to

---

[104] Loserth, *Stubenberg*, 205–9.

[105] Her intercession is mentioned in Ferdinand's decree of 30 June 1602, STMLA, 'Stubenberg-Archiv', Sch. 95, H. 587.

[106] Cf. Ferdinand's letter of 2 June 1619. Ferdinand informs Stubenberg that the confederates' army under Count Thurn had crossed the Danube at Fischamend and was now advancing on Vienna. Stubenberg is instructed to barricade the routes to the north and order a peasant levy to take position. On 27 June 1620, Stubenberg confirmed that he had received Ferdinand's orders for a meeting to deliberate on the defence of the eastern border, ibid., Sch. 96, H. 588.

[107] 'Das wir in dergleichen Gottes ehr und sein heillige Catholische Religion antreffenden fällen den Ungehorsamb mit nichten gedulden khünen.' Decree of 29 Dec. 1598, ibid., Sch. 95, H. 586.

[108] Ibid., Sch. 95, H. 587. A paraphrase of Prättinger's letter is printed in *FRA/60*, 238–9.

favour.[109] The proceedings against Stubenberg are reminiscent of the Hoffmann case in 1587. This time, however, the charge was not part of a plot to force the archduke's hand, but expressed the prince's determination to punish both the spiritual offence and the challenge to his authority. In 1613, Ferdinand resumed his efforts to further and control the progress of the Counter-Reformation. On 18 April 1613, the parish priests and vicars of Inner Austria were ordered to send lists of all those parishioners who had failed to confess and receive the sacrament of communion during the past Easter week. When Bishop Jakob of Seckau embarked on a visitation of the Salzburg parishes of Styria in 1616, Ferdinand urged him to enquire into the state of religion in this region. The parish priests should provide the bishop with the names of all local heretics, so that he could examine and instruct them. Eberlein should order the 'Halsstarrige' to pay the tenth penny and emigrate, and should send a separate account to the archduke.[110] The bishop's reports confirm the previously quoted evidence for the essentially unchanged situation in Upper Styria. Lists of heretics are extant for Murau, Unzmarkt, Pusterwald, Scheifling (more than forty), Pöls, Oberwölz, Niederwölz, St Peter at Judenburg, and Gröbming. It emerges that only very few of the recorded heretics had fulfilled their religious obligations more than once after the reform of 1599–1600. The vast majority had never complied with the commissioners' orders.

As in 1599–1600, a number of the peasants and burghers who were summoned resorted to evasive strategies, for example the parishioners of Scheifling. Twelve of them are listed as absent. The brewer Caspar Kaniz and his wife had fled to Murau, 'Mertt am Platz' was in Austria, and the grocer at the market had disappeared during Lent, presumably to evade his Easter duties.[111] Similar to Stubenberg's town of Mureck in Lower

---

[109] Decree of 30 June 1602. The archduchess's intervention is mentioned in this letter. STMLA, 'Stubenberg-Archiv', Sch. 95, H. 587. Ibid. a copy of Zrinyi's petition, dated 28 June 1602. Stubenberg's sisters had married into the families of Zrinyi and Erdödy, see Loserth, *Stubenberg*, 218.

[110] 'Separate', that is, from the general record which Eberlein had to send to the archbishop of Salzburg. Decrees of 18 Apr. and 12 June 1616, DA, 'Religionsberichte Protestantismus', 1598–1730, XV-b-23. The archduke's request for confidential reports was not compatible with Eberlein's obligations towards Salzburg. He solved the problem by delegating the interrogations to the parish clergy, and reported the findings from July to Oct. 1616 to Graz. The official visitation record for Salzburg begins with a report for 19 Oct. 1617.

[111] For the concept of Eberlein's summary account, dated Oct. 1616, and the separate reports for the above parishes from 29 June 1616 onwards see DA, 'Religionsberichte Protestantismus', 1598–1730, XV-b-23.

Styria, Murau offered at least temporary refuge to heretics. The Upper Styrian town was subject to the jurisdiction of Carl von Teuffenbach. In April 1603, a reform commission had ordered the magistrates to enforce the decrees concerning the conversion or emigration of those burghers who still eluded the commission and failed to comply with their religious obligations. However, Teuffenbach accepted the fugitives as settlers on his estates, and tried to pass them off as Catholic subjects. Teuffenbach was fined heavily for this attempt, but the above evidence proves that he continued to tolerate refugees in his town.[112]

In the smaller, scattered settlements of the mountainous region of the duchy, it was even easier to evade the authorities. Throughout Styria, the population of most villages was subject to several seigneurs (*Grundherren*). Moreover, the scope of seigneurial rights rendered it impossible for the local clergy to establish control over domestic religious practices.[113] Although he might refer to the overriding authority of a ducal or governmental order, the parish priest in practice needed the co-operation of the respective seigneurs and their officials to punish offenders and to coerce fugitives. The above list of Protestants in Scheifling illustrates the problem. The lord or estate owner (*Herrschaft*) is not always mentioned, but at least six *Grundherren* exercised seigneurial rights over the forty or so recorded heretics. Five of these seigneurs belonged to the Protestant nobility.[114]

Nor was the latter's influence the only source of difficulties in the parishes. The slow progress of clerical reform likewise caused problems. As previously mentioned, there were comparatively few reports from the

---

[112] Decree of the reformation commissioners for Murau, 15 Apr. 1603, and copy of the Catholic burgher oath. Ducal decrees for Carl von Teuffenbach, 28 May and 14 July 1603. The market town was eventually reformed by the Catholic Georg von Schwarzenberg, who strictly controlled the burghers' observance of the religious decrees, cf. his instructions for the magistrates, dated 11 June 1631. All documents from STMLA, 'Archiv Murau', Sch. 131, H. 272.

[113] In Styria, there were practically no 'geschlossene Herrschaften', i.e. village communities which were subject to a single seigneur. During the 18th century, probably not more than one-tenth of all taxable communities belonged in this category. The punishment of criminal offences which were committed in the house of his subjects was reserved to the respective seigneur, see A. A. Klein, 'Landgemeinde und Dorfherrschaft in Steiermark', *ZHVST* 46 (1955), 85, 89.

[114] Report for Scheifling, 5 July 1616, DA, 'Religionsberichte Protestantismus', 1598–1730, XV-b-23. The authorities mentioned are Georg von Stubenberg, the parish priest of St Lorenzen ob Scheifling, Gottfried von Stadl, Adam and Anna von Neuhaus, the Styrian estates, and 'Frau Welzerin im Mürztal', probably meaning Anna Amalia Weltzer who emigrated in 1629, see Loserth's excerpt from Sötzinger's list of emigrants, *FRA/60*, 859.

parish clergy during the first decade of the seventeenth century. Ferdinand's decrees of 17 March 1604 and 18 April 1613 had increased the pressure on them. The earlier decree had even implied a charge of collusion. This suspicion was not unfounded, as the evidence for Eisenerz suggests. In 1607, the Catholic parish priest who had been installed by the commissioners in November 1599 died. In his will, he ordered that the heretical books in his library should be destroyed after his death. Furthermore, he made provision for his wife and three daughters, claiming that he had been wedded by the chaplain of the prelate of Admont. He appended a dispensation which he had recently obtained to secure legitimate status for his family.[115] His case sheds light on the collusion among members of the 'unreformed' lower clergy, while the episcopal dispensation might have been granted to hush up the scandal and prevent unrest among the parishioners. In any case, the evidence shows that concubinage and heresy or the teaching of a 'mixed doctrine' had not been stopped by the reformation of 1599–1600.[116]

A report on the state of religion in Carinthia in 1623 blamed the lack of education and the immoral conduct of the Catholic parish clergy for the futility of the commissioners' efforts.[117] Again, there was comparable evidence from Styria to indicate similar shortcomings.[118] The issue was taken up by Ferdinand II in connection with his preparations for a general reformation. On 14 May 1626, he sent a decree to the bishops and archdeacons of Inner Austria to inform them that he had deputed specially instructed commissioners for every municipality. He repeated his earlier decrees of 1598 and 1625 concerning the parish clergy's obligation to recover alienated ecclesiastical property, and reminded the prelates of their responsibility for the spiritual and material welfare of the Church. Above all, he urged the bishops to take measures for the reform

[115] The will is summarized in *FRA/60*, 441.

[116] A study for the Lower Austrian part of the archduchy ('Unter der Enns') points to the uneven progress of Catholic reform in the hereditary lands. The author thus states that in the 1590s, a new generation of parish clergy who had been educated by the Jesuits was taking over in Lower Austria, see F. Schragl, *Glaubensspaltung in Niederösterreich* (Vienna, 1973), 153. However, it should be borne in mind that the dynastic conflict after 1606 was to encourage a resurgence of Protestantism; likewise, Lower Austria became briefly involved in the Bohemian rebellion, see above, Ch. 4.

[117] Memorandum by an anonymous author, *FRA/60*, 746–7. See also the pessimistic assessment of the Counter-Reformation in Carinthia by the *Landeshauptmann* of this duchy, Christoph David Urschenbeck, in 1616, ibid. 674–82, 686–93.

[118] Cf. the complaint of the parishioners of Kindberg, dated 3 Mar. 1607. They countered the parish priest's charge of heresy with a complaint about his immoral conduct and physical assaults on parishioners, ibid. 428–31. The charge was essentially confirmed by the government commissioners, see the note by Loserth, ibid. 431.

of the parish clergy, claiming that the scandalous life of the majority of them was causing their parishioners to apostatize from the Catholic faith.[119]

Special commissions continued to operate until March 1628, when Ferdinand II created an Inner Austrian reformation commission to co-ordinate and supervise the envisaged general reform. Christoph Moritz von Herberstein, Hans Ferdinand von Khuenburg, and the lawyers Karl Kuglmann and Eitl Johann Ziglmüller were appointed commissioners at the suggestion of the Inner Austrian government. No member of the clergy was added, a decision which confirmed the commission's character as a government council. Ferdinand nevertheless arranged for close co-ordination with the clergy. Thus, he sent detailed instructions for a joint proceeding to the bishop of Seckau and all ecclesiastical authorities in Styria. The bishop was to begin the reformation with an examination of his diocesan clergy. If he encountered resistance, he was to ask the government for support. Secondly, he should supply the local commissioners with lists of obstinate heretics and exiles who had stealthily returned so that the officials could arrange for their exemplary punishment. The bishop was exhorted to give particular attention to the religious instruction of repentant heretics. Confessional slips were to be sent to the government as evidence of success. Thirdly, the local commissioners were ordered to examine the schoolteachers and expel suspects. New candidates needed the approval of the bishop, except for the teachers of Graz, who would henceforth be examined by the local Jesuits. The next point concerns the supervision of the observance of general religious regulations concerning Lenten fare, prohibition of work on Sundays and feast-days, etc. This was followed by instructions regarding the recovery and administration of ecclesiastical property and pious foundations. Probably with an eye to further support for the Jesuits' institutions, the bishop was asked to report specifically on donations and scholarships for indigent students. The instructions concluded by demanding that the diocesan clergy send annual lists of those parishioners who had failed to perform their religious duties at Easter.[120]

The decree concerning the recently ennobled persons was issued on 6 May 1628, and on 15 May a reformation charter for all Styrian towns was

---

[119] Copy for the bishop of Seckau in DA, 'Religionsberichte Protestantismus', 1598–1730, XV-b-23.

[120] Ferdinand II to Bishop Jakob of Seckau, 27 Mar. 1628, DA, 'Religionsberichte Protestantismus', 1598–1730, XV-b-23. Similar instructions were sent to all ecclesiastical authorities in Styria.

proclaimed which repeated and generalized the previous charters.[121] Eventually, on 1 August 1628, a general decree (*Generalmandat*) for the Protestant nobility of Inner Austria was issued. Further orders concerning the present reformation, dated 27 August 1628, were probably motivated by fears of a large-scale emigration. Ferdinand II urged the bishop of Seckau and his subordinate clergy to spare no effort to further the religious instruction of the population.[122]

Building on the experience of Karl II's urban campaign in the 1580s, Ferdinand resumed the battle against urban and rural Protestantism. Administrative reforms and the systematic use of reformation commissions were instrumental in transmitting the aims of his religious policy. Conversely, the policy of recatholicization provided the impetus for reforms of the central and local government machinery which strengthened the power of the prince, e.g. the appointment of Catholic town judges and permanent magistrates, which completed the subjection of the municipal corporations. At the centre, far-reaching powers of control over the progress of the Counter-Reformation were given to the new reformation council (created in 1628) which was composed exclusively of government officials.

Ferdinand's achievement by this date was nevertheless incomplete. Between 1598 and 1628, he was able to destroy the Protestant school and church ministry that was indispensable for the survival of Protestantism as a competing faith. By contrast, he was unable to check foreign heretical influences which resulted from the geographical position and economic links of his lands. The final decrees of 1628 concluded the political Counter-Reformation by imposing a legal ban on Protestantism. This policy succeeded in forcing the duchies' elite into submission, but the progress of spiritual reconquest had only just begun. The evidence for the state of religion at local level and the conduct of some of the parish clergy revealed that substantial efforts would have to be made to achieve a genuine recatholicization of the Emperor's Inner Austrian dominions.

---

[121] *FRA/60*, 804–5, 806–9.
[122] Decree of 27 Aug. 1628, DA, 'Religionsberichte Protestantismus', 1598–1730, XV-b-23. The decree of 1 Aug. 1628 is printed in *FRA/60*, 814–21.

6

Reform, Mission, and Propaganda
(1580–1630)

As previously demonstrated, the Counter-Reforming initiative between 1580 and 1600 had rested first with the Catholic alliance shaped in 1579 and a nucleus of clerical reformers centred on the court in Graz. With the accession of Ferdinand in 1596, the Catholic court became the headquarters from which the Counter-Reformation was devised and directed under the leadership of a resolute prince who set himself successfully to the task of recovering control of the government apparatus, with the temporary exception of the War Council. The roving reformation commissions that had operated as ad hoc inquisitions in the reign of Karl II were turned into the regular device of a systematic policy. In the final stages of the Counter-Reformation, their activity was co-ordinated and directed by a new executive council, the government board of the Inner Austrian reform commission acting on the orders of the then Emperor Ferdinand II. If the prince's Counter-Reformation had thus cleared the political stage and prepared the ground for a recatholicization at local level, both clerical and secular reformers were agreed on the crucial importance of a sustained missionary and self-reforming effort of the clergy for the completion of this work.

As shown earlier, the related issues of ecclesiastical reform and the combat of heresy in the church province of Salzburg, of which Styria formed part, had since the beginning of the Protestant Reformation been the subject of intermittent and occasionally acrimonious debate between the secular and clerical authorities involved.[1] For both political and administrative reasons, the progress of ecclesiastical reforms in the suffragan bishoprics of Inner Austria remained closely linked to developments in the archdiocese of Salzburg. Of particular relevance was the fact that the vast majority of Styrian parishes was directly subject to the archbishop until Bishop Martin Brenner of Seckau was appointed vicar general for the Salzburg district of Styria in 1591.[2] The fate of ecclesiastical reform in the

---

[1] See above, Ch. 2.   [2] Schuster, *Martin Brenner*, 276–90.

duchy was therefore largely dependent on the policy and attitude adopted by the archbishop. Since the 1520s, the issue of clerical reform had been recognized as crucial for the combating of heresy and had figured on the agenda of successive archbishops from the accession of Matthäus Lang onwards.[3] However, the permanent contest of power between the archbishop and the cathedral chapter quickly stunted these initiatives. The conflict reached a climax during the reign of Archbishop Wolf Dietrich von Raittenau (1587–1612), who temporarily succeeded in subjecting the canons to his authority by the so-called 'Statuta Perpetua' of 1605–6. During a spell of reform activity until about 1600 he effected a recatholicization of his residence city of Salzburg, but his attempt to introduce the Jesuits to further the education of clerics foundered on the opposition of the local Benedictines. In the following years, the reform initiative petered out when Wolf Dietrich began to indulge in the worldly pursuits and lifestyle of a secular prince. From the beginning, he refused to tackle the problem of clerical concubinage which had been a major concern of the synods of 1549 and 1569. Quite to the contrary, the archbishop himself indulged this failing, and continued to live with his concubine Salome Alt, who bore him fifteen children. His political adventures, above all the attempt to annex the territory of the convent and chapter (*Fürstpropstei*) of Berchtesgaden, eventually provoked the military intervention of Bavaria in 1611, and in the following year, Wolf Dietrich was deposed and imprisoned for the rest of his life.

His decision to empower the bishop of Seckau as vicar general in 1591 was, however, an important administrative innovation which facilitated the implementation of reforms at the local level. As the archbishop's representative, the bishop exerted full authority and jurisdiction in spiritual matters. This enhancement of power proved a valuable tool in the hands of a reform-minded suffragan bishop like Martin Brenner of Seckau and his equally zealous successor, his nephew Bishop Jakob Eberlein. Co-operation between Salzburg and Seckau became closer under Archbishop Markus Sittich, Count Hohenembs (1612–19), who concentrated his efforts on the issue of clerical reform.[4] Both he and his successor Paris Lodron (1619–53) decided to postpone a general expulsion of the Protestant salt miners and peasants because they feared the outbreak of rural unrest on the scale of the peasant uprisings in neighbouring Austria

---

[3] See above, Ch. 2, last section. For the following see F. Ortner, *Reformation, Katholische Reform und Gegenreformation im Erzstift Salzburg* (Salzburg, 1981), esp. 102–9, and H. Widmann, *Geschichte Salzburgs*, vol. iii (Gotha, 1914), 150–251.

[4] See Loserth, 'Gegenreformation in Salzburg', 676–96.

in 1594–7 and 1626. Instead, they concentrated on preserving the precarious political neutrality of Salzburg, beginning with the refusal to join the Catholic League in 1609 in spite of considerable pressure from the Catholic princes of the Empire, especially from Bavaria.[5]

On the whole, relations between the archbishop and the archduke of Inner Austria were good. Salzburg tolerated the successive appointment of five Inner Austrian suffragan bishops as ducal governors (*Statthalter*) in the period 1569 to 1630.[6] Similarly, Bishop Brenner of Seckau was allowed to act as Imperial and archducal commissioner in Tyrol (1604–5) and Passau (1605).[7] There was nevertheless friction over two issues, namely the right of disposition over ecclesiastical property and the exertion of jurisdictional power by a foreign ecclesiastical authority. The concordats of 1583 and 1592 settled similar disputes between the Wittelsbach dynasty and Salzburg and between the Emperor and Passau. The frequency of such conflicts between Catholic princes and prelates indicated that the medieval contest for power between the ecclesiastical and the secular authorities had multiplied rather than diminished as a result of the fragmentation of secular power. Shortly after the Munich conference, the recently appointed nuncio Malaspina had to mediate between the archbishop of Salzburg and Archduke Karl II. In December 1580, he received a complaint from Salzburg listing a number of encroachments on archiepiscopal rights. According to this statement, Karl II had usurped control over the *temporalia* of benefices, and attempted to limit the archbishop's authority to the supervision of the spiritual administration of these offices. It was also claimed that he prevented the suffragan bishops from inquiring into the income and revenues of the benefices. Furthermore, it was urged that the archduke should refrain from granting licences to the lower clergy for the sale of church property, and should cease to mortgage ecclesiastical property for his current needs.[8]

As previously described, Karl II's pressing financial needs forced him to resort to expedients which were reminiscent of Ferdinand I's policy, for example, when Karl levied a quinquennial contribution on ecclesiastical

[5] Ortner, *Salzburg*, 110–29.

[6] Urban von Österreich, bp. of Gurk (governor in 1569–73), Christoph Andreas von Spaur, bp. of Gurk (governor in 1581–5), Georg Stobaeus von Palmburg, bp. of Lavant (governor in 1596–1609), Johann Jakob von Lamberg, bp. of Gurk (governor in 1611–14), Leonhard Goetz, bp. of Lavant (governor in 1621–30), see Thiel, 'Zentralverwaltung', I, 205.

[7] Schuster, *Martin Brenner*, 555 nn. 3 and 4.

[8] Salzburg commissioners to Malaspina, 17 Dec. 1580, *Nb i*, 155–7.

property in 1574. Such encroachments on the material basis of the Church ran counter to the objectives of his religious policy, but it was not before the beginning of Archduke Ferdinand's reign that a determined effort was made to restore and preserve ecclesiastical property.[9]

The remaining points concerned infringements of jurisdictional rights, such as the summoning of clerics before secular courts without express permission of their superiors. Like the complaints regarding ecclesiastical property rights, this latter grievance had been voiced previously at the provincial synods of 1549 and 1569, where it had been rejected by the Lower Austrian government.[10] A further point was the archduke's claim not only to choose and install incumbents in those parishes over which he claimed temporal wardship (*ius advocatiae*), but also to exert complete control and the right of disposition over the parishes' property.[11] On the surface, Karl II's reply, dated 31 December 1580, was essentially a repetition of the position adopted by the Austrian side at the provincial synod of 1549. Thus, the complaints are either dismissed as untrue, or else rejected as an unwarranted attack on rights which the Austrian princes had exerted 'from time immemorial' such as the right of investiture with the *temporalia*.[12] There was nevertheless a significant modification of the earlier argument. No mention is made of the ancient claim that church property was demesne (*Kammergut*) and therefore at the prince's disposal. By contrast, it is now argued that ecclesiastical property had never been sold or mortgaged to serve the financial needs of the prince, but exclusively for the benefit of the Church, more precisely for the defence of Christendom against the Turks.[13]

In spite of the archduke's insistence on his rights of control over the *temporalia*, the omission of the more radical statements of 1549 and 1569 could be seen as a conciliatory gesture which indicated a modification of the ducal position on this issue. It seems likely that this change resulted from the influence of Malaspina or Karl II's Jesuit confessor, P. Heinrich Blyssem. In a letter of 18 March 1581 to the General of the Society, Blyssem reported on the conflict between the archduke and the ecclesiastical authorities, 'quae res bonum religionis statum vel successum multum

---

[9] Loserth, *Kirchengut*, 153–61.

[10] Hübner, 'Provinzialsynoden', 110–12, 122–3, and Loserth, 'Salzburger Provinzialsynode', 158–9, 167–8, and Ferdinand I's reply on 10 May 1549, which led to a standstill in negotiations over the reform issue. For the rejection of the clerical *gravamina* by the Lower Austrian government, who confirmed Ferdinand's position that ecclesiastical property was *Kammergut*, see ibid. 175–195.   [11] *Nb i*, 157.

[12] The reply is reprinted in ibid. 166–8.   [13] Ibid. 167.

impedivit'. Now, however, the archduke had been persuaded to seek a complete reconciliation with the archbishop and a settlement of the contentious issues on equitable terms for the good of the Church. Both sides had appointed commissioners to work out this agreement, and the nuncio was to act as mediator. Malaspina was empowered to leave the final decision to the pope as supreme judge on earth.[14] It is unlikely that this concession was approved by Rudolf II, and no formal concordat between Salzburg and Graz was concluded. Nevertheless, some kind of provisional agreement must have been reached as the sources for the following years record no disputed cases involving the contentious issues.

By contrast, no satisfactory solution was found to regulate the procedure of archiepiscopal visitations in the ducal lands.[15] In the end, these visitations were conducted jointly by the archbishop or his delegate and a government official.[16] In 1592, Pope Clement VIII informed the new nuncio for Graz, Girolamo Porcia, that the Austrian princes claimed a special privilege granted in connection with the concordat of Vienna in 1448. By virtue of this alleged privilege, the procedure during archiepiscopal visitations had to be agreed upon in a consultation with the archduke who would also appoint secular commissioners as assistants. The Habsburgs' claim was helped by the fact that the papal records were unclear on this point, so that Clement VIII instructed Porcia to inquire closely into this question.[17]

With his episcopal powers enhanced by the arrangement of 1591, and the major points of dispute between the secular and ecclesiastical authorities settled, the bishop of Seckau should have been in a better position to address the issues of clerical reform and heresy. However, his jurisdictional power and hence his power of implementing reforms was still limited by the exis-

---

[14] Blyssem to General Acquaviva, 18 Mar. 1581, AGR, 'Germ. (159)', fo. 113.

[15] A similar conflict over the procedure during visitations occurred in the recatholicized territory of the Upper Palatinate. The issue of control over the administration of the *temporalia* was not settled by the series of agreements between the dukes of Bavaria and the bishops of Regensburg, Eichstätt, and Bamberg in the years 1629–60, see A. Schosser, *Die Erneuerung des religiös-kirchlichen Lebens in der Oberpfalz nach der Rekatholisierung (1630–1700)* (Düren, 1938), 6–8.

[16] Cwienk, 'Kirchliche Zustände', 21, for the visitation of 1615. During his general visitation of Styrian parishes in 1678, the archbishop was accompanied by two councillors of the Inner Austrian *Hofkammer*, who were instructed to report on the administration of the *spiritualia* as well as the *temporalia*, STMLA, 'Miszellen', Karton 202. There is no evidence that Ferdinand (II) had made similar demands in connection with the local prelates' visitations.

[17] Second papal instruction for Girolamo Porcia, 1 Apr. 1592, printed in Klaus Jaitner (ed.), *Die Hauptinstruktionen Clemens' VIII. für die Nuntien und Legaten an den europäischen Fürstenhöfen 1592–1605*, vol. i (Tübingen, 1984), 39.

tence of exempt enclaves. Most notable among these was the diocese of Seckau itself, which remained subject to the jurisdiction of the provost of Seckau as head of the cathedral chapter. Visitations were therefore conducted jointly by both prelates, for example by Bishop Martin Brenner and Provost Sebastian of Seckau in 1598.[18] Further enclaves were formed by some of the Upper Styrian parishes, like Haus and Gröbming in the Enns valley, which remained directly subject to the archbishop. Likewise exempt were the twenty-four incorporated parishes of the Benedictine monastery of St Lambrecht, most of them in Upper Styria. Neither the suffragan bishop nor Salzburg was able to subdue the Benedictines' resistance, and their parishes were visited only by the papal nuncios and the abbots.

By contrast, the abbots of Neuberg permitted the visitation of their dispersed parishes. There was similar co-operation with the bishops of Gurk for the visitation of Marburg, and, after initial opposition, with the Knights of the Teutonic Order for the east Styrian parishes of Friedau, Groß-Sonntag, and Fürstenfeld.[19] Such agreements reduced the practical relevance of jurisdictional privileges, and permitted a uniform proceeding in the parishes. Conversely, insistence on these rights could create blank spots on the map of episcopal power. This happened not only in the case of the parishes incorporated to St Lambrecht, but also where the Jesuits' possessions were concerned. In 1598/1602, Archduke Ferdinand and Pope Clement VIII had invested the Jesuits with the estate (*Herrschaft*) of Millstatt in Carinthia, a possession of the then extinct Order of the Knights of St George. The Upper Styrian parishes of St Lorenzen in the Mürz valley, Kindberg, Kapfenberg, Krieglach, Stanz, Pürgg with Niederhofen, and Mitterndorff were incorporated to Millstatt, and the jurisdictional power of the *Komtur* as *ordinarius loci* was transferred to the rector of the Jesuit college in Graz.[20] On the basis of this claim, the Jesuits succeeded in staving off episcopal control from Salzburg and Seckau. In 1616 and 1619, rector Guilelmo Lamormaini got the full support of General Mutius Vitelleschi (1615–45) for refusing a parish visitation by archiepiscopal commissioners.[21]

---

[18] Schuster, *Martin Brenner*, 429.

[19] The enclaves and resulting negotiations are described by Cwienk, 'Kirchliche Zustände', 36–40.

[20] The official deed for this donation dates from 1602. For the donation of Millstatt see Peinlich, *Geschichte*, i. 45, and Franz von Krones, *Geschichte der Karl-Franzens-Universität in Graz* (Graz, 1886), 248–50. The papal bull of 28 Jan. 1600 transferred the quasi-episcopal rights for Millstatt and its dependencies to the rector of Graz, see Krones, *Geschichte*, 250.

[21] Mutelleschi to Lamormaini, 9 July 1616 and 8 June 1619, AGR, 'Epp. Gen., Austr. 2/II (1601–1620)', fos. 741, 1029.

The Jesuits' opposition did, in fact, run counter to the spirit if not to the letter of the Tridentine decree 'De Regularibus et Monialibus' (Conc. Trid. sess. 25), which aimed at the enhancement of the regular bishops' power to effect reforms. Gregory XV's decree 'De Exemptorum Privilegiis' of 1622 further reduced the scope of exemptions, especially those of incorporated benefices, whose incumbents were subjected to the authority of the local bishop in matters of both spiritual and temporal administration. However, neither this nor the earlier Tridentine decree had abolished such privileges as were held by the Jesuits.[22] The progress of reform and recatholicization in these jurisdictional enclaves therefore depended on the initiative of the prelates and was removed from the direct supervision of the bishops. As will be seen, this situation contributed to the survival of crypto-Protestant communities in Millstatt and Upper Styria as a result of the Jesuits' negligence.

A more obvious obstacle to episcopal reforms at parish level resulted from the continuing pressure exerted by the Protestant nobility and Protestant parishioners. In 1616, Bishop Jakob of Seckau informed Ferdinand that a number of 'disobedient' subjects in the parishes of Murau, Unzmarkt, Pusterwald, Scheifling, and St Oswald at Pöls still refused to confess and receive the sacrament according to the Catholic rite. He complained that it was impossible to enforce obedience because the Lutheran *Grundobrigkeit* of these heretics, meaning the families of Stubenberg, Neuhaus, Welzer, and Stadl, refused to co-operate.[23] In July 1616, he recorded thirty-eight individual cases of disobedience in the parish of St Lorenzen ob Scheifling. Most of the parishioners had been subject to the recently deceased Protestant Anna von Neuhaus, and her servants and estate officials at the castle of Neuhaus are listed as notoriously heretical.[24] As previously described, evasion and recourse to the services of Protestant preachers in the neighbouring archduchy of Austria and in Hungary were widespread, and most parishioners lapsed after they had been obliged to receive the Catholic sacraments during the 'reformation' of 1599–1600. In his report for the archduke, Bishop Eberlein demanded that Hans Pichler, a wealthy innkeeper at

[22] The regulations of the Tridentine decree 'De regularibus' and Gregory XV's decree 'De exemptorum Privilegiis' of 5 Feb. 1622 are printed in *Sacrosanctum Concilium Tridentinum Additis Declarationibus Cardinalium Concilii Interpretum, ex Ultima Recognitione Joannis Gallemart . . .*, (Augustae Vindelicorum (Augsburg), 1746), 608–20.

[23] Copy of the letter of Oct. 1616, DA, 'Religionsberichte Protestantismus', 1598–1730, XV-b-23.

[24] Ibid., report of 5 July 1616.

Niederwölz, be fined and banned as a 'troublesome heretic' ('ärgerlicher Ketzer'). Pichler frankly admitted that he had never confessed or received the sacrament according to the Catholic rite. Though he had at the time heard of a general reformation, he had not cared much for it, because he hoped that things would change again ('dan er verhoffte es soll wider anderst werden').[25] It seems that this optimism rested on the attitude adopted by their Lutheran seigneurs, most of whom hoped to be spared their Austrian co-religionists' fate as a reward for their unfailing loyalty. Visible proof of this false sense of security was the Inner Austrians' acquisition of emigrants' property shortly before the general emigration decree was issued in 1628.[26]

The intervention of the Protestant nobility frequently obstructed or delayed the enforcement of episcopal orders at parish level, but it could not prevent recognizable, if slow, progress in the field of clerical reform. As has been seen, the removal of Lutheran incumbents by the reformation commissions of 1599–1600 had not been complete, partly for lack of suitable Catholic substitutes.[27] Likewise, the problem of concubinage continued. Both problems were closely linked, and a strategy of gradual replacement was adopted during the next decades. The papal instruction for nuncio Porcia, dated 1 April 1592, ordered him to investigate the problem of concubinage or 'matrimonia putativa', adding that very few members of the lower clergy were celibate. It is further stated that this vice was widespread among the regular clergy as well, 'and this is the fuel that keeps all kinds of evil going' ('estque is omnium malorum fomes'). Clement VIII instructed Porcia to secure the assistance of the government for his visitation, because otherwise it was to be feared that the culprits would resort to appeals to their heretical noble patrons. The possibility of a wholesale expulsion of the offenders was ruled out because this would have left Inner Austria virtually without parish priests.[28] A gradual approach, reminiscent of the secular October programme of 1579 for the recovery of court and government offices, was therefore advised.

---

[25] Pichler's statement is quoted in Eberlein's report of 16 Oct. 1616. For further examples see the inquisition protocols for Judenburg, Niederwölz, and Pöls, 29 June to 4 July 1616, DA, 'Religionsberichte Protestantismus', 1598–1730, XV-b-23.

[26] See above, Ch. 4.

[27] In his correspondence with the rector of the college in Graz, P. Bartholomäus Viller, General Acquaviva referred to the lack of qualified priests among the province's secular and regular clergy, Acquaviva to Viller, 1 Sept. and 20 Oct. 1601, AGR, 'Epp. Gen., Austr. 2/I (1601–1620)', fos. 17, 28.

[28] Second papal instruction for Girolamo Porcia, 1 Apr. 1592, in Jaitner, *Hauptinstruktionen*, i. 41.

Before he started his visitation, Porcia was to obtain a list of suitable candidates from the Jesuit college or from other places, notably from the German seminary (Germanicum) in Rome.[29] Failing the recruitment of an adequate number of priests from these sources, he should entrust two or three parishes to one incumbent, because it was still better that there were few orthodox than plenty of heretical priests. The final instruction reveals that Clement VIII had little hope of a short-term solution. As a result he was willing to adopt a thoroughly pragmatic attitude to preserve at least the residue of Catholicism at parish level. Thus, Porcia was instructed to tolerate priests who did not strictly observe the rule of chastity if they were otherwise orthodox Catholics, and if their parishioners did not take offence at their conduct.[30]

During his visitation in 1607, Bishop Brenner examined 216 parish priests, vicars, and curates. On this occasion and over the following seven years, Brenner took action in at least thirty-six cases of clerical concubinage. It turned out that most of the offenders had already been reprimanded several times and had promised to make amends, but had nevertheless kept their 'wives' and children in their household, obviously with the connivance or even active support of their parishioners. This could be seen as indicative of the persistence of more tolerant attitudes towards clerical matrimony as opposed to the new Tridentine standards of clerical conduct. Successful intervention depended therefore on the co-operation of the local population, and some of the above proceedings were indeed set in motion by denunciations, as in the case of the trial against the parish priest of Stallhofen, Johann Khaindorfer, who was eventually deposed and banned from the church province of Salzburg in 1614. The examination revealed that he had lived with his concubine for thirty years and had been married by the parish priest of Piber. During the visitation of 1607, when he had been the incumbent of St Pancratius in Upper Styria, he had been denounced by members of his parish, who claimed that he had a concubine in the nearby parish of St Stephan. He was nevertheless spared severe punishment because he promised to mend his ways. In 1611, he was installed as parish priest of Stallhofen. Like St Pancratius, this parish was incorporated to the monastery of St

---

[29] Ibid. 41–2. Ferdinand's adviser Bishop Georg Stobaeus of Lavant, for example, had been a seminarist at the Germanicum in 1575–9, see the table of names in P. Schmidt, *Das Collegium Germanicum in Rom und die Germaniker* (Tübingen, 1984), 304.

[30] Jaitner, *Hauptinstruktionen*, i. 42. The previously described case of the priest of Eisenerz who was installed in 1599 and died in 1607, leaving a wife and several children, suggests that this strategy was still applied during the parish reform of 1599–1600.

Lambrecht, and it emerged during the trial that Khaindorfer had been able to conceal the earlier reprimand for immoral conduct because the abbot of St Lambrecht had failed to seek episcopal approval for his investiture. Khaindorfer was eventually arrested after he and his wife had been seen in a tavern in Graz, where his drunkenness and scandalous behaviour had brought him to the attention of the authorities.[31]

Brenner's successor, the previously mentioned Bishop Jakob Eberlein, examined 160 clerics and detected ten concubines during his visitation in 1617–19. It could be argued that the number of recorded cases was probably below the actual number of 'married' priests. Also, the government continued to denounce cases of concubinage and unpriestly conduct in the following years. It is nevertheless obvious that progress had been made since Clement VIII's orders for Porcia in 1592. Eberlein also recorded no vacancies, though it seems that the previously described dearth of adequately trained and orthodox candidates from Inner Austria was still a problem. As a result, the number of foreign clergy remained high. Of 144 parish priests, only forty came from Styria, six from Carinthia, four from the archduchy of Austria, three from Salzburg; the majority (91), however, came from various other parts of the Empire.[32] Some progress had been made in the field of clerical education and training. By 1619, most of the parish priests had attended the higher classes of a Catholic grammar school and had received a brief instruction in moral theology, and their chaplains and curates had attended at least the lower classes.[33] The notable bias in favour of a brief, practical instruction as opposed to a thorough academic theological training was the result of necessity rather than choice, permitting the rapid promotion and ordination of students who could then be used to replace suspect parish priests.

The papal instructions of 1592 had demanded proof of Catholic orthodoxy rather than evidence of theological training as the minimal requirement for a candidate's investiture.[34] Moreover, a focus on practical, pastoral training of priests was laid down by the Tridentine decree 'Cum adolescentium aetas' of 15 July 1563.[35] By this statute, archbishops,

---

[31] For the findings of Brenner's visitation see Schuster, *Martin Brenner*, 555–63. Khaindorfer's case is related ibid. 563–6. By a decree of 28 Aug. 1602, Brenner had sought to enforce the regulations demanding episcopal approval of candidates presented to vacant parishes, see Cwienk, 'Kirchliche Zustände', 209.

[32] Cwienk, 'Kirchliche Zustände', 283 n. 67.   [33] Ibid. 205–7.

[34] Jaitner, *Hauptinstruktionen*, i. 42.

[35] The decree is paraphrased and quoted in part by H. Tüchle, 'Das Seminardekret des Trienter Konzils und Formen seiner geschichtlichen Verwirklichung', in Bäumer, *Concilium Tridentinum*, 527–31.

bishops, and cathedral chapters were ordered to create seminaries for the education of priests. Candidates for admission to these colleges had to be at least 12 years old, and had to be of legitimate birth. They were expected to possess reading and writing skills, a very modest requirement considering that a Jesuit pupil of the same age would normally have passed at least the lower two classes of the grammar school. Clerical reform was now attempted from the root by raising suitable candidates for priesthood in the spirit of the Tridentine Council. It was hoped that the secluded life in the seminary would shut out morally corrupting and heretical influences, so that the seminarists would be brought up to lead an exemplary life. If children had previously been placed in monasteries to fulfil the pious vows of their parents, there was now a strong emphasis on the aptitude and inclination of candidates for religious vocations.[36]

The Tridentine decree was put into practice by the archbishop and cathedral chapter of Salzburg who made an endowment for the support of twenty pupils in 1579.[37] A smaller seminary in Straßburg (Carinthia) had been created by Bishop Christoph Spaur of Gurk in 1576 to recruit parish priests for his diocese.[38] Eberlein's visitation record of 1619 listed very few incumbents from Carinthia or Salzburg, but given the general preponderance of foreigners among the clergy, it is still possible that some of the duchy's priests had been trained in the neighbouring seminaries, especially in Salzburg. More directly relevant for the training of a native Styrian clergy was the Convict in Graz. Founded in 1576 and extended by a papal donation in 1577, it was intended as the equivalent of a seminary. Nevertheless, it was open to the nobility as paying students as well. Admission as a *Convictist* did not entail an obligation to take up a clerical vocation, although it was hoped that a large proportion of the students would become priests. A binding obligation existed only for the papal alumni and for those seminarists who held one of the ten scholarships that were founded between 1578 and 1630.[39] Eight further endowments were made for priests or students of theology at the seminary which Karl II had founded in 1574 to cater for needy students. It was subsequently extended and renamed (Ferdinandeum). In the years 1618

---

[36] The relevant prescriptions are quoted ibid. 528.

[37] Ortner, *Salzburg*, 92.

[38] For a general survey, though not a quantitative analysis, see P. G. Tropper, 'Die Erneuerung des Pfarrklerus in Salzburgisch-Kärnten zur Zeit der Gegenreformation', in Dolinar et al., *Katholische Reform*, 331–44.

[39] The founders were Archduchess Maria of Austria (two scholarships in 1578), Queen Anna of Poland, archduchess of Austria (six in 1596), and the parish priest of Cilli, Dr Michael Kuppitsch (two in 1597), see Peinlich, *Geschichte*, ii. 73.

and 1629/1633, both colleges had about the same number of students (100 and 125–30). By 1634, however, the Convict had run up such debts that a drastic reduction to around thirty to forty pupils had to be made, suggesting that it was by now the Ferdinandeum rather than the clerical Convict which attracted paying students.[40]

In spite of fiscal restraints, the Jesuit-directed institutes in Graz helped to provide for an adequately trained secular clergy, and thus contributed to the progress of clerical reform. Constant episcopal supervision and a considerable amount of pressure were nevertheless required to shape a new parish clergy. In response to the defects he had noticed during a visitation of his diocese, Archbishop Markus Sittich devised a set of statutes and decrees as directives for his subordinates. The 'Statuta et Decreta Generalia Visitationis per Archdioecesim Salisburgensem' were printed as a booklet in 1616 and were subsequently sent to the suffragan bishops for implementation in their dioceses.[41] His instructions concerning the conduct and duties of parish priests permit inferences regarding the abuses he had encountered. The presumed applicability of these regulations to Inner Austria implied that the denounced practices were not unknown in the suffragan bishoprics, though Eberlein's findings for 1617–19 suggest that the situation in some parts of Styria, i.e. Upper and 'middle' Styria, at least had improved. As will be shown, however, the issue of clerical conduct did not disappear from the agenda: in the second half of the seventeenth century, the development of a numerous, indigent, and poorly trained clerical 'proletariat' in Lower Styria and parts of Carinthia caused considerable disciplinary problems.[42]

The archbishop's statutes were nevertheless proof of a new episcopal concern with the moral conduct of the clergy and the relationship between the parish priest and his flock. The gist of his orders was that the priest was to lend credibility to his teachings by the example of his own irreproachable conduct. Protestant anticlerical propaganda in the Empire

---

[40] These endowments were made by the parish priest of Graz and Imperial councillor Dr Matthäus Scholasticus (two in 1611), by Veronika, Ursula, Regina, and Johanna von Hollenegg (two in 1611), by Dr Mathias Kielenhofer, parish priest in Hartberg (two in 1612), and Bishop Thomas Hren of Laibach (two in 1620), see Peinlich, *Geschichte*, iii. 71. For the origins of the Convict and the Ferdinandeum see ibid. i. 11–14. For the student numbers see ibid. iii. 81.

[41] They were applied by Bishop Eberlein during his visitation in 1617–19, see Cwienk, 'Kirchliche Zustände', 20. His copy of the *Statuta et Decreta* (Salzburg, 1616) can be found in DA, 'Synode' 1568–1722, XV-a-4. On 31 Dec. 1616, Eberlein confirmed the receipt of 500 copies for distribution among the Styrian parish clergy, DA, 'Synode' 1568–1722, XV-e-5.

[42] This problem is discussed below, Ch. 7.

concentrated on the vices of the clergy, and had shattered the nimbus of the sacerdotal office. If the authority of the parish priest as the representative of the Roman Church was to be restored, external distinguishing marks such as clerical dress and tonsure, and a careful separation of his life from the life of the parish community, were of utmost importance. Thus, the priests were prohibited from attending baptism and wedding feasts and suchlike conviviality, especially if these were held in hostels or taverns. Likewise, they should abstain from 'traditional games', i.e. games of dice, and from poaching. Numerous prescriptions regarding their moral conduct follow. Priority was given to the abolition of concubinage, and priests were peremptorily ordered to send away their concubines and children, unless the latter were allowed to stay with them by a special episcopal licence. Likewise, they should avoid the company of ill-reputed females 'like the plague' ('veluti pestem'). There is repeated reference to the vice of drunkenness, suggesting that this was a most common failing and the source of further misdemeanours. The clergy were severely warned not to dare attend or say mass in this state. In general, they were to abstain from all vices, brawls, tumults, scandals, and blasphemies and any other behaviour that was morally reprehensible and disgraceful for a priest.

Some of the instructions shed light on the material situation of the parish clergy, and if this information is added to the above statements it emerges that, so far, neither the private life nor the economic situation and pursuits of the priest, nor his role in the social life of the parish, had marked him off as a person who was outside, let alone above the parish community. There were regulations which prohibited the renting of additional land to supplement the priest's income. Likewise, he was not allowed to keep a tavern in his house or in the parsonage, trade in wine and other goods, or engage in any other pursuits for worldly gain.[43]

The latter reproaches raise the question of the lower clergy's material situation. Fiscal pressure and thus the need to alienate parochial property (*Gülten*) had continued to some extent in Karl II's reign. More significant losses of parochial rights and property were inflicted by the usurpations of the Protestant nobility. The papal instructions of 1592 stated that the nobility and their subjects refused to pay tithes to Catholic incumbents.[44] Shortly after his accession, Ferdinand therefore began to take steps to effect a restoration. Acting on the archduke's orders, Bishop Thomas

---

[43] 'De Vita, Honestate, ac Officiis Clericorum & Sacerdotum', from the *Statuta et Decreta* (1616), 11–13, DA, 'Synode' 1568–1722, XV-a-4.
[44] Second instruction, dated 1 Apr. 1592, in Jaitner, *Hauptinstruktionen*, i. 42.

Hren of Laibach set about recovering alienated ecclesiastical property from November 1598 onwards.[45] To support the parish reformation of 1599–1600, Ferdinand issued a decree for the Styrian estates on 31 July 1600 by which recently installed Catholic incumbents were discharged from tax debts incurred by their Protestant predecessors.[46] Moreover, Ferdinand urged the parish priests to recover alienated property.[47]

The confessional conflict was exacerbated by Ferdinand's willingness to countenance even dubious legal claims of the Catholic clergy, as the following case illustrates. In 1587, a long-drawn-out struggle began between the Jesuit college and a Protestant nobleman, Hans Adam von Schratt. The document which recorded the eventual decision is not extant, but the case itself shows the Jesuits as belligerent defenders of the clergy's rights and property to the point of breaking the law of the land and circumventing the judicial power of the estates. At the instigation of the rector in Graz, the Jesuits' vicar at Kindberg forcibly collected the tithe from the fields near Schratt's castle in 1601. Schratt contested the right to levy tithes from these grounds which formed part of his manorial estates (*Hofgründe*), basing the validity of his claim on the alleged evidence of the tithe register and the foundation deed for the parish (*Pfarrstiftsbrief*), which, however, seem to have been lost by that date. His complaint to the estates' court was rejected by the *Landeshauptmann* at the orders of the government. The *Landeshauptmann* nevertheless sought to mediate by suggesting an amicable settlement in 1603. It seems that there was a temporary agreement, but in 1614 a fresh quarrel broke out when the vicar of Kindberg undertook a nocturnal raid at the instigation of the Jesuit rector Lamormaini and collected thirteen measures (*Schober*) of oats from an extension of Schratt's fields (*Neubruch*). Schratt demanded the sum of 100 florins gold as compensation for damages caused by this raid, and the estates' court (*Landschranne*) found in his favour. In May 1619, however, Lamormaini successfully applied to Archduke Ferdinand, soon to be Emperor Ferdinand II, for the 'beneficium revisionis', by which the decision of the estates' court was suspended. Litigation continued at least until 1624, when the new incumbent of Kindberg urged the Jesuits to settle their argument with Schratt's heirs.[48]

---

[45] Bishop Thomas Hren of Laibach to Bartlme Höritsch zum Thurm und Wöllau, 14 Nov. 1598, printed in *FRA/58*, 412–14.

[46] The decree is mentioned in *FRA/60*, 15.

[47] Such orders were issued by the reformation commissioners for parishes in Styria (Judenburg) and Carinthia (Wolfsberg), see Loserth, preface to *FRA/60*, pp. ci–cii and the relevant documents on p. 21 and p. 66.

[48] The documents relating to Schratt's case are taken from DA, 'Jesuiten (5)', XIX-c-34.

In general, the recovery of parochial rights and property and the educational and moral improvement of the parish clergy were by no means completed by the time of the nobility's emigration in 1628. As has been shown, the presence of the Protestant nobility hampered or delayed the implementation of episcopal decrees at parish level before this date. However, substantial progress was made in the years 1580–1630 in the field of both administrative and clerical reform in spite of these obstacles. As previously demonstrated, the authority of the bishop of Seckau was enhanced by his appointment as vicar general for Salzburg, while agreements with Karl II and the majority of the exempt prelates removed most, though not all, jurisdictional barriers to a thorough reform of the clergy.[49] Likewise, Ferdinand's decrees encouraged the recovery of lost parochial rights and property, and hence contributed to the restoration of the parishes' material basis. Episcopal control and an improvement of the priests' material situation were important preconditions for the shaping of a new type of Tridentine clergy. The visitation findings of 1617–19 and the later complaints by the Inner Austrian government prove that not all of the clerical abuses had been remedied, but the decline of concubinage was an indicator of progress in this direction. Likewise, the creation of seminaries and above all of Jesuit-directed institutes in Graz had improved the level of education. The large group of foreigners among the incumbents showed that the number of Inner Austrian candidates for priesthood was insufficient. However, the proportion of Styrians listed by Bishop Eberlein in 1619 suggested that the pattern of recruitment was beginning to change.

The activity of the Jesuits as the vanguard of the Counter-Reformation is partly shown by this evidence. Jesuit influence was deployed in three main ways: the provision and training of parish clergy, and the exposition of doctrine. A closer look at the development of the Jesuit mission until 1630 reveals the initial difficulties encountered by the Society, and the shift in the focus of their activity towards the end of this period.

The mixed national composition of the first group of Jesuits who came to Graz in 1572 was evidence of the fact that the Austrian province was not yet provided with a sufficient number of priests to supply the new settlement. Complaints from Graz in 1601 and from the college in Leoben in 1624 prove that the Society was also affected by the general

---

[49] The remaining exemptions included the Benedictines' parishes in Upper Styria and the Jesuits' property in the same region and in Carinthia, with considerable consequences for the survival of crypto-Protestants in these places, see below, Ch. 7.

lack of priests.[50] In 1625, the Austrian province had 443 members, out of which a mere 120 were ordained priests. Apart from the general dearth of candidates for priesthood, it seems that the Society's exceptionally high standards for admission, and the long period of subsequent education, aggravated the problem. By way of reply to a complaint about the slow progress of the college in Graz, General Vitelleschi revealed his discontent with the quality of the Austrian Jesuits by stating that the entire province suffered from a want of able members.[51] The influx of refugees from Bohemia to Graz in 1618–20 temporarily increased the number of priests, though at the price of causing pressing financial problems. The annual report of the college in Graz records the presence of thirty-two priests, twenty coadjutors, and 110 Jesuit Bohemian refugees.[52]

With the encouragement of Ferdinand II, the Society nevertheless continued its institutional expansion by opening colleges with grammar schools in Leoben (1615) and Judenburg (1621), the first serving in this period mainly as a house for novices, while the latter became a complete college in 1629 and from 1632 onwards catered for novices who prepared for the taking of the final vows (*Tertiarier*). These houses continued to be financially dependent on Graz, whereas the two colleges in Klagenfurt (1604) and Laibach (1597) remained completely separate institutions, Klagenfurt being an archducal foundation in the wake of the 'reformation' at the turn of the century. The college in Laibach was opened with the support of Archduke Ferdinand and Bishop Stobaeus.[53] In 1613,

---

[50] The first Jesuit priests in Graz were P. Gerard Pastel from Belgium, P. Johann Herman from Swabia, P. Bernhard Koch from Westphalia, P. Johann Reinel from Bohemia and at least one Inner Austrian, P. Nikolaus Coprivitz from Carniola, see Peinlich, *Geschichte*, i. 8. The complaints are mentioned in the General's letters to P. Bartholomäus Viller in Graz, 1 Sept. 1601, and to a member of the college in Leoben, P. Johannes Janus, 4 Mar. 1623, AGR, 'Epp. Gen., Austr. 2/I', and 'Epp. Gen., Austr. 3/I (1620–28)'. Vitelleschi informed Janus that he had ordered the provincial to supply Leoben, but that the latter had been unable to comply for want of priests.

[51] The figures for 1625 are taken from Peinlich, *Geschichte*, iii. 87. Vitelleschi's reply to P. Michael Summerecker in Graz, dated 8 Mar. 1625, can be found in AGR, 'Epp. Gen., Austr. 3/II (1620–28)', fos. 601–2.

[52] 'Litterae Annuae' for Graz, 1618, ÖNB, 'Litterae Annuae', 1617–19, MS 13562. The report for 1617 mentions a total number of 110 members in the college in Graz, the residence in Millstatt and the mission in Gorizia. Out of these, twenty-seven were priests, seven graduates (*Magistri*), and fifty-seven students. The remaining were presumably coadjutors and secular 'familiares' of the houses. The refugee problem is mentioned in Vitelleschi's letter to Lamormaini, 9 May 1620, AGR, 'Epp. Gen., Austr. 3/I', fo. 53. Peinlich, *Geschichte*, iii. 86, estimates an average number of 120–40 members in Graz if the students (*Scholastiker*) are included, with an average number of 30 priests.

[53] For a brief survey of the beginnings in Leoben and Judenburg see Duhr, *Geschichte*, ii/1. 337–40.

Ferdinand donated the building of his ducal residence (*palatio*) in Leoben to encourage Jesuit activity among the Protestant burghers of this town. The abbot of Admont and former reformation commissioner Johann Jakob Hofmann contributed a generous 10,000 fl. for the college.[54] An additional ducal donation of 5,000 fl. from the revenues of the customs office in Eisenerz, however, was apparently never paid out to the Jesuits.[55] No support was forthcoming from the local parish and its wealthy artisans, merchants, and iron dealers, and in the years 1618–21, the rector of Leoben, Bartholomäus Wetzger, complained that grave financial problems hampered the settlement's main task—the education of novices— and obstructed the general progress of the college. In 1618, Leoben nevertheless admitted fourteen candidates in addition to the twenty-nine novices from Brno (Brünn) in Moravia who had been transferred in 1615, raising the number of priests, coadjutors, and novices in Leoben temporarily to fifty-three in all. Part of the new burden was immediately shifted to Rome by sending eight novices to the Italian noviciate. The annual report for 1617 states that there were usually forty-four members in Leoben, four of whom were priests.[56]

This was a sizeable Jesuit colony for a small Catholic community like Leoben's, with an estimated 350–400 communicants in 1617, as compared to Judenburg's 2,000–2,400.[57] Moreover, governmental pressure on the town had not relented since the reformation commission of 1610 had severely punished thirty-five burghers for attending Protestant services abroad. In April 1613, Ferdinand inquired into the magistrates' wardships and peremptorily ordered the councillors to call back wards who had been sent abroad to ensure their Protestant upbringing. In December the same year, two burghers were ordered to send away their preceptors

---

[54] Ferdinand's and Hofmann's donations are mentioned by Duhr, ibid. 337, and in the General's letters to the provincial Bartholomäus Viller, 22 June 1613, and to the rector in Graz, Guilelmo Lamormaini, in the latter case without expressly mentioning the abbot's name, AGR, 'Epp. Gen., Austr. 2/I', fo. 526, 'Austr. 2/II', fos. 790–1.

[55] This emerges from a letter of Vitelleschi to rector Marco Noelio in Leoben, 4 Mar. 1623, AGR, 'Epp. Gen., Austr. 3/I', fo. 357. On 20 July 1653, the rector of Leoben, Adam Aböed, in vain petitioned the *Hofkammer* for the execution of the late archduke's orders, DA, 'Jesuiten (13)', XIX-c-42. There is no evidence that the sum was ever paid.

[56] For the transfer of Moravian novices see Duhr, *Geschichte*, ii/1. 337. The rector's complaints and possible means of alleviating the burden are discussed in the General's letters to Wetzger, dated 11 Aug. 1618, 8 June 1619, AGR, 'Epp. Gen., Austr. 2/II', fo. 942 and fo. 1029, and in the letters to Wetzger and Lamormaini, dated 27 Mar. 1621 and 27 Mar. 1621, 'Austr. 3/I', fos. 132–4. For the average number of residents see the 'Litterae Annuae' for 1617, ÖNB, MS 13562.

[57] Round figures based on Straka, 'Bevölkerungsentwicklung', table c, between pp. 17 and 18.

who refused to obey the Catholic parish school teacher. A decree was issued in 1621 to enforce the Sunday and Lenten regulations, and in 1627, the burghers were sharply rebuked for preventing the ducal bailiff (*Landprofoß*) from tracking down a Carinthian preacher who had stayed in the town.[58]

The Society's presence in the town therefore met with considerable opposition from the Protestant faction. There was bitter resistance when the Jesuits opened a grammar school at the request of the Catholic burghers of nearby Eisenerz in 1620. Until 1630, student numbers remained very low, so that the school consisted only of the basic grammar classes, the remaining two higher classes (*Humanität* and *Rhetorik*) being added at five-year intervals in 1635 and 1640.[59] The Jesuits responded to this situation by avoiding any action which might antagonize the population. In 1617, they admitted a burgher's son as novice who falsely asserted that he was acting with the knowledge and consent of his parents. A conflict ensued between the student and his family, supported by a further burgher, who claimed that the Jesuits had abducted the youth. To effect a reconciliation, the Jesuits arranged for a meeting between the young man and members of his family in the presence of two members of the college. No attempt was made to keep the novice, who nevertheless confirmed his decision in spite of his family's protests. In the end, his determination and the conciliatory attitude of the Jesuits seem to have persuaded the burghers of the voluntary nature of his action, and the incident had no adverse effect on the Society's activity.[60]

No mention is made of controversial preaching. Instead, the Jesuits engaged in spiritual missions of a more charitable character, e.g. they looked after prisoners and delinquents sentenced to capital punishment. Their novices were dispatched to help the priests of neighbouring parishes, and were allegedly very successful in hearing confessions and giving catechetical lessons to the children of these rural parishes. This

---

[58] For the above decrees see *FRA/60*, 592–3 (punishment of 35 burghers), 620, 735, 792.
[59] Duhr, *Geschichte*, ii/1. 337–8.
[60] The case is related in the 'Litterae Annuae' for 1617, ÖNB, MS 13562. A similar case involving an aristocratic youth had played into the hands of the Jesuits' adversaries in Rome in the first half of the 16th century, see H. Stoeckius, 'Ottaviano Cesare, ein Rechtsstreit zwischen Gesellschaft Jesu und Elternhaus', in *Sitzungsberichte der Heidelberger Akademie der Wissenschaften, Phil.-hist. Klasse*, v. 7: *Abhandlung* (Heidelberg, 1914). More celebrated cases involving clashes of individual religious vocation with the duty of obedience to parental authority are discussed by B. Diefendorf, 'Give Us Back Our Children: Patriarchal Authority and Parental Consent to Religious Vocations in Early Counter-Reformation France', *JMH* 68 2 (June 1996), 265–307.

approach had repercussions on the Jesuits' position in the town. While only twenty-three burghers had attended their services in 1614 to obtain a special indulgence, there were several hundred attendants in 1616 from the town and the surrounding municipalities. In 1625, there were allegedly 600 communicants at Christmas, and 2,500 at the Easter services in the Jesuit church at Leoben.[61] As previously described, there is evidence that a Protestant faction among the burghers still existed in the 1620s. Nevertheless, the Jesuits' efforts were obviously having an impact on the religious practice of the population in and around Leoben, even if an element of coercion in the shape of increasing governmental pressure on those who defaulted on fulfilling their religious obligations is taken into account.[62]

By comparison, conditions in Judenburg were more favourable to a Jesuit settlement. Though the bishop of Seckau had reported on Protestants in the nearby parish of St Peter at Judenburg, there was at this time (1621) no evidence directly from the burghers of the town. The town had become confessionally divided in 1570, with a majority of Protestant burghers congregating at St Martin's church, and a small Catholic community, led by the parish priest, at the parish church of St Nikolai. The local Protestants' hegemony was strengthened by the terms of the 'Pacification' of 1578, which sanctioned the confessional status quo in Judenburg and in the three duchies' capitals (Graz, Klagenfurt, Laibach). A Protestant grammar school was opened, and the buildings and remaining property of the impoverished monasteries were henceforth administered by the town magistrates. In 1596–8, the priest of Pöllau, Sigismund Rephuen, who administered the parish of Judenburg, stated that the parish had contracted huge debts to the burghers of Judenburg, and that most of the parish property had been confiscated by the estates and distributed to various owners.[63] Ferdinand therefore issued orders to effect the restoration of alienated parish lands and church treasures (*Kirchenkleinodien*) to the new incumbent, Leonhardt Todtseisen.[64] The

---

[61] The Jesuits' activities in and near Leoben are recorded in the 'Litterae Annuae' for 1617, ÖNB, MS 13562. The figures are taken from Duhr, *Geschichte*, ii/1, based on the 'Litterae Annuae' for 1620–50. They should be read as a rough estimate illustrating a tendency.

[62] Confessional slips as proof of compliance with the ducal decrees were not introduced before 1628.

[63] J. Andritsch, *Unser Judenburg* (Judenburg, 1975), 79–84. Rephuen's statement is paraphrased ibid. 81. For the monasteries see P. Dedic, *Das Schicksal der Judenburger Klöster und Spitäler in der Reformationszeit* (Graz, 1930), 1–8.

[64] *FRA/60*, 4, 21, 239–40.

latter was succeeded by the belligerent Magister Paul Erber, who successfully appealed to the Emperor in 1625–6 in his struggle to recover full
control over the administration of the churches and hospitals, and in his
persecution of crypto-Protestants, most of whom belonged to the local
nobility's officials.

The Catholic cause was helped by the fact that Protestants' educational efforts had come to an end with the abolition of their school on 3
October 1598.[65] It was further strengthened by the presence of Archduke
Ferdinand and members of the ducal family, who spent part of the year
in Judenburg. A castle was built in the years 1596–1600 as a second ducal
residence, and in 1603–4, three Jesuits from Graz were sent as tutors of
the archduke's younger brothers Leopold and Karl.[66] In 1620,
Ferdinand's privy counsellor, Baron Balthasar von Thanhausen, bought
the abandoned Augustinian monastery in Judenburg and donated it, with
papal consent, to the Jesuits. Adding property and capital for the support
of twenty-four residents, Balthasar von Thanhausen and his wife Ursula
laid the foundation for the Jesuit college that was opened in 1621. 2,000
fl. interest from the Thanhausen estate of Castua in Carniola was added.
These generous endowments were rounded off by Ferdinand's donations,
consisting largely of revenues from property in Carniola.[67] Although the
settlement numbered only three priests and two coadjutors from Graz in
1621, building works to create room for forty residents were begun immediately. A grammar school was opened in November 1621 and admitted
thirty-five children.[68] In the following year, the General congratulated
the superior of the small Jesuit community, Balthasar Nymptsch, on the
auspicious beginnings of the house. The superior's report of 26

[65] *FRA/60*, 761, 771–2, and 803. For the decree see ibid. 187.

[66] For the ducal residence see Andritsch, *Unser Judenburg*, 84–5. The appointment of
Jesuit tutors is mentioned by Duhr, *Geschichte*, ii/1. 338–9.

[67] The donation is first mentioned in a letter by the General to rector Lamormaini in
Graz, 7 Dec. 1619, AGR, 'Epp. Gen., Austr. 2/II', fo. 1091, in which he speaks of
Thanhausen's wish to found a Jesuit college, but states that the location had not yet been
decided upon. In his letter of 9 May 1620 to Lamormaini, he confirms that he had received
the foundation deed, AGR, 'Epp. Gen., Austr. 3/I', fo. 53. The Thanhausens' generous
endowment of the college is referred to in his letter of 21 Jan. 1621 and 17 July 1621, AGR,
'Epp. Gen., Austr. 3/I', fos. 116, 164, see also the description in Peinlich, *Geschichte*, ii. 19,
and the more detailed statements in Andritsch, *Unser Judenburg*, 90. The contract of sale
was signed on 8 Apr. 1620, see ibid. The captainship and revenues of Castua/Kesten had
previously been granted to the ducal (vice-)chancellor, Wolfgang Schranz, see below, this
chapter.

[68] Andritsch, *Unser Judenburg*, 90. On 25 Dec. 1621, the General approved the plans for
a new college building, AGR, 'Epp. Gen., Austr. 3/I', fo. 23.

December 1622 was able to point even to the town magistrates' support of the Jesuits' efforts.[69]

Although student numbers remained low in the next years and delayed the completion of the grammar school until 1646, the progress made was sufficient to warrant at least the addition of the *Humanität* to the elementary and lower grammar classes in 1626.[70] It remains dubious whether the weak response can be put down exclusively to Protestant opposition. Rather, it seems that the Jesuits were confronted with the same problems as their Protestant adversaries, namely the proximity of a complete grammar school in Graz which promised greater prestige and better training to the minority who aspired to academic education. In 1630, the Jesuits recorded 3,000 communicants at Judenburg, rising to 4,600 four years later. A Marian congregation for the burghers of Judenburg was created in 1632, and its members asked General Vitelleschi for incorporation into the Roman confraternity in the same year. The petition was signed by members of the town council and urban elite on behalf of the noble and civic *sodales*.[71] Obviously, the Jesuits' labours for a revival of Catholic religious practice were bearing fruit.

By contrast, it proved rather difficult to provide for a sufficient number of residents to turn the settlement into a complete college. Judenburg was elevated to this rank in 1629 and its then superior, Johann Melzer, became the first rector. In 1631, there were only twelve members, five of them *Patres*, and three *Magistri* at the Jesuits' grammar school.[72] As previously mentioned, the Austrian province suffered from a shortage of novices as well as full members (*Professen*) who could educate further candidates. To remedy the difficulties of Judenburg, third-year novices preparing for their final vows (*Tertiarier*) were transferred to this house. At the beginning of November 1632, P. Christian Bertschiada reported that the number of third-year novices was exiguous, but expressed his hope of better progress and urged the sending of further candidates. To

---

[69] Vitelleschi to Nymptsch, 11 June 1622, AGR, 'Epp. Gen., Austr. 3/I', fos. 273–4. The information on the town's support emerges from the General's reply of 4 Feb. 1623, ibid. 348.

[70] Duhr, *Geschichte*, ii/1. 339.

[71] The number of communicants is mentioned by Duhr, ibid. 341. For the burghers' petition of 20 Oct. 1632, see AGR, 'Austria (21), Epp. (1601–1660)', fo. 175. The General's approval is stated in his letter to rector Johann Melzer, 11 Dec. 1632, AGR, 'Epp. Gen., Austr. 4/II (1628–35)', fo. 721.

[72] For the number of residents see Duhr, *Geschichte*, ii/1. 339. A list of superiors and rectors of Judenburg 1603–47 can be found ibid. 340 n. 1. The title 'rector' does not appear in the General's letters before Melzer's appointment in 1629.

give weight to this request, Bertschiada praised the advantages of the site, which was remote and quiet enough to permit the performance of the spiritual exercises as prescribed for the novices, but was surrounded by villages and towns which would give them ample opportunity for missions. His praise of Judenburg's advantages persuaded the General, and a further group of nine novices arrived in November 1632.[73]

Later reports on the progress of the college and *Tertiorat* stand in contrast to the above evidence for the years 1620–34 which proved that at least moderate success was achieved in the missionary and educational field. From the General's correspondence with Bertschiada and the Austrian provincial, Johannes Rumer, in July 1635 to January 1637, it emerges that the former now urged the transfer of the college. Bertschiada sharply criticized the *Patres* for concentrating on household affairs at the expense of their pastoral and missionary obligations. Moreover, he claimed that the colleges' achievements ('fructus') were so minute that it was barely worth the effort to maintain a Jesuit settlement there. His accusations impressed the General sufficiently to ask the provincial for his opinion on this matter. In his letter to Johann Rumer, the General wondered whether the Society could really carry out such a transfer without encountering much opposition, and without incurring a reputation for fickleness. Clearly, the General was loath to jeopardize the Society's reputation for constancy and to sanction retreat in the face of difficulties. His own expectation of protest from the population of Judenburg suggested that he was not fully persuaded of the validity of Bertschiada's arguments. It seems that Rumer's reply or else the protests of the rector of Judenburg, Andreas Cobavius, supported him in this, because, in February 1637, Vitelleschi informed Cobavius that he could not bring himself to believe that the college was useless in this place if the *Patres* devoted so much effort to the cure of souls.[74] In the end, the college remained in Judenburg, but the *Tertiorat* was transferred to Leoben in the years 1637–42.[75] The General took care to discuss this step

---

[73] P. Christian Bertschiada to General Vitelleschi, 2 Nov. 1632, Rector Johann Melzer to Vitelleschi, 14 Nov. 1632, AGR, 'Austria (21), Epp. (1601–1660)', fo. 187 and fo. 198. Bertschiada's rank as superior of the novices in Judenburg emerges from the correspondence. In this function, he was subject to the local rector's authority.

[74] For Bertschiada's accusations and demand for transfer see AGR, 'Austr. 5/I (1635–48)', Vitelleschi to P. Christian Bertschiada, 21 July 1635, fos. 13–14, and 25 Oct. 1636, fos. 188–9. The above quotation is taken from Vitelleschi's letter to Rumer, 3 Jan. 1637, ibid. 216. For the letter to Cobavius, dated 7 Feb. 1637, see ibid. 229–30.

[75] Duhr, *Geschichte*, ii/1. 339.

with Ursula von Thanhausen, widow of the founder of the college,[76] and another huge donation of 50,000 fl. from the same benefactress in the years 1642–4 encouraged the final transfer of the now increased *Tertiorat* back to Judenburg in 1645.[77]

Apart from illustrating communication and co-operation between the General and the lower ranks of the Society, the episode also points to the existence of diverging concepts of the Jesuits' task. It emerges that the leading officials of the Society, the rector of Judenburg, the provincial, and the General, considered the achievement of steady if slow progress in terms of institutional growth and missionary success as the most important task. Domestic stability and the continuity of the college's work were not to be sacrificed, not least because such actions might have repercussions on the work of the Society in other parts of the province. By contrast, the superior of the *Tertiorat* seems to have envisaged a different kind of mission for the Jesuits. His assertion that the Judenburg college was utterly ineffective is not borne out by the evidence, and should be interpreted in the light of his further statement that the college might be more useful elsewhere.[78] The Society had provided the shock-troops for the Counter-Reformation in the Empire in the sixteenth century, and Bertschiada seems to have thought that the Jesuits should not waste their efforts on a mission which neither achieved spectacular successes nor offered the opportunity for heroic feats.

He was not the only Styrian Jesuit who felt that the remaining labours did not satisfy his missionary zeal. Between 1617 and 1640, at least sixteen Jesuits from Judenburg, Graz, and Leoben asked for transfer to other missions.[79] In three cases, no geographic preferences are stated, but six asked to be sent to Asia or Africa, four volunteered for missions among

---

[76] This emerges from his letter of 14 Mar. 1637 to Johannes Rumer, AGR, 'Epp. Gen., Austr. 5/I', fo 245.

[77] For the deliberations with the Countess von Thanhausen see Vitelleschi's letter of 14 Mar. 1637 to Johann Rumer. The details of her donation are related in the foundation deed of 1 May 1645, copy in DA, 'Jesuiten (9)', XIX-c-38, 'Fam. Thanhausen betreffend'.

[78] His argument as stated by the General, Vitelleschi to Rumer, 3 Jan. 1637, AGR, 'Epp. Gen., Austr., 5/I', fo. 216.

[79] The following is based on an evaluation of the General's letters, AGR, 'Epp. Gen., Austr., Austr. 2/II–5/I', and the letters from members of the province, 'Austria (21), Epp. (1601–1660)'. The applicants were Johannes Gans (1617), P. Martin Santinus (1620), Everhard Erthal (1621), Johannes Zentgeorgy (1622), P. Johannes Rumer (1625), Wolfgang Sigismund Fuerthenstain (1626), P. Julius Magnana (1627), Nicolaus Posarelli (1629), Franciscus Basellus (1632), P. Jakob Durandus on behalf of an unmentioned applicant (1633), Karl Schiechel (1635), P. Stephan Cornis (1636), P. Jakob Reiss (1637), P. Georg Lofferer (1637), Caspar Sännigk (1639), P. Stephan Suberle (1640).

heretics or unbelievers in the Habsburg lands or related eastern missions (one Bohemia, two Transylvania, one Turkish mission), and three expressed less specific wishes to work either among heretics or natives (1), in Saxony and other parts of Protestant Germany, or elsewhere in Europe (2). By 1639, such appeals had become so frequent that the General already kept a register with the names of applicants who came to be called, for short, 'Indipetae'.[80] The motives for these requests emerge partly from the applicants' statements, and partly from the geographical preferences they expressed. Both are revealing of their missionary ideal, and permit inferences regarding their perception of the situation in Styria.

The list of non-European missionary fields to which transfer was requested, for example, reads like a survey of Francis Xavier's travels, mentioning India, Japan, and even China, which had been his final but unattained goal. The cult of this missionary saint was especially furthered by the college in Graz. In 1622, the college and university celebrated the canonization of Ignatius and Francis Xavier by a procession and feast in Graz, attended by the governor, the bishop of Seckau, the regular clergy, nobility, and burghers of the town. At the height of these celebrations, the Jesuits declared the two saints patrons of the House of Austria, of Styria, and of its capital in particular, and the assembled students took a public vow of special worship.[81] Hence, it seems likely that the Jesuits' novices were acquainted with Francis Xavier's life and missionary achievements, and their interest in overseas missions suggests that the appeal of this notion of mission was strong enough to encourage emulation.

Appropriate as it had been for one of the founding fathers of the Jesuit order to emulate the early apostles and follow his own path in his missionary work, such a proceeding was no longer compatible with the tight hierarchical organization and the tasks of the Society in the seventeenth century. The General therefore invariably declined such applications, sometimes consoling the applicant by hinting at the possibility of a later call.[82] Instead, he referred the applicants to the importance of continuing the mission in the Empire, for example when declining the repeated

---

[80] Vitelleschi promised to enter the name of one applicant, Caspar Sännigk, in this register, 12 Mar. 1639, AGR, 'Epp. Gen., Austr. 5/I', fo. 456.

[81] The celebrations are described in Peinlich, *Geschichte*, i/2, 20.

[82] The General's rejection of applications for overseas missions are recorded in AGR, 'Austr. 2/II', fo. 889; 'Austr. 3/II', fos. 602, 729–30, 923–4, 'Austr. 4/I', fo. 197, 'Austr. 5/I', fos. 267–8.

requests of a novice, Johannes Gans, for transfer to the Indian or Chinese mission. On 19 May 1618, the General explained his final decision, so that the novice might concentrate his efforts entirely on the task at hand, i.e. the mission in the German lands, which, the General thought, offered no lesser field than India for the exercise of virtues and the performance of good deeds.[83] In the same vein, he sought to comfort another unsuccessful applicant 'that even though you cannot go to India, Germany offers you open fields, or fields that need to be explored yet, which are of equal size, and not unlike those [in India]' ('quod etiamsi ad Indos ire non possis, campi tamen aeque magni, et regionibus illis non absimiles in Germania iam aperti videantur, vel aperiendi').[84]

The Styrian 'Indipetae' showed a marked preference for dangerous missions, e.g. P. Georg Lofferer, who desperately appealed for his transfer 'to some more arduous mission' ('ad arduam quamcumque missionem') in India, or else in Saxony or any other heresy-infested European province.[85] Such appeals prove that some Jesuits who strove to get away from Styria were moved by other considerations than merely the wish to follow the example of Francis Xavier, and had motives beyond the fascination of the exotic which seems to have captured the imagination of some applicants. The firm wish to undertake missions among 'heretics or natives'[86] could imply a willingness to embrace martyrdom. It is unclear whether the Styrian colleges possessed such vivid pictorial representations of martyrdom as were used in the Jesuit college churches in Rome to prepare the minds of future missionaries,[87] but biblical and early Christian examples frequently formed the plot of theatrical plays in Graz.[88]

[83] 'ut studia tua omnia ad divinam gloriam in Germanicis provinciis propagandam dirigere possis, ubi non minorem tibi virtutis et meritorum segetem quam in Indiae regionibus offerendat puto.' AGR, 'Epp. Gen., Austr. 2/II', fo. 912.

[84] Letter to P. Jakob Reiss in Graz, 9 May 1637, AGR, 'Epp. Gen., Austr. 5/I', fo. 267.

[85] Ibid. 268.

[86] See the request of Everhard Erthal, mentioned in the General's letter of 26 June 1621, AGR, 'Epp. Gen., Austr. 3/I', fo. 156.

[87] See the instructive passage in the article by E. Levy, ' "A Noble Medley and Concert of Materials and Artifice": Jesuit Church Interiors in Rome, 1567–1700', in T. M. Lucas, SJ and Biblioteca Vaticana (eds.), *Saint, Site, and Sacred Strategy*, catalogue of the exhibition (Vatican City, 1990), 51.

[88] R. Hofer, 'Das Grazer Jesuitendrama, 1573–1600' (doctoral thesis, University of Graz, 1931), 83, mentions three plays for the years before 1600, namely one 'Eustachius' play in 1594, a 'Catharina' play in 1597, and an unspecified martyr's drama in Sept. 1598. Biblical themes and panegyric plays for the House of Habsburg became more prominent in the programme of the following decades, ibid. 28. There were apparently no theatrical performances until 1630 either in Judenburg or Leoben.

The veneration of martyrs of the Diocletian reign was furthered both in Graz and Judenburg. In 1617, Ferdinand effected the transfer of the relics of the martyrs Martin, Vincent, Maxentia, and Agatha from Rome to the Jesuits' church in Graz, and special celebrations were performed by the university's senate and the highest prelates. The Jesuits had begun to further the cult of two local martyrs, Cyriacus and Propertius, two peasant children from Strettweg near Judenburg who had allegedly died for the Christian faith in 304–5. From 1626 onwards, the Jesuits began to further their cult and represented them as local patron saints of Judenburg. With the help of the bishop of Seckau, Jakob Eberlein, and the provost of the cathedral chapter, Antonius de Potiis, the Jesuits were able to bring back the relics, which were enshrined and placed in front of the high altar in the local Jesuit church.[89] In both cases, the intention must have been to encourage the revival of the cult of saints as a Catholic devotional practice among the population, but it can hardly be doubted that such propaganda had an even greater effect on the Jesuits' students and novices as the most receptive spectators. Likewise, Catholic propaganda had probably acquainted them with the life and work of the English Jesuit Edmund Campion (1540–81), who had started his career as a missionary working in Prague and Brünn (Brno) in the 1570s before embarking on his fateful journey to England in June 1580. Following the example of earlier translations which circulated in the Empire, the abbot of Pöllau Peter Muchitsch published his translation of Campion's 'Rationes Decem' (1580), a vindication of the Catholic faith which led to Campion's arrest and execution in London in 1581. Supplemented with a preface by Muchitsch, this work was published at the court and university press of Georg Widmanstetter in Graz in 1588.[90]

As previously mentioned, the General usually declined to consider appeals for transfer to non-European missions, and sought to direct the applicants' missionary zeal to objectives in the Empire or Habsburg lands, as in the case of Johann Rumer, who had asked frequently to be sent to India, Japan, or Ethiopia in the 1620s. Having risen in the hierarchy as rector of the college in Graz, and Austrian provincial in the 1630s and 1640s, he came to adopt the General's notion of the Jesuits' missionary obligation and supported his argument in the discussion about

---

[89] Peinlich, *Geschichte*, i. 11. Andritsch, *Unser Judenburg*, 92.
[90] T. Graff, *Bibliographia Widmanstadiana* (Graz, 1993), no. 14, p. 11. For earlier translations of this work see Evans, *Making of the Habsburg Monarchy*, 46 n. 12.

Judenburg's fate.[91] By contrast, Vitelleschi readily encouraged suitably qualified candidates who applied for missions in Bohemia, Hungary, and Transylvania or else volunteered for the Turkish mission.[92] In 1646, this policy was continued by his successor, General Vincent Carrafa (1645–9), who referred at least ten applicants from Judenburg, Leoben, Graz, and even from the small residence in Millstatt, which numbered not more than five priests in 1633, to the missions in Hungary, Transylvania, and Moldavia.[93] A link between Graz and the eastern missions had been established in the late sixteenth century by the university's intake of students from Hungary, Croatia, and Transylvania. They often returned to their home countries as priests, frequently as members of the Society.[94] Most famous among these was the professor of theology in Graz, future archbishop of Gran, primate of Hungary and cardinal, Peter Pázmány (1570–1637).[95]

While the Jesuits' institutes in Graz helped supply priests for Inner Austria and the neighbouring lands, they were less successful in their missionary work among the elite of the Protestant Styrian nobility. The overall impression given by the fragmentary evidence for confessional shifts suggests that the gentry was more amenable to the Jesuits' efforts, presumably because conversion was now the precondition for access to court and government offices and hence to social promotion. Conversely, it seems that the more prosperous and politically independent higher Protestant nobility (*Herrenstand*) was less easily persuaded to return to the Catholic faith. An analysis of the group of noble students who attended the university in Graz in the years 1586 to 1630 would seem to confirm this assumption. Where the higher echelons were concerned, the findings reveal the prominent part played by the court nobility, some of

---

[91] See the General's negative answer to Rumer's last application, 8 Mar. 1625, AGR, 'Epp. Gen., 3/II', fo. 602. For Judenburg see above.

[92] AGR, 'Epp. Gen., Austr. 3/I', letters to Martin Santinus, 20 Feb. 1620, fo. 125, Johannes Zentgeorgy, 4 June 1622, fo. 267, and 'Austr. 5/I', letters to Stephan Cornis, 2 Aug. 1636, fo. 165, and Stephan Suberle, 14 Jan. 1640, fo. 530.

[93] Carrafa to P. Johann Georg Harman, 30 June 1646, AGR, 'Epp. Gen., Austr. 5/II', fo. 1043. The records in 'Austr. 5/I–II' list 10 'Indipetae' from Styria. In 1643 and 1648, Vitelleschi and Carrafa complained that the mission in Temesvar still relied on Jesuit missionaries from Rome, because there were hardly any applicants from the Austrian province, see the letters to the visitor of the province, P. Martin Summerecker, 25 July 1643, 'Austr. 5/I', fos. 812–13, and to the new provincial Georg Turcovic, 1 Feb. 1648, 'Austr. 5/II', fos. 1141–2. The size of the Millstatt colony is stated by Peinlich, *Geschichte*, iii. 87.

[94] See the list by Andritsch, 'Grazer Jesuitenuniversität', 252–4.

[95] Andritsch, ibid. 257–8, gives a brief description of Pázmány's life and work until 1600.

whom were of recent creation.[96] There were, in all, fifty-two students from twenty-one Styrian families who belonged to the *Herrenstand*. Six of these families had, with few and brief aberrations, been Catholic throughout this period, and belonged to the group of court and government officials, namely the Attems, Eggenberg, Jöchlinger, Paar, Thanhausen, and Breuner. They supplied no less than twenty of the fifty-two students recorded. To these might be added the family of Schrattenbach, whose Catholic branch is recorded from the 1580s, and who sent nine students between 1589 and 1627.[97] The remaining fourteen families who sent twenty-three students seem to have been split into Catholic and Protestant branches, and there is in each case evidence for both Catholic and Protestant members of these families.[98] Demographic vagaries notwithstanding, there seems to have been a change in the nobility's attitude towards Jesuit education after the politically fateful year 1620. Of the above fourteen confessionally mixed families, eight began to send their children to the Jesuit university in the decade 1620–30, namely the Prank (1621), Radmansdorf (1621), Pfeilberg (also 'Pfeilwerg', 1625), Wagensberg (1625), Wexler (1625), Eibiswald (1630), Falbenhaupt (also 'Falmhaupt', 1630), and Rindsmaul (1630). It is most likely that the political crisis of 1618–19, and the subsequent fate of the Bohemian and Austrian rebels, acted as a catalyst for a confessional reorientation among the conciliatory majority of the Styrian estates. Attendance at the Jesuits' school and university eased this adaptation. However, no Barons Windischgrätz or Hoffmann von Grünbüchel are recorded in the student register. Moreover, the names of the leading Protestant families of the ancient nobility did not appear before the middle of the seventeenth century, when a new Catholic generation succeeded to their emigrated relatives' positions: members of the families of Stubenberg, Teuffenbach, and Stadl are thus mentioned in the university register for the first time in 1651.

If Jesuit education was beginning to make headway among the elites, especially after 1620, it did not, to all appearances, bring about a more

---

[96] The following is based on an evaluation of the list of Inner Austrian and foreign students from the aristocracy (princes, counts, and barons) who attended the university in 1586–1773 in Peinlich, *Geschichte*, iii. 93–105.

[97] Balthasar was the head of the elder line of the Thanhausen family, which had remained Catholic. Balthasar had apostatized, but converted in 1597, and his family became eminent patrons of the Jesuits. The Barons Franz and Gottfried von Schrattenbach were Protestants, see the evidence in *FRA/60*, 208 (for the year 1601), 627 (for 1614).

[98] This is based on an evaluation of *FRA/58* and *FRA/60* as well as my own findings in the Styrian State Archive and the Diocesan Archive.

strenuous commitment to the Society. In fact, the colleges received strikingly little material support from the civic and noble elites of Styria. Such donations as were made to the Ferdinandeum and the Convict came from members of the dynasty or from the clergy.[99] For the period 1610–30, there is little evidence to suggest that members of the laity made donations or bequests to the Jesuit colleges in Graz, Judenburg, or Leoben, while donations for the interior decoration of the Jesuit university church were made by court officials and members of the court nobility only.[100] A spectacular deviation from this rule occurred in 1619, when the Styrian estates made a donation of 2,000 fl. to the college in Graz. However, this was an isolated instance, and a collective action. It seems most likely that this was a politically motivated gesture, intended as an expression of loyalty as part of the celebrations on the occasion of Ferdinand's Imperial election.[101]

With few exceptions, the Catholic nobility conformed to the rule and made no material contribution to support the work of the Jesuits. Two spectacular deviations from the general pattern deserve to be mentioned here, namely the cases of the Schranz and Thanhausen families. The rise of the first illustrates the career opportunities open to those members of the nobility who opted for Catholicism and thrived on the developing symbiosis of Church and dynasty. The second example, however, is a reminder that genuine religious conviction was a powerful driving force in itself which could and *did* cause the sacrificing of social and economic gains derived from conversion, to the point of jeopardizing the very existence of an aristocratic family.

The rise of the Schranz family was largely the achievement of Wolfgang Schranz, privy counsellor and court vice-chancellor of Karl II.[102] His family belonged to the lower nobility, with property in Styria

[99] The sum of *c*.318 fl. was donated by the magistrates of Judenburg in 1611 for the support of three students of theology or philosophy. For donations to the Ferdinandeum and Convict see the tables in Peinlich, *Geschichte*, iii. 71–3.

[100] This is based on an evaluation of the Jesuit records in the Diocesan Archive of Graz-Seckau, especially the documentation in 'Jesuiten, XIX-c-42, XIX-c-43, Inventare und Testamente von Laien, Schenkungen, Erbschaften, 1610–1667'. Donations by members of the court are mentioned in Peinlich, *Geschichte*, ii. 15. The 'Litterae Annuae' for 1617 mention a donation of 1,000 fl. for the novitiate in Leoben by Balthasar von Schrattenbach, see below.

[101] The donation is mentioned by Peinlich, *Geschichte*, ii. 16.

[102] The information which follows is taken from the manuscript 'Genealogia der Herren Schranzen von Schranzenegg und Forchtenstain, von Hanns Phillibert Schranz Freiherr von Schranzenegg . . .' n.d. [c. 1677], STMLA, 'Archiv Schranz von Schranzenegg', Sch. 1/1. The precise dates for Wolfgang Schranz's appointment as privy counsellor etc. are stated in Thiel, 'Zentralverwaltung', I, 206.

and Carinthia. He was sent to Siena, where he obtained his doctorate in law sometime between 1555 and 1559. His first marriage in 1559 to Catharina Ostermayer, the daughter of an Austrian nobleman (*Landmann*), added a house in Vienna and property in the archduchy to his possessions. Schranz's Catholicism and legal training combined to make him a suitable candidate for a career in the service of the archduke, a prospect which he furthered by marrying Anna Walther, daughter of the government chancellor (*Regimentskanzler*) Bernhard Walther, after the death of his first wife in 1570. Wolfgang subsequently acted as a go-between in the communications between the courts in Graz and Munich, and became adviser and confidant to Karl II's wife Archduchess Maria after 1571. In the following years, he rose from privy counsellor without special commission (1574–6) to court vice-chancellor, an office which he held from 1576 to 1591. Wolfgang was granted the title of baron and assumed the title 'von Schranzenegg' in 1572. Schranz's social rise was crowned by the conclusion of an even more prestigious match after the death of his second wife in 1585. His patroness Maria and her brother Duke Wilhelm V of Bavaria procured his marriage to one of Maria's ladies-in-waiting, Margarethe von Pappenheim, daughter of a high-ranking Imperial court official, *Reichserbmarschall* Hans von Pappenheim.

Schranz's close relation with the Jesuits had been established as a result of his Bavarian contacts. Allegedly, the young duke-designate Wilhelm (V) had arranged for the mission of P. Bartholomäus Viller and another Jesuit in 1571 from Munich to Graz to strengthen the Catholic party there, and Schranz had escorted them and arranged for their introduction to Karl II.[103] As head of the Catholic party at the court in Graz, Schranz was closely in touch with the nuncio and the archduke's Jesuit confessor. At his death in 1594, Schranz left 180,000 fl. to his heirs, protected against waste and dispersal by a ducal privilege of entail granted in 1591.[104] Schranz bequeathed a house in Graz as well as 1,500

---

[103] The details are related in the 'Genealogia'. The author claims that Wilhelm (V) had sent the Jesuits disguised as Bavarian noblemen so that they could further the Catholic cause at the court under the pretext of 'political discourse'. The idea must have been to strengthen the archduchess's position and to put pressure on Karl II, perhaps in connection with the negotiations for a Jesuit settlement which began in 1571, see Peinlich, *Geschichte*, i. 7, and Duhr, *Jesuiten an deutschen Fürstenhöfen*, 24–5.

[104] The 'Genealogia' states that Schranz was also captain (*Hauptmann*) of 'Kesten', presumably meaning Kastav/Castua in the Carniolan–Croatian confines close to the Adriatic Sea, which was subject to the archduke. Schranz also had the castle of Forchtenstain in Upper Styria, and the ducal castle of Marburg with the adjoining estates.

fl. and a heavy cross of gold with precious stones to the Jesuits. His will stipulated that the money should be used for the building of an altar in the Jesuit church of St Ägidi in Graz, and that the cross should be displayed on this altar on each feast-day to commemorate the benefactor. However, the author of the 'Genealogia' noted that none of these stipulations had been fulfilled by that date, i.e. the second half of the seventeenth century, in spite of his family's frequent requests. It is stated that the rector of the college now excused himself on account of lack of funds, but this does not explain why the Jesuits refused to display the cross. The reason seems to have been that the Society was unwilling to permit aristocratic ostentation in their churches, especially if it was likely to distract the parishioners' attention during the celebration of holy mass. In 1658, the first German general of the Society, Goswin Nickel (1652–64), refused a request by the rector of the college in Judenburg, Count Ferdinand Herberstein, for a licence to cede the right of sepulture in their church to noble families. The General argued that such concessions suggested venality, and that exceptions could only be made to honour outstanding benefactors of the Society.[105] As a special patron of the Jesuits, Schranz received these honours, and was buried, together with his deceased two wives and children, behind the high altar in the Jesuits' church.[106] The Jesuits' policy about burials expressed the new Tridentine concept of devotion, but it ran counter to practices which had their roots in late medieval piety. Above all, it hardly increased the Society's popularity among the Styrian nobility and civic elites, who turned to the more obliging mendicant orders.[107]

During the reign of Ferdinand II, the family of Thanhausen became the most devoted supporters of the Society. Balthasar von Thanhausen was the only son of the Catholic Conrad, Baron of Thanhausen, who held various high court offices (councillor, chamberlain, *Obristjägermeister*) in the reign of Karl II. In 1598, Conrad's daughter Maria Sidonia married

---

After his death, this property was transferred to another Catholic favourite, Karl II's *Obristjägermeister* Conrad von Thanhausen, father of Balthasar.

[105] Letter of 12 Jan. 1658, AGR, 'Epp. Gen., Austr. 7 (1656–1663)', fos. 93–4. For Goswin Nickel see the article in L. Koch, SJ, *Jesuiten-Lexikon* (Paderborn, 1934), cols. 1292–3.

[106] Noted in the 'Genealogia'.

[107] In 1672, the priest of St Peter at Graz protested against the building of another Augustinian monastery in Graz, claiming that the wealthier parishioners already turned to the existing convent, founded in 1656, to obtain tombs in their church, thus depriving the parish of all income from grants of sepulture, bequests, etc., Johann Baptista Benutius to the bishop of Seckau, 30 May 1672, DA, 'Augustiner-Mönche' (2), XIX-b-44, Monastery 'St. Anna am Münzgraben' in Graz.

another member of the Catholic court nobility, Hans Ulrich von Eggenberg, then chamberlain and cupbearer of Ferdinand. Balthasar had initially adopted the Lutheran faith, a decision that was probably influenced by contacts with the younger Protestant line of the house.[108] In 1597, however, he reverted to Catholicism and, like Eggenberg, was drawn to the inner circle of court officials by his appointment as court chamberlain. His conversion caused a stir among the Protestant party, and the estates' preacher Salomon Eginger was banned from Inner Austria for castigating Thanhausen's decision in his sermons.[109] As ducal chamberlain and confidant, von Thanhausen accompanied Ferdinand to Italy in 1598.[110] Balthasar was married to Ursula von Hollenegg, who in the following decades became an eminent benefactress of the Counter-Reformation clergy.[111] He was able to round off his property by acquisitions and ducal donations of estates in Istria and Hungary. In 1624, the title of count was conferred on him.[112]

More spectacular than its social career, however, was the family's profound dedication to the Counter-Reformation cause in general, and to the support of the Jesuits in particular.[113] At his death in 1627, Balthasar left a wife and seven children, five of whom entered religious orders.[114] With the express permission of the head of the family, two of the three sons, Johann Bernhard and the younger Johann Ignatius, joined the Jesuits while they were their students in Graz. Johann Bernhard became a novice in Leoben in 1626, but was rapidly promoted and became a professor of philosophy at the university in Graz in 1633. He died of the plague in 1634. A year after this, his younger brother Johann Ignatius was

---

[108] See Raab, 'Thannhausen', 3–33.   [109] Peinlich, *Geschichte*, i. 45.
[110] Loserth in *FRA/60*, p. xliv.
[111] See ibid. 97 for the reforming activities of the Catholic Justina Benigna von Hollenegg, widow of the Protestant baron Friedrich von Hollenegg. Ursula was probably Justina's daughter. Together with her sisters Veronika, Regina, and Johanna, Ursula von Hollenegg (Thanhausen) donated 2,000 fl. in 1611 for the support of two clerical students, see Peinlich, *Geschichte*, iii. 71. Ferdinand II's decree of 9 Mar. 1630 which ordered a number of Protestant Styrian noblemen to comply with the general decree of Aug. 1628 is addressed to one Hans Adam von Hollenegg, presumably a Protestant relative of the above, *FRA/60*, 862.
[112] Raab, 'Thannhausen', 29–30.
[113] The following concentrates on the Thanhausen's special relation to the Jesuits, but Countess Ursula Thanhausen made several less spectacular donations to other religious orders as well, e.g. 1,000 fl. for the Carmelite nuns in Graz according to a receipt of 6 Dec. 1655, DA, 'Jesuiten (9)', XIX-c-38, 'Familie Thanhausen betreffend'. Together with the bishop of Bamberg and Count Franz von Hatzfeld, she founded a Capuchin monastery in Wolfsberg (Carinthia) in 1634, see A. Zák, *Österreichisches Klosterbuch* (Vienna, 1911), 194.
[114] Three of his four daughters entered Styrian convents, Raab, 'Thannhausen', 30.

allowed to enter the Society, leaving only one further male heir, Johann
Anton, to continue the elder line of the family. Ignatius joined the college
in Judenburg in 1635 and was subsequently sent to the college in Rome,
accompanied by his tutor, P. Zacharias Trinkell from Graz, because he
had formed and educated the Count's mind from childhood.[115] As previously mentioned, Balthasar and Ursula von Thanhausen had founded the
college in Judenburg, a donation which was hugely expanded by Ursula
von Thanhausen in 1642–3. With the support of his mother, Johann
Bernhard gave 55,050 fl. of his paternal heritage for the foundation of a
college in Steyr in Upper Austria. The college in Fiume (*Rijeka*) was likewise a Thanhausen foundation. To these were added Johann Ignatius'
donation of his share of his patrimony (55,050 fl.) for the college in
Zagreb. He donated a further 10,000 fl. for the college, church, and
library in Graz, for the German provinces (*Assistentiae Germaniae*), and
another 1,000 fl. to support the process for the beatification of Petrus
Canisius in Rome.[116] Countess Ursula von Thanhausen's will of 1654
made such extravagantly generous stipulations for the Jesuit colleges of
Zagreb, Steyr, Fiume, Judenburg and Linz, which was to receive a
Francis Xavier chapel, that the widow of Johann Anton sued the Society
to obtain at least the legal portion of her husband's share of his patrimony.[117]

The case of the Thanhausen, though exceptional, is evidence that
conversion and confessional allegiance could be more than just a stepping
stone for a career in the service of the prince. On the whole, however,

[115] On 27 June 1626, General Vitelleschi instructed the Jesuits in Graz to accept Johann
Bernhard only if his parents fully approved, to avoid any suspicion that the Society had
enticed away the son of a distinguished family. By September, it was clear that Johann
Bernhard's parents fully backed his decision, and Vitelleschi ordered the novice's dispatch
to the college in Rome. The journey, however, did not come about as a result of Johann
Bernhard's illness; see the letters by Vitelleschi to P. Philipp Alegambe, 27 June 1626, 24
Oct. 1626, and 5 Dec. 1626, Vitelleschi to rector Marcellus Pollardt in Graz, 19 Sept. 1626,
and to Johann Bernhard von Thanhausen in Leoben, AGR, 'Epp. Gen., Austr. 3/II', fos.
719, 742–3, 755, 770. Johann Bernhard's death is mentioned in the General's letter to P.
Philipp Alegambe on 16 Sept. 1634, ibid. 973. For Johann Ignatius see the letter by
Vitelleschi to P. Johann Rumer in Graz, 7 Apr. and 9 June 1635, fos. 1060 and 1079. For
Johann Bernhard's appointment as professor in Graz see Peinlich, *Geschichte*, i. 102.
[116] The above information has been taken from an account entitled 'Plena Informatio' in
DA, 'Jesuiten' (9) XIX-c-38, 'Familie Thanhausen betreffend'. Thanhausen's stipulation
suggests that funds were being raised by the Jesuits in the German provinces to further
Canisius' process. Canisius was beatified in 1869 and canonized in 1925, but he was vener-
ated as a saint soon after his death in 1597, a cult that was furthered by the Jesuits, see J.
Brodrick, SJ, *Petrus Canisius*, German trans. by Karl Telch (Vienna, 1950), ii. 581.
[117] The relevant documents can be found in DA, 'Jesuiten (9)', XIX-c-38, 'Familie
Thanhausen betreffend (2)'.

Ferdinand's court nobility seems to have expressed their allegiance to the Catholic cause in terms that did not interfere with their worldly ambitions, e.g. in the case of the Schrattenbach family, whose Catholic branch supplied privy counsellors and court officials from the late sixteenth century onwards, beginning with the appointment of Balthasar von Schrattenbach as the young archduke's *Obersthofmeister* in 1597. He acquired a reputation as patron of the Jesuits by less ruinous donations for the church in Graz and the noviciate in Leoben.[118] Another member of the family, Maximilian, had been privy counsellor and *Obersthofmeister* to Karl II's widow Maria of Bavaria. In 1598, he was granted the title of baron, and Ferdinand II later on conferred the title of count on Maximilian's younger brother Johann Friedrich, whose name appears in the Jesuits' university register in 1616.[119]

As previously described, the Jesuits' educational mission was beginning to score successes among the elite of the nobility from the 1620s onwards, while direct support for their work was still provided only by members of the dynasty, the higher clergy, and a few members of the court nobility. After the transfer of the court to Vienna in 1619–20, there was a brief decline in the number of nobility who participated in the Jesuits' feast-day processions in Graz, indicating the importance of immediate ducal control. The number of conversions recorded by the Jesuits in Graz rose from a mere fifteen in 1620 and nine in 1621 to forty-two in 1622, numbering ninety-seven in 1629, though the social and national background of these converts is unclear.[120] It seems that, by comparison, the Jesuits were more successful in addressing the civic elite of the capital. In 1622, General Vitelleschi joined the Jesuits' Marian congregation for the burghers 'sub titulo Purificationis B(eatae) Mariae Virginis' to the first congregation in Rome, so that the *sodales* in Graz would share in the special privileges and indulgences granted to this congregation if they fulfilled their religious duties.[121] By this time, there were already three students' congregations as well as a civic 'Congregatio Beatae Virginis ab archangelo salutatae', numbering all in all 435 members, who contributed to the revival of the Marian cult and to the

[118] 'Litterae Annuae' for 1617, ÖNB, MS 13562.
[119] See Thiel, 'Zentralverwaltung', i. 203–4, Peinlich, *Geschichte*, ii. 8, 16, iii. 102, and the article on the Schrattenbach family in C. V. Wurzbach, *Biographisches Lexikon des Kaiserthums Österreich* (Vienna, 1856–90).
[120] Krones, *Karl-Franzens-Universität*, 281–4, on the basis of the 'Litterae Annuae' for these years.
[121] Confirmation by General Mutius Vitelleschi, 15 Apr. 1622, DA, 'Jesuiten, XIX-d-1, Kongregationen'.

spread of Jesuit directed devotional practices.[122] A 'Spiritus Sanctus' congregation had been founded in the Convict in 1576, which had staged processions for the defence of the Catholic faith and for the propagation of the Society while the town was still thoroughly heretical.[123] The necrology of this congregation for the years 1600–12 suggests that around two-thirds of its members belonged to the clergy. This is hardly surprising in view of the Convict's main function, clerical education. The high proportion of prelates and regular clergy from a variety of orders whose recorded 'Sterb-Ort' (place of death) was situated outside Inner Austria, e.g. in Croatia, Poland, Tyrol, and the Empire (Cologne), is further evidence of the Jesuits' importance for the recruitment of the clergy and the development of the Catholic mission in the Empire and adjoining territories. The remaining third of secular members consisted mainly of court officials, like Ferdinand's secretary Peter Casal, and one Leonard Liechtenberger who died in 1611 as 'inferioris Austriae Camerae Officialis'—an indication that the seminary in Graz also supplied Catholic officials for other institutions of the Monarchy. Of the twenty-six secular members who died in the years 1600–12, sixteen were noblewomen, among whom a 'Domina Regina Rintscheitin auf Schloß Wolkenstein', a member of the otherwise Protestant family of Rindscheidt, is described as an eminent benefactress of the congregation.[124]

If the students' theatrical performances and the activity of the congregations were directed mainly at the noble and civic elites, there were nevertheless public celebrations and devotions which sought to involve all strata of the urban population, e.g. the processions and celebrations on the occasion of the canonization of Ignatius, Francis Xavier (1622), and Francis Borgia (1624).[125] In 1594, the Jesuits introduced the 40-hours

---

[122] The 'Sodalitas Beatae Mariae Virginis' was founded in 1595 and joined to the Roman congregation in that year, see the confirmation by General Acquaviva in DA, 'Jesuiten, XIX-d-1, Kongregationen'. The confraternities of the students and pupils in Graz counted 210 and 135 members in 1622, while the congregation for non-academics had 90 members. The composition of this latter group is unfortunately not stated. To these should be added the civic congregation founded in 1622, which is not mentioned by Krones, see id., *Karl-Franzens-Universität*, 62.

[123] 'Litterae Annuae' for 1576, AGR, 'Austr. 132', fo. 19.

[124] The necrology for 1600–12 can be found in DA, 'Vereine-Bruderschaften, 1600ff, XVI-a-3'. Regina Rindscheidt withdrew capital from the Styrian *Landschaft* in 1629, presumably in connection with the emigration of Protestant members of the family, *FRA/60*, 859. For the Protestants Ernreich and Andreas Rindscheidt see ibid. 298, 312.

[125] Peinlich, *Geschichte*, ii. 20–1. The college's theatrical performances are dealt with by Hofer, 'Grazer Jesuitendrama', and M. Rader, 'Das Grazer Barocktheater (1600–1700)' (doctoral thesis, University of Graz, 1964), 21–134.

prayer in Graz as a petitionary and penitential prayer 'to avert the Turkish threat'.[126] This religious exercise continued throughout the years of the 'Long Turkish War' until 1606, and became popular among the lower strata of the urban population. By 1615, they had given up their customary Shrovetide revelries, and the Jesuits' penitential prayer had become a firmly established devotional practice in Graz.[127]

The introduction of new types of devotional practices which expressed the spirit of Tridentine piety was but one way of spreading the true faith. From the 1580s onwards, written propaganda was developing into an important means of diffusing Counter-Reformation doctrines in Inner Austria. At the conference of Munich in October 1579, the Catholic princes, led by Bavaria, had attached great importance to the restoration of the archduke's control over the printing press in his capital.[128] One of the twelve Jesuits who founded the settlement in Graz in 1572, the Bohemian P. Johannes Reinel, quickly acquired a reputation for his polemical sermons and invectives against the Lutherans in Graz, activities which endeared him to the Archduchess Maria, who made him her confessor and protégé.[129] Presumably at her request, he accompanied the court on a journey through Swabia and Bavaria in 1582,[130] and he subsequently became the Bavarian duke's confidant and 'agent' in Graz. In October 1582, Duke Wilhelm V instructed Reinel to make good use of his influence on Karl II, presumably to ensure the implementation of the decisions of Munich, but urged him to take care 'so that it does not seem as if we wanted to govern there entirely'.[131]

It seems likely that Reinel took the initiative in suggesting the transfer of the Catholic printer Georg Widmanstetter from Munich to Graz in 1585.[132] Georg was the son of Johann Albrecht Widmanstetter (1506–57), a zealous Catholic who rose from modest origins to become

---

[126] 'Litterae Annuae' for 1594, AGR, 'Austr. 132', fo. 220.

[127] 'Tertius hic annus est, quod insana dierum Liberalium licentia ab Urbe Graecensi extorris, quadraginta horarum Supplicationi locum cessit . . .' 'Litterae Annuae' for 1617, ÖNB, MS 13562.

[128] Decisions of the conference of Munich, 14 Oct. 1579, in *FRA/50*, 37.

[129] For Reinel see Peinlich, *Geschichte*, i. 8, Duhr, *Jesuiten an deutschen Fürstenhöfen*, 29–30, 35.

[130] Duhr, *Jesuiten an deutschen Fürstenhöfen*, 30.

[131] 'das es nit auch das Ansehen hab, als wollten wir dasselbs gannz und gar regiren.' Letter of 20 Nov. 1582, quoted in Cerwinka, 'Graz und München', 106.

[132] A. Schlossar, 'Grazer Buchdruck im 16. Jahrhundert', *AGDBH* 4 (1879), 26–7, states that Widmanstetter was called to Graz at the request of the Jesuits. Given the special relationship between Reinel and the Bavarian court, it seems likely that the idea originated either with him or Duke Wilhelm V.

Imperial knight in 1548, and privy counsellor, government chancellor, and court printer of Ferdinand I in the 1550s. He eventually married into a collateral branch of the Wittelsbach family (Bayern–Landshut). In 1585, Georg Widmanstetter became court printer to Karl II, and received an annual pension of 100 ducats to support his work. In 1591, the *Hofkammer* discontinued the payment of this subsidy, but the Jesuit rector Emmerich Forsler persuaded Archduke Ernst to resume its payment by pointing to the importance of Widmanstetter's press for the university and for the fight against Protestant propaganda.[133] The appointment of Widmanstetter was accompanied by a campaign against the estates' printer, Zacharias Bartsch. Bartsch had on an earlier occasion incurred Karl II's wrath for printing an anti-papal pasquinade, and in 1586 his refusal to print the lecture list of the university was used as a pretext for his arrest and eviction from Inner Austria. His successor Hans Schmid fared no better. In 1599, he was banned for having printed an allegedly seditious Protestant prayer.[134] The abolition of the Protestant school and church ministry in Graz by the decree of 23 September 1598[135] and the work of the reformation commissions destroyed the Protestants' educational institutions, so that from about 1600 onwards, the Jesuits and their printer enjoyed a virtual monopoly in the field of propaganda and education.

These changes are to some extent reflected by the literary production of the Widmanstetter press.[136] In the years 1586 to 1600, at least 135 titles were issued, including several reprints. Sixteen of these prints were items with secular contents, e.g. ducal decrees, guild statutes, almanacs, and news of the Turkish War, so-called 'Türken-Zeytungen', all of these written in German. The majority of prints was divided into roughly equal shares of German religious works and Latin treatises on theological questions.

[133] Ibid. 26–34. Forsler's letter of 4 May 1592 is reprinted ibid. 33–4. Georg Widmanstetter became a member of the civic elite in Graz as town councillor and administrator of the almshouse, see T. Graff, 'Die Offizin Widmanstetter 1585–1806', in id. and S. Karner, *Leykam: 400 Jahre Druck und Papier* (Graz, 1985), 23–90.
[134] See the Styrian estates' complaint to Archduke Ferdinand, 24 Apr. 1599. They protested the inoffensive nature of the text, *FRA/58*, 556–7. For Schmid and the appointment of Widmanstetter see also F. Ahn, 'Die Druckerpresse Widmanstetters zu Graz', *MÖVBW* 8 (1904), 144–5.
[135] *FRA/58*, 324–5.
[136] The following calculations are based on the information provided by Theodor Graff's *Bibliographia*, 9–44 (1586–1600) and 44–86 (1601–29). A closer description of Widmanstetter's production can be found in id., *Die Entwicklung des steirischen Buchdrucks bis zum Ende des 18. Jahrhunderts und ihre Auswirkungen in den innerösterreichischen Raum* (Maribor, 1988). The second half of the title is unfortunately misleading.

218   *Reform, Mission, and Propaganda*

Almost all of these latter publications were prints of academic disserta-
tions, or the written version of disputations held at the university of Graz
or one of the other Catholic universities in the Empire. Arguably, they
were not only published for the benefit of the Jesuits' students at the
university in Graz, but also aimed at the instruction of the provincial
clergy, and candidates for priesthood. In 1588, there was, for example, an
edition of the *Tractatus Brevis de Censuris Ecclesiasticis, Omnibus
Praesertim Clericis Perutilis ac Necessarius* by the Dominican Sebastian
Cattaneo, theological adviser of the archbishop of Salzburg.[137] Academic
theses on the sacraments of penitence and the Eucharist in 1588 and 1591
were published presumably not only for the instruction of the Catholic
clergy. It is likely that it was hoped to arouse the interest of the Protestant
students at the *Stiftsschule* in Graz and of the apostatized rural priests as
well.[138]

By 1600, Widmanstetter had published at least fifty-six German-
language religious writings. This group could be subdivided into works of
polemical character which engaged in a controversy with the Lutheran
theologians in Graz and Tübingen, and those publications which
explained the main articles of the Catholic faith and all controversial
issues to the Catholic and Protestant laity. Among the latter group of
pamphlets, there was, for example, a vindication of the Catholic doctrine
against the Lutheran position on the question of communion in both
kinds, which seeks to persuade the Protestant reader that it is sufficient to
receive the sacrament according to the Catholic rite.[139] Direct appeals
presented in the shape of public letters to individuals are used to encourage the return of straying sheep to the Catholic fold, e.g. the 'candid
letter' ('trewhertzigs Sendschreiben') of the parish priest of Pettau,
Sebastian Khobl, 'to his lost sheep Benedict Tottung' ('An sein verlornes
Schäfflein Benedicten Tottung'), a Protestant burgher and merchant of
Pettau who had left the town, presumably heading for Hungary. Tottung

---

[137] Title page reprinted in Graff, *Bibliographia*, 11, no. 15.
[138] *Theses Theologicae de Poenitentiae Sacramento*, printed in 1588. The author is one
Magister Georg Empristius, student at the university in Graz and preacher in the town
parish, see the title page in Graff, *Bibliographia*, 12, no. 17. The *Assertiones Theologicae de
Sacrosancto Eucharistiae Sacramento et Sacrificio* by Nikolaus Eczeth, a Hungarian student
of theology and alumnus of the cathedral chapter of Gran (Esztergom), had been presented
for discussion at the Jesuit college in Vienna, and were printed twice by Widmanstetter in
1591 and 1592, see Graff, *Bibliographia*, 22 and 24, nos. 65 and 73.
[139] *Examen oder fleissige Erörterung | dessen zu unsern Zeiten allermaisten strittigen Artickels
von der Communion . . . Durch Magister Blasius Ellander* (Graz, 1588). Reprint of the title
page in Graff, *Bibliographia*, 12, no. 19.

is urged to reconsider his decision and revert to the Catholic faith, and with him all of those among the readers who likewise belong to the 'straying sheep' ('Irrende . . . Schäfflein').[140] For the Catholic faithful, there were several German devotional tracts before 1600, e.g. the prayer book by the rector of the college in Graz, P. Emmerich Forsler, published in 1588.[141] A Catholic catechism by Johann Baptist Romanus, a Jesuit theologian at the college in Rome, presented the main articles of the Catholic faith to the reader, adding pictures to explain the meaning of the text to the simple, illiterate folk ('dem gemeinen einfältigen Volck | so nicht lesen kan | zu nutz mit schoenen newen Figuren für Augen gestellt | und eingebildet'). This tradition of illustrated catechisms dated back to 1550, but Canisius and his successors like Romanus were the first to make systematic use of this means of teaching the illiterate.[142] Anti-Lutheran propaganda was contributed by the Jesuit Georg Scherer, a renowned Viennese controversial preacher whose sermons and polemical writings in defence of Catholic doctrines and devotional practices were in part reprinted by the Widmanstetter press in the years 1588–90.[143]

At the same time, the Jesuits in Graz launched a particularly ingenious campaign to undermine the authority of their theological adversaries and cause confusion among their less erudite followers. In 1587, Widmanstetter published a booklet which was ostensibly a reprint of Luther's small catechism, enlarged and amended, as the title claimed, by explanations from his own writings, and prefaced by a vindication ('Schutzred') for the Lutheran priests and preachers.[144] The 'amendments'

---

[140] Full title in Graff, *Bibliographia*, 17, no. 45 (Graz, 1589).

[141] Ibid. 15, no. 36.

[142] *Doctrina Christiana: Das ist | Ein Christlicher Bericht unnd Lehr . . .*, by Johann Baptist Romanus, SJ (Graz, 1589). Title page reprinted in Graff, *Bibliographia*, 17, no. 44. In 1589, the Plantin press published a Canisian catechism with 107 octavo-size illustrations, each of which had a brief subtitle from the text. For this and the above information on illustrated catechisms see Duhr, *Geschichte*, i. 461–2.

[143] For a detailed description of Scherer's life and works see Duhr, *Geschichte*, i. 798–820. Widmanstetter printed Scherer's works on the Corpus Christi procession (1588) and the ceremony of baptism (1588), as well as his attack on the Protestant preacher Maximilian Biber who had been preaching in Upper Austria and Styria (1589), and his controversy with the Protestant theologian Paul Florenius in Vienna (1590), see Graff, *Bibliographia*, 12, no. 20, 13, no. 22, 16, 41 and 21, no. 59. Scherer was probably also the author of a polemical treatise entitled *Der Lutherisch Bettlers Mantel*, see Duhr, *Geschichte*, i. 820, n. 2, which was published by Widmanstetter in 1588, see Graff, *Bibliographia*, 13, no. 21.

[144] *Enchiridion; Das ist | Der kleine und raine Catechismus | mit schönen newen Figuren | sampt einer Nothwendigen Schutzred | für die Gemaine Pfarrherrn unnd Prediger gemehrt und gebessert | Auß D. M. Lutheri Schrifften und Büchern | zu Wittenberg gedruckt* (Graz, 1589),

in fact consisted of interspersed quotations from Luther's early orthodox writings, so that their addition to the questions and answers of the later catechism infused it with a Catholic meaning. The sources for these interpolations were in each case indicated in the margin, adding to its air of authenticity for those who were ignorant, and impairing Luther's authority among those who compared these to the positions of the original version. The attack was especially upsetting for the Protestant party because the small catechism was used as a primer at their grammar school in Graz. Its author was the Jesuit Sigismund Ernhofer, then archducal confessor in Graz, and his opponents thought it wise to avoid a direct confrontation.[145] Instead, they turned to the University of Tübingen for help, and, over the next two years, the Protestant theologian Jakob Heerbrand engaged in a pamphlet war with Ernhofer. The controversy quickly deteriorated into the usual exchange of calumnies and abuse among opposed controversialists. Moreover, Heerbrand's scholarly argument in his first reply was too long-winded and sophisticated to deflect the blow dealt to the Protestant cause by the denunciation of Luther's inconstancy.[146]

By 1600, confessional competition in the educational field had stopped and the political Counter-Reformation was making progress. A corresponding change can be detected in the character of printed propaganda after this date. Although the alleged novelty of the Protestant faith, Lutheran fickleness, and discord among the Protestant theologians remained recurrent themes in the writings of Catholic propagandists, there were fewer direct polemical challenges to Protestant theologians, and more elaborate arguments for conversion. To facilitate this step, these arguments were often presented as the advice of former Protestants turned zealous Catholics.[147]

see Graff, *Bibliographia*, 16, no. 42. For the following details concerning the controversy see Loserth, *Gegenreformation*, 486–501, who mentions the first edition of 1587. The full titles of Ernhofer's and Heerbrand's subsequent pamphlets are stated ibid.

[145] Ernhofer had joined the Society in Munich in 1562 and was subsequently sent to Vienna and Graz. For a brief characterization see Duhr, *Jesuiten an deutschen Fürstenhöfen*, 68–9 n. 2.

[146] This point is made by Loserth, *Gegenreformation*, 493.

[147] e.g. in the *Außrauschung der Augspurgischen Confusion* . . . (Graz,1606), which used this device extensively. The preface to the 'Christian reader' is signed by one Conradus Doschius, 'geweßner Lutherischer Predicant', and the text claims to be the speech of a converted Calvinist preacher, delivered in Antwerp on the occasion of his public abjuration of the reformed faith in 1586. Copy in the Styrian State Library, C 518043 I. Similarly, the *Gute Zeitung | für die Christlichen Layen*, published in 1604, presented its arguments for conversion in the form of a fictive conversation between Lucas Osiander (1534–1603), son

The extant evidence for the production of the Widmanstetter press in the years 1600 to 1630 suggests that the volume of overall literary production actually diminished. There were *c*.170 titles issued in these three decades, as compared to *c*.135 in the period 1586–1600. The proportion of secular items remained very small (*c*.17), but the number of German-language theological or devotional treatises seems to have decreased (*c*.36) in favour of a growing proportion of Latin prints for the university, panegyrical works for the dynasty, and devotional tracts for the academic sodalities.[148]

In view of Widmanstetter's peculiar position as court printer and subsidized propagandist of the Counter-Reformation, it remains unclear how far the composition of the enterprise's production reflects the influence of readers' predilections. It could nevertheless be argued that reprints, especially of recent publications, are indicative of a work's popularity, so for example in the case of the collection of 'new and hitherto unprinted' Catholic chants 'to be sung not only during Holy Mass, processions and pilgrimages, but also at home', by Nikolaus Beuttner, schoolmaster in the Jesuits' Upper Styrian parish of St Lorenzen in the Mürz valley.[149] This hymn book was published by Widmanstetter in 1602 and went through several further editions until 1630.[150]

The changes in the volume and focus of printed Catholic propaganda in the later decades of the period under consideration could be seen as reflecting a growing sense of security among the Counter-Reformers. The previously described evidence for a shift in the focus of Jesuit missionary activity seems to point in the same direction. Progress had been made in the field of clerical reform and lay education, and the previously described evidence

of the famous Andreas Osiander and court preacher to the Lutheran duke of Württemberg, and 'many thousand' converted Calvinists, Lutherans, Zwinglians, and other sectarians. Copy in the Styrian State Library, C 518025 I. The full titles can be found in Graff, *Bibliographia*, 58, no. 220, 53, no. 199.

[148] This is based on an evaluation of Graff, *Bibliographia*, 44–86, with the same modifications as before. In Munich, the Jesuits directed a pious foundation for the production and distribution of devotional literature to support their missionary effort in south Germany. An analysis of the catalogue of the 'Golden Alms' reveals that, as in the case of the Widmanstetter press, the number of German-language as compared to Latin publications steadily declined after the subsiding of religious controversy, see W. Brückner, 'Zum Literaturangebot des Güldenen Almosens', *Zeitschrift für bayerische Landesgeschichte*, 47 (1984), 121–39, and the further research quoted ibid.

[149] Title page reprinted in Graff, *Bibliographia*, 48, no. 177. The information on Beuttner's occupation is taken from K. Amon, 'Religiöse Literatur des 16. Jahrhunderts in der Steiermark', in *Literatur in der Steiermark*, catalogue of the *Landesausstellung* in Graz (Graz, n.d. [1976]), 48.

[150] Graff, *Bibliographia*, 64, no. 260 (1609), 75, no. 303 (1615–19), 84, no. 342 (1625).

for Judenburg and Graz illustrates that traditional Catholic piety revived, and new devotional practices like the 40-hours prayer became popular among the urban population. Furthermore, the evidence for the Jesuits' activity in Leoben proves that urban missionary work had an impact on the religious life of the surrounding rural communities as well. On the other hand, Protestant enclaves survived in the remoter regions of Upper Styria and on the borders of the duchy in the absence of efficient control by the secular and ecclesiastical authorities.

The decisive change in the confessional orientation of the political elite set in only during the final decade of the period under consideration, and it was not until about the middle of the seventeenth century that the former Protestant aristocracy was represented among the students of the university. Like the previously described timing of the further 'reformations' in the 1620s, these dates indicate the degree to which the progress of the Counter-Reformation in Inner Austria was influenced by the course of the military confrontation in the Empire. The imposition of confessional conformity in 1628 marked the end of the political Counter-Reformation, but the spiritual reconquest was far from being completed. Its shortcomings were to cause the temporary return of religious persecution, but also the eventual rejection of the Counter-Reformation in the eighteenth century.

7

The Limits of the Counter-Reformation

With the general edict of emigration of 1 August 1628, Ferdinand II terminated a Counter-Reformation campaign that had received its first impetus from the meeting of Habsburg and Wittelsbach princes in Munich in October 1579, but which had failed to achieve its main objectives in the reign of Karl II as a result of the combined obstructive effects of the personal shortcomings of the prince and adverse military and financial circumstances. After a period of inconclusive legislative and reforming activity in the 1580s and a temporary setback during the ducal minority, it was the energetic young Archduke Ferdinand who resumed the battle over the confessional issue at the height of the military crisis, and as Emperor Ferdinand II brought it to its conclusion in the wake of military successes. The political Counter-Reformation was supported by the reforming activity of the nuncios, the Jesuits, and Jesuit-trained prelates like Georg Stobaeus and Martin Brenner, who strove to bring about a thorough reform of the clergy and a revival of Catholic devotional practices among the laity. This process was obstructed in many ways by the activity of the Protestant nobility, who used their rights as feudal seigneurs to protect their Protestant subjects. Although there were signs of a confessional reorientation of the elite from 1620 onwards, it took the final decree of 1628 to remove this obstacle definitely. A residue of secret heretical activity by noblemen was recorded until the mid-seventeenth century, but any lingering hopes of a Protestant revival were dashed by the constitutional settlement between Ferdinand III and his adversaries in 1648.

The following survey of the confessional development from the general expulsion in 1628 to the abolition of religious persecution in 1780–1 attempts to assess the achievements and shortcomings of the Ferdinandean Counter-Reformation. In addressing the first issue, particular attention is given to the activity of the protagonists of the process of confessional consolidation which roughly spanned the century from the

Inner Austrian edict of emigration to the resumption of *systematic* persecution in 1731. The imperfections of the Catholic achievement are discussed more fully in the subsequent section which deals with the governmental and ecclesiastical response to the problem of crypto-Protestantism in the Austrian lands and Bohemia in the eighteenth century. This discussion of the fate of the Catholic mission and the course of governmental religious policy after 1630 intends to put the Ferdinandean Counter-Reformation into perspective. As will be demonstrated, the crypto-Protestant crisis in the eighteenth century undermined the consensus on the political assumptions which supported the Counter-Reformation approach towards religious dissent, thus foreshadowing the repudiation of religious persecution as a device of governmental politics. It is hoped thereby to contribute to an assessment of the Counter-Reformation's ambivalent heritage to the nascent modern Habsburg Monarchy.

A qualification must be made regarding the scope of the picture presented. A summary treatment of the period from the end of the Ferdinandean Counter-Reformation to the official termination of religious intolerance by Joseph II cannot attempt to give an adequate assessment of those complex political and intellectual constellations which formed the background to the eighteenth-century response to the Counter-Reformation. Thus, it is beyond the scope of the present book to discuss the influence of the acquisition of the 'second Habsburg empire' in Italy and the Netherlands, which in 1714 made the Belgian Jansenist controversy a political issue for the Viennese government, while the Italian acquisitions brought a current of enlightened 'reform Catholicism' from Milan from the middle of the eighteenth century onwards. Reform-minded bishops in the Empire and the archbishopric of Salzburg rose to the challenge of the secular enlightenment by introducing liturgical and educational reforms to end extrovert devotional practices that were now disapproved as abuses. The importance of Austrian Jansenism is well documented, but anti-Jesuitism was not as prominent in the Austrian reform debate as it was in the Empire, presumably because Maria Theresia maintained until its dissolution in 1773 an essentially benevolent attitude towards the Society, in spite of her Jansenist inclinations. Nevertheless, the criticism of enlightened and Jansenist reformers systematically discredited characteristic forms of Counter-Reformation piety which had been introduced by the Society and other reform orders.[1]

---

[1] The acquisition of the 'second Habsburg empire' in the west and Maria Theresia's dynastic policy in Italy are discussed by Ingrao, *Habsburg Monarchy*, 105–77, 193–4. For the

For the purposes of the present study, the range of issues has been limited with an eye to the direct relevance of the material presented. This means that Maria Theresia's ambitious but largely abortive institutional and administrative reform plans of the 1750s, for example, are not discussed here.[2] Instead, the following discussion concentrates on the problem of crypto-Protestantism and the fate of the Counter-Reformation mission in Styria, issues that were raised in the preceding analysis of the Counter-Reformation in the sixteenth and seventeenth centuries.

As previously indicated, a brief consideration of the terms of the Westphalian peace treaty must form the starting point for a discussion of these issues since they sealed the fate of Austrian Protestantism and marked the beginning of a century of confessional consolidation in the Empire and the Habsburg lands. To facilitate the territorial settlement and to obtain a constitutional guarantee for the Protestant population of the rest of the Empire, based on the state of confessional allegiances in the year 1624, Sweden abandoned the cause of the Protestants in the hereditary lands. The Emperor's right to impose confessional conformity was not restrained, except for a saving clause granting freedom of worship to the Silesian Protestants.[3] In Lower Austria, the remaining Protestant nobility was ceded the right to attend Protestant services

---

Italian link see E. Zlabinger, *Lodovico Antonio Muratori und Österreich* (Innsbruck, 1970) as well as A. Wandruszka, 'Die katholische Aufklärung Italiens und ihr Einfluß auf Österreich' in E. Kovacs (ed.), *Katholische Aufklärung und Josephinismus* (Vienna, 1979), 62–9. A survey of the Austrian government's changing attitude towards Jansenism can be found in J. Rogiers, 'Die Bestrebungen zur Ausbildung einer belgischen Kirche und ihre Analogie zum österreichischen (theresianischen) Kirchensystem', ibid. 78–83. For the Jansenist influence in Austria see P. Hersche, *Der Spätjansenismus in Österreich* (Vienna, 1977), who seeks to demonstrate that Maria Theresia's policy after 1760 was influenced by Jansenist views, see ibid. 134–50. For the catalytic function of anti-Jesuitism in the German context see R. van Dülmen, 'Antijesuitismus und katholische Aufklärung in Deutschland', in *HJb* 89 (1969), 52–80. Biographical information on the leading enlightened reformers in Vienna, Salzburg, and Passau, like Archbishop Count Leopold Anton Firmian, Count Johann Trautson, or Joseph Maria, Count Thun, can be found ibid. 50–69. In Inner Austria, enlightened ecclesiastical reforms were delayed until the accession of Joseph Adam von Arco as bishop of Seckau (1780–1802), see A. Posch, *Die kirchliche Aufklärung in Graz und an der Grazer Hochschule* (Graz, 1937).

[2] The most important preliminary measures for a comprehensive ecclesiastical reform as envisaged by the Empress are outlined by R. Reinhardt, 'Zur Kirchenreform in Österreich unter Maria Theresia', *Zeitschrift für Kirchengeschichte*, 77 (1966), 105–19.

[3] This privilege was ceded to the Protestants in the Silesian principalities of Liegnitz-Brieg-Wohlau, Münsterberg-Oels, and in the town of Breslau. So called 'Peace Churches' near the towns of Glogau, Jauer, and Schweidnitz were built for the Habsburgs' Protestant subjects in the hereditary principalities of Lower Silesia (Schweidnitz-Jauer, Glatz, Breslau, Oppeln-Ratibor, Teschen, and Glogau), see Press, *Kriege und Krisen*, 264 and G. Köbler, *Historisches Lexikon der deutschen Länder* (Munich, 1988), 491–2.

abroad, a privilege which perpetuated the earlier favour bestowed on the loyal faction of the Lower Austrian estates. Neither the Swedish ambassadors nor the Protestant princes of the Empire were able to negotiate further religious concessions for the Habsburgs' subjects, and the Counter-Reformation regime established in the archduchy, Bohemia and Moravia, and Inner Austria in the 1620s remained in full force. Likewise, the Protestant allies were unable to make sure that the favourable terms of the Westphalian Peace regarding the right of emigration were enforced in the Habsburg lands. The religious settlement granted a *ius emigrandi* to Protestant subjects of Catholic rulers, and a period of three or even five years for the necessary arrangements, e.g. for the sale of their farmsteads and livestock at a fair price. Emigrants were furthermore allowed to take their families and property with them.[4]

None of these generous terms were in fact applied to the Habsburgs' subjects, and after the conclusion of the Peace, Ferdinand III sought to complete the expulsion of the remaining heterodox population. He had previously renewed the religious decrees of his father,[5] and on 2 June 1650 he ordered the general dispossession (*Abstiftung*) and eviction of Protestant peasants in Upper Austria. In 1652–3, reformation commissions continued the confessional purge of Upper and Lower Austria. Those who refused to convert to Catholicism were ordered to emigrate at short notice. Children under age were forcibly taken away and entrusted to Catholic guardians.[6]

In Inner Austria, Ferdinand II had initially granted his loyal Protestant estates a year's grace to settle their affairs,[7] and the course of the military confrontation after 1630 brought a reprieve for the remaining Protestant noblemen, who managed to postpone their emigration year after year. The correspondence between the Styrian *Landeshauptmann* Karl von Saurau and the Inner Austrian government in the years 1635 to 1652 is mainly concerned with the problems of crypto-Protestantism and the lack of religious enthusiasm among aristocratic converts.[8] By way of reply

---

[4] For the details of the above negotiations and the terms of the 'normative year' settlement see F. Dickmann, *Der Westfälische Frieden* (3rd edn., Münster, 1964), 462–3.

[5] Renewal of the general decrees and special resolutions of 1628 and 1631 concerning the expulsion of the Protestant nobility, printed patent, Preßburg, 3 Mar. 1638, DA, 'Religionsberichte Protestantismus', 1598–1730, XV-b-23.

[6] Haider, *Oberösterreich*, 187, Gutkas, *Niederösterreich*, 250.

[7] Emigration decree of 1 Aug. 1628, *FRA/60*, 818.

[8] The correspondence is dispersed among STMLA, 'Archiv Saurau', Sch. 230, H. 1600, STMLA, 'Landschaftliches Archiv, Religion und Kirche', Sch. 29–30, and STMLA, 'Meillerakten', XIX-h.

to Saurau's report of 26 September 1636 and his denunciations of 'uncatholic' noblewomen who continued to educate their children in the Lutheran faith, held conventicles, and read Lutheran literature to their servants, Ferdinand II issued a decree on 31 October 1636 which ordered the severe—though unspecified—punishment of these women. Their children were to be entrusted to Catholic teachers, and annual reports certifying their Catholic education and fulfilment of their Easter duties had to be submitted to the *Landeshauptmann*. The decree also deals with the persecution of preachers who ministered to members of these households and their servants, and exhorts the parish clergy and the bishop to keep an eye on the rural and urban population.[9] In January 1638, Saurau sent strict orders to eight Styrian noblemen who had refused to send their children to Catholic schools and to Easter communion. He furthermore denounced several Upper Styrian Protestant noblemen, including two members of the Protestant branch of his family, Ernreich and Christoph Alban von Saurau, and complained of the proselytizing activity of four noblewomen, again implicating a member of his family (Anna Maria, Baroness of Saurau, widow of Baron von Radmansdorf).

The draft of a report of February 1639 gives further evidence of a Protestant residue among the Upper and east Styrian nobility, and confirms the geographical pattern of heterodoxy which had emerged in the course of the Ferdinandean reformation of the years 1599/1600–1628.[10] It proved exceedingly difficult to stamp out heresy among the population of the Hungarian confines and the mountainous regions of Upper Styria and Upper Carinthia. In 1644 and 1646, an inquiry was made and Imperial decrees were issued to extirpate crypto-Protestantism in Upper Carinthia. It turned out that large numbers of

---

[9] Catharina Engelprunner, a member of the lower nobility, is singled out for especially sharp criticism for proselytizing among the nobility in Fehring and Spielfeld in Lower Styria. For Saurau's report and the above decree see STMLA, 'Meillerakten', XIX-h. Ibid. a government memorandum of 13 May 1639, which recommends the expulsion of the large number of 'uncatholic' widows of Carniolan noblemen. On 19 Nov. 1642, the Inner Austrian government ordered Karl von Saurau to enquire into reports incriminating the wives of Gündhart von Herberstein, Hans Christoph von Mündorf, Wilhelm von Radmansdorf, and several other noblewomen who instructed their servants in the Lutheran faith and had persuaded their husbands to apostatize once more, STMLA, 'La. Arch., Religion und Kirche', Sch. 29.

[10] Letter of 12 Jan. 1638 to Hans Jacob von Herberstein, Gottfried von Eibiswaldt, Salomon von Meilegk, Georg Andre von Prank, Otto von Teuffenbach, Jacob von Falbenhaupt, Veit von Steinach, and Achaz Hagen. Copy of a denunciation to the government, n.d. [1638–9]. Concept of Saurau's report on the inquisition of Upper and East Styrian noblemen, Feb. 1639. All documents in STMLA, 'La. Archiv, Religion und Kirche', Sch. 29.

peasants, especially from the Herrschaft Sommeregg, were using the grain trade as a pretext for frequent travels to Hungary, where they attended Lutheran services.[11] There were also suspicious signs of slackness, or worse, among the population of Upper Styria: in 1651, the abbot of Admont reported that large numbers of commoners and noblemen among the parishioners of his archdeaconry had failed to attend confession and communion in the past year.[12]

The remoteness of the rural settlements in the mountainous regions of Inner Austria and the proximity of Hungary were clearly of great importance for the survival of crypto-Protestantism among the population of Upper and east Styria, but a brief Protestant revival occurred among a larger proportion of the Styrian elite during the later stages of the war. From about 1636 onwards until the middle of the century, the amount of evidence for crypto-Protestant and proselytizing activities of recent converts from the former Protestant elite increased, suggesting that the almost uninterrupted series of Imperial and Spanish defeats since 1636 was giving rise to hopes of a reversal. In June 1650, there were rumours of meetings between the crypto-Protestants and emigrants from Inner Austria and Protestant noblemen and magnates from the archduchy, Hungary, and Croatia.[13]

In the same year, Ferdinand III announced his decision to complete the expulsion of the remaining Protestant nobility, stating that the earlier decrees had been temporarily suspended only to further the peace negotiations. Toleration of 'uncatholics' was to end forthwith, and emigrants and Protestant widows were to leave the country at short notice. Those Protestants who had so far failed to sell their estates, like Paul von Eibiswald, had to complete this transaction within two months, on pain of severe punishment. No foreign Protestants were allowed to stay in the duchy without special permission from the Emperor. Ferdinand then

---

[11] Inner Austrian Government to the Emperor, 18 June 1641, STMLA, 'Meillerakten', XIX-h. Imperial decrees of 27 June 1644 and 1 Dec. 1646, STMLA, 'La. Arch., Religion und Kirche', Sch. 30.

[12] The abbot's account is related in the government's report for Ferdinand III, 28 Jan. 1651, STMLA, 'Meillerakten', XIX-h.

[13] Examples for the proselytizing activities of Wolf von Stubenberg (who is not to be confused with the previously mentioned Catholic ducal cupbearer, see above, Ch. 4), Franz von Welz and further members of the Styrian nobility are stated in a denunciation of June 1650. Ibid. also the reference to clandestine meetings, which are dealt with in the Imperial decree of 3 Sept. 1650. Both documents in STMLA, 'La. Arch., Religion und Kirche', Sch. 30. The government records also contain a list of names of 'uncatholics' and the charges brought against them in 1650, modern copy in STMLA, 'Regierungsakten', Expedita', 1650-VI-16.

expressed his suspicion that, judging from their lack of enthusiasm, most converts had accepted the Catholic faith merely as a result of coercion and intended to persist in their heretic faith. To establish a permanent control of their conduct, the archdeacons were ordered to arrange for annual or biannual interrogations of all parishioners, regardless of their rank and past confessional record. Strict control should be exerted to ensure attendance at Easter confession and communion, and confessional slips were to be sent to the Privy Council as proof of compliance.[14] A determined effort was made to detect and expel emigrants who had secretly returned to Styria, and the last entry in the government records relating to this subject dates from 1657.[15]

As regards the progress of clerical reform, there were still reports of clerical concubinage and even of severe abuses by Styrian and Carinthian priests during the second half of the seventeenth century. This would suggest that the increase in the number of clergy was not always matched by an equal improvement of their moral and educational quality. In the years 1670–4, the government urged the ecclesiastical authorities to take vigorous action against clerical delinquency, adducing fourteen cases of immoral conduct as evidence, for example the case of the parish priest of Radkersburg, who had fathered two children, and in general scandalized the Catholic community by his conduct, to the delight of the Lutheran and Calvinist merchants from neighbouring Hungary. The parish priest of Wildon who maltreated his parishioners and even mutilated a peasant woman was undoubtedly an extreme case, but his example fits the picture emerging from the bulk of evidence, suggesting a poor moral and educational standard of the Lower Styrian clergy. The poverty of their parishioners had obvious consequences for the income of the clergy, and complaints against parish priests who engaged in trade and transgressed on communal rights, like the picking of firewood, could be seen as indicative of the lower clergy's precarious material situation.[16]

---

[14] Imperial decree of 3 Sept. 1650, STMLA, 'La. Arch, Religion und Kirche', Sch. 30. The extent to which these regulations were enforced is now difficult to assess, as the government records contain none of the obligatory reports and collected confessional slips.

[15] A government register of emigrants still resident in Styria, dated 12 June 1652, lists twenty-two noblemen. They were ordered to leave the duchy by 4 Jan. 1653, STMLA, 'La. Arch., Religion und Kirche', Sch. 30. The notice on Hans Adam von Praunfalk's sale of his estates in Styria in 1657, mentioned by Schnabel, *Exulanten*, 475, seems to be the last entry in this matter.

[16] Visitation record for parishes of the diocese of Lavant, 1657–8, DA, 'Religionsberichte Protestantismus', 1598–1730, XV-b-23. For the government's charges against the parish priests of Radkersburg, Luttenberg, St Andrä and St Nicolai 'im Sausal', Preding near Deutschlandsberg, St Florian and Kleinsonntag (all of these in Lower Styria), Hitzendorf

Clerical poverty at the lower levels of the hierarchy was, of course, endemic in early modern Europe. As in the Austrian Monarchy, the growth of an impoverished clerical surplus population which concentrated in the towns continued into the next century in the kingdom of Spain and in Italy, posing financial and disciplinary problems to town magistrates and clerical authorities alike. In France, the wars of religion had caused a sharp reduction in the number of secular clergy from the 1580s onwards. Subsequent recovery was regionally uneven and had to be regulated by a rigorous enforcement of the Tridentine requirements concerning proof of adequate funding for prospective priests. The charitable foundation of 'Queen Anne's Bounty', created for the support of destitute parish clergy in England in 1704, indicates that structural problems, like a 'top-heavy' financial hierarchy within the Church and a general change in the attitude of parishioners, rather than any confession-related problems, were at the root of this evil.[17]

In Styria and Carniola, the clergy's economic situation deteriorated further as a result of peasant uprisings in the first half of the seventeenth century. In 1635, a large-scale uprising against war taxation and the arbitrary increase of labour services (*Robot*) spread among the peasantry of the district of Cilli in Lower Styria and Carniola. The estates of lay and ecclesiastical lords were ravaged, and contemporaries claimed that as many as sixty-seven castles and manors were plundered or destroyed, to which must be added the Dominican nunnery of Studenitz and the Carthusian monasteries of Seitz and Geirach. The revolt was put down in October 1635, but there were outbreaks of unrest in the district of Cilli until 1675, in which the clergy's attempt to increase their income from ecclesiastical fees formed one of the peasants' major grievances.[18]

---

and St Peter near Graz, and St Georgen near Radkersburg, see DA, consistorial record of the diocese of Seckau, 1670–4, fos. 757–65. Pressure was brought on the bishop of Seckau to proceed more rigorously against clerical delinquents, see letters by the Inner Austrian government, 6 Apr. 1674, and by the archbishop of Salzburg, 19 June 1677, DA, 'Synode', XV-e-5.

[17] Theresian and Josephinian attempts to assess the wealth of the Catholic Church and effect structural reforms are analysed in P. G. M. Dickson, *Finance and Government under Maria Theresia 1740–1780* (Oxford, 1987) i. 59–77, ii, Chs. 2 and 3 *passim*, and id., 'Joseph II's Reshaping of the Austrian Church', *HJ* 36/1 (1993), 89–114. For the south-west European clergy see J. Bergin, 'Between Estate and Profession: The Catholic Parish Clergy of Early Modern Western Europe', in M. L. Bush (ed.), *Social Orders and Social Classes in Europe since 1500: Studies in Social Stratification* (London, 1992), 66–85. For Queen Anne's charitable fund see A. Savidge, *The Foundation and Early Years of Queen Anne's Bounty* (London, 1955).

[18] For details see Mell, 'Der windische Bauernaufstand', 205–87, and Pferschy,

A different, administrative shortcoming acted as a brake on the progress of the Counter-Reformation in Upper Styria. In 1695, the Consistory of Salzburg informed the bishop of Seckau of its observations on the quality of the Upper Styrian clergy. They had noticed that highly qualified candidates were reluctant to apply for vacant chaplaincies and vicarages in Upper Styria because of the low chance of advancement. The candidates had argued that in Lower Styria the bishop picked new incumbents for parish benefices mainly from the local clergy who had previously ministered as chaplains and curates in these places. By contrast, the majority of Upper Styrian parishes were subject to the prince, the nobility, or the religious orders as patrons, who usually rewarded foreigners with these benefices.[19] This practice aggravated the problem of *de facto* vacancies. An inquiry into unlicensed absenteeism of parish priests who also failed to appoint a vicar had therefore already been on the agenda of the episcopal visitation in 1657. In 1706, a dispute arose between the ecclesiastical and secular authorities in Salzburg and Styria over an Imperial mandate which ordered the bishop of Seckau to hand in a list of all parishes that were administered by vicars on behalf of the actual incumbent.[20] Above all, the way in which patronage rights over Upper Styrian parishes were being exercised diminished the prospects of attracting able and ambitious candidates who would further the process of recatholicization.

Gradual progress was made in the field of organizational reform at parish level, but it nevertheless took almost two centuries before the relevant Tridentine statutes were applied consistently throughout the duchy. From the beginnings of the Counter-Reformation in the towns and villages in the late sixteenth century, both ducal and episcopal decrees had

---

'Bauernaufstände', 50–4. The income of Geirach had been ceded to the Jesuit Convict in Graz, and the college was forced to dismiss several pupils as a result of the monastery's destruction in 1635, see Peinlich, *Geschichte*, ii. 31. In 1675, the Consistory in Salzburg instructed the archpriest for Lower Styria, Sebastiano Porth, to ensure that those incumbents who left wills made bequests to their parish churches, DA, 'Synode', XV-e-5, letter of 24 May 1675.

[19] Letter of 26 Aug. 1695, DA, 'Synode', XV-e-5. At an earlier stage of his career, before 1668, the Imperial adviser and bishop of Wiener Neustadt, Cristóbal de Rojas y Spinola (1626–95), had been invested with the lucrative benefice of the parish of Hartberg in (Upper) east Styria, which he resigned in 1676, see the parish inventory of 8 Sept. 1676, STMLA, 'Geistliche Stiftungsakten', fasc. 494, part ii, no. 8. For a note on Spinola see Evans, *Making of the Habsburg Monarchy*, 305–6.

[20] Episcopal *Interrogatorium* of 1657, DA, 'Religionsberichte Protestantismus', 1598–1730, XV-b-23. Archbishop Johann Ernst von Thun to Bishop Franz Anton von Wagensperg, 1 Dec. 1708, DA, 'Synode', 1568–1722, XV-e-5.

concentrated on the recovery, reform, and material restoration of the parish as the central institution which supervised and regulated the religious life of the community. Provisions for an administrative improvement at parish level were made by the Council of Trent and the revised *Rituale Romanum* of 1614, which ordered the keeping of separate registers to record baptisms, weddings, and burials in each parish. The register of the names of all parishioners (*Hauptbuch*) was to be supplemented by the dates of their first holy communion and confirmation. Registration of the age or date of birth was necessary to enforce the regulations of the *Rituale*, which prescribed that children between 7 and 12 years should be admitted to these sacraments.[21] The introduction of parish registers helped establish closer control over the life of the parishioners in general, and further episcopal decrees pointed in the same direction. In 1629 and 1662, the parish clergy received orders which aimed at the control of premarital relations and the prevention of abortions or infanticide.[22] Illegitimate births were recorded in the parish registers.

The surviving evidence suggests that only very few Styrian parishes possessed such registers before 1600. By the end of the seventeenth century, however, they had been introduced in at least 181 of the 374 Styrian parishes which existed in 1779, and only a few (16) still failed to comply by 1750.[23] In the eighteenth century, the state was to profit from this 'modernization'. The parish continued to form the basic unit for administrative purposes, and the registers provided the government with essential demographic information which facilitated its assessments for fiscal and military purposes.[24]

The implementation of the Tridentine decrees for an administrative reorganization of the parishes was thus a slow process. By contrast, earlier efforts at a thorough reform of the regular clergy were bearing fruit and

---

[21] K. Eder, *Die Kirche im Zeitalter des konfessionellen Absolutismus (1555–1648)* (Freiburg im Breisgau, 1949), 208, 355.

[22] Archbishop Paris Lodron to the clergy under his jurisdiction, letters of 4 and 11 Aug. 1629, STMLA, 'Meillerakten', XIX-g-45. A later decree by Archbishop Guidobald von Thun to the archpriest in Graz, n.d. [1662], orders that pregnant women should be warned against the 'periculum oppressionis'.

[23] See K. Brandner, 'Überblick über die Pfarrmatriken in Steiermark', *Blätter für österreichische Familienkunde*, 1 (June 1927), 19. A list of the 374 parishes existing in 1779 can be found in H. Pirchegger, 'Die Pfarren als Grundlage der politisch-militärischen Einteilung der Steiermark', *AÖG* 102 (1913), 72–81.

[24] See the examples quoted by M. Straka, 'Die Ortschaften- und Seelenzählung von 1761 in der Steiermark', in *ZHVST* 14 (1967), 82–106, as well as the quotation from a Theresian decree in 1753, which ordered that these data were to be forwarded to the government for conscription etc., see Pirchegger, 'Pfarren', 10–11.

a monastic revival began to manifest itself already during the first half of the seventeenth century. In the 1580s, the general decline of the religious orders had been a matter of great concern to the ecclesiastical and secular authorities, but by the mid-seventeenth century, the regular clergy outdid their secular counterparts in their efforts to revive Catholic devotional practices. The question of monastic reform had been addressed most vigorously by the papal nuncio Germanico Malaspina, who relied on the Jesuits' assistance to conduct a thorough visitation in 1581. Malaspina concluded his description of deserted monasteries and decaying ecclesiastical property with a sharp critique of the foreign superiors whose immoral conduct and inept administration of the orders' property lay, in his view, at the root of the evil. In 1608 and 1635, the communities of the Dominican and Augustinian orders in Styria drew the prince's attention to various practical problems arising from the appointment of foreigners who lacked a basic knowledge of the German language. A government commission was set up to inquire into the Augustinians' complaint in 1635, and its findings strengthened the petitioners' case. They reported that only one of the ten Augustinians in Graz spoke German, while the rest belonged to various nations and were unable to perform any clerical functions apart from celebrating mass. The commissioners supported the Augustinians' appeal for the appointment of German superiors and confessors who would minister to the burghers and thus win their affection and hence some means of sustenance from donations and bequests.[25] However, during the early stages of the Counter-Reformation, a substantial intake of Italian, Spanish, and Belgian regular clergy had been of vital importance for the resumption of monastic life in the duchy.[26]

Among the new religious orders who settled in Inner Austria, the Capuchins deserve closer attention because of their rapid expansion and the direction of their missionary activity. The fact that the first generation of Capuchins consisted almost entirely of Italian clergy from the Venetian province explains why they initially settled in Gorizia (1596) and in those Styrian towns where they could rely on the support of an Italian administrative or merchant elite. Such elites existed in the prince's residential town

---

[25] For the letter by the Dominican community of Graz in 1608 and the government's report dated 14 Apr. 1635, relating the Augustinians' complaint and the commission's recommendation, see STMLA, 'Meillerakten', XIX-f-13 and XIX-h.

[26] The importance of Spanish and Italian support for the restoration of the Franciscan Order in this period is emphasized by F. E. Löffler, 'Reformation und Gegenreformation in ihrer Auswirkung auf die österreichische Franziskanerobservanz des 16. Jahrhunderts' (graduate thesis at the Faculty of Theology, University of Salzburg, 1970).

of Graz, where convents were created in 1600 and 1648, the first being founded by Laurence of Brindisi, presumably at the request of the papal nuncio Paravicini who wished to provide for the small community of Italians among the burghers and court officials in Graz.[27] Further convents were created in Cilli, Pettau, Marburg, and Radkersburg, all of which possessed Italian merchant communities.

To overcome the obstacles resulting from this linguistic barrier and to facilitate the raising of a native regular clergy, the Inner Austrian Capuchins obtained a licence to ordain priests at an earlier age than their statutes prescribed, so that the first Slovenian priest of the order was ordained in 1613.[28] Between 1600 and 1711, fifteen Capuchin monasteries were founded in the duchy, eight of them in Lower and east Styria, namely Cilli (1611), Pettau (1615) Radkersburg (1617), Marburg (1620), Leibnitz (1634), Hartberg (1654), Mureck (1667), and Schwanberg (1706).[29] The order concentrated on providing bilingual preachers who were able to minister both to the German and to the Slovenian population of the duchy. In the course of the seventeenth century, an increasing proportion of the *Patres* obtained an episcopal licence to preach and hear confession.[30] Capuchins were soon present in most Lower Styrian towns,

---

[27] M. Benedik, *Die Kapuziner in Slowenien 1600–1700* (Rome, 1974), 9–14. The relevant letter by Paravicini, dated 9 Mar. 1615, is quoted ibid. 14 n. 19. The initial dependence on the Venetian province also emerges from the account of a fragmentary 18th-century chronicle for the first Capuchin monastery in Graz. It states that a community of six Venetian Capuchins moved into the convent after its completion in 1605, the first *Guardian* being one P. Damian from Venice. From 1630 onwards, however, the *Guardian* was usually a German, see the modern translated manuscript copy of the 'Acta Conventus Graecensis ad S. Antonium Pad[uavinu]m' (post-1731), 43 pp., in the STMLA, MS XII/5, fos. 9 and 43. There is also a brief fragmentary history of the foundation of the Radkersburg monastery by the *Guardian* P. Virgilius from Marburg, dated 1761. Virgilius states that the monastery was founded in 1617 by Abbot Rosolenz with the support of Archduke Ferdinand, Archbishop Markus Sittich, and the magistrates of Radkersburg, STMLA, MS 624, 2 pp. (19th-century copy).

[28] Benedik, *Kapuziner in Slowenien*, 12. The Congregation for the Propagation of Faith granted licences and dispensations to Capuchin and Franciscan priests, e.g. to absolve heretics, see the decrees of 5 Nov. 1627, Feb. 1630, 15 Apr. 1630, 12 Dec. 1637, 27 Mar. 1638, printed in H. Tüchle (ed.), *Acta SC de Propaganda Fide Germaniam Spectantia (1622–1649)* (Paderborn, 1962), 171, 271, 282, 439–40, 443. For the immigration of Italian merchants in the 16th and 17th centuries see H. Valentinitsch, 'Italienische Unternehmer im Wirtschaftsleben der innerösterreichischen Länder 1550–1650', in *Wirtschaftswege und Wirtschaftskräfte: Festschrift für Hermann Kellenbenz*, vol. i (Stuttgart, 1978), 696–708.

[29] Pirchegger, *Geschichte der Steiermark*, ii. 9.

[30] In 1643, 44 of the 120 Styrian Capuchins possessed this licence. In 1684, however, the ratio was 276 licensed priests to 159 without this permission, and the ratio for the following years confirms this trend (301 : 100 in 1721, 408 : 87 in 1749), see Benedik, *Kapuziner in Slowenien*, 16.

for example in the recently recatholicized town of Radkersburg. With the financial support of the chronicler of the urban Counter-Reformation, Abbot Jakob Rosolenz of Stainz, a monastery was built near the town at the request of the Catholic community. There were occasional conflicts with the Protestant burghers, though, resulting in one case even in the murder of a Capuchin, P. Benedikt from Krapina (Carniola), near Radkersburg in 1635. He was a member of the local convent and had been sent to convert the heretic residue among the town's population.[31]

In general, the Capuchins' activity seems to have gained them a reputation as gifted preachers among the urban population, though it has been pointed out that this did not always apply to those who were sent to assist in Slovenian parishes and whose training was often poor.[32] Moreover, the Capuchins seem to have given no catechetical instructions to the population of the rural parishes and small municipalities. By contrast, famous preachers of the later seventeenth and early eighteenth centuries, like Amandus and Aemilian of Graz, were renowned for their erudite sermons. Aemilian produced a German-language homiletic work for catechetical purposes, while P. Amandus embellished his elegant sermons with allusions and Latin quotations for the educated, a manner of preaching which was designed to attract the civic elites rather than a rustic audience.[33] Their efforts were not futile, and the involvement of commoners as benefactors testifies to the Capuchins' popularity.

Among the nobility, it was the elite of converts and foreigners who gave visible proof of their allegiance to the Roman faith by conspicuous support of the religious orders. At least six of the fifteen Capuchin monasteries in Styria were founded by the nobility, three of them by members of the convert families of Saurau (Hartberg, 1654), Stubenberg (Mureck, 1667), and Falbenhaupt (noviciate in Schwanberg, 1706). The convents of Leibnitz (1634), Murau (1643), and Irdning (1711) were founded by the Catholic families of Kollonich, Schwarzenberg, and Welsersheim, who did not belong to the local nobility and had only recently acquired property in Styria.[34] The Stubenberg's foundation in

---

[31] Benedik, ibid. 20, cites from the *Mortuarium Styriae* of the province. There is a government report for Ferdinand II, dated 13 Sept. 1635, which speaks of an attack on two Capuchins, summarized in *FRA/60*, 909. Benedik's sources nevertheless state that the Capuchins practically took over from the parish priest, see Benedik, *Kapuziner in Slowenien*, 10.

[32] This point is made by Benedik, *Kapuziner in Slowenien*, 27.

[33] For P. Amand, a former student of the Jesuits in Graz, and P. Aemilian, who wrote a lengthy homiletic treatise on catechetical sermons, see Benedik, ibid. 48–53.

[34] Zák, *Österreichisches Klosterbuch*, 194–6.

Mureck was motivated above all by the urgent requests of the local burghers.[35] Similarly, local support was strong enough in Graz to effect the foundation of a second Capuchin monastery in 1648 for the population of the suburb. In the Upper Styrian town of Knittelfeld, a convent was founded jointly by the burghers and the provost of the cathedral chapter of Seckau, Paul Frantz Poitz, in 1705.[36] In most cases, the activity of Capuchin preachers in the municipalities accounts for these requests by urban communities. The ducal town of Leoben, however, constitutes an exception that deserves brief consideration. In this initially recalcitrant municipality, it was the Jesuit mission which had prepared the ground for the thorough recatholicization and religious activity of the community. As previously described, the local Jesuits had at the beginning taken great care to avoid any confrontation with the burghers—though evidence for legal disputes over property abounds for the second half of the seventeenth century—and their novices' missionary activity in the neighbouring villages and in Eisenerz was slowly winning over the remaining Protestants. Thanks to the activity of the Jesuit college in Leoben, the cult of Francis Xavier was thriving by the middle of the seventeenth century.[37] In 1637, plans were made for the construction of an *alumnat* for poor students, and put into practice with the opening of the Josephinum in 1640. For its support, a donation of property worth more than 5,000 fl. was made by a local government official, the imperial councillor and director of the ore mines in Eisenerz, Christoph Jantschitsch. His son Christoph entered the Jesuit order, and, together with his mother Magdalena, endowed the seminary with a further 6,000 fl. in 1642.[38] The Capuchin monastery in Leoben

---

[35] This emerges from a letter by the Capuchin provincial P. Hyazinth to Archbishop Max Gandolph von Khuenburg, 26 July 1665, DA, 'Kapuzinerkloster Mureck', XIX-d-17. Apart from smaller sums donated by local burghers for the support of the Capuchins, the sources mention a donation of 1,000 fl. capital, made in 1714 by Maria Standegg, widow of the local burgher and master mason Joseph Schmerlaib, to be administered by the local magistrate, see STMLA, 'Geistliche Stiftungsakten', fasc. 600.

[36] Provincial's letter to the bishop of Seckau, Johann Markus Count Altringen, 6 Feb. 1648, DA, 'Kapuzinerkloster Graz-Stiege', XIX-d-17. For Knittelfeld see Zák, *Österreichisches Klosterbuch*, 195.

[37] For evidence on legal disputes with the burghers of Leoben see AGR, 'Epp. Gen., Austr. 7', General's letters of 22 May and 28 Aug. 1660, fos. 187, 196. However, in the letter of 28 Aug., the General praises their generous support for the Jesuits, and their religious zeal for the promotion of the Marian cult at Maria Neustift, a Jesuit-directed place of worship. The reference to the saint's cult is made in the letter of 13 Sept. 1659, ibid. 163.

[38] The plan is mentioned in the General's letter of 21 Feb. 1637, AGR, Epp. Gen., Austr., 5 I', fo. 245. For the above donations see Peinlich, *Geschichte*, ii. 34, 40, and iii. 75. Christoph Jantschitsch the Elder also made a contribution to visual Counter-Reformation

was likewise founded by local benefactors of the Church, Johann Georg and Maria Thessalon, at the request of the burgher community in 1684–9. A government document makes mention of their noble status, and it seems that Johann Georg Thessalon belonged to the group of higher government officials who obtained a patent of nobility. His widow Maria subsequently donated 10,000 fl. to the Josephinum for the support of poor students at the Jesuit school in Leoben. In honour of the Holy Virgin, they were to be dressed in light-blue garments and should be called 'foster-children of Our Lady' ('Nährkinder unserer lieben Frau'), stipulations that bear witness to the Jesuits' successful promotion of the Marian cult.[39]

As previously demonstrated, the Catholic revival was often helped by the presence of Catholic merchants and officials of foreign, mostly Italian, origin in the trading towns of the duchy. In 1642, one of them, a wealthy burgher of Eisenerz named Pandulph Andreae, petitioned the Propaganda Congregation in Rome for a Capuchin mission to Eisenerz whose upkeep he was willing to finance. In the following year, three missionaries were actually sent to Styria and Carinthia, and the instructions made specific mention of Eisenerz as one of their destinations.[40]

In terms of the sheer number of foundations, the Capuchin Order's success was unparalleled, even if set against the background of an overall growth of the religious orders from thirty-one Styrian convents before the Reformation to seventy-three in 1773.[41] In most cases, missionary activities paved the way for permanent settlements, and the frugality of the mendicants helped spread the order. Modest means were sufficient to

propaganda. He commissioned a votive tablet, painted as part of a series for the Marian pilgrimage church of Mariazell in Upper Styria by Markus Weiß in 1622–6. The picture commemorated the great fire in Eisenerz in the year 1615, during which Jantschitsch's house was miraculously spared after he had made a vow to Mariazell, see the commented survey of Weiß's pictures in H. Valentinitsch, 'Religiöse Propaganda, Kunst und Politik', in *Schatz und Schicksal*, catalogue of the *Steirische Landesausstellung* 1996 (Graz, 1996), 128–9.

[39] The relevant government documents are a letter by the Inner Austrian Aulic Chamber to the *Landeshauptmann* Georg Christoph von Saurau, 1 Dec. 1685, and the government memorandum of 12 Dec. 1685. The Imperial permission was given at the petition of P. Marcus d'Aviano on 17 Oct. 1688, STMLA, 'Landrecht', Sch. 637, H. 7, Leoben-Kapuziner. A copy of Maria Thessalon's foundation deed for the Jesuit scholarship is kept in AGR, 'Austr. Epp., 22', fos. 44–6. The stipulations are also mentioned by Peinlich, *Geschichte*, ii. 75. The documents relating to the Thessalon's donation of their property (*Freihof*) and mill near Leoben, dated 30 Dec. 1684 and 22 Nov. 1689, can be found in STMLA, 'Archiv Leoben', Sch. 172, H. 937.

[40] Records of the Congregation for the Propagation of Faith, dated 11 July 1642 and 30 June 1643, in Tüchle, *Acta*, 527 and 549.

[41] Pirchegger, *Geschichte der Steiermark*, ii. 10. This includes the Jesuits' settlements.

found and support a monastery whose religious remained for their subsistence and for the conduct of their temporal affairs permanently dependent on their benefactors. By virtue of their statutes, the Capuchins, like the older Franciscan orders, appointed magistrates and other local notables as 'spiritual fathers' or 'spiritual mothers' who acted on their behalf in all temporal matters such as litigation or the administration of donations. In 1760, Maria Elisabeth Schulze, widow of a local burgher and 'spiritual mother' of the Capuchin monastery in Leoben, informed the government that there was only one permanent source of income, derived from a mill, which the founder Maria Thessalon had donated and which was administered by the magistrates of Leoben. A similar donation was entrusted to the administration of the magistrates of Leibnitz. Among other things, they were responsible for the maintenance of the monastery's buildings, and for the inspection and repair of the Loreto chapel.[42]

The regular clergy who depended mainly, and in the case of the mendicants even exclusively, on alms and fees for their support were consequently more amenable to their benefactors' requests, for example for the right of burial at a conspicuous place in or near the convent's church. It seems that the greater scope for control exercised by the laity and the public prestige deriving from supervisory functions rendered the mendicant orders more attractive to potential benefactors. This impression is strengthened by the fact that the Franciscan Observants and Minorites likewise achieved a substantial, if less spectacular growth, with the foundation of six new monasteries in the years 1632 to 1669.[43]

Both Jesuit activity and the related monastic revival in the duchy contributed to the resuscitation of the medieval confraternities which had fallen into disuse in the sixteenth century, and numerous new religious organizations of this kind were introduced by the orders. The monastery's chapel or the Jesuits' church became the focus of the lay community's life. In the course of the seventeenth century, they substantially strengthened the Counter-Reformation at parish level by absorbing the rural population into a more intensive form of religious life, and on the eve of the Josephinian reforms, there were no less than 330 confraternities in the

---

[42] STMLA, 'Geistliche Stiftungsakten', fasc. 600.

[43] Zák, *Österreichisches Klosterbuch*, 163, 167, 186. For the spread of the Franciscan orders see also *Die Minderbrüder: Minoriten—Franziskaner—Kapuziner in der Steiermark. Begleitheft zur Ausstellung 16. Mai bis 30, September 1990*, ed. the Episcopal *Ordinariat* of Graz-Seckau (Graz, 1990).

Styrian parishes and religious houses.[44] In 1669, a list of all confraternities in Graz was drafted for the bishop of Seckau, mentioning no less than twenty congregations supervised by the parish priest, the Jesuits, the Dominicans, Franciscans, Augustinians, and Carmelites. Ten of these congregations had been introduced by the Jesuits, including the diverse Marian congregations of the students and clerics, the *Herrenbruderschaft* for the nobility, higher officials, and burghers, and the St Michael's confraternity, whose members assisted the Jesuits in the cure of souls among the local prisoners. Apart from this duty, the obligations prescribed by the statutes of this confraternity included, for the men, the wearing at public functions of the confraternity's garb, which combined the insignia of the crusader and the pilgrim: a white robe with a blue cross, and a staff. Furthermore, men and women were to wear the 'St Michael's penny' as a visible token of their membership, and as a blessing against demons. A fixed number of further religious obligations was to be performed to benefit from the special indulgences granted to the confraternity.[45] Significantly, no charitable obligations are stated beside a general concern for the spiritual well-being of prisoners. Instead, the regulations focus on the achievement of individual perfection and salvation. Apart from this, they had the propagandistic effect of providing frequent occasions for public statements of orthodoxy by the members.

These statutes were by no means exceptional, but in fact representative of the direction of religious activities and devotional practices in the wake of the Counter-Reformation. Its protagonists' overriding concern had been the recatholicization of the duchy, and success was measured in the number of registered converts and communicants. Participation in public ceremonies and religious associations which performed or supported these demonstrations had become obligatory for the elite, and in turn prestigious for the mass of the faithful. The new brand of Counter-Reformation piety which developed on these foundations was spectacular in its public expressions, and almost obsessively concerned with individual salvation, perhaps as a result of its being a product of the

---

[44] Although the confraternities did not have to make up for deficient parochial organization in the villages, as was the case in the diocese of Veszprém in Hungary, see G. Tüskés and É. Knapp, 'Bruderschaften in Ungarn im 17. und 18. Jahrhundert', *Bayerisches Jahrbuch für Volkskunde* (1992), 1–23, at 9. Lists (*Fassiones*) of Styrian confraternities in 1781 are kept in DA, 'Vereine-Bruderschaften, 1600ff', XVI-a-3.

[45] 'Specification' of the confraternities in Graz, May 1669, and 'Obligationen und Verrichtungen der Brüder und Schwestern' of the St Michael's confraternity, copy enclosed in a fascicle of documents dated 1731, DA, 'Vereine-Bruderschaften 1600ff', XVI-a-3.

battle with heresy. The elites in particular responded readily to the new emphasis on spiritual perfection. Works of charity concerned with the physical well-being of one's neighbour had been a characteristic feature of medieval piety, but were now relegated to subordinate rank in the hierarchy of virtues as expressed in such programmatic statements as confraternity rules. With few exceptions, contemporary wills stated exiguous sums as donations for the poor and infirm, frequently not more than a few florins or pennies to be distributed as alms among the poor who attended the funeral.[46]

The fate of the first settlement of the Monk Hospitallers (*Barmherzige Brüder*) in Graz is a further case in point. The order had been introduced in the Habsburg lands in 1605 on the estates of Karl von Liechtenstein (1569–1627), a further spectacular example of the emergence of a new convert elite in the Austrian hereditary lands.[47] In 1615, Archduke Ferdinand founded a monastery and hospital in Vienna and Graz, and a further settlement was opened in Prague in 1620.[48] By the middle of the seventeenth century, benefactions had been made by one Bernhard Walther, probably a member of the family of Karl II's *Regimentskanzler* of the same name, and his cousin Erhard (1624), and by Hans Ulrich von Eggenberg and his son Johann Anton (1627, 1637). In 1630, the Inner Austrian government chancellor Johann Kaspar von Dornsperg and a member of the Aulic Chamber (*Oberhofkammerrat*), Andreas Edler von Khainpach, made a donation for the support of twelve poor women who were to look after the plague-sick in the suburb of Graz. Significantly, all of these benefactors belonged to the court nobility and elite of government officials, and their contributions could not make up for the lack of support from the burghers and the estates. As a result, Ferdinand was forced to issue licences for the collection of alms throughout the Empire and Habsburg lands in 1624 and 1627. In the 1640s, donations were made not for the support of the hospital, but for the reading of masses by the

---

[46] This is based on an evaluation of the wills among the Jesuit records in the diocesan archive, DA, 'Jesuiten', XIX-c-42 and 43. An exceptionally huge bequest of 60,000 fl. for the burghers' hospital in Graz is mentioned, without reference to the testator, in a petition by the Monk Hospitallers' prior in the mid-17th century (*c.*1655). He contrasts this largesse with the burghers' and magistrates' habitual unwillingness to contribute to the support of the sick, insane, poor, and orphaned. Quoted and transcribed in V. Prangner, *Geschichte des Klosters und des Spitales der Fr. Fr. Barmherzigen Brüder in Graz und der innerösterreichischen Ordensprovinz zum heiligsten Herzen Jesu* (Graz, 1908), 69.

[47] For Liechtenstein's career and the rise of the family see Evans, *Making of the Habsburg Monarchy*, 171–2.

[48] Prangner, *Barmherzige Brüder*, 23.

monks. At the same time, the magistrates refused the prior's petitions for the opening of an orphanage, in spite of the fact that the presence of sick and abandoned children had become a problem for the town. A favourable Imperial decision in 1649 remained ineffective because no donations were made for a new construction and the support of the orphans. Eventually, Ferdinand III ordered the magistrates to sell the dilapidated building at a modest price, but the magistrates continued their obstruction by fixing an extortionate sum for the sale and future taxes, which caused the exasperated prior to comment that he would have fared better even with the Lutheran magistrates of Nuremberg. The orphanage was opened in 1658, and was finally saved by the intervention of a member of the Scherffenberg family, who refounded the orphanage on his estates in the suburb in 1679.[49]

The prior's criticism chimes with the previously described obsession with individual salvation achieved by prayer, penitence, and symbolical sacrifice rather than by works of charity. This was arguably the motive that inspired the dissemination of Marian worship which became the most conspicuous feature of seventeenth- and early eighteenth-century piety. Most of these places of worship, like Maria Buch (near Judenburg), Maria Rehkogel (near Bruck), and Mariazell (close to the Lower Austrian border in the north), had been notable places of worship in the Middle Ages. After the disruption of the Reformation era, these churches were of particular importance for the revival and spread of Catholic devotional practices among the population of the duchy from the mid-seventeenth century onwards, though, as will be seen, the crypto-Protestant rural settlements of the mountainous region of Upper Styria remained impervious to this kind of propaganda. The geographical situation and tradition of Mariazell, a Benedictine church belonging to the monastery of St Lambrecht, rendered this place the obvious starting point for a joint effort of the clergy and the dynasty which turned Mariazell into the most important place of Marian worship in the Habsburg lands. In 1599, the Lower Austrian Counter-Reformer Melchior Khlesl started the campaign by accompanying in person a procession of 23,000 pilgrims from Lower Austria to the Styrian church. The Habsburgs subsequently helped reconstruct and extend the building by exceptionally large donations, devoting great care to its embellishment and turning it into a sanctuary

---

49 For the above see Prangner, *Barmherzige Brüder*, 43–84. The author does not state the full name of the founder, but again, a link with the court nobility seems likely. A member of the family, Ulrich Christoph von Scherffenberg, held the office of Inner Austrian privy counsellor in 1632–48, see Thiel, 'Zentralverwaltung', II, 623.

for the special Marian devotion which came to characterize the 'Pietas Austriaca'. Ferdinand III in particular furthered the cult, and paid frequent visits to the church. Henceforth, Marian devotion was to be the uniting formula which expressed the ideological consensus between the prince, his ally, the Catholic Church, and the new Catholic-convert elites in the Habsburg lands. Public statements of Marian devotion were to encourage this ideological fusion. Following the conclusion of the Peace of Westphalia, Ferdinand III ordered the raising of a Marian column in Vienna in 1649, and in a public ceremony, he dedicated his family, his subjects, and his provinces to the Holy Virgin as ruler and patroness of the House of Austria. The ceremony was repeated by Leopold I at the height of the Turkish War in 1693, and he especially dedicated the kingdom of Hungary to the Virgin as 'Magna Hungariae Domina', a title which tradition had associated with the Virgin of Mariazell. A similar symbolical 'transfer of power' was once more staged by Charles VI.[50]

In the course of the seventeenth century, steps were taken to strengthen the ties which linked Mariazell to Hungary and Moravia, thus providing a focus of Marian devotion for the Habsburg lands.[51] With the progress of the Counter-Reformation in Hungary, the Hungarian links became more and more dominant, and the rebuilding of the church during the second half of the seventeenth century is associated with the names of Hungarian and Croatian magnates, like the Nádasdy, Esterházy, and Draskovic, a list that could be supplemented with the names of the leading Transylvanian families, like the Catholic branch of the Thököly, for the early eighteenth century. Mariazell was likewise frequented by an increasing number of pilgrims from the rural and urban population of Hungary and Croatia, bearing witness to the success of the Jesuits' missionary efforts.[52]

[50] For a survey of the Styrian votive sites see Gugitz, *Österreichs Gnadenstätten*, iv. *Schatz und Schicksal*, the catalogue of the Styrian exhibition of 1996, is devoted almost entirely to Mariazell. For the Habsburgs' relation to Mariazell see the article by A. Stillfried, 'Der barocke Umbau der Mariazeller Wallfahrtskirche', ibid. 51–61, esp. 52–4.

[51] In the 14th and 15th centuries, King Louis I of Hungary and the margraves of Moravia had built a chapel and a church for the Benedictine foundation. The Moravian and Hungarian motif was taken up by Markus Weiß, who received a commission for the painting of a series of thirty-two pictures commemorating major miracles associated with vows to this place of worship, some of which bear a direct relation to the Counter-Reformation, see Valentinitsch, 'Religiöse Propaganda', 127–9.

[52] See G. Barna, 'Mariazell und Ungarn', in *Schatz und Schicksal*, 281–94. Four of the twelve chapels of the church were built by Hungarian magnates. The St Ladislaus chapel was commissioned in 1685 by the Primas of Esztergom (Gran), György Szelepcsényi, and was destined for his burial, ibid. 283.

As a result of Jesuit propaganda, Marian churches and chapels in Styria were founded by the Inner Austrian nobility and members of the civic elite, for example the church of Maria Schnee near the town of Knittelfeld in Upper Styria, which was founded by the families of Dietrichstein and Eggenberg at the beginning of the eighteenth century, or Maria Grün near Graz, an Augustinian hermitage and popular place of Marian worship, founded by Hans Fritz, a wealthy innkeeper and burgher of Graz.[53] In 1660, the General of the Society praised the zeal of the Jesuits of Leoben in promoting the Marian cult at Maria Neustift, a Slovenian parish which had been transferred to the care of the Jesuits in 1615 and was turned successfully into a place of pilgrimage by them. The object of devotion was a Marian picture of recent origin, showing the Virgin as protectress (*Schutzmantelmadonna*), adored by members of the different estates, next to whom knelt a Jesuit.[54] A less subtle attempt to combine Marian propaganda with the promotion of the Society foundered on the General's opposition. In 1660, he sharply rebuked the rector of Leoben for suggesting the title of 'B[eatissi]ma Maria a Corde Ignatiano' for a recently founded church in the *Herrschaft* of Freienstein, and ordered him to avoid in future 'suchlike novel and exotic titles' ('istiusmodi novos, et exoticos pietatis titulos') which were repugnant to God and the saints.[55]

Apart from promoting pilgrimages and confraternities, the Jesuits played an important part in the popularization of penitential religious practices. So-called calvaries were founded as meeting places for public prayer and penitential processions by Baron Ferdinand von Maschwander in Graz in 1596–1606 and by the magistrates of Judenburg in 1719–22.[56] The Turkish threat and periodic plague epidemics which

---

[53] *Dehio: Steiermark*, 175–6. For Maria Grün and further places of worship in and near Graz see H. Moser, 'Marianische Volksfrömmigkeit im 17. Jahrhundert am Beispiel der Grazer Marienkirchen', *HJbG* 7–8 (1975), 75–88.

[54] General's letter to rector Cornelius Gentilotti, 28 Aug. 1660, AGR, 'Epp. Gen., Austr. 7', fo. 196. For the Jesuits' campaign and a description of the picture see Simon Povoden, 'Beytrag zu einer steyermärkischen Kirchengeschichte von allen Slovenen . . .', (1826), STMLA, MS 481, fo. 277–8.

[55] Letter of 28 Feb. 1660, AGR, 'Epp. Gen., Austr. 7', fo. 177.

[56] The joint administration of a civic foundation for Judenburg by the Jesuits' Marian congregation 'Maria Reinigung' and the magistrates led to a dispute in the 18th century, General's letter to the provincial Franziskus Molindes, 24 Apr. 1734, AGR, 'Epp. Gen., Austr. 12/II', fos. 457–8. For Maschwander's donation see *Dehio: Steiermark*, 80. Two barons of Maschwander (also: Maßwander, Moschwander), Johann Gabriel and Johann Jakob, matriculated as students in Graz in 1621 and 1653. The family was subsequently elevated to the rank of count, and a Count Georg Sigmund is registered as a student in 1692, see Peinlich, *Geschichte*, iii. 99.

swept the Habsburg lands to the west from the Hungarian plains in the
second half of the seventeenth and in the early eighteenth centuries
encouraged the spread of such practices among the population of Styria.
Marian statues, often accompanied by representations of the plague
patrons St Roch and St Sebastian, were raised in the capital and larger
municipalities of Styria.[57] However, considerable governmental pressure
had to be exerted to maintain discipline once the immediate danger had
subsided, so that some of the most conspicuous expressions of the
Marian cult were presumably transient rather than permanent features of
religious life in the duchy.[58]

. Nevertheless, a high degree of mass participation in new devotional
practices and religious congregations characterized the era of confessional consolidation in the seventeenth and early eighteenth centuries. A
limiting factor for more substantial ideological permeation was the
neglect of doctrinal instruction of the rural population. Repeated episcopal decrees, for example in 1612 and 1651, had ordered the parish clergy
to provide for regular catechetical instruction of the children and young
people on Sundays and feast-days. However, the level of compliance especially among the Lower Styrian clergy was so unsatisfactory that the
government began to put pressure on the bishop of Seckau, Franz Anton,
Count Wagensperg, who in turn issued strict orders to his commissioner
in Lower Styria in January 1709. He complained that, as a result of the
clergy's negligence, even the adult rural population was often ignorant of
the main articles of faith ('mithin das gemäine ainfältige Landvolkh
höheres Alther erräichet, ohne das es auch nur die zur Seeligkheit noth-
wendige glaubens puncten wisse'). To forestall government intervention,
he urged his officials to exert strict control over the parish clergy, and
threatened severe punishment for defaulters.[59]

[57] e.g. in Graz (1665–71), Murau (1717), Knittelfeld (1720), Hartberg (Marian statue in
1675, St Roch statue in 1680), Radkersburg (1680), Wildon (1682), Mureck (1665–8), see
Dehio: Steiermark. The burghers of Leibnitz in Lower Styria who wished to raise a Marian
column in the market place in 1678 had to overcome the opposition of the parish priest who
feared that the introduction of new devotional practices would diminish attendance at the
regular parish services, see G. Christian and E. Holzmann, 'Ein Beitrag zur Baugeschichte
von Leibnitz', in *1000 Jahre Leibnitz* (Graz, 1970), 81–2.

[58] Imperial and episcopal decrees ordering obligatory public prayers in the towns in
connection with the Turkish wars and plague bouts were issued in 1677–8, 1684, 1686, 1693,
and 1709–10 (plague epidemic in Hungary). A governmental decree of Dec. 1684 criticized
that public and private devotions were falling into disuse again, see DA, 'Synode',
1568–1722, XV-e-5.

[59] Episcopal decrees for the archpriests of Styria by Bishop Martin Brenner of Seckau,
3 Mar. 1612, Bishop Johann Markus von Altringen, 24 Feb. 1651, and Bishop Franz Anton
von Wagensperg, 19 Jan. 1709, DA, 'Synode', 1568–1722, XV-e-5. Wagensperg's fear of

The existence of stark differences in the secular and religious educational standards of the north and south of the duchy was thrown into sharp relief in 1752, when Maria Theresia commissioned an inquiry by the Inner Austrian government into the state of schooling, which was intended to form the basis of a thorough educational reform. The returns received from the local ecclesiastical authorities in the Styrian administrative circles of Graz, Bruck, Judenburg, Marburg, and Cilli are revealing of an imbalance in the level of schooling between the towns and the countryside, and the German and Slovenian parts of the duchy. The parish priests and government officials of the Lower Styrian districts of Marburg and Cilli uniformly reported that none of the local peasants and labourers in the vineyards could afford to dispense with the help of their children and pay the school fees. Besides, there were few parish schools anyway. In the parish of Marburg, which numbered 4,000 souls in 1752, there was a small school at which fifty-five burgher children between 6 and 11 years of age received instruction in reading, writing, arithmetic, and Latin, supplemented by catechetical instruction once a week by the parish priest. It emerged that, on the whole, access to elementary schooling was limited to the urban population. The creation of additional schools, however, was vigorously opposed by the secular and ecclesiastical authorities of both Lower Styrian circles, who considered further education dangerous to the social order and subversive of orthodoxy. By way of proof, they pointed to the connection between literacy and heterodoxy observable among the recently discovered crypto-Protestant population in Salzburg, Upper Styria, and Upper Carinthia.

The evidence for Upper Styria would indeed bear out this claim. In this region, the size of the parishes and the remoteness of the farms (*Einödhöfe*) rendered systematic and regular catechetical instruction of the population difficult. Moreover, often poor remuneration and bleak prospects of promotion dampened the clergy's missionary fervour. Instead, these conditions encouraged the survival of autonomous educational structures such as unlicensed teaching by literate members of the local population ('Winkelschulen'), and hence the persistence of heterodoxy. Parish schools which had been established in the Reformation era

government intervention reflects the changed climate under the new 'interventionist' Emperor Joseph I. In 1708–9, Joseph began to prune and contest ecclesiastical jurisdictional rights and privileges in Bohemia and Austria, see the decrees prohibiting the excommunication of his subjects without Imperial consent, 5 Dec. 1708, and the projected application of the Bohemian regulations regarding church asylum in the hereditary lands, memorandum of 18 Dec. 1708, both documents in STMLA, 'Meillerakten', XIX-h.

by Upper Styrian noblemen like Hans Hoffmann continued to exist, though under Catholic direction. However, in those places where no sustained catechetical effort was made, parish schools failed to become an effective tool of recatholicization. Instead, they helped maintain the tradition of widespread literacy among the partly heterodox population of this region. Reports for the Upper Styrian circles of Judenburg and Bruck revealed a high level of schooling: there were forty-nine regular parish schools, whose staff were employed exclusively as teachers—unlike the teaching sextons of the Lower Styrian parishes—and received a fixed salary, free lodgings, as well as a plot of land for their support. In addition to this, illicit private teaching which defied both secular and ecclesiastical supervision continued in spite of repeated Imperial prohibitions, issued on 6 February 1750, 8 January 1753, and 16 August 1757, and vociferous protests from the Jesuit director in Graz.[60]

This was in stark contrast to the orthodox, but rudimentary, educational structures in Lower Styria. As previously mentioned, the missionary activity of the urban-based Capuchins had a different focus, and could not compensate for the lack of secular and religious elementary instruction by the parish clergy, especially in the rural parishes. High levels of attendance at public sermons and penitential processions was therefore not indicative of a corresponding degree of doctrinal awareness among the Slovenian rural population. Moreover, the findings of the Josephinian inquiry into the linguistic skills of the Capuchins in 1783 suggest that knowledge of the Slovenian language was on the wane among those who had joined the order after the middle of the eighteenth century. It is conceivable that this change reflected a greater degree of linguistic adaptation by the Slovenian peasantry who engaged in trade with the mostly German-speaking market towns. However, in the absence of corroborative evidence, it could also be interpreted as indicative of a contraction of the order's missionary activity. The close links between the Capuchins of Leibnitz and the magistrates of the town, for example, render a preoccupation with the concerns of the German-speaking burghers likely, and by the late eighteenth century none of the resident monks had a knowledge of the Slovenian language. In the small market town of Mureck, only five of the seventeen Capuchins were able to preach in the Slovenian idiom

---

[60] The reports and the clergy's arguments can be found in STMLA, 'Repräsentation und Kammer, Sachabteilung', fasc. 109. The circular which ordered the inquiry is dated 10 Jan. 1752. For the intellectual and cultural background to the Theresian educational reforms see J. Van Horn Melton, *Absolutism and the Eighteenth-Century Origins of Compulsory Schooling in Prussia and Austria* (Cambridge, 1988), esp. 60–83.

spoken by the surrounding rural population. A parallel development can be observed for the monastery of Hartberg near the Hungarian border, which accommodated fifteen German-speaking Capuchins. The monasteries of Radkersburg and Pettau were better furnished, with five of the fifteen monks in Radkersburg being proficient in Slovenian, and two of them having a knowledge of Hungarian and Croatian as well. In Pettau, there were still no less than eight preachers with a knowledge of Slovenian, and four monks were also able to preach to the Italian community.[61]

The issue of elementary doctrinal instruction was raised once more in the 1730s, and catechetical missions, followed by the introduction of catechetical confraternities in the parishes, formed part of a missionary revival spreading from Italy to the hereditary lands and Hungary over the following four decades. A change in the missionary method occurred in the course of the first half of the eighteenth century, by way of response to lay criticism of baroque devotional practices. Penitential missions along the lines recommended by the Italian Jesuit Paolo Segneri, which involved participants in often spectacular demonstrations of contrition, were gradually abandoned in favour of educational, i.e. catechetical, activities. The subject cannot be discussed in detail here, but it should be noted that missions of the former type were conducted by the Jesuit P. Bernhard Cerroni, onetime superior of the Imperial field mission in Italy, who indefatigably travelled Hungary, Bohemia, Moravia, Inner Austria, and the archduchy from about 1706 onwards, established a mission in Belgrade in 1734, and left a fund for missions in Hungary and Croatia, amounting to the sum of 4,060 fl., in 1760.[62] Cerroni's missions were attended by thousands of the faithful, but the local Jesuits were incensed by his activity, which they felt implied a reproach. Moreover, his method was sharply criticized by those Carinthian and Styrian Jesuits who knew of the population's Protestant leanings and considered the dramatic

---

[61] See the tables of 1783 for the composition of the clergy in the monasteries of Hartberg, Radkersburg, Mureck, Leibnitz, and Pettau, in DA, 'Kapuziner', XIX-d-17. The table for Marburg (Maribor) is missing.

[62] The 18th-century missionary revival is discussed by L. Chatellier, *La Religion des pauvres* (Paris, 1993), 87–121 and 245–68. Chatellier describes the missionary movement in Spain, Italy, France, Poland, and the Habsburg Monarchy in the period 1720–70. He is able to demonstrate that the first half of the 18th century was the 'golden age' of rural missions. The scope of Cerroni's activity emerges from his correspondence with the General, see the General's letters in the years 1706–34, AGR, 'Epp. Gen.', Austr. 11/I–II, 12/I–II', *passim*. The sum of Cerroni's fund is stated in the 'Billance der samentlichen Activ, Passiv und Stiftungs Capitalien der I.Ö. Provinz= des aufgelösten Jesuiten=Ordens zu Gratz . . .', 1773, see DA, 'Jesuiten (21), Aufhebung, Verordnungen, Exjesuiten', 1773–4, XIX-d-2.

Italian-style missions unsuitable for the combat of heresy. A Styrian Jesuit was arrested and removed from all clerical offices for denouncing Cerroni as a 'damned actor' ('sacrem histrionem'), alluding to the theatrical staging of these missions, which encouraged the populace to emulate the missionaries in public acts of penitence.[63]

As a result of this internal debate in the Society, a new missionary method devised by the Upper Austrian Jesuit Ignaz Parhamer brought the issue of catechetical teaching once more to the attention of the Austrian Jesuits. In the 1750s, Maria Theresia arranged for missions by Parhamer and his pupils in Styria, Carinthia, and the Austrian archduchy. However, his peculiar method of instruction with its military organization into catechetical 'regiments' as well as the demoralizing effects of his harsh penitential sermons on the peasantry led to the prohibition of his missions in the diocese of Passau in 1760.[64] The idea of basic religious instruction by laymen who acted under the strict supervision of the clergy actually dated back to the sixteenth century. So called 'Schools of Christian doctrine' had been active in the duchy of Milan since 1536. With the support of St Charles Borromeo, these institutions expanded rapidly, and at the time of his death in 1584, there were 740 schools at which 3,000 teachers taught about 40,000 pupils in the diocese of Milan. Similarly, the Jesuits had founded a catechetical confraternity, which was confirmed by Pius V in 1571 and spread in the Catholic monarchies, with the curious exception of the Austrian Habsburgs' lands, where the first association was formed in Vienna as late as 1711.[65]

---

[63] The General criticized the slackening of discipline and missionary fervour among the Austrian Jesuits in a letter to the provincial Stephan Dinarich, dated 7 Aug. 1723. He ordered that all *missionarii vagi*, of whom there were five in 1719, should follow Cerroni's example in applying Segneri's method, letters of 7 Aug. 1723, 30 July 1718, and similarly his letter to Cerroni, dated 6 Dec. 1732, AGR, 'Epp. Gen., Austr. 12/I', fo. 141, '11/II', fos. 912–13, '12/II', fo. 409. For the quoted incident involving the preacher P. Joseph Fleischer from Leoben and the critique uttered by the missionary P. Carl Scherer from Klagenfurt see AGR, 'Epp. Gen., Austr. 12/I', fos. 80–4, 2 Aug. and 20 Sept. 1721, and '12/II', letter to P. Scherer, fo. 456, 10 Apr. 1734. The life and missionary method of Paolo Segneri (1624–94) are described by A. Guidetti, SJ, *Le missioni popolari* (Milan, 1988), 104–6, 114–25.

[64] For Parhamer's missions in Carinthia and his rejection in the diocese of Passau see Tropper, *Staatliche Kirchenpolitik*, 209–14 and K. Baumgartner, *Die Seelsorge im Bistum Passau . . .* (St Ottilien, 1975), 37 n. 50. The Imperial decree of 6 Sept. 1755 ordered the institution of catechetical missions after Parhamer's method in Lower Styria and Gorizia, STMLA, 'Hofkammermiszellen', Sch. 352.

[65] P. F. Grendler, 'Borromeo and the Schools of Christian Doctrine', in J. M. Headley, J. B. Tomaro (eds.), *San Carlo Borromeo* (Washington, 1988), 158–71. For the quoted figures see ibid. 165. For the Jesuit confraternity see Engelbrecht, *Geschichte des österreichischen Bildungswesens*, iii. 31–3.

The primacy of military and spiritual reconquest plausibly accounts for the delay of catechetical activity in Hungary, where confraternities for the teaching of the doctrine became an important instrument of recatholicization and confessional consolidation in the 1750s and 1760s.[66] Likewise, it seems that the lull in the government's legislative activity in religious matters in the hereditary lands and Bohemia at the end of the seventeenth and the beginning of the eighteenth centuries resulted from the need to concentrate forces on the military defence and subsequent campaign against the Turks in 1683–99 and the suppression of the Hungarian conspiracy and revolts in 1671, 1682, and 1703–11.[67]

In Inner Austria, sporadic manifestations of episcopal concern for the extirpation of heresy testify to an awareness in principle that crypto-Protestantism lingered on. In 1673, the bishop of Seckau, Wenzel Wilhelm, Count Hofkirchen, urged his subordinate parish clergy to devote themselves to the doctrinal instruction of their flock, and to keep their local superiors informed on cases of heresy. If necessary, they should seek the assistance of the secular authorities for further inquisitions. They were especially exhorted to keep an eye on immigrants, and to prevent the smuggling and sale of Protestant literature.[68] A list of parish priests who applied for the episcopal licence to absolve from heresy suggests that, by 1671, converts were gained solely from the group of foreigners, i.e. merchants, Protestant soldiers, and members of the nobility, etc., who temporarily stayed in the capital. Most of the Lower and east Styrian market towns and border settlements, like Weiz, Hartberg, Pettau, Radkersburg, Burgau, or Waltersdorf, were represented as well, pointing to the existence of a Protestant residue among the local population, but indicating also that the Catholic clergy was making converts among the neighbouring Hungarian population who frequented these places. As for the situation in Upper Styria, the synodal reports mentioned neither

---

[66] There were at least 220 of them, see Tüskés and Knapp, 'Bruderschaften in Ungarn', table 3 on p. 6.

[67] For Bohemia see M. É. Ducreux, 'La Reconquête catholique de l'espace bohémien', *RES* 60/3 (1988), 685–702. Ducreux points to the overall decrease of legislative activity and governmental persecution of heresy in the reign of Leopold I. The penal code issued by Joseph I in 1707–8 made no mention of heresy except for the crime of 'seduction' by the sale of heretical books, ibid. 687–8. Ducreux's assessment of Leopold's reign must be qualified to take account of the period of religious persecution following the magnates' conspiracy in 1671, see Ingrao, *Habsburg Monarchy*, 69–71, and F. von Krones, *Zur Geschichte Ungarns (1671–1683): Mit besonderer Rücksicht auf die Thätigkeit und die Geschicke des Jesuitenordens* (Vienna, 1894).

[68] 'Remedia. Pro Curatis ad tollendas occultas Haereses, quae inter Alpes grassantur', 1673. DA, 'Synode', 1568–1722, XV-a-4.

requests for absolution nor conflicts with the local clergy. It was in fact the clandestine emigration of crypto-Protestants from the parish and *Herrschaft* of Pürgg, both of which were subject to the Jesuits in Graz, which led to the resumption of legislative activity. Between 1670 and 1707, there were sporadic reports to the government about the circulation of heretical books among the population of Pürgg and the clandestine emigration of several families to the Protestant towns of the Empire. Government decrees ordering frequent catechetical teaching and threatening severe punishment for heretics were issued in 1700 and 1710, but the Jesuit rector of Graz as temporal as well as spiritual authority over this parish did his best to play down these incidents. However, further reports on the survival of Protestantism in Upper Styria, especially in the Enns valley, came from the owner of the *Herrschaft* Wolkenstein in Upper Styria, Count Carl Adam von Saurau. Probably at his request, Jesuit missions had been held, in the course of which heretical books had been collected and burnt in public, but there was evidence that heresy lingered on among his subjects. Allegedly, the local Protestants had even sent for a Lutheran preacher from Saxony. Saurau urged his bailiff to take action against any conspiracies.[69]

In spite of these alarming reports, there was no systematic inquiry by the ecclesiastical or secular authorities until 1731–2, when the anti-Protestant edict of Archbishop Leopold, Baron Firmian, led to a mass emigration of more than 20,000 Protestants from Salzburg.[70] Over the following fifty years, the Imperial government fought an ultimately unsuccessful battle for the extirpation of heresy in Austria and Bohemia.[71] Begun by Imperial order as a precautionary inquiry into the state of religion in the adjoining regions of Upper Austria, Styria, and Carinthia, the findings were such as to bring about large-scale inquisitions in 1733–4.

---

[69] DA, 'Religionsveränderungen', 1633–1817, XV-c-2. For Pürgg see P. Dedic, 'Die Bekämpfung und Vertreibung der Protestanten . . .', offprint from *Buch der deutschen Forschung in Ungarn* (Budapest, 1940), 27–33. For the decree of 18 July 1710 and Saurau's instructions of 29 June 1712 see DA, 'Religionsberichte Protestantismus', 1598–1730, XV-b-23.

[70] There are numerous narrowly focused studies of the subject, but two recent works offer a comprehensive analysis, see G. Florey, *Geschichte der Salzburger und ihrer Emigration 1731/2* (Vienna, NY, 1977) and the instructive study by M. Walker, *The Salzburg Transaction* (Ithaca, 1993), which gives special attention to the Imperial dimension of this conflict.

[71] The following summary account of the Styrian persecution is based on the government and episcopal records in DA, 'Religionsberichte Protestantismus', 1731–80. Copies of the religious patents can be found here and among the government records in STMLA, 'Hofkammermiszellen', Sch. 348–56.

Crypto-Protestant communities existed in the Jesuits' parish of Pürgg with the settlements of Kulm and Ramsau and the surrounding scattered settlements of Zlem, Dörfl, and Tauplitz, in the nearby market town of Irdning, in the parishes of St Georgen and Stadl near the market town of Murau, formerly a Teuffenbach possession and bulwark of the Lutheran faith, and in several parishes that were subject to the jurisdiction of the Benedictines of Admont and St Lambrecht. Government commissioners were sent to the larger suspect parishes, and the resulting reports formed the basis for the deliberations of mixed committees of government officials and local ecclesiastical authorities in the three duchies concerned.

This arrangement became the model for subsequent religious inquisitions in the reign of Maria Theresia, until the Empress decided to divest the ecclesiastical authorities of their share in the government's deliberations and decisions. In 1773, she dissolved the joint committees and transferred their power to act in religious matters to the reorganized Inner Austrian government (*Gubernium*) and its subdelegate officials, the *Kreishauptleute*, who supervised the new administrative units (*Kreise*). There was no continuous campaign against crypto-Protestantism in the years 1733 to 1780. Fears of a Protestant conspiracy of rebellious subjects and foreign Protestant powers and the need to concentrate forces led to the suspension of persecution during military confrontations, most notably during the Seven Years War (1756–63). Moreover, the laity's attitude towards the problem changed in the course of this largely futile campaign, and the resulting debate which began in the mid-eighteenth century helped prepare the ground for a complete break with the Counter-Reformation in 1781. As will be shown, it was Maria Theresia's firm opposition which delayed the decisive change.

In the 1730s, crypto-Protestantism had been interpreted as the result of both clerical neglect and seditious activity by foreign agitators. The Imperial decree of 29 August 1733 showed considerable perception on Charles VI's part by acknowledging the existence of a heretical tradition in this region: crypto-Protestantism is characterized as a residue ('Yberbleibsel') of the Reformation which had survived the Catholic inquisitions at the beginning of the seventeenth century. A sharp critique of the clergy's, especially the mendicants', shortcomings resulted from this assessment. Thus, the decree states that the present scandals could have been prevented if the clergy had extended their activities to the mountainous regions instead of imposing themselves on the overburdened towns. The clerical *Grundherren*, meaning the Jesuits and the regular clergy of the Upper Styrian monasteries of Admont, St Lambrecht, and Rottenmann, had defaulted on their duty to look after the spiritual welfare of their subjects, for which purpose they had been entrusted with possession of these places in the first place.[72] The decree makes a further important point in criticizing the detrimental effects of clerical estate owning, which obstructed the clergy's spiritual mission. The clergy should resign the administration of property to the neighbouring secular landowners to avoid disputes over this issue which tended to undermine the mutual trust and faith that should prevail between the priest and his flock.[73]

The pertinency of this criticism is demonstrated by the example of the Jesuits' conduct as estate owners in Styria and Carinthia. From the late seventeenth century, the General of the Society received complaints about the Jesuits in Millstatt, who administered the college of Graz's property in Carinthia and were likewise entrusted with the cure of souls in the incorporated parishes. In 1699, the local Jesuits were accused of arbitrarily raising the registered dues and labour services, and of inventing new ones. The superior Ignatius Keck was denounced for reigning 'in a most despotic manner' ('plus quam despotice'), and was feared as a 'singular oppressor of the poor, orphans, and widows' ('singularis oppressor pauperum, pupillorum, et viduarum').[74] Matters came to a head in 1737–8, when a peasant uprising temporarily forced the Jesuits to flee.[75] In the seventeenth century, the Jesuits had successfully defended their right of exemption from episcopal visitations, and had subsequently furthered their economic interests at the expense of their missionary

[72] 'die dermahligen praeiudicia und Scandala religionis gar wohl hötten können vermiden werden, wann der Clerus das profitierende Apostolat ein wenig in das gebürg, ia wann einige geistlich grundt Herren solches nur auf eigne Unterthanen erstreckhet hötten, welche doch denen selben religionis causa ybergeben worden', quoted from the Imperial *Resolution* for the delegated commissioners and members of the Inner Austrian Aulic Chamber, Joseph Ignaz Jöchlinger von Jochenstein, Johann Philipp von Gabelkoven, Johann Christoph von Waitmannstorff, and Johann Adam Felix von Mainersperg, 29 Aug. 1733, DA, 'Religionsberichte Protestantismus', 1731–5, XV-b-23.

[73] 'damit nemblich das zwischen dem Pfarrer und Pfarr-Kindern obwaltende Miß vernemben desto besser gehoben werde, wäelches offt grossen Thails von dene herriehret, das die Pfarrer zu gleich deren Pfarrgenossen grundtobrigkheiten seindt, womit in divisione mei et tui ienes verthrauen zerfahlet, so zwischen einem Pfarrer und dessen Pfarrgenossen nötig ist', Imperial *Resolution* of 29 Aug. 1733, DA, 'Religionsberichte Protestantismus', 1731–5, XV-b-23.

[74] General's letter to Provincial Albert Mechtl, 9 May 1699, AGR, 'Epp. Gen., Austr. 10', fo. 292.

[75] H. Glaser, 'Die Herrschaft der Jesuiten in Millstatt 1600–1773' (doctoral thesis, University of Vienna, 1967), 149–82. The government's sentence eventually confirmed the legality of the Jesuits' seigneurial claims, ibid. 182.

obligations, so that heresy survived and even spread further among their parishioners. As in the case of Pürgg, the Jesuits concealed the fact that traces of crypto-Protestantism had been found in 1710 and 1728, and denied the existence of a confessional motive for the revolt in 1737–8. In 1752, Protestants from Millstatt engaged in the clandestine book trade and acted as emissaries to Regensburg. At the same time, the Jesuits' subjects were among the signatories of a petition for the readmission of the Lutheran faith in Carinthia.[76]

In Styria, the Jesuits forced the successive parish priests of Pürgg as vicars of the rector in Graz to resign the revenues from the estates (*Herrschaft*) pertaining to this parish. As a result, the vicars were unable to employ chaplains who would minister to the Catholic parishioners of the affiliated villages of Steinach, Niederhofen, Meittschern, Wörschach, and Weissenbach.[77] Moreover, the Jesuits failed to respond to earlier reports on the survival of heresy in Pürgg. In the course of the inquiry in 1737, the Upper Styrian archdeacon and member of the government commission Maximilian Heipl maintained that all of the 3,140 parishioners of Pürgg were heretics. In March 1752, three peasants were arrested for submitting a petition for religious toleration on behalf of the Lutheran population, and in the same year a delegation was sent to petition the representatives of the Protestant estates in Regensburg. However, the rector of the Jesuit college in Graz as *ordinarius loci* still refused to provide for additional curates and quarrelled with the government over the admission of missionaries and the financing of a missionary residence in Tauplitz in the district of Pürgg. The fact that the rectors of the college in Graz declined to attend the sessions of the joint commissions in the 1730s and 1750s gave additional weight to the charge of neglect.[78]

However, this preoccupation with the shortcomings of the clergy since the Ferdinandean Counter-Reformation was not a permanent feature of

[76] Koller-Neumann, 'Protestantismus unter der Jesuitenherrschaft', 147, 151–9.

[77] Petition of the five village communities, n.d. [forwarded to Vienna on 4 July 1752], STMLA, 'Hofkammermiszellen', Sch. 348. The signatories state that the length and breadth of the parish measured a distance of five hours' walk.

[78] Maximilian Heipl to bishop Jakob Ernst Count Liechtenstein, 1 July 1737, DA. 'Religionsberichte Protestantismus', 1736–50, XV-b-23. The Jesuits' absence is commented on disapprovingly in the various protocols of the committee's sessions in the 'Religionsberichte' of these years. For the documents relating to the quarrel over Tauplitz see the Imperial decree of 29 July 1752, DA, 'Religionsberichte Protestantismus', 1751–3, XV-b-24, and the Inner Austrian government's letter of 22 Oct. 1753 to the rector of the college in Graz, P. Willibald Krieger, STMLA, 'Hofkammermiszellen', Sch. 350. Documents relating to the petition from Pürgg can be found ibid., Sch. 348, and the government's report on the incident, dated 18 Mar. 1752, STMLA, 'Meillerakten', XIX-h.

the governmental campaigns of 1732 to 1780. Rather, it was characteristic of the beginning and the final period of persecution in the eighteenth century. In the 1730s, the government had given priority to persuasion through catechetical instruction by missionaries, though coercion was used in particularly severe cases, as in the years 1734–6, when at least 624 Upper Austrian and 180 Carinthian crypto-Protestants were forcibly transferred as settlers to Transylvania.[79] The Imperial decree of 29 August 1733 prescribed corporal or even capital punishment for dangerous agitators. Otherwise, they were to be drafted into the Italian regiments.[80] The added explanation that this was more desirable because military service could not be considered a penal sentence and hence did not require a formal inquisition and condemnation for heresy points to the political considerations behind this surprisingly benevolent solution. Charles VI wished to avoid any activity that was bound to provoke a reaction among the Protestant estates in the Empire and beyond and might jeopardize the recently obtained safeguards for the Pragmatic Sanction. This was arguably also the reason why no death sentences were pronounced in the hereditary lands. A similar approach was adopted in Bohemia, where the draconian punishments threatened by the Imperial instructions for the court of appeal in Prague in 1725, ranging from forced labour to capital punishment, were enforced only in a small number of the reported cases.[81]

The limited number of 'transmigrations' from Carinthia and the benevolent treatment of the Styrians were in line with the Emperor's conviction that the extirpation of heresy could not be achieved by force, but required gentle means and skilful persuasion by the local secular and ecclesiastical authorities who exerted jurisdictional power (*Jurisdicenten*). He opposed the prelates' defensive argument that education led to heresy, expressed for the first time by the Lower Styrian archdeacon in Cilli who argued that Lower Styria was not jeopardized because the Slovenian children could neither read nor write. By contrast, Charles VI ordered that the literate peasants should not be deprived of 'their skill and the pleasure they take in

[79] E. Buchinger, *Die 'Landler' in Siebenbürgen* (Munich, 1980), 81–102, 121–5, 144–6. The number of refugees who fled to the Protestant towns and principalities of the Empire is unclear, but there is evidence for the flight of at least another fifty Protestants who were related to the Carinthian emigrants, ibid. 142.

[80] DA, 'Religionsberichte Protestantismus', 1731–5, XV-b-23.

[81] Ducreux, 'Reconquête', 688. The author states no absolute figures, but the discrepancy between the severity of the laws and the actual number of deaths and penal sentences is pointed out. The Imperial *Rescript* of 28 Dec. 1725 is reprinted in A. Gindely, *Die Processierung der Häretiker in Böhmen unter Kaiser Karl VI.* (Prague, 1887), 24–6.

it' ('an dießer ihrer Khunst und darob haltender Lust').[82] Instead, the Jesuits were ordered to compile a Catholic devotional book which should replace the popular Lutheran booklets (*Hauspostillen*).[83]

A similar campaign had been launched in Bohemia, and the considerable success scored in terms of the reception of these books presumably raised hopes of comparable achievements in Austria. This turned out to be an illusion. None of the confessional ambiguity which arguably facilitated the conversion of the Czech heretics characterized the views of the Inner Austrian Protestants. By 1740, not one of the 2,000 copies printed in 1734 had been sold, so that it was decided to distribute them without charge. Nevertheless, the missionaries managed to press not more than 400 copies on the reluctant heretics. In 1751, it was suggested that the government should force the bibliophile heretics in the district of Schladming to buy copies of a Catholic booklet from Salzburg by way of exchange for the confiscated Protestant books.[84] In spite of a similarly

[82] Charles further denounced the use of force to effect conversions: 'that this is no matter that can be put right by force; rather, it depends on the right measure of forbearance' ('daß nemblich dißes keine Sach, so sich mit gewalt richten lasse, sondern auf die glimpfingkheit und deroselben anebtierung ankhome'), decree of 29 Aug. 1733, DA, 'Religionsberichte Protestantismus', 1731–5, XV-b-23, and similarly in his letter of 18 Apr. 1736 to the Upper Austrian *Landeshauptmann* von Thürheim, in which he implicitly criticized the clergy for demanding massive secular intervention and the use of coercion, a method which the Emperor considered an 'unanstendige bekherungsarth'. Quoted in R. Weiß, *Das Bistum Passau . . .* (St Ottilien, 1979), 359. The archdeacon's statement is recorded in the protocol of the commission's session of 23 Nov. 1733, DA, 'Religionsberichte Protestantismus', 1731–5.

[83] Protocol of the religious commission's session of 22 Mar. to 3 Apr. 1734, DA, 'Religionsberichte Protestantismus', 1731–5, XV-b-23.

[84] Imperial instructions for the Inner Austrian government, 9 and 11 Mar. and 4 and 8 June 1740. Abbot Anton of Admont to the Salzburg *Provikar* Aloysius Bertholdi, 13 Feb. 1751, DA, 'Religionsberichte Protestantismus', 1731–5, XV-b-23, 1751–3, XV-b-24. The crypto-Protestants' attitude towards the printed word cannot be discussed here, but it should be noted that the government and episcopal records testify to the eminent importance of the circulation of Lutheran bibles, catechisms, and Pietist devotional literature. In 1757, the Austrian provincial Paul Zetlacher admitted the futility of the seventeen Jesuit missionaries' work in Upper Austria, Styria, and Carinthia. Several hundred books had been extorted with great difficulty from the heretics who held suchlike literature dearer than gold, AGR, 'Austr. 229, Fructus Missionum, Varia (1566-1763)'. The Imperial commissioners in Haus reported that two crypto-Protestants had threatened the curates who had taken away their Lutheran books and had subsequently fled from the parish 'and had declared that, as they were not allowed to keep their books, they would leave their fatherland' ('mit Vermelden: die Bücher Lasse man Ihnen nit, derowegen wollen Sie lieber das Vatterland verlassen'). Letter of 4 Mar. 1752, DA, 'Religionsberichte Protestantismus', 1751–3, XV-b-24. The parish priest of Stadl near Murau, which numbered 3,248 souls in 1746, received no less than 914 Protestant books from his parishioners in the years 1773–8. The number of successfully concealed books is unclear. Letters by the bishop of Seckau to

futile campaign in 1755, Maria Theresa's position on this issue was consistent with her father's policy. In 1773, the prelates' argument for a connection between literacy and heresy eventually persuaded the Inner Austrian government to support their proposal for the abolition of rural elementary schools. However, this attempt met with a swingeing rebuke from the Empress. The Imperial decree of 4 September 1773 confirmed the enlightened position on the general usefulness of primary education as 'allgemein nützlich, und das Mittl . . . den Menschen zu bilden'. The government was ordered to report on the state of elementary schooling and was instructed to submit a memorandum for further improvement.[85]

Maria Theresa's policy deviated from her father's approach in her assessment of the role of the nobility and her greater willingness to use coercion. Although she did not dispute the clergy's particular obligation, she was nevertheless amenable to complaints about the lack of support from the estate owners. The Imperial circular of 31 August 1752 provided a detailed plan for the institution of permanent missions in Upper Styria, which operated, with interruptions, in the 1750s and 1760s and were financed by the local clergy. On the other hand, the instructions for the government's and the nobility's officials in Upper Styria stressed their responsibility for the enforcement of the laws against heresy. They were to exert close control over the conduct of the population, and were threatened with severe punishment if they defaulted on their duties. The nobles were in turn warned against employing heretical officials, and were ordered to demand a written certificate of orthodoxy from the respective parish priest before they accepted foreigners as subjects. A decree of 27 May 1752 had furthermore reprimanded the lay patrons for using benefices as rewards for protégés, regardless of their often poor quality.

the Upper Styrian archdeacon in Pöls, 1 Jan. 1746, DA, 'Religionsberichte Protestantismus', 1736–50, XV-b-23, and 'Nachricht von dem Religions=Zustand der Pfarr Stadl . . .' by the parish priest Martin Gletler, MS 1778, DA, 'Gebundene Quellen', XIX-b-9. There is also evidence for the belief in the supernatural powers of the book, see Gletler's report of 25 May 1779, DA, 'Religionsberichte Protestantismus', 1779–80, XV-c-1. For a general discussion of this problem see the collection of articles in E. Bödeker, G. Chaise, and P. Veit (eds.), *Le Livre religieux et ses pratiques* (Göttingen, 1991) and D. Cressy, 'Books as Totems in Seventeenth-Century England and New England', *Journal of Library History*, 21/1, winter 1986, 92–106.

[85] For the campaign in 1755 see the instructions of the Imperial *Resolution* of 6 Sept. 1755, STMLA, 'Hofkammermiszellen', Sch. 352. A copy of the Imperial decree of 4 Sept. 1773 is kept in DA, 'Religionsberichte Protestantismus', 1771–3, XV-b-24. The argument in favour of the abolition of elementary schooling can be found ibid., report of the archdeacon in Pöls on the commission in Stadl, 29 Aug. 1772.

The Inner Austrian government was empowered to exert closer control over the relations between the clergy and the lay authorities.[86] When the anti-heresy campaign was resumed in October 1764, a decree was issued which sharply attacked the secular authorities for their slackness or downright refusal to co-operate. Steps were taken to render inquisitions more effective and to minimize the risk that suspects had time to flee or else hide their books. Henceforth, the delegated commissioners were empowered to institute proceedings among the rural population without prior notification of their seigneurs. An explanatory clause was added to forestall protests on grounds of principle. Thus, it was stated that it was by no means intended to detract from the seigneurial rights, 'and the commissioners' full power and authority shall therefore be limited strictly to religious matters' ('und wird eben derohalben dieser freye Gewalt und Authorität auf die alleinige Causas Religionis hiemit deutlich eingeschränket'). In spite of these decrees, the government and ecclesiastical authorities received little support from the laity. Quite to the contrary, the latter often obstructed the authorities' work. A report of November 1778 for the summer missions in Pichl, Kulm, Schladming, and Haus drew attention to this problem and complained that nothing was done about the Lutheran miners and day labourers. In spite of evidence to the contrary, the local administrator of the ducal mines (*Bergamtsverwalter*) denied that Lutherans had ever been accepted, and defended the right of free movement (*Zu- und Abzugsrecht*) for the miners.[87]

The evidence suggests a secret but fierce struggle between the government and the nobility for the power of disposition over the subjects and therefore indirectly over the resources of the Monarchy. In the sixteenth and seventeenth centuries, the Counter-Reformation and recatholicization in Bohemia and the hereditary lands had offered the prospect of social and economic advancement and had provided the disciplinary means for the consolidation of seigneurial power over the estates acquired. This process had involved a mutual reinforcement of governmental and seigneurial authority. By the mid-eighteenth century, however, rising taxation and the removal of manpower by recruitment

---

[86] Copies of the decrees of 27 May and 31 Aug. 1752 in STMLA, 'Hofkammermiszellen', Sch. 348, and DA, 'Religionsberichte Protestantismus', 1751–3, XV-b-24.
[87] Decree of 3 Oct. 1764, STMLA, 'Hofkammermiszellen', Sch. 356. Summary report by the missionary of Stadl, Martin Gastner, and the deputy captain (*adjungierter Kreishauptmann*) for Judenburg, Franz Karl von Preitenau, 9 Nov. 1778, DA, 'Religionsberichte Protestantismus', 1775–8, XV-c-1.

diminished the nobility's share of the estates' revenues. Hence, there was little support for a policy which entailed government interference and threatened further losses. In Upper Austria, the local seigneurs therefore openly refused to report the names of 'obstinate' Protestant peasants whom the government wished to deport to Transylvania, stating that these were often their wealthiest and most industrious subjects whose emigration would mean a considerable loss of revenue. On the whole, seigneurial authority was not an agent of confessional consolidation beyond the level reached in 1700, and began to work as a brake on attempts to tighten governmental control over the rural population afterwards.[88]

As for Maria Theresia's attitude towards the use of force, it seems that the failure of Charles VI's diplomacy and the constant threat of Prussian intervention had persuaded her to take vigorous action against a potential 'fifth column' of Protestants in the Monarchy. The missionary campaigns in Upper Austria, Styria, and Carinthia were backed by the rigorous use of coercion. An effort was made to distinguish between different types of heretics, and to develop a graded system of sanctions, ranging from capital punishment for foreign, especially Prussian agents—a threat which never materialized—to forced labour, imprisonment, or transmigration for unrepentant or backsliding heretics. In the 1750s, so-called 'Houses of Conversion' were built in Judenburg and Rottenmann, which were in use until 1775. Avowed heretics were imprisoned there for several months or even years, during which they were interrogated and instructed in the Catholic doctrine. Such 'instruction' frequently meant economic ruin for the prisoners, who were to pay for their support and were kept from their farms even over the harvest season.[89] Those who refused to abjure, or failed to persuade their instructors of their genuine conversion, were eventually deported to Hungary or Transylvania. Between 1752 and 1774, at least 3,180 Protestants from Upper Austria (2,059), Carinthia (851), and Styria (270) were sent to Transylvania. The proportion of 'obstinate' heretics in Styria was obviously low, even if the first transportations of

---

[88] For the imposition of confessional discipline by the landowning nobility during the earlier period see T. Winkelbauer, 'Sozialdisziplinierung und Konfessionalisierung durch Grundherren in den österreichischen und böhmischen Ländern im 16. und 17. Jahrhundert', *ZHF* 19/3 (1992), 317–39. The conflict in Upper Austria is mentioned in the Imperial instructions for the Upper Austrian government, 11 Mar. 1752, DA, 'Religionsberichte Protestantismus', 1751–3, XV-b-24. For the assessment of a similar development in Bohemia see Ducreux, 'Reconquête', 699.

[89] The relevant decrees can be found in DA, 'Religionsberichte Protestantismus' for the years 1752–75.

perhaps 100–50 Styrian 'transmigrants' to the estates of the Hungarian magnates of Podmaniczky and Ráday in Iklad and Keresztúr are added.[90] These figures suggest that the Counter-Reformation and subsequent confessionalization had been more successful in the duchy of Styria than in the Inner Austrian heartland, the recatholicization of which had formed the immediate objective of the resident prince (until 1619–20) and his clerical advisers. They could also be interpreted as testifying to the influence of a greater density of monastic settlements and more vigorous, though urban-based, educational and missionary activity by the Jesuits and the Capuchin Order in Styria, with Jesuit schools and colleges settling in Graz, Leoben, Judenburg, and in Marburg, where a settlement (*Residenz*) was established in 1753.

However, even the use of transmigrations failed to settle the problem of heresy. Counter-strategies of dissimulation were devised by the Lutheran preachers of Ortenburg in Bavaria, and circulated among the crypto-Protestants in the three duchies concerned.[91] Moreover, the harsh conditions imposed on the transmigrants, involving loss of property through precipitate sale and above all separation from their below-age children, proved counter-productive even in the short run because they led to a radicalization among the crypto-Protestants and embroiled the Empress in a constitutional dispute with the Protestant estates of the Empire. In 1752, a petition was submitted in Graz and Regensburg on behalf of 200 confessed Lutherans in Pürgg, and in 1772, more than 300 signatories from Stadl and St Georgen near Murau petitioned the Empress for religious tolerance.

The latter incident provoked a reaction which testified to the intransigence of the clergy. In his report on the findings of the religious

---

[90] For the number of Theresian transmigrants to Transylvania and Hungary see Buchinger, *Landler*, 221, 235, 267, 315, 336, and P. Brandtner, 'Beitrag zur Geschichte der Transmigration inner- und oberösterreichischer Protestanten . . .', *Deutsche Forschungen in Ungarn*, 4 (1939), 71–84.

[91] The interception of such an instruction is mentioned in the bishop of Seckau's report for the Empress, 27 Nov. 1754, and a manuscript copy is added, DA, 'Religionsberichte Protestantismus', 1754–70, XV-b-24. The involvement of Ortenburg illustrates the extension of the Protestant network in the Empire and beyond. The Imperial county of Ortenburg formed a Protestant enclave in Bavaria, bordering on the territory of the bishopric of Passau. Until 1602, the dukes of Bavaria repeatedly contested its exempt jurisdictional status (*Reichsunmittelbarkeit*), but full subjection and incorporation was achieved only with the dissolution of the Holy Roman Empire in (1803–) 1806. From 1698, Ortenburg belonged to the north-western association of Calvinist princes, the 'Wetterauer Reichsgrafenkollegium', members of which (Nassau-Dillenburg) had dynastic links with the House of Orange and were in touch with the Dutch republic, see Press, *Kriege und Krisen*, 127 and Köbler, *Historisches Lexikon*, 392–3.

commission in Stadl, the Upper Styrian archdeacon, Maximilian Heipl, once more urged the abolition of elementary schooling for the rural population. To elicit confessions of heresy from suspects, he suggested that the government should issue a declaration promising the allocation of a place of public worship to all avowed Protestants, without stating that this promise referred to some place in Hungary or Transylvania.[92] Both suggestions met with sharp criticism from the Empress and the Viennese government, but a similar strategy was nevertheless employed by three ex-Jesuit missionaries in Moravia, whose false proclamation of religious tolerance led to a final wave of religious unrest among the Wallachian population. Maria Theresia's decision to enforce the full measure of the law against the Moravian Protestants led to a decisive confrontation with Joseph II, who threatened to abdicate. The resulting compromise solution, which passed into law by the decrees of 14 November 1777 for Bohemia, Moravia, and the hereditary lands, amounted to a *de facto* toleration through connivance at secret heretical practices, even if these involved meetings of conventicles and the neglect of the prescribed religious duties.[93]

However, it would be misleading to interpret these decrees as indicative of a change of principle in Maria Theresia's attitude towards the confessional issue. Until the very end of her reign, she pursued a religious policy that was based on the assumption that confessional pluralism was incompatible with the requirements of stable government. Hence, there could only be tactical concessions, and persecution remained a legitimate response to the threat of heresy. The November decrees expressly stated that the regulations were to be kept secret on pain of severe punishment, so that toleration would not officially transcend the level of individual acts of grace by the local clergy and government officials. Likewise, the

---

[92] All documents in DA, 'Religionsberichte Protestantismus', 1752–73. The documents exchanged with the Imperial Protestants are collected in STMLA, MS 1302, 'Reichstagsakten', 1752–6. A brief survey of the clash with the Imperial Protestants is provided by F. Reissenberger, 'Das Corpus evangelicorum und die österreichischen Protestanten (1685–1764)', *JGGPÖ* 17 (1896), 207–22, though this article is mainly concerned with the Salzburg Protestants.

[93] R. J. Wolny, *Die josephinische Toleranz unter besonderer Berücksichtigung ihres geistlichen Wegbereiters Johann Leopold Hay* (Munich, 1973), 37–70, G. Trautenberger, 'Zur Geschichte der Religionsbewegung in der mährischen Wallachei', *JGGPÖ* 1 (1880), 141–9, and ibid. 150–65 the reprinted report of the government commissions, edited by F. Preidel, 'Bericht Hay's über die Unruhen in der mährischen Wallachei vom 3 September 1777'. The decrees for Moravia and Austria have been published by J. Loserth, 'Grundsätze der Kaiserin Maria Theresia, nach welchen die Religionsschwärmer in Mähren zu behandeln seien', *ZVGMS* 18 (1914), 297–300, and G. Loesche, 'Maria Theresias letzte Maßnahmen gegen die "Ketzer" ', *ZVGMS* 20 (1916), 411–44.

Houses of Conversion were abolished in 1775, but their inmates were transferred to various monasteries in Graz, and in May 1780, it was still discussed whether they should be dispatched to Hungary.[94] It was not before the accession of Joseph II in December 1780 that the inevitable break with the principles of the Counter-Reformation was made. Even before the proclamation of the Edict of Toleration ('Toleranzpatent') on 13 October 1781, orders were issued which signalled the end of the Counter-Reformation era. A decree of 25 November and 8 December 1780 ordered the dismissal of the permanent missionaries, who were to be replaced by secular parish clergy, and prohibited the official use of the term 'missionary' which had become odious to the population. The parish priest of Stadl aptly characterized the change in a brief retrospective entry in his parish chronicle: 'NB: on 29 November died the ever memorable Empress Maria Theresia, and with her death the entire religious constitution [of the Monarchy] changed.'[95]

[94] DA, 'Religionsberichte Protestantismus', 1775–80.

[95] 'NB: den 29ten: 9ber 1780 starb die unvergessliche Kaiserin Maria Theresia, und mit ihrem Tod änderte sich die ganze bisherige Religions=Verfassung.' All documents in 'Religionsberichte Protestantismus, 1779–80, XV-c-1.

8

Conclusion

For a period of nearly two centuries from the accession of Archduke Ferdinand to the beginning of Josephinian rule, the alliance between the Catholic Church and the dynasty had operated successfully and had established the cultural hegemony of Catholicism in the Monarchy. Favoured by the conciliatory confessional outlook and political orientation of the majority of the Inner Austrian nobility, the process of recatholicization and the accompanying changes in the relations between the ruler and the estates were accomplished without a military confrontation. Ferdinand's victory over the Protestant estates in this contest for power permanently strengthened the position of the prince and his provincial executive, the Inner Austrian government. It is true that the estates' tax-granting right remained intact until 1748, when acceptance of a system of decennial contributions sharply reduced its value as a political pawn in negotiations with the Viennese government.[1] However, the nobility's power was decisively pruned well before that date as a result of the confessional streamlining of the Inner Austrian diets in the Counter-Reformation, which was accompanied by the creation of a 'robe' nobility of courtiers and officials. In addition, the composition and operations of the estates' executive committees were brought under closer control when Ferdinand II forced admission of a member of the clergy and made convocation of the committees dependent on his consent. By way of compensation, prospects of social and economic improvement were opened to the recatholicized elite. Holding out a promise of exclusive temporal advancement to those who accepted political submission spelt out in terms of confessional loyalty, Ferdinand II and his successors were able to create a politically reliable elite composed of the 'old' Catholic minority, the recatholicized nobility, and a group of Catholic 'new men', consisting of nobles and commoners from the rest of the Empire and Italy who were co-opted to the provincial elites by ducal or Imperial favour.[2]

---

[1] See Mell, *Verfassungs- und Verwaltungsgeschichte*, 586–7.

[2] Ferdinand II's policy of granting estate membership to Catholic courtiers and officials was continued by his successors, so that towards the end of the 17th century, the new nobil-

From the reign of Ferdinand II onwards, Habsburg religious policy was guided by the political principles that had found poignant expression in the princes' agenda of October 1579. Though unattainable in practice, the imposition of confessional uniformity throughout the Monarchy was considered the indispensable precondition for political stability. By the mid-eighteenth century, this assumption was coming increasingly under pressure from enlightened critics, but Maria Theresia's intransigence delayed the readjustment of religious policy. By the 1770s, religious intolerance had become a definite encumbrance for her programme of educational reform, and had created sources of unrest in the Austrian and Bohemian lands.

The fate of the alliance between the Catholic Church and the Habsburg dynasty had implications for the situation of the Church in Styria and Inner Austria at large. Since the reign of Ferdinand II, the secular power's intervention had helped effect the material restoration of the Church, and had enabled Catholicism to become the all-pervasive ideology. In the course of the seventeenth and eighteenth centuries, Catholicism shaped the province's intellectual life through the educational monopoly of the Jesuits' schools and universities. It likewise influenced the artistic production of this era. Through the normative influence of favoured architectural styles and its prescriptions for the visual arts, the Counter-Reformation made a lasting imprint on public aesthetic judgement. The means of art and architecture were enlisted for the propagation of the faith, and products of sacred art were subjected to the theological verdict of the Tridentine decrees.[3]

However, as a concomitant of this success, the Church became more directly dependent on the secular power, which in the long run made a reworking of the alliance inevitable. Resting on Ferdinand II's absolutist claims as protector of the Catholic Church and faith, the balance struck between ecclesiastical and dynastic interests had been precarious from the

---

ity (*Hof- und Beamtenadel*) constituted a politically significant part of the estates, see ibid. 573 ff. For the further measures see the present study, Ch. 4.

[3] The relation between the political and spiritual Counter-Reformation and contemporary artistic production in general continues to be a matter of dispute, see for example the assessment in R. Bösel, 'Typus und Tradition in der Baukunst gegenreformatorischer Orden', in *Römische historische Mitteilungen*, 31 (1989), 239–53, esp. 239–42, 253. Recent contributions to the subject include the previously quoted collection edited by T. Lucas, *Saint, Site and Sacred Strategy* (Vatican City, 1990) and T. DaCosta Kaufmann, *Court, Cloister and City: The Art and Culture of Central Europe 1450–1800* (London, 1995), ch. 9, pp. 204–31. The relevant Tridentine prescriptions are reprinted in H. Jedin, 'Entstehung und Tragweite des Trienter Dekrets über die Bilderverehrung', *THQS* 116 (1935), 181–6.

start. During the first half of the eighteenth century, frequent jurisdictional contests and the anticlerical tenor of Charles VI's crypto-Protestant campaign raised the prospect of a readjustment on terms dictated by the dynasty. This threat temporarily subsided as a result of the more pressing military and political concerns of this period. Over the following decades, Maria Theresa's attitude towards the religious question meant that secularizing tendencies inherent in her reform policy were kept in check. However, this did not prevent the balance from tilting gradually in favour of the secular powers, represented by the provincial and central governments, who extended their competences at the expense of the ecclesiastical authorities.

The Church preserved its autonomy to some extent in the field of ecclesiastical reform. In Styria, the modernization of the institutional framework was furthered by the creation of an intermediary power in the shape of a vicar general for Salzburg's Styrian parishes in the sixteenth century, and by the implementation of the Tridentine regulations for a tighter control and more efficient administration at parish level.[4] In spite of this progress, the remaining clerical exemptions and the jurisdictional rights of the lay patrons continued to mark the limits of episcopal power. This defect formed part of a legacy of unresolved problems which the Counter-Reformation bequeathed to the restored Church. Among the graver shortcomings were the moral and educational defects of the Lower Styrian clergy, which had dire consequences for the doctrinal instruction of the Slovenian population. The survival of crypto-Protestantism in Upper Styria likewise exposed the ecclesiastical authorities to charges of neglect, and strengthened the cause of their enlightened critics.[5]

By 1780, the traditional alliance between the State and the Church had outlived its primary political purpose of effecting a Catholic restoration as the basis of stable monarchical rule. Since Ferdinand II, the indubitable personal piety and genuine religious commitment of the Habsburg princes had proved compatible with an instrumentalization of the religious question as a vehicle for the implementation of dynastic policy. However, the case of the Hungarian Counter-Reformation indicated the limitations of

---

[4] A 'Max-Weberian' interpretation of Counter-Reformation ecclesiastical reforms as part of a process of modernization is put forward by W. Reinhard, 'Gegenreformation als Modernisierung? Prolegomena zu einer Theorie des konfessionellen Zeitalters', *Archiv für Reformationsgeschichte* 68 (1977), 226–52.

[5] The relation between the Church and the Enlightenment, and the question of a genuine 'Catholic enlightenment' are discussed in the previously quoted collection of articles edited by E. Kovács, *Katholische Aufklärung*. See also the contributions in H. Klueting, *Katholische Aufklärung: Aufklärung im katholischen Deutschland* (Hamburg, 1993).

this approach when Leopold I's attempt to impose a reign of confessional absolutism caused a political crisis in the relations between the Hungarian nobility and the dynasty. The conspiracy and uprising in 1671 and 1682 should have warned the dynasty that any attempt to use the religious issue as a pretext for subjecting the nobility of this kingdom to an absolutist regime would result in uniting the magnates' opposition against the dynasty, regardless of their confessional affiliations. Religious persecution created a permanent source of instability by alienating the Protestant part of the elite,[6] but there is no indication that this experience led to a reassessment of the validity of the political assumptions which underlay the Emperor's Counter-Reformation policy.

On the other hand, the process of ideological and political fusion among the hereditary lands and Bohemia was sufficient to warrant a uniform religious policy in the eighteenth century. Measures adopted for the struggle against heresy in one province were deemed suitable to deal with comparable phenomena elsewhere. The exchange of information between the local reform commissions and Vienna furthered the homogenization of policies, so that a change of method in one part had repercussions on the proceedings in the rest of the provinces. In general, the rationalization of governmental politics entailed an extension of the state's administrative and jurisdictional powers at the expense of the ecclesiastical authorities, and the exposure of the Counter-Reformation's defects provided a lever for preliminary reforms in the reign of Maria Theresia.

On the basis of the above, it could be argued that the Counter-Reformation contributed to the process of state-building in several important ways: first of all, it strengthened the position of the prince at

---

[6] For the conspiracy of 1671 and the decade of religious persecution which, in spite of an Imperial decree of 9 Nov. 1681 offering a modest degree of toleration, caused an uprising led by the Transylvanian prince Imre Thököly in 1682, see Krones, *Zur Geschichte Ungarns (1671–1683)*. The repressive Counter-Reformation measures adopted in the aftermath of the conspiracy included the condemnation of twenty-two Lutherans and thirty-nine Calvinists, among them several preachers, to the galleys. Contemporary Protestant reactions in England, the Dutch Republic, and the Empire focused on the Jesuits as the likely instigators, and castigated Emperor Leopold I's submissiveness, see the pertinent quotations from contemporary pamphlets in B. Köpeczi, *Staatsräson und christliche Solidarität: Die ungarischen Aufstände und Europa in der zweiten Hälfte des 17. Jahrhunderts* (Budapest, 1983), 134–7, 331, 165 n. 85, and in H. von Zwiedineck-Südenhorst, *Die öffentliche Meinung in Deutschland im Zeitalter Ludwigs XIV. 1650–1700* (Stuttgart, 1888), 60, 62–4, 102. For the general pattern of 17th- and early 18th-century Hungarian uprisings and the problem of Catholic participation see Evans, *Making of the Habsburg Monarchy*, 261–6.

the expense of the estates. Related to this was the formation of loyal and, in the case of the urban corporations, pliable Catholic 'power elites' in the various provinces of the Monarchy.[7] As previously shown, the process of 'confessionalization' at parish level entailed a tightening of control over every aspect of the social life of the community. Concomitant administrative improvements, most notably the introduction of birth and marriage registers, provided the government with a valuable source of supplementary demographic data that could be tapped, for example, for purposes of recruitment and taxation. Further, the necessity of co-ordinating government action to effect the implementation of religious policy in the different parts of the Monarchy tended, again, to a homogenization of approach in the eighteenth century. On the other hand, disputes over the infringement of the nobility's privileges and economic interests in the course of the campaign against crypto-Protestantism revealed a potentially destabilizing tendency of state expansion. The protests of the landed nobility against transgressions on their seigneurial rights on this occasion foreshadowed the more serious confrontation in the reign of Joseph II. His centralizing reform policy temporarily jeopardized the political consensus between the provincial nobilities and the dynasty which proved the truly indispensable foundation of Habsburg rule. In this, Joseph II failed to heed the lessons to be learned from his predecessors' mistakes. Beginning with the Empire of Charles V, the Habsburgs' fortunes had thrived and deteriorated depending on their ability to harness the fiscal and human resources of the various parts of their composite monarchies to dynastic aims by negotiating working agreements with the entrenched political elites of their dominions.

By the mid-sixteenth century, it proved impossible to master the 'centrifugal' forces of territorial particularism in the Empire and unite them with the gradually diverging interests of the Spanish and Austrian monarchies. The crises and revolts which shook the Spanish Empire in the sixteenth and first half of the seventeenth centuries were caused mainly by the dynasty's inability successfully to integrate the provincial political elites, and negotiate a politically acceptable agreement for the allocation of the fiscal and military burden of its sprawling Empire. In the case of the Netherlands, Habsburg commitment to the Catholic cause meant that the power contest between centre and province fused with the

---

[7] The concept of power elites and their significance for the transformation of dynastic into modern states is discussed in the contributions to W. Reinhard (ed.), *Power Elites and State Building* (Oxford, 1996).

ongoing confessional struggle, providing the rebels with a distinct ideological armoury to support their revolt against 'tyranny'.

After 1620, the Austrian Habsburgs gradually succeeded in establishing Catholicism as the basis of elite consensus, which in turn helped sustain the fabric of the developing Austrian monarchy. The persistence of Protestantism in the kingdom of Hungary and the principality of Transylvania formed a notable exception to this rule. Likewise, a measure of confessional pluralism in the shape of religious minorities at the periphery constituted an unacknowledged reality of the Monarchy in the eighteenth century.[8]

It would seem that, in the rival monarchies of France and Prussia, state-building during the seventeenth and eighteenth centuries was achieved largely through the extension of the Monarchy's bureaucracy and acquisitive apparatus as well as its armed forces, which encouraged elite support for the dynasty as the provider of new careers and sources of income. By contrast, the costs and demographic strains of mostly defensive or recuperative campaigning by the Austrian Monarchy acted as a limiting factor upon the political gains to be reaped by the dynasty from comparable processes of state-building. In the period under consideration, the Austrian Monarchy remained anchored in Imperial power and pursued frequently chimerical projects for a western Empire while actually making lasting acquisitions in the east. For its survival, eighteenth-century dynastic government continued to rely on the balancing of structural flaws by a skilful mixture of coercion and manipulation of the local political elites.[9]

The present study has sought to demonstrate that the Counter-Reformation of the sixteenth and seventeenth centuries contributed to the process of state building in various ways, most important among which were the enhancement of monarchical power and the devising of an ideological formula for the consensus between the dynasty and the provincial nobilities who represented the political nation.

---

[8] See the stimulating article by G. Klingenstein, 'Modes of Religious Tolerance and Intolerance in Eighteenth-Century Habsburg Politics', *Austrian History Yearbook*, 24 (1993), 1–16. The emphasis must be on the repressive quality of this policy, though, in view of the limited and even secretive nature of the quoted concessions, which Maria Theresia hedged in with provisos and evidently perceived as individual and revocable acts of grace.

[9] It could be argued that the constraints on domestic power had an equivalent in the field of foreign policy, where the priority of negotiation over direct military action was beginning to be acknowledged by the lavish efforts bestowed on the recruitment and training of an increasingly refined diplomatic corps.

On the other hand, there was the case of Hungary and the unsolved problem of crypto-Protestantism which illustrated the dialectics of a confessional policy that already carried the germ of self-destruction. In the course of the eighteenth century, it was to succumb to the dissolvent, secularizing forces of the Enlightenment, whose 'cosmopolitan' expansionism was in turn checked by the countercurrents of nascent nationalism.

The age of confessionalization and aspiring confessional absolutism hence left an ambivalent legacy of repression and revolt, to be rejected or assimilated by the modern national movements of the peoples in the Habsburg Monarchy.[10]

---

[10] The literature on the roots of modern nationalism is vast, and rapidly increasing as a result of the recent revival of (political) interest, but a brief general appraisal of the popular origins can be found in E. J. Hobsbawm's stimulating essay on 'Popular proto-nationalism', in id., *Nations and Nationalism since 1780* (2nd edn., Cambridge, 1992), 46–79.

BIBLIOGRAPHY

I. MANUSCRIPT SOURCES

Archivio Generale della Compagnia di Gesù, Rome:

'Austria' (21–2) (1601–60).
'Austria (132)', 'Litterae Annuae', 1575–99.
'Austria (229)', 'Fructus Missionum', 'Varia' (1566–1763).
'Epistolae Generalium, Austria', 1/I–12/II (1573–1736), 15 vols.
'Germania (159–60) (1581–2)'.

Diözesan-Archiv Graz-Seckau, Graz, episcopal records:

'Konsistorialprotokoll', 1670–4.
'Religionsberichte Protestantismus, 1598–1780, XV-b-23/4, XV-c-1 (8 Schuber).
'Religionsveränderungen', 1633–1817, XV-c-2.
'Synode', 1568–1722, XV-a-4, XV-e-5.
'Vereine-Bruderschaften', 1600 ff, XVI-a-3.
MS 1778, 'Nachrichten von dem Religions-Zustand der Pfarr Stadl . . .', XIX-bB-9.

Religious orders and congregations:

'Augustiner-Mönche' (2), XIX-b-44.
'Kapuziner' (=miscellaneous), 'Kloster Mureck', 'Kloster Graz-Stiege', (3 Schuber) XIX-d-17.
'Jesuiten' (5), (9), (13), XIX-c-34/38/42/43.
'Jesuiten—Kongregationen', XIX-d-1.
'Jesuiten' (21), XIX-d-2.

Österreichische Nationalbibliothek, Vienna:

'Litterae Annuae' (1617–19), MS 13562.
Guilelmo Lamormaini, 'Ferdinandi II Romanorum Imperatoris Virtutes' (Vienna, 1638), MS 7378.

Steiermärkisches Landesarchiv, Graz:

Government records:

'Geistliche Stiftungsakten', fascicles 494, 600.
'Hofkammermiszellen', Sch. 202, 348–56.
'Meillerakten', XIX-e (1–23), f-13, h, XX-a–f, t–v.
'Regierungsakten, Expedita, 1650'.
'Repräsentation und Kammer, Sachabteilung', fasc. 109.

Estates' records:

'Landschaftliches Archiv', IV, 3.
'Beziehungen zu Ungarn', Sch. 705.
'Religion und Kirche', Sch. 29–30.
'Landrecht', Sch. 637.

Town archives:

'Archiv Leoben', Sch. 172.
'Archiv Murau', Sch. 131.

Family archives:

'Archiv Saurau', Sch. 230.
'Archiv Schranz von Schranzenegg', Sch. 1/1.
'Stubenberg Archiv', Sch. 11, 12, 95, 96.

Manuscripts:

MS 31 'Gründlicher Gegenbericht auf den falschen Bericht und vermeinte Erinnerung Davids Rungii, wittenbergischen Professors, von tyrannischer päbstischer Verfolgung des H. Evangelii in Steyermarkt, Kärnten und Krain, von Jacob Rosolenz, Propst von Stainz' (Graz, 1606) (MS copy).

MS XII/5, 'Acta Conventus Graecensis ad S. Antonium Pad(uavinu)m' (after 1730).

MS 481, Simon Povoden, 'Beytrag zu einer steyermärkischen Kirchengeschichte von allen Slovenen . . .' (1826).

MS 506, 'Georgii Stobaei de Palmaburgo Episcopi Lavantini Epistolae ad diversos', n.p., n.d. (18th-century copy).

MS 624, Chronicle of the Capuchin monastery in Radkersburg (1761) (19th-century copy).

2. PRINTED SOURCES

(*a*) *Primary Sources*

Außrauschung der Augspurgischen Confusion, oder wichtige und starcke Ursachen/warumb es gefährlich inn Augspurgischer Confession zuleben unnd zusterben (Graz, Widmanstetter press, 1606), copy in the Styrian State Library C 518043 I.

Gute Zeitung/für die Christlichen Layen . . . (Graz, Widmanstetter press, 1604), copy in the Styrian State Library, C 518025 I.

(*b*) *Secondary Sources*

ACHBERGER, L., 'Die innere Entwicklung der evangelischen Kirche in der Steiermark im 16. Jahrhundert', in *Evangelisch in der Steiermark*, 25–32.

AHN, F., 'Die Druckerpresse Widmanstetters zu Graz', *MÖVBW* 8 (1904), 144–9.

ALBRECHT, D., *Maximilian I. von Bayern 1573–1651* (Munich, 1998).

—— 'Wilhelm V. (1579–1598)', *HbBG* ii. 351–63.

AMON, K. (ed.), *Die Bischöfe von Graz-Seckau, 1218–1968* (Graz, 1969).

—— 'Die geistige Auseinandersetzung', in *Evangelisch in der Steiermark*, 39–43.

—— 'Innerösterreich', in Schindling and Ziegler, *Die Territorien des Reichs*, i. 102–16.

—— 'Religiöse Literatur des 16. Jahrhunderts in der Steiermark', in *Literatur in der Steiermark*, 43–62.

—— *Die Steiermark vor der Glaubensspaltung: Kirchliche Zustände 1490–1520* (Graz, 1960).

——and PRIMETSHOFER, B. (eds.), *Ecclesia Peregrinans: Josef Lenzenweger zum 70. Geburtstag* (Vienna, 1986), 361–70.

ANDRITSCH, J.,'Die Grazer Jesuitenuniversität und der Beginn der katholischen Restauration im Karpatenraum', in Pickl (ed.), *800 Jahre Steiermark*, 247–94.

—— *Unser Judenburg* (Judenburg, 1975).

—— *Studenten und Lehrer aus Ungarn und Siebenbürgen an der Universität Graz (1586–1782)* (Graz, 1965).

AUERBACH, I., *Stände in Ostmitteleuropa: Alternativen zum monarchischen Prinzip in der frühen Neuzeit* (Munich, 1997).

BAHLCKE, J. (ed.), *Ständefreiheit und Staatsgestaltung in Ostmitteleuropa: Übernationale Gemeinsamkeiten in der politischen Kultur vom 16.–18. Jahrhundert* (Leipzig, 1996).

—— and STROHMEYER, A. (eds.), *Konfessionalisierung in Ostmitteleuropa: Wirkungen des religiösen Wandels im 16. und 17. Jahrhundert in Staat, Gesellschaft und Kultur* (Stuttgart, 1999).

BAK, J. (ed.), *The German Peasant War of 1525* (London, 1976).

BARNA, G., 'Mariazell und Ungarn', in *Schatz und Schicksal*, 281–94.

BÄUMER, R. (ed.), *Concilium Tridentinum* (Darmstadt, 1979).

—— (ed.), *Reformatio Ecclesiae: Festgabe für Erwin Iserloh* (Paderborn, 1980).

BAUMGARTNER, K., *Die Seelsorge im Bistum Passau zwischen barocker Tradition, Aufklärung und Restauration* (St Ottilien, 1975).

BENEDIK, M., *Die Kapuziner in Slowenien 1600–1700* (Rome, 1974).

BERGIN, J., 'Between Estate and Profession: The Catholic Parish Clergy of Early Modern Western Europe', in Bush, *Social Orders*, 66–85.

BETTS, R. R., 'Poland, Bohemia and Hungary', in Elton, *Reformation*, 198–222.

BIBL, V., *Die Einführung der Katholischen Gegenreformation in Niederösterreich durch Kaiser Rudolf II. (1576–1580)* (Innsbruck, 1900).

—— 'Erzherzog Ernst und die Gegenreformation in Niederösterreich (1576–1590)', *MIÖG*, supplementary volume 6 (1901), 575–96.

—— *Die Religionsreformation Kaiser Rudolfs II. in Oberösterreich*, offprint from *AÖG*, 109 (Vienna, 1921).

BIRELEY, R., 'Ferdinand II: Founder of the Habsburg Monarchy', in Evans and Thomas, _Crown, Church and Estates_, 226–44.

—— _Maximilian von Bayern, Adam Contzen S.J. und die Gegenreformation in Deutschland 1624–1635_ (Göttingen, 1975, also Harvard University dissertation).

BITSKEY, I., 'The Collegium Germanicum in Rome and the Beginning of Counter-Reformation in Hungary', in Evans and Thomas, _Crown, Church and Estates_, 110–22.

BLICKLE, P., _Die Revolution von 1525_ (2nd rev. and enlarged edn., Munich, 1981).

BÖDEKER, G., CHAISE, G., and VEIT, P. (eds.), _Le Livre religieux et ses pratiques_ (Göttingen, 1991).

BORN, K. E., 'Moritz von Sachsen und die Fürstenverschwörung gegen Karl V.', _HZ_ 191 (1966), 23–4.

BÖSEL, R., 'Typus und Tradition in der Baukunst gegenreformatorischer Orden', _Römische historische Mitteilungen_, 31 (1989), 239–53.

BOSSY J., 'The Counter-Reformation and the People of Catholic Europe', _P&P_ 47 (1970), 51–70.

BRANDNER K., 'Überblick über die Pfarrmatriken in Steiermark', _Blätter für österreichische Familienkunde_, 1 (June 1927), 18–60.

BRANDTNER, P., 'Beitrag zur Geschichte der Transmigration inner- und oberösterreichischer Protestanten nach Ungarn: Iklád und Keresztur', _Deutsche Forschungen in Ungarn_, 4 (1939), 71–84.

BRODRICK, J., SJ, _Petrus Canisius_, German trans. by Karl Telch (Vienna, 1950).

BRÜCKNER, W., 'Zum Literaturangebot des Güldenen Almosens', _Zeitschrift für bayerische Landesgeschichte_, 47 (1984), 121–39.

BUCHINGER, E., _Die 'Landler' in Siebenbürgen_ (Munich, 1980).

BÜCKING, J., 'The Peasant War in the Habsburg Lands as a Social Systems-Conflict', in Scribner and Benecke, _German Peasant War_, 160–73.

BURGESS, G., _The Politics of the Ancient Constitution_ (University Park, Pa., 1992).

BURGSTALLER, K., 'Zur Geschichte der Gegenreformation in Kärnten: Die Gegenreformation in Kärnten bis zum Tode Kaiser Ferdinands II.' (doctoral thesis, University of Vienna, 1910).

BURKERT, G., _Landesfürst und Stände: Karl V., Ferdinand I. und die österreichischen Erbländer im Ringen um Gesamtstaat und Landesinteressen_ (Graz, 1987).

—— 'Protestantism and Defence of Liberties in the Austrian Lands under Ferdinand I', in Evans and Thomas, _Crown, Church and Estates_, 58–69.

BUSH, M. L. (ed.), _Social Orders and Social Classes in Europe since 1500: Studies in Social Stratification_ (London, 1992).

BUSZELLO, H., _Der deutsche Bauernkrieg von 1525 als politische Bewegung_ (Berlin, 1969).

—— BLICKLE, P., and ENDRES, R. (eds.), _Der deutsche Bauernkrieg_ (Paderborn, 1984).

CAVAZZA, S., 'La controriforma nella contea di Gorizia', in Dolinar et al., _Katholische Reform_, 143–55.

CERWINKA G., 'Die politischen Beziehungen der Fürstenhöfe zu Graz und München im Zeitalter des konfessionellen Absolutismus 1564–1619' (doctoral thesis at the Faculty of History, University of Graz, 1966).

CHATELLIER, L., *La Religion des pauvres* (Paris, 1993).

CHRISTIAN, G., and HOLZMANN, E., 'Ein Beitrag zur Baugeschichte von Leibnitz', in *1000 Jahre Leibnitz, 970–1970: Festschrift zum Gedenkjahr* (Graz, n.d. [1970]), 78–81.

CORETH, A., *Pietas Austriaca* (2nd edn., Vienna, 1982).

CRESSY, D., 'Books as Totems in 17th-Century England and New England', *Journal of Library History*, 21/1 (Winter 1986), 92–106.

CWIENK, D., 'Kirchliche Zustände in den Salzburger Pfarren der Steiermark in der Gegenreformation nach dem Visitationsprotokoll des Seckauer Bischofs Jakob Eberlein aus den Jahren 1617–19' (doctoral thesis at the Faculty of Theology, University of Graz, 1966).

DALHAM, F., *Concilia Salisburgensia Provincialia et Dioecesana* (Augustae apud Vindelicos (Augsburg), 1788).

DEDIC, P., 'Die Bekämpfung und Vertreibung der Protestanten aus den Pfarren Pürgg und Irdning im steirischen Ennstal', offprint from *Buch der deutschen Forschung in Ungarn* (Budapest, 1940).

—— 'Besitz und Beschaffung evangelischen Schrifttums in Steiermark und Kärnten in der Zeit des Kryptoprotestantismus', offprint from *Zeitschrift für Kirchengeschichte*, 3rd ser. 9/58, pts iii–iv (1939), 476–95.

—— *Geschichte des Protestantismus in Judenburg* (Graz, 1932).

—— *Der Protestantismus in Steiermark im Zeitalter der Reformation und Gegenreformation* (Leipzig, 1930).

—— 'Der Kärntner Protestantismus vom Abschluß der "Hauptreformation" bis zur Adelsemigration (1600–1629/30), *JGGPÖ* 58 (1937), 70–108.

—— 'Reformation und Gegenreformation in Bruck an der Mur und im Mürztal', *JGGPÖ* 63–4 (1942–3).

—— *Das Schicksal der Judenburger Klöster und Spitäler in der Reformationszeit* (Graz, 1930).

Dehio: Handbuch der Kunstdenkmäler Österreichs. Steiermark (Vienna, 1956).

DICKMANN, F., *Der westfälische Frieden* (3rd edn., Münster, 1964).

DICKSON, P. G. M., *Finance and Government under Maria Theresia 1740–1780*, 2 vols. (Oxford, 1987).

—— 'Joseph II's Reshaping of the Austrian Church', *HJ* 36/1 (1993), 89–114.

DIEFENDORF, B., 'Give us Back our Children: Patriarchal Authority and Parental Consent to Religious Vocations in Early Counter-Reformation France', *JMH* 68/2 (June 1996), 265–307.

DIMITZ, A., *Geschichte Krains*, ii: *1493–1564* (Ljubljana, 1875).

DIRNBERGER, G., 'Geschichte der landesfürstlichen Stadt Radkersburg vom Beginn der Neuzeit bis zum Regierungsantritt Maria Theresias' (doctoral thesis at the Faculty of History, University of Graz, 1973).

DOLESCHALL, E. A., 'Die Kirchenordnung Innerösterreichs im 16. Jahrhundert', *JGGPÖ* 5 (1884), 163–83.

DOLINAR, F. M., LIEBMANN, M., and RUMPLER, H. (eds.), *Katholische Reform und Gegenreformation in Innerösterreich 1564–1628* (Graz, 1994).

DOTZAUER, W., *Die deutschen Reichskreise in der Verfassung des alten Reiches und ihr Eigenleben (1500–1806)* (Darmstadt, 1989).

DUCREUX, M. É., 'La Reconquête catholique de l'espace bohémien', *RES* 60/3 (1988), 685–702.

DUHR, B., *Geschichte der Jesuiten in den Ländern deutscher Zunge*, vols. i–ii/1 (Freiburg im Breisgau, 1907–13).

—— *Die Jesuiten an den deutschen Fürstenhöfen des 16. Jahrhunderts* (Freiburg im Breisgau, 1901).

DÜLMEN, R. VAN, 'Antijesuitismus und katholische Aufklärung in Deutschland', *HJb* 89 (1969), 52–80.

—— *Reformation als Revolution* (2nd edn., Frankfurt am Main, 1987).

EBERHARD, W., *Konfessionsbildung und Stände in Böhmen 1478–1530* (Munich, 1981).

—— *Monarchie und Widerstand: Zur ständischen Oppositionsbildung im Herrschaftssystem Ferdinands I. in Böhmen* (Munich, 1985).

—— 'Reformatorische Gegensätze, reformatorischer Konsens, reformatorische Formierung in Böhmen, Mähren und Polen', in Bahlcke, *Ständefreiheit und Staatsgestaltung*, 187–215.

EDELMAYER, F., and KOHLER, A. (eds.), *Kaiser Maximilian II: Kultur und Politik im 16. Jahrhundert* (Vienna, 1992).

EDER, K., *Glaubensspaltung und Landstände in Österreich ob der Enns, 1525–1602* (Linz, 1936).

—— *Die Kirche im Zeitalter des konfessionellen Absolutismus (1555–1648)* (Freiburg im Breisgau, 1949).

—— 'Die Visitation und Inquisition von 1528 in der Steiermark', *MIÖG* 63 (1955), 312–22.

ELTON, G. R. (ed.), *The Reformation 1520–1559, New Cambridge Modern History*, vol. ii (2nd edn., Cambridge, 1990).

ENGELBRECHT, H., *Geschichte des österreichischen Bildungswesens*, vols ii–iii (Vienna, 1983–4).

Epistolae Mixtae ex Variis Europae Locis ab Anno 1537 ad 1556 Scriptae nunc Primum a Patribus Societatis Jesu in Lucem Editae (Monumenta Historica Societatis Jesu) vol. v (Madrid, 1901).

Evangelisch in der Steiermark, catalogue of the exhibition (Graz, 1981).

EVANS, R. J. W., *The Making of the Habsburg Monarchy 1550–1700* (Oxford, 1979).

—— and THOMAS, T. V. (eds.), *Crown, Church and Estates* (Basingstoke, 1991).

FABIAN, E., *Die Entstehung des Schmalkaldischen Bundes und seiner Verfassung 1529 bis 1531/33*, Schriften zur Kirchen- und Rechtsgeschichte 1 (Tübingen, 1962).

FEDOROWICZ, J. K. (ed.), *A Republic of Nobles: Studies in Polish History to 1864* (Cambridge, 1982).

FLOREY G., *Geschichte der Salzburger und ihrer Emigration 1731/2* (Vienna, 1977).

FUCHS, W. P., *Das Zeitalter der Reformation* (8th edn., Munich, 1986).

GELMI, J., *Kirchengeschichte Tirols* (Innsbruck, 1986).

GINDELY, A., *Geschichte des dreißigjährigen Krieges*, vol. ii (Leipzig, 1882).

—— *Die Processierung der Häretiker in Böhmen unter Kaiser Karl VI.* (Prague, 1887).

GLASER, H.,'Die Herrschaft der Jesuiten in Millstatt 1600–1773' (doctoral thesis at the Faculty of History, University of Vienna, 1967).

—— (ed.), *Um Glauben und Reich: Kurfürst Maximilian I* (Munich, 1980).

GOETZ, H.-J., *Religiöse Bewegungen in der frühen Neuzeit* (Munich, 1993).

GOMILSCHAK, J., 'Zünfte in Radkersburg und Materialien zu ihrer Geschichte', *BKSTGQ* 16 (1879), 51–82.

GRADAUER, P., 'Vom "Münchner Konkordat" zum "Wiener Rezeß" (1675)', in Amon and Primetshofer (eds.), *Ecclesia Peregrinans*, 361–70.

Grafenauerjev Zbornik (Ljubljana, 1996).

GRAFF, T., *Bibliographia Widmanstadiana* (Graz, 1993).

—— *Die Entwicklung des steirischen Buchdrucks bis zum Ende des 18. Jahrhunderts und ihre Auswirkungen in den innerösterreichischen Raum* (Maribor, 1988).

—— 'Die Offizin Widmanstetter 1585–1806', in T. Graff and S. Karner, *Leykam: 400 Jahre Druck und Papier* (Graz, 1985), 23–90.

GRELL, O. P., and SCRIBNER, R. (eds.), *Tolerance and Intolerance in the European Reformation* (Cambridge, 1996).

GRENDLER, P. F., 'Borromeo and the Schools of Christian Doctrine', in Headley and Tomaro, *Borromeo*, 158–171.

GUGITZ, G., *Österreichs Gnadenstätten in Kult und Brauch*, vol. iv (Vienna, 1956).

GUIDETTI, A., SJ, *Le missioni popolari* (Milan, 1988).

GUTKAS, K., *Geschichte des Landes Niederösterreich* (St Pölten, 1973).

HABERLEITNER, O., *Handwerk in Steiermark und Kärnten vom Mittelalter bis 1850* (Graz, 1962).

HAIDER, S., *Geschichte Oberösterreichs* (Vienna, 1987).

Handbuch der bayerischen Geschichte, ed. H. Lutz and M. Spindler, vol. ii (Munich, 1966).

HEADLEY, J. M., and TOMARO, J. B. (eds.), *San Carlo Borromeo* (Washington, 1988).

HEILINGSETZER G., 'Die Bayern in Oberösterreich (1620–1628)', in Glaser, *Um Glauben und Reich*, 416–23.

HEISS, G., 'Konfession, Politik und Erziehung: Die Landschaftsschulen in den nieder- und innerösterreichischen Ländern vor dem Dreißigjährigen Krieg', in Klingenstein et al. (eds.), *Bildung, Politik und Gesellschaft*, 13–63.

HELCZMANOVSKI, H. (ed.), *Beiträge zur Bevölkerungs- und Sozialgeschichte Österreichs* (Munich, 1973).

HERSCHE, P., *Der Spätjansenismus in Österreich* (Vienna, 1977).

HERTLING, L., *Die Jesuiten in Kärnten* (Klagenfurt, 1975).

HERZIG, A., *Reformatorische Bewegung und Konfessionalisierung: Die habsburgische Rekatholisierung in der Grafschaft Glatz 1530–1730* (Hamburg, 1996).

HILLERBRAND, H. J. (ed.), *The Oxford Encyclopedia of the Reformation*, 4 vols. (Oxford, 1996).

HOBSBAWM, E. J., 'Popular Proto-nationalism', in Hobsbawm, *Nations and Nationalism since 1780* (2nd edn., Cambridge, 1992), 46–79.

HOFER, R., 'Das Grazer Jesuitendrama 1573–1600' (doctoral thesis, University of Graz, 1931).

HÖFER, R., 'Bischof Martin Brenner als Gegenreformator und katholischer Reformer', in Dolinar et al., *Katholische Reform*, 21–40.

——— 'Die kirchlichen Zustände in Bruck an der Mur und seiner Umgebung nach den Visitationsprotokollen von 1524, 1528 und 1544' (graduate thesis at the Faculty of Theology, University of Graz, 1977).

——— *Die landesfürstliche Visitation der Pfarren und Klöster in der Steiermark 1544/1545* (Graz, 1992).

HSIA, R. PO-CHIA, *Social Discipline in the Reformation: Central Europe, 1550–1750* (London, 1989).

——— *The World of Catholic Renewal, 1540–1770* (Cambridge, 1998).

HÜBEL, I., 'Die Ächtung von Evangelischen und die Konfiskationen protestantischen Besitzes im Jahre 1620 in Nieder- und Oberösterreich', *JGGPÖ* 58 (1937), 17–28.

HUBER, W., 'Hanns Friedrich Hoffmann, Freiherr von Grünbüchel und Strechau, der bedeutendste Vertreter des Protestantismus in Innerösterreich im 16. Jahrhundert', *JGGPÖ* 48 (1927), 58–165.

HÜBNER, K., 'Die salzburgischen Provinzialsynoden im XVI. Jahrhundert', *Deutsche Geschichtsblätter*, 12 (1911), 7–126.

HUTTER F., *Geschichte Schladmings und des steirisch-salzburgischen Ennstales* (Graz, 1906).

INGRAO, C., *The Habsburg Monarchy 1618–1815* (Cambridge, 1994).

JAITNER, K. (ed.), *Die Hauptinstruktionen Clemens' VIII. für die Nuntien und Legaten an den europäischen Fürstenhöfen 1592–1605*, vol. i (Tübingen, 1984).

——— 'Die päpstliche Kirchenreformpolitik von Gregor XIII. bis Gregor XV. (1572–1623)', in Dolinar et al., *Katholische Reform*, 279–88.

JEDIN, H., 'Entstehung und Tragweite des Trienter Dekrets über die Bilderverehrung', *THQS* 116 (1935), 181–6.

JÜRGENSMEIER, F., 'Kurmainz', in Schindling and Amon, *Die Territorien des Reichs*, iv. 60–95.

KAUFMANN, T. DaCosta, *Court, Cloister and City: The Art and Culture of Central Europe 1450–1800* (London, 1995).

KERN, A., *Ein Kampf ums Recht: Grundherren und Weinbauern in Steiermark im 16. und 17. Jahrhundert* (Graz, 1941).

KERN, F., *Gottesgnadentum und Widerstandsrecht im früheren Mittelalter: Zur Entwicklungsgeschichte der Monarchie* (6th edn., Darmstadt, 1973).

KLEIN, A. A., 'Landgemeinde und Dorfherrschaft in Steiermark', *ZHVST* 46 (1955), 82–111.

KLEIN, K., 'Die Bevölkerung Österreichs vom Beginn des 16. bis zur Mitte des 18. Jahrhunderts', in Helczmanovski, *Beiträge*, 47–112.

KLINGENSTEIN, G., 'Modes of Religious Tolerance and Intolerance in Eighteenth-Century Habsburg Politics', *Austrian History Yearbook*, 24 (1993), 1–16.

—— LUTZ, H., and STOURZH, G. (eds.), *Bildung, Politik und Gesellschaft: Studien zur Geschichte des europäischen Bildungswesens vom 16. bis zum 20. Jahrhundert* (Munich, 1978).

KLUETING, H., (ed.), *Katholische Aufklärung: Aufklärung im katholischen Deutschland* (Hamburg, 1993).

—— ' "Quidquid est in territorio: etiam est de territorio": Josephinisches Staatskirchentum als rationaler Territorialismus', *Der Staat*, 37/3 (1998), 417–34.

KÖBLER, G., *Historisches Lexikon der deutschen Länder* (Munich, 1988).

KOCH, L., SJ, *Jesuiten-Lexikon* (Paderborn, 1934).

KOHLER, A., 'Bayern als Vorbild für die innerösterreichische Gegenreformation', in Dolinar et al., *Katholische Reform*, 387–403.

—— 'Bildung und Konfession: Zum Studium der Studenten aus den habsburgischen Ländern an Hochschulen im Reich (1560–1620)', in Klingenstein et al., *Bildung, Politik und Gesellschaft*, 64–123.

KOLLER-NEUMANN, I., 'Zum Protestantismus unter der Jesuitenherrschaft Millstatt', *Carinthia*, 1/178 (1988), 143–63.

KOOPS, T., *Die Lehre vom Widerstandsrecht des Volkes gegen die weltliche Obrigkeit in der lutherischen Theologie des 16. und 17. Jahrhunderts* (Kiel, 1968).

KÖPECZI, B., *Staatsräson und christliche Solidarität: Die ungarischen Aufstände und Europa in der zweiten Hälfte des 17. Jahrhunderts* (Budapest, 1983).

KOVÁCS, E. (ed.), *Katholische Aufklärung und Josephinismus* (Vienna, 1979).

KRASENBRINK, J., *Die Congregatio Germanica und die katholische Reform in Deutschland nach dem Tridentinum* (Münster, 1972).

KREUZIGER, D., 'Rechts- und sozialhistorische Entwicklung des ländlichen Dienstboten- und Gesindewesens in der Steiermark . . .' (doctoral thesis at the Faculty of Law, University of Graz, 1969).

KRONES, F. von, 'Aktenmäßige Beiträge zur Geschichte des windischen Bauernaufstandes vom Jahre 1573', *BKSTGQ* 5 (1868), 3–34.

—— *Geschichte der Karl-Franzens-Universität in Graz* (Graz, 1886).

—— *Zur Geschichte Ungarns (1671–1683): Mit besonderer Rücksicht auf die Thätigkeit und die Geschicke des Jesuitenordens* (Vienna, 1894).

LAUBE, A., 'Precursors of the Peasant War: *Bundschuh* and *Armer Konrad*—Movements at the Eve of the Reformation', in Bak, *German Peasant War*, 49–53.

LEIDENFROST, R., 'Zur Geschichte der Gegenreformation in Steiermark', *JGGPÖ* 6 (1885), 51–80.

—— 'Religionsbeschwerden der evangelischen Stände von Steiermark, Kärnten und Krain', *JGGPÖ* 4 (1883), 26–30.

LEVY, E., ' "A Noble Medley and Concert of Materials and Artifice": Jesuit Church Interiors in Rome, 1567–1700', in Lucas et al. (eds.), *Saint, Site and Sacred Strategy*, 47–61.

LIEBMANN, M., 'Die Anfänge der Reformation in der Steiermark', in *Evangelisch in der Steiermark*, 7–15.

Literatur in der Steiermark, catalogue of the *Landesausstellung* in Graz (Graz, n.d. [1976]).

Litterae Quadrimestres ex Universis Praeter Indiam et Brasiliam Locis in Quibus Aliqui de Societate Jesu Versabantur Romam Missae, (1546–1552), Monumenta Historica Societatis Jesu, vol. i (Madrid, 1894).

LOESCHE, G., 'Maria Theresias letzte Maßnahmen gegen die "Ketzer" ', *ZVGMS* 20 (1916), 411–44.

—— 'Die reformatorischen Kirchenordnungen Ober- und Innerösterreichs', *Archiv für Reformationsgeschichte*, 18 (1921), 3–4: 35–55, 121–54.

LÖFFLER, F. E., 'Reformation und Gegenreformation in ihrer Auswirkung auf die österreichische Franziskanerobservanz des 16. Jahrhunderts' (graduate thesis at the Faculty of Theology, University of Salzburg, 1970).

LOJEWSKI, G. von, 'Bayerns Kampf um Köln', in Glaser, *Um Glauben und Reich*, 40–7.

LOSERTH, J. (ed.), *Acten und Correspondenzen zur Geschichte der Gegenreformation in Innerösterreich unter Erzherzog Karl II. (1578–1590)*, Fontes rerum Austriacarum 50 (Vienna, 1898).

—— (ed.), *Akten und Korrespondenzen zur Geschichte der Gegenreformation in Innerösterreich unter Ferdinand II.*, pts. i–ii, Fontes rerum Austriacarum 58–60 (Vienna, 1906–7).

—— *Die Beziehungen der steiermärkischen Landschaft zu den Universitäten Wittenberg, Rostock, Heidelberg, Tübingen, Straßburg und anderen in der zweiten Hälfte des 16. Jahrhunderts* (Graz, 1899).

—— *Erzherzog Karl II. und die Frage der Errichtung eines Klosterrathes für Innerösterreich* (Vienna, 1897).

—— 'Eine Fälschung des Vizekanzlers Wolfgang Schranz: Kritische Untersuchung über die Entstehung der Brucker Pazifikation von 1578', *MIÖG* 18 (1897), 341–61.

—— 'Der Flacianismus in Steiermark und die Religionsgespräche von Schladming und Graz', *JGGPÖ* 20 (1899), 1–13.

—— 'Die Gegenreformation in Innerösterreich und der innerösterreichische Herren- und Ritterstand', offprint from *MIÖG*, supplementary volume 6 (Vienna, 1901).

—— 'Die Gegenreformation in Salzburg unter dem Erzbischof Marx Sittich, Grafen von Hohenembs (1612–1619)', *MIÖG* 19 (1898), 676–96.

—— *Geschichte des altsteirischen Herren- und Grafenhauses Stubenberg* (Graz, 1911).

—— 'Zur Geschichte des Brucker Libells', *JGGPÖ* 53 (1932), 7–23.

—— 'Grundsätze der Kaiserin Maria Theresia, nach welchen die Religionsschwärmer in Mähren zu behandeln seien', *ZVGMS* 18 (1914), 297–300.

—— 'Das Haus Lobkowitz und die Gegenreformation', *MVGDB* 43 (1905), 511–18.

—— 'Ein Hochverratsprozeß aus der Zeit der Gegenreformation in Innerösterreich', *AÖG* 88 (1900), 315–65.

—— 'Der Huldigungsstreit nach dem Tode Erzherzog Karls II.', 1590–1592', *FVVGST*, ii/2 (Graz, 1898).

—— *Innerösterreich und die militärischen Maßnahmen gegen die Türken im 16. Jahrhundert: Studien zur Geschichte der Landesdefension und der Reichshilfe* (Graz, 1934).

—— *Das Kirchengut in Steiermark im 16. und 17. Jahrhundert* (Graz, 1912).

—— 'Matthes Amman von Ammansegg, ein innerösterreichischer Staatsmann des 16. Jahrhunderts', *AÖG* 108 (1920), 1–68.

—— 'Miscellen zur steiermärkischen Religionsgeschichte', *JGGPÖ* 20 (1899), 185–92.

—— *Die protestantischen Schulen der Steiermark im 16. Jahrhundert* (Berlin, 1916).

—— *Reformation und Gegenreformation in den innerösterreichischen Ländern im 16. Jahrhundert* (Stuttgart, 1898).

—— 'Die Reformationsordnungen der Städte und Märkte Innerösterreichs aus den Jahren 1587–1628', *AÖG* 96 (1907), 99–190.

—— 'Die Salzburger Provinzialsynode von 1549', *AÖG* 85 (1898), 131–357.

—— 'Die steirische Religionspazifikation und die Fälschung des Vizekanzlers Dr. Wolfgang Schranz', *JGGPÖ* 48 (1927), 1–57.

—— 'Wiedertäufer in Steiermark', *MHVST* 42 (1894), 118–45.

LOUTHAN, H., *The Quest for Compromise* (Cambridge, 1997).

LUCAS, T. M., SJ, and Biblioteca Vaticana (eds.), *Saint, Site and Sacred Strategy, catalogue of the exhibition* (Vatican City, 1990).

LUTTENBERGER, A., 'Innerösterreich und das Reich im Zeitalter der Gegenreformation', in Dolinar et al., *Katholische Reform*, 357–71.

MACHILEK, F., 'Böhmen', in Schindling and Ziegler, *Die Territorien des Reichs*, i. 136–46.

MAKKAI, L., 'The Crown and the Diets of Hungary and Transylvania in the Sixteenth Century', in Evans and Thomas, *Crown, Church and Estates*, 80–91.

MAYER F., 'Materialien und kritische Bemerkungen zur Geschichte der ersten Bauernunruhen in Steiermark und den angrenzenden Ländern', *BKSTGQ* 13 (1876), 1–32.

MECENSEFFY, G., *Geschichte des Protestantismus in Österreich* (Graz, 1956).

MELL, A., *Grundriß der Verfassungs- und Verwaltungsgeschichte des Landes Steiermark* (Graz, 1929).

—— *Die Lage des steirischen Unterthanenstandes seit Beginn der neueren Zeit bis in die Mitte des 17. Jahrhunderts* (Weimar, 1896).

—— 'Der windische Bauernaufstand des Jahres 1635 und dessen Nachwehen', *MHVST* 44 (1896), 205–87.

MELTON, J. VAN HORN, *Absolutism and the Eighteenth-Century Origins of Compulsory Schooling in Prussia and Austria* (Cambridge, 1988).

MENSI, F., *Geschichte der direkten Steuern in Steiermark bis zum Regierungsantritte Maria Theresias*, vol. iii, pt. 3 (Graz, 1936).

MEZLER-ANDELBERG, H. J., ' "Diß ist der beste weg, den ich auß gottes wort in diser schweren sache zeigen khan" ', in Mezler-Andelberg, *Kirche in der Steiermark*, 199–210.

—— 'Erneuerung des Katholizismus und Gegenreformation in Innerösterreich', in Mezler-Andelberg, *Kirche in der Steiermark*, 175–98.

—— 'Der Obrigkeit gehorsam', in Mezler-Andelberg, *Kirche in der Steiermark*, 211–30.

—— *Kirche in der Steiermark* (Vienna, 1994).

—— (ed.), *Festschrift Karl Eder* (Innsbruck, 1959).

Die Minderbrüder: Minoriten—Franziskaner—Kapuziner in der Steiermark. Begleitheft zur Ausstellung 16. Mai bis 30. September 1990, ed. the Episcopal See (*Ordinariat*) of Graz-Seckau (Graz, 1990).

MOSER, H., 'Marianische Volksfrömmigkeit im 17. Jahrhundert am Beispiel der Grazer Marienkirchen', *HJbG* 7–8 (1975), 75–88.

MÜLLER, M. G., *Zweite Reformation und städtische Autonomie im königlichen Preußen: Danzig, Elbing und Thorn in der Epoche der Konfessionalisierung (1557–1730)* (Berlin, 1997).

NERI, D. (ed.), *Nuntiaturberichte aus Deutschland*, viii: *Nuntiatur Giovanni Dolfins (1575–1585)* (Tübingen, 1997).

NEUMANN, H.-B., 'The Styrian Estates during the Counter-Reformation, 1578–1628' (doctoral thesis at the Faculty of History, University of Toronto, 1976 (?)).

NISCHAN, B., *Prince, People and Confession: The Second Reformation in Brandenburg* (Philadelphia, 1994).

NOFLATSCHER, H., 'Tirol, Brixen, Trient', in Schindling and Ziegler, *Die Territorien des Reichs*, i. 86–101.

ORTNER, F., *Reformation, katholische Reform und Gegenreformation im Erzstift Salzburg* (Salzburg, 1981).

PÁNEK, J., 'Maximilian II. als König von Böhmen', in Edelmayer and Kohler, *Kaiser Maximilian II.*, 55–69.

PANTZ, A., *Beiträge zur Geschichte der Innerberger Hauptgewerkschaft* (Graz, 1903).

PAOLIN, G., 'La visita apostolica di Bartolomeo da Porcia nel Goriziano nel 1570', in Dolinar et al. (eds.), *Katholische Reform*, 133–42.

PARKER, G. (ed.), *The Thirty Years' War* (2nd edn. London, 1987).

PASTURE, A., *La Restauration religieuse aux Pays-Bas catholiques sous les archiducs Albert et Isabelle (1596–1633)* (Louvain, 1925).

PEINLICH, R., *Geschichte des Gymnasiums in Graz*, pts. i–iii (Graz, 1869–72).

PÉTER, K., 'Tolerance and Intolerance in Sixteenth-Century Hungary', in Grell and Scribner, *Tolerance and Intolerance*, 249–61.

PETTEGREE, A., 'Confessionalization in North Western Europe', in Bahlcke and Strohmeyer, *Konfessionalisierung in Ostmitteleuropa*, 105–20.

PFERSCHY, G., 'Die steirischen Bauernaufstände', in Posch, *Bauerntum in der Steiermark*, 50–4.

PICKL, O. (ed.), *800 Jahre Steiermark und Österreich, 1192–1992* (Graz, 1992).

—— 'Grazer Finanzkaufleute und Fernhändler im 15. und 16. Jahrhundert', in *850 Jahre Graz* (Graz, 1978), 147–65.

—— 'Die wirtschaftliche Lage der Städte und Märkte der Steiermark im 16. Jahrhundert', in Rausch, *Die Stadt*, 93–128.

PIRCHEGGER, H., *Geschichte der Steiermark*, i: *1282–1740*; ii: *1740–1919* (Graz, 1931–4).

—— 'Die Pfarren als Grundlage der politisch-militärischen Einteilung der Steiermark', *AÖG* 102 (1913), 1–81.

POPELKA, F., 'Der "ewige" Rat: Eine Episode aus dem Kampf um die städtische Demokratie', *ZHVST* 46 (1955), 150–61.

POSCH, A., *Die kirchliche Aufklärung in Graz und an der Grazer Hochschule* (Graz, 1937).

POSCH, F., 'Bauer und Grundherrschaft', in Posch, *Bauerntum in der Steiermark*, 11–16.

—— (ed.), *Das Bauerntum in der Steiermark* (Graz, 1963).

—— *Flammende Grenze: Die Steiermark in den Kuruzzenstürmen* (Graz, 1968).

PRANGNER, V., *Geschichte des Klosters und des Spitales der Fr. Fr. Barmherzigen Brüder in Graz und der innerösterreichischen Ordensprovinz zum heiligsten Herzen Jesu* (Graz, 1908).

PREIDEL, F., 'Bericht Hay's über die Unruhen in der mährischen Wallachei vom 3 September 1777', *JGGPÖ* 1 (1880), 150–65.

PRESS, V., *Calvinismus und Territorialstaat: Regierung und Zentralbehörden der Kurpfalz 1559–1619* (Stuttgart, 1970).

—— *Kriege und Krisen: Deutschland 1600–1715* (Munich, 1991).

—— 'Die "Zweite Reformation" in der Kurpfalz', in Schilling, *Reformierte Konfessionalisierung*, 104–29.

RAAB, R., 'Die Thannhausen', *Mittheilungen der Gesellschaft für Salzburger Landeskunde*, 12 (1872), 3–33.

RABENLECHNER, M., *Der Bauernkrieg in der Steiermark* (Freiburg, 1901).

RADER, M., 'Das Grazer Barocktheater (1600–1700)' (doctoral thesis, University of Graz, 1964).

RAINER, J., 'Die Grazer Nuntiatur 1580–1622', in Dolinar et al., *Katholische Reform*, 289–94.

—— (ed.), *Nuntiaturberichte, Sonderreihe: Grazer Nuntiatur, i: 1580–2* (Vienna, 1973); *ii: 1582–7* (Vienna, 1981).

—— and WEIß S., *Die Visitation steirischer Klöster und Pfarren im Jahre 1581* (Graz, 1977).

RAUSCH, W. (ed.), *Die Stadt an der Schwelle zur Neuzeit* (Linz, 1980).

REINHARD, W., 'Gegenreformation als Modernisierung?', *Archiv für Reformationsgeschichte*, 68 (1977), 226–52.

—— (ed.), *Power Elites and State Building* (Oxford, 1996).

—— 'Zwang zur Konfessionalisierung? Prolegomena zu einer Theorie des konfessionellen Zeitalters', *ZHF* 10/3 (1983), 257–77.

—— and SCHILLING, H. (eds.), *Die katholische Konfessionalisierung* (Gütersloh, 1995).

REINHARDT, R., 'Zur Kirchenreform in Österreich unter Maria Theresia', *Zeitschrift für Kirchengeschichte*, 77 (1966), 105–19.

REISSENBERGER, F., 'Das Corpus evangelicorum und die österreichischen Protestanten (1685–1764)', *JGGPÖ*, 17 (1896), 207–22.

RIEMENSCHNEIDER, R. (ed.), *Schlesien und Pommern in den deutsch-polnischen Beziehungen vom 16. bis 18. Jahrhundert* (Braunschweig, 1982).

RITTER M., 'Der Ursprung des Restitutionsediktes', *HZ* 76 (1895), 62–102.

ROGIERS J., 'Die Bestrebungen zur Ausbildung einer belgischen Kirche und ihre Analogie zum österreichischen (theresianischen) Kirchensystem', in Kovacs, *Katholische Aufklärung*, 78–83.

RUBLACK, H.-C. (ed.), *Die lutherische Konfessionalisierung in Deutschland* (Gütersloh, 1992).

RUPEL, M., *Primus Truber*, German transl. by Balduin Saria (Munich, 1965).

Sacrosanctum Concilium Tridentinum Additis Declarationibus Cardinalium Concilii Interpretum, ex Ultima Recognitione Joannis Gallemart . . . (Augustae Vindicorum (Augsburg), 1746).

SAKRAUSKY, O., 'Der Einfluß der deutschen Theologie auf die südslawische Reformation', *Südostdeutsches Archiv*, 13 (1970), 77–96.

—— 'Der Flacianismus in Oberkärnten', *JGGPÖ* 76 (1960), 83–109.

SARIA, B., 'Die slowenische Reformation und ihre Bedeutung für die kulturelle Entwicklung der Slowenen', in Trofenik, *Geschichte, Kultur und Geisteswelt*, 23–49.

SAVIDGE, A., *The Foundation and Early Years of Queen Anne's Bounty* (London, 1955).

SCHAAB, M. (ed.), *Territorialstaat und Calvinismus* (Stuttgart, 1993).

SCHÄFFER, R., *Der obersteirische Bauern- und Knappenaufstand und der Überfall auf Schladming 1525* (Vienna, 1989).

Schatz und Schicksal, catalogue of the *Steirische Landesausstellung* 1996 (Graz, 1996).

SCHELLHASS, K., *Der Dominikaner Felician Ninguarda und die Gegenreformation in Süddeutschland und Österreich 1560–1583,* 2 vols. (Rome, 1930–9).

—— 'Zum richtigen Verständnis der Brucker Religionspacification vom 9. Februar 1578', *QF* 17 (1924), 266–77.

SCHILLING, H., *Kirchenzucht und Sozialdisziplinierung im frühneuzeitlichen Europa* (Berlin, 1994).

—— 'Die Konfessionalisierung im Reich', *HZ* 246 (1988), 257–77.

—— (ed.), *Die reformierte Konfessionalisierung in Deutschland: Das Problem der 'Zweiten Reformation'* (Gütersloh, 1986).

SCHINDLING, A., and ZIEGLER, W. (eds.), *Die Territorien der Reichs im Zeitalter der Reformation und Konfessionalisierung,* 5 vols. (Münster, 1989–93).

SCHLOSSAR, A., 'Grazer Buchdruck im 16. Jahrhundert', offprint from *AGDBH* 4 (Leipzig, 1879).

SCHMIDT, H., 'Pfalz-Neuburgs Sprung zum Niederrhein: Wolfgang Wilhelm von Pfalz-Neuburg und der Jülich-Klevische Erbfolgestreit', in Glaser, *Um Glauben und Reich,* 77–89.

SCHMIDT, H. R., *Konfessionalisierung im 16. Jahrhundert* (Munich, 1992).

—— 'Sozialdisziplinierung? Ein Plädoyer für das Ende des Etatismus in der Konfessionalisierungsforschung', *HZ* 265 (1997), 639–82.

SCHMIDT, P., *Das Collegium Germanicum in Rom und die Germaniker* (Tübingen, 1984).

SCHNABEL, W. W., *Österreichische Exulanten in oberdeutschen Reichsstädten* (Munich, 1992).

SCHNEIDER, B., SJ, *Die Jesuiten als Gehilfen der päpstlichen Nuntien und Legaten in Deutschland zur Zeit der Gegenreformation* (Rome, 1959).

SCHNURRER, C. F., *Slavischer Bücherdruck in Württemberg im 16. Jahrhundert* (Tübingen, 1799).

SCHOLZ, G., 'Aspekte zur Situation des niederen Klerus in Innerösterreich während der Reformationszeit', in Bäumer, *Reformatio Ecclesiae,* 629–40.

—— *Ständefreiheit und Gotteswort: Studien zum Anteil der Landstände an Glaubensspaltung und Konfessionsbildung in Innerösterreich (1517–1564)* (Frankfurt am Main, 1994).

SCHORMANN, G., *Der Dreißigjährige Krieg* (Göttingen, 1985).

SCHOSSER, A., *Die Erneuerung des religiös-kirchlichen Lebens in der Oberpfalz nach der Rekatholisierung (1630–1700)* (Düren, 1938).

SCHRAGL, F., *Glaubensspaltung in Niederösterreich* (Vienna, 1973).

SCHRAMM, G., *Der polnische Adel und die Reformation, 1548–1607* (Wiesbaden, 1965).

SCHULZE, W., *Landesdefension und Staatsbildung: Studien zum Kriegswesen des innerösterreichischen Territorialstaates 1564–1619* (Vienna, 1973).

SCHULZE, W., 'Zur politischen Theorie des steirischen Ständetums der Gegen-reformationszeit', *ZHVST* 62 (1971), 33–48.

SCHUSTER, L., *Fürstbischof Martin Brenner* (Graz, 1898).

SCRIBNER, B., and BENECKE, G. (eds.), *The German Peasant War 1525: New Viewpoints* (London, 1979).

SEIFERT, A., 'Die "Seminarpolitik" der bayerischen Herzöge im 16. Jahrhundert und die Begründung des jesuitischen Schulwesens', in Glaser, *Um Glauben und Reich*, 125–32.

SKINNER, Q., *The Foundations of Modern Political Thought*, vol. ii (4th edn., Cambridge, 1988).

SOCHER, A., SJ, *Historia Provinciae Austriae Societatis Jesu* (Vienna, 1740).

STEINWENTER, A., 'Der Friede von Zsitvatorok (1606)', *AÖG* 106 (1918), 157–240.

STEPISCHNEG, J., 'Georg III. Stobaeus von Palmburg, Fürstbischof von Lavant', *AÖG* 15 (1856), 71–132.

STILLFRIED, A., 'Der barocke Umbau der Mariazeller Wallfahrtskirche', in *Schatz und Schicksal*, 51–61.

STOECKIUS, H., 'Ottaviano Cesare, ein Rechtsstreit zwischen Gesellschaft Jesu und Elternhaus', in *Sitzungsberichte der Heidelberger Akademie der Wissenschaften, Phil.-hist. Klasse*, v 7: *Abhandlung* (Heidelberg, 1914).

STÖKL, G., *Die deutsch-slavische Südostgrenze des Reiches im 16. Jahrhundert* (Breslau, 1940).

STRAKA, M., 'Die Bevölkerungsentwicklung der Steiermark von 1528 bis 1782 auf Grund der Kommunikantenzählungen', *ZHVST* 52 (1961), 3–53.

—— 'Die Ortschaften- und Seelenzählung von 1761 in der Steiermark', *ZHVST* 14 (1967), 82–106.

STUPPERICH, R., *Die Reformation in Deutschland* (2nd rev. edn., Gütersloh, 1980).

STURMBERGER H., *Adam Graf Herberstorff: Herrschaft und Freiheit im konfessionellen Zeitalter* (Munich, 1976).

—— *Georg Erasmus Tschernembl: Religion, Libertät und Widerstand. Ein Beitrag zur Geschichte der Gegenreformation und des Landes ob der Enns* (Graz, 1953).

—— 'Jakob Andreae und Achaz von Hohenfeld: Eine Diskussion über das Gehorsamsproblem zur Zeit der Rudolfinischen Gegenreformation in Österreich', in Mezler-Andelberg (ed.), *Festschrift Karl Eder*, 381–94.

TASSIN, F., 'La situazione religiosa ed ecclesiastica del Goriziano negli atti della curia patriarcale (1570–1616)', in Dolinar et al., *Katholische Reform*, 123–31.

TAZBIR, J., 'The Fate of Polish Protestantism in the Seventeenth Century', in Fedorowicz, *Republic of Nobles*, 198–217.

THIEL, V., 'Die innerösterreichische Zentralverwaltung, 1564–1749', I, *AÖG* 105 (1916), 1–210, II '1625–1749', *AÖG* 111 (1930), 497–670.

TILL, J., 'Stifter und Springer' (doctoral thesis at the Faculty of Theology, University of Graz, 1977).

TOIFL, L., and LEITGEB, H., *Die Türkeneinfälle in der Steiermark und in Kärnten vom 15. bis zum 17. Jahrhundert* (Vienna, 1991).

TRAUTENBERGER, G., 'Zur Geschichte der Religionsbewegung in der mährischen Wallachei', *JGGPÖ* 1 (1880), 141–9.

TREMEL, F., 'Beiträge zu einer Handelsgeschichte Leobens in der frühen Neuzeit', *ZHVST* 60 (1969), 107–26.

—— *Der Frühkapitalismus in Innerösterreich* (Graz, 1954).

—— 'Grundzins, Robot und Zehent', in Posch, *Bauerntum in der Steiermark*, 35–42.

—— 'Die oberdeutschen Kaufleute in der Steiermark im 15. und 16. Jahrhundert', *ZHVST* 40 (1949), 13–35.

—— 'Der österreichische Kaufmann im 16. Jahrhundert', in Mezler-Andelberg (ed.), *Festschrift Karl Eder*, 119–40.

TROFENIK, R. (ed.), *Geschichte, Kultur und Geisteswelt der Slowenen*, vol. i (Munich, 1968).

TROPPER, G., 'Die Erneuerung des Pfarrklerus in Salzburgisch-Kärnten zur Zeit der Gegenreformation', in Dolinar et al., *Katholische Reform*, 331–44.

—— *Staatliche Kirchenpolitik, Geheimprotestantismus und katholische Mission in Kärnten (1752–1780)* (Klagenfurt, 1989).

TÜCHLE, H. (ed.), *Acta SC de Propaganda Fide Germaniam Spectantia (1622–1649)* (Paderborn, 1962).

—— 'Das Seminardekret des Trienter Konzils und Formen seiner geschichtlichen Verwirklichung', in Bäumer, *Concilium Tridentinum*, 522–39.

TÜSKÉS, G., and KNAPP, É., 'Bruderschaften in Ungarn im 17. und 18. Jahrhundert', *Bayerisches Jahrbuch für Volkskunde* (1992), 1–23.

VALENTINITSCH, H., 'Die Bedeutung der steirischen Wirtschaft im Zeitalter des Absolutismus für Österreich', in Pickl (ed.), *800 Jahre Steiermark*, 343–58.

—— 'Italienische Unternehmer im Wirtschaftsleben der innerösterreichischen Länder 1550–1650', in *Wirtschaftswege und Wirtschaftskräfte*, 696–708.

—— 'Religiöse Propaganda, Kunst und Politik: Die Mirakelbilder des Markus Weiß (gest. 1641) in Mariazell', in *Schatz und Schicksal*, 117–29.

—— 'Willkür und Widerstand: Die wirtschaftliche und rechtliche Lage der Untertanen der untersteirischen Herrschaft Schönstein in der frühen Neuzeit', in *Grafenauerjev Zbornik*, 469–82.

VILFAN, S., 'Crown, Estates and the Financing of Defence in Inner Austria, 1500–1630', in Evans and Thomas, *Crown, Church and Estates*, 70–9.

WACHA, G., 'Georg Stobäus, Pfarrer von Linz, Bischof von Lavant', *Carinthia*, 1/175 (1985), 215–28.

WAGNER, O., 'Der Einfluß von Reformation, Gegenreformation und Barock auf die Nationsbildung in Schlesien', in Riemenschneider, *Schlesien und Pommern*, 119–45.

WALKER, M., *The Salzburg Transaction* (Ithaca, NY, 1993).

WANDRUSZKA, A., 'Die katholische Aufklärung Italiens und ihr Einfluß auf Österreich', in Kovács, *Katholische Aufklärung*, 62–9.

WEIß, R., *Das Bistum Passau unter Kardinal Joseph Dominikus von Lamberg, 1723–1761* (St Ottilien, 1979).

WEITLAUFF, M., 'Die Reichskirchenpolitik des Hauses Bayern im Zeichen gegenreformatorischen Engagements und österreichisch-bayerischen Gegensatzes', in Glaser, *Um Glauben und Reich*, 48–76.

WERNER, G., *Sprache und Volkstum in der Untersteiermark* (Stuttgart, 1935).

WIDMANN, H., *Geschichte Salzburgs*, vol. iii (Gotha, 1914).

WIEDEMANN, T., *Geschichte der Reformation und Gegenreformation im Lande unter der Enns*, vol. i (Prague, 1879).

WINKELBAUER, T., 'Sozialdisziplinierung und Konfessionalisierung durch Grundherren in den österreichischen und böhmischen Ländern im 16. und 17. Jahrhundert', *ZHF* 19/3 (1992), 317–39.

WINKELMANN, E., 'Geschichte des Luthertums im untersteirischen Mur- und Draugebiet', *JGGPÖ* 54 (1933), 98–117; 55 (1934), 155–72; 56 (1935), 88–119; 57 (1936), 79–116; 58 (1937), 35–69.

—— 'Springersekte und Bergkirchen in der alten Südsteiermark', *JGGPÖ* 62 (1941), 33–7.

WINKLER, G. B., *Die nachtridentinischen Synoden im Reich: Salzburger Provinzialkonzilien 1569, 1573, 1576* (Vienna, 1988).

Wirtschaftswege und Wirtschaftskräfte: Festschrift für Hermann Kellenbenz, vol. i (Stuttgart, 1978).

WOLGAST, E., *Die Religionsfrage als Problem des Widerstandsrechts im 16. Jahrhundert* (Heidelberg, 1980).

WOLNY R. J., *Die josephinische Toleranz unter besonderer Berücksichtigung ihres geistlichen Wegbereiters Johann Leopold Hay* (Munich, 1973).

WURM, H., *Die Jörger von Tollet* (Linz, 1955).

WURZBACH, C. VON, *Biographisches Lexikon des Kaiserthums Österreich*, vols. i–lx (Vienna, 1856–90).

ZAHN, J. VON, *Styriaca: Gedrucktes und Ungedrucktes zur steiermärkischen Geschichte und Kulturgeschichte* (Graz, 1894).

—— 'Über Materialien zur inneren Geschichte der Zünfte in Steiermark', *BKSTGQ* 14–15 (1877–8), 51–80, 74–128.

ZÁK, A., *Österreichisches Klosterbuch* (Vienna, 1911).

ZEEDEN, E. W., 'Salzburg', in Schindling and Ziegler, *Die Territorien des Reichs*, i. 72–85.

—— *Das Zeitalter der Glaubenskämpfe* (7th edn., Munich, 1986).

ZIEGLER, W., 'Nieder- und Oberösterreich', in Schindling and Ziegler, *Die Territorien des Reichs*, i. 118–33.

ZIMMERMANN, B., 'Die Bedeutung Wiens für die Reformation und Gegenreformation bei den Kroaten und Slowenen', *JGGPÖ* 65–6 (1944–5), 21–53.

ZLABINGER, E., *Lodovico Antonio Muratori und Österreich* (Innsbruck, 1970).

ZOVATTO, P., 'La controriforma a Trieste', in Dolinar et al., *Katholische Reform*, 171–89.

ZWIEDINECK-SÜDENHORST, H. VON, *Hans Ulrich von Eggenberg* (Vienna, 1880).

—— *Die öffentliche Meinung in Deutschland im Zeitalter Ludwigs XIV. 1650–1700* (Stuttgart, 1888).

INDEX